A HISTORY OF
ACCOUNTING AND ACCOUNTANTS

GEORGE WATSON
1645–1723

A History of Accounting

and Accountants

EDITED AND PARTLY WRITTEN BY

RICHARD BROWN

Routledge
Taylor & Francis Group

LONDON AND NEW YORK

First published by
FRANK CASS AND COMPANY LIMITED

This edition published 2013 by Routledge

2 Park Square, Milton Park, Abingdon, Oxfordshire OX14 4RN
711 Third Avenue, New York, NY 10017

First issued in paperback 2014

Routledge is an imprint of the Taylor and Francis Group, an informa business

First edition	1905
New impression	1968

ISBN 13: 978-0-714-61279-9 (hbk)
ISBN 13: 978-0-415-76039-3 (pbk)

PART I.—HISTORY OF ACCOUNTING

PART II.÷HISTORY OF ACCOUNTANTS

PREFACE

THE occurrence of the Fiftieth Anniversary of the incorporation of Accountants in Scotland—in which country the Chartered Accountant first saw the light — suggested the propriety of writing an account of the origin and growth of the profession while it was still possible to ascertain the facts and describe the circumstances with some degree of fulness. The idea having been heartily approved of by the Scottish Societies of Accountants, the project soon expanded, and it was decided to include a history of Accounts, Auditing, and Book-keeping; in short, to treat of Accounting— as well as Accountants—from the historic standpoint.

So ambitious a scheme could not well have been carried out singly by any one who had at the same time to attend to the daily demands of a somewhat exacting profession, but, by the division of labour shown on the sub-title page, the work projected has now been completed, and the volume, such as it is, is ready for publication within a short time of the events which it was intended to commemorate.

The reader is asked to bear in mind that the writers of this book are men engaged in active business, who have little time to cultivate literary accomplishments, but who have endeavoured to compose a full and faithful history of an important profession and of the things which pertain to it, believing that in so doing they are rendering a service to that profession as well as adding something, however little, to the sum total of useful historical research.

To the history proper there have been added several appendices: *First*, a bibliography of all printed books on book-keeping in European languages up to the year 1800 which the Editor has been able to authenticate; *Second*, a record of past Accountants in Scotland useful for purposes of reference, and *Third*, accounts of the meetings held in Edinburgh and Glasgow to celebrate the Fiftieth Anniversaries of the Incorporation of the Societies there, which, if not perhaps of much general interest, are of special importance to the not inconsiderable body of Scottish Chartered Accountants.

The Editor makes grateful acknowledgment to his fellow-workers not only for their hearty co-operation as regards the special portions of the volume undertaken by them, but for valuable help in other ways; particularly to Mr. Boyd, for compiling the Index, and Mr. Patrick, for reading the proofs. For the information collected in the later chapters of the book he is indebted to British Ministers and Consular representatives in foreign countries, to the Presidents and Secretaries of the various Societies of Accountants referred to, and to other Accountants resident in different parts of the world. It would be impossible to mention so many by name, but to all of them the Editor tenders his sincere thanks for their invariable courtesy and willing response to his sometimes troublesome inquiries. To the following also his best thanks are given:—Mr. W. H. Hamilton, W.S., Edinburgh; Lieut. Robertson, No. 6 (Accountants) Company, Q.R.V.B., R.S.; Mr. Horatio F. Brown, LL.D., Venice; M. Gabriel Faure, Paris; M. Panayotopoulo, Greece; and Mr. J. N. Hayward, Shanghai; as well as to those others whose kindness, whether in the way of furnishing information or permitting illustrations to be reproduced, has been referred to in the text.

Edinburgh, 1905

CONTENTS

PART I

HISTORY OF ACCOUNTING

CHAPTER I

NUMERATION

CHAPTER II

ANCIENT SYSTEMS OF ACCOUNTING

CHAPTER III

EARLY FORMS OF ACCOUNTS

CONTENTS

CHAPTER IV

HISTORY OF AUDITING

CHAPTER V

HISTORY OF BOOK-KEEPING

CHAPTER VI

HISTORY OF BOOK-KEEPING—(*Continued*)

PART II

HISTORY OF ACCOUNTANTS

CHAPTER I

EARLY ITALIAN ACCOUNTANTS

CONTENTS

xii CONTENTS

CHAPTER V
THE BRITISH COLONIES, ETC.

CHAPTER VI
THE UNITED STATES OF AMERICA

CHAPTER VII
THE CONTINENT OF EUROPE

CHAPTER VIII
OTHER FOREIGN COUNTRIES

CHAPTER IX

DEVELOPMENT OF THE PROFESSION

CHAPTER X

THE POSITION AND PROSPECT

APPENDICES

LIST OF ILLUSTRATIONS

PART I

HISTORY OF ACCOUNTING

A HISTORY OF ACCOUNTING
AND ACCOUNTANTS

CHAPTER I

NUMERATION

PRIMITIVE, GREEK, ROMAN, MODERN

THE art of numeration, or the method of counting, whether
by words or signs or symbols, goes back to the dawn of
intelligence among human beings, though it can hardly be
said to begin with the moment when one thing is distinguish-
able from another. How the process of numbering did begin
can only be conjectured from the habits of those lower races
who are still uncivilised, and from the results reached by
comparative philologists in their study of language.

It is probable that methods of indicating small numbers
by some sort of signs preceded the giving of names, and
that indeed the names given denoted the signs employed.
Thus the words for *ears, wings, hands* have been used by
the Chinese, the Tibetans, and the Hottentots respectively
to denote *two*. The Brazilians generally count by the joints
of the fingers, and consequently only to *three*. Every
greater number they express by the word for *many*. The
African Bushmen are said to have no names for any numbers
beyond two, and among some of the Papuan islanders two
is the basis of their numeration; they do not go beyond
six, three twos signifying both six and an indefinite number.

3

It is abundantly evident from the narratives of travellers that the majority of savage races learned to make use of their fingers and toes in helping them to count, and hence the bases of their systems were five or ten or twenty. The Mexicans have a primitive or uncompounded name for twenty, and as we count from ten upwards by the multiples and powers of ten, so they count by the multiples and powers of twenty. For example, they express 100 by a word which means 5 times 20, and 1000 by twice 400 plus 10 times 20. The Peruvians, who employed knotted strings, called *quipus*, probably the earliest form of abacus, for expressing numbers and retaining them in memory, had a decimal system. With them a single knot signified 10, two single knots 20, a double knot 100, a triple knot 1000, and so on to higher numbers. Among the early Greeks a quinary system seems to have been in use, as may be seen from the verb πεμπάζειν, to count by fives, and then generally to count. After the establishment of a decimal system of numeration, a corresponding nomenclature would follow with comparatively little difficulty.

The cardinal numbers in Greek are—εἷς, one; δύο, two; τρεῖς, three; τέσσαρες, four; πέντε, five; ἕξ, six; ἑπτά, seven; ὀκτώ, eight; ἐννέα, nine; δέκα, ten.

The names for the numbers 11–19 are formed by conjoining the *units* with *ten*, with in general an intervening *and* (καί). A few of the higher numbers are εἴκοσι, twenty; τριάκοντα, thirty; ἑκατόν, a hundred; χίλιοι, a thousand; μύριοι, ten thousand. The last number, often termed a myriad (μυριάς), was the highest denomination used by the Greeks, though they could without difficulty express numbers higher than 10,000. Thus 100,000 would be δέκα μυριάδες, and a billion (that is, a million millions) would be μυριάκις μύριαι μυριάδες.

In the statement of large and also of comparatively small numbers it was common to begin with the units and to ascend to the tens, hundreds, but the reverse order was frequently adopted. Thus they could say *five and twenty* as well as *twenty and five;* when *and* was omitted they put the tens first, thus *twenty five* (εἴκοσι πέντε).

Instead of *eighteen* or *nineteen* the Greeks (and the Romans also, as we shall see) often said *twenty wanting two* or *twenty wanting one.* A similar mode of expression was employed for 28, 29; and Thucydides uses a *myriad wanting three hundred* for *nine thousand seven hundred.*

Some peculiarities, which are not easy to account for, occur in the names of the cardinal numbers. Thus the words for 1, 2, 3, 4 are declinable, those for 5 to 199 inclusive are indeclinable, while those for 200, 300–1000, 2000–10,000 are declinable.

The names for the ordinal numbers are mostly derived from those of the cardinal by a process which is in general uniform throughout. The first of the ordinals (πρῶτος from πρό) has the ending of the Greek superlative—compare the form πρόατος and the comparative πρότερος—and the second (δεύτερος) has the ending of the comparative. It may here be noted, however, that some tribes exist which have names for many cardinal numbers, but the only names they have for ordinals are *first* and *last.*

The Greeks expressed fractions whose numerator is unity much as we do; thus $\frac{1}{2}$ = τὸ ἥμισυ, $\frac{1}{3}$ = τὸ τρίτον, $\frac{1}{4}$ = τὸ τέταρτον. Sometimes they conjoined the name for the ordinal with a word for *part;* thus $\frac{1}{3}$ = τριτημόριον, $\frac{1}{5}$ = πεμπτημόριον. Fractions with other numerators than unity they expressed by stating the denominator first and then the numerator:

thus $\frac{3}{5}$ = τῶν πέντε τὰ τρία μέρη
(of the five the three parts);
$\frac{2}{7}$ = τῶν ἑπτὰ αἱ δύο μοῖραι
(of the seven the two portions).

Fractions whose numerator was one less than the denominator they expressed by stating the numerator only with the word for *parts;* thus $\frac{2}{3}$ = τὰ δύο μέρη, the two parts (out of three).

The way in which they expressed certain mixed numbers may be seen from such a phrase as ἕβδομον ἡμιτάλαντον. It means *the seventh a half talent,* and is equivalent to six whole talents and the seventh a half talent, that is, to 6$\frac{1}{2}$ talents.

The cardinal numbers in Latin are *unus*, one; *duo*, two; *tres*, three; *quatuor*, four; *quinque*, five; *sex*, six; *septem*, seven; *octo*, eight; *novem*, nine; *decem*, ten.

The names for the numbers 11–19 are formed by prefixing the *units* to *ten*, the word *decem* being modified to *decim*. A few of the higher numbers are *viginti*, twenty; *triginta*, thirty; *centum*, a hundred; *mille*, a thousand. The last number, *mille*, is the highest denomination of the Romans.

The numbers between 20 and 100 are expressed either by the larger number first and the smaller number after it without a connecting *et* (and), or by the smaller number first and the larger number after it with a connecting *et*. Thus 21 is *viginti unus*, or *unus et viginti*. Numbers above 100 always have the larger number first.

The numbers 18, 19, 28, 29, &c., are often expressed by *two from twenty, one from twenty*, &c. The smaller number is put first, and *de* is inserted for *from;* thus 18 = *duodeviginti*, 19 = *undeviginti*, 28 = *duodetriginta*, 29 = *undetriginta*, and so on to *undecentum* for 99. 98 however is either *nonaginta octo* or *octo et nonaginta*.

As in Greek, the names of the ordinal numbers are derived from those of the cardinal, with the exception of *primus* and *secundus*. *Primus* is the superlative of *prae* or *pro* (before), and *secundus* the present participle of the verb *sequor* (follow).

Fractions are expressed by the ordinal numbers, with part or parts (*pars* or *partes*) expressed or understood; thus $\frac{1}{3}$ = *tertia pars*, $\frac{3}{7}$ = *tres septimae*. Other forms are employed when the numerator is one less than the denominator; thus $\frac{2}{3}$ = *duae partes* (two parts out of three), $\frac{3}{4}$ = *tres partes* (three parts out of four). Sometimes a fraction is expressed as the sum of two fractions; thus *pars quarta et septima* = $\frac{1}{4} + \frac{1}{7} = \frac{11}{28}$: sometimes as the product of two fractions; thus *quarta septima* = $\frac{1}{4} \times \frac{1}{7} = \frac{1}{28}$.

The Roman unit of weight, length, area was called *as* (our *ace*), and it was divided into twelve equal parts, called *unciae*, whence came our *ounce* and *inch*. The names of the parts are—

Uncia	$=\frac{1}{12}$ of the unit.	Septunx	$=\frac{7}{12}$ of the unit.	
Sextans	$=\frac{2}{12}$ or $\frac{1}{6}$,, ,,	Bes	$=\frac{8}{12}$ or $\frac{2}{3}$,, ,,	
Quadrans	$=\frac{3}{12}$ or $\frac{1}{4}$,, ,,	Dodrans	$=\frac{9}{12}$ or $\frac{3}{4}$,, ,,	
Triens	$=\frac{4}{12}$ or $\frac{1}{3}$,, ,,	Dextans	$=\frac{10}{12}$ or $\frac{5}{6}$,, ,,	
Quincunx	$=\frac{5}{12}$,, ,,	Deunx	$=\frac{11}{12}$,, ,,	
Semis	$=\frac{6}{12}$ or $\frac{1}{2}$,, ,,			

Here we have the first occurrence of duodecimal fractions.

In the expression of mixed numbers the fractional part is followed by that ordinal number which is one more than the given integer; thus $3\frac{1}{4} = $ *quadrans quartus*, the fourth a quarter (three wholes being understood), $2\frac{1}{2} = $ *semis tertius*, the third a half (two wholes being understood). *Semis tertius*, contracted to *sestertius*, was written with the symbol for two (II), and S, the initial of *semis*, after it (IIS). The horizontal stroke that was drawn through the whole symbol, as in our ℔, £ for pounds, is represented by the printer's HS.

The names of the cardinal numbers in French are derived from the corresponding Latin names transformed more or less regularly according to the laws of phonetics.

The numbers 17, 18, 19 were in classical Latin *septemdecim, octodecim, novemdecim,* but in popular Latin they were *decem et septem, decem et octo, decem et novem,* and these popular forms have given rise to the French terms *dix-sept, dix-huit, dix-neuf.* Among the multiples of 10, the first five are formed regularly from the Latin, but the usual names for 70, 80, 90 are not *septante, octante, nonante,* but *soixante-dix, quatre-vingts, quatre-vingt-dix.* The name *septante* occurs in *La Version des Septante,* the Greek version of the Hebrew Bible, called by us the Septuagint; along with *octante* and *nonante* it is found in certain provinces of the north and east of France, and in some parts of Belgium.

The forms *soixante-dix,* &c., are vestiges of the vigesimal system which was in use among the ancient Gauls. This vigesimal system and the Roman decimal system were used concurrently during the Middle Ages; thus 32 was either *trente et deux* or *vingt et douze*, 43 either *quarante et trois* or *deux vingts et trois*, 158 either *cent cinquante et huit* or *sept-vingts et dix-huit.* In the seventeenth century *six vingts* was a common expression for 120, and at the present day there is an hospital in Paris for three hundred blind people called *Les Quinze-Vingts.*

The same adoption of the popular Latin words for 17, 18, 19 is seen in Italian *diciassette, diciotto, diciannove,* ánd for 16, 17, 18, 19 in the Spanish *diez y seis, diez y siete, diez y ocho, diez y nueve.* The names for 70, 80, 90 in Latin become *settanta, ottanta, novanta* in Italian, and *setenta, ochenta, noventa* in Spanish.

The word million, derived from the Italian *milione,* means a big thousand, just as balloon means a big ball, saloon, derived from *salone,* a big *sala.*

For 1000 millions the French now use the word milliard as well as billion. In the sixteenth and seventeenth centuries a French billion was a million of millions; its present meaning in France dates from the eighteenth century.

In old French, numbers expressed by thousands, hundreds, tens, and units had the various denominations connected by *et* (and). This conjunction is now suppressed except before *un* and *onze.*

The names of the ordinal numbers come from the corresponding cardinals, except in the case of *premier.* Twenty-first, however, is *vingt et unième.*

In German the names of the cardinal numbers from 1–20, 30–100, 1000 closely resemble our own. For 21, 22, Germans say *ein und zwanzig, zwei und zwanzig,* and not *zwanzig ein.*

As in Greek and Latin, so in German there is found the idiom *viertehalb* (the fourth a half) for 3½, *elftehalb* (the eleventh a half) for 10½. Instead, however, of *zweitehalb* for 1½ they use *anderthalb,* from *ander* (other), in the sense of second.

The Germans still retain what seems to us a peculiarity in their expression of time. Thus they say *halb zwei* (half two) for half-past one, *halb zehn* (half ten) for half-past nine

This mode of expression is exactly paralleled in the Scottish dialect, where half twelve means half-past eleven, and so on. A similar idiom is found in French, in some Eastern languages, and in Icelandic, where half the fourth hundred = 350, half the fourth ten = 35, and so on.

Our own names for numbers show few peculiarities in their composition, the exceptions being the names for the cardinal numbers *eleven* and *twelve*, and the ordinals *first* and *second*. Eleven is obviously the same word as Anglo-Saxon *endlufon*, Gothic *ainlif*, German *eilf* or *elf*, but whether it stands for *one left* (after the base, ten, is taken away) is somewhat doubtful. Twelve is supposed to stand for *two left* (after ten is taken away), and is derived from the Teutonic base, *twalif*. First is the superlative of a word meaning *before*, and second is derived from the Latin *secundus*.

With regard to the earliest Greek notation for numbers our information is scanty, for the oldest inscriptions contain no numerals. There is reason to believe that a set of symbols where 1, 2, 3, 4 were denoted by upright strokes, 5 by Π, the initial letter of πέντε, 10 by Δ (δέκα), 100 by H (ἑκατόν), 1000 by X (χίλιοι), 10,000 by M (μυρίοι), was widely used in Greece before the letters of the alphabet were adopted for numeral expression.[1]

Among the letters of the alphabet the Greeks inserted three strange letters, ς (sigma), Ϙ or Ϟ (koppa), ϡ (sampi), in order to obtain the twenty-seven symbols [2] necessary to express all the numbers from 1 to 999.

The following table gives their scheme for representing numbers:—

α′	β′	γ′	δ′	ε′	ς′	ζ′	η′	θ′
1	2	3	4	5	6.	7	8	9
ι′	κ′	λ′	μ′	ν′	ξ′	ο′	π′	ϟ′
10	20	30	40	50	60	70	80	90
ρ′	σ′	τ′	υ′	φ′	χ′	ψ′	ω′	ϡ′
100	200	300	400	500	600	700	800	900

[1] See illustration opposite page 26.
[2] Nine for units, nine for tens, and nine for hundreds.

To denote thousands they began the alphabet again and put a short stroke at the left of the letter. Thus

$$,a = 1000 \qquad ,\beta = 2000 \qquad ,\gamma = 3000, \&c.$$

To denote 10,000 they generally employed Mv or M, and if there were several tens of thousands they wrote the number of them above the M; thus $\overset{\beta}{M} = 20,000$.

Their notation for whole numbers will be understood from the following examples:—

$$\kappa\gamma' = 23,\ \tau\mu' = 340,\ \rho\nu\gamma' = 153,\ ,\delta\chi o\gamma' = 4673,\ \overset{\omega\mu\varsigma}{M},\gamma\lambda\kappa a' = 8,473,921.$$

Fractions whose numerator was unity were expressed by writing the denominator and affixing two accents; thus $\frac{1}{3} = \gamma''$, $\frac{1}{14} = \iota\delta''$. If the numerator was not unity, it was written to the left of the denominator; thus $\frac{8}{13} = \eta'\ \iota\gamma''$. The symbol for $\frac{1}{2}$ in Archimedes resembles L, in Heron a capital S.

The numerical notation of the Romans is much inferior to that of the Greeks, though far fewer symbols are employed in it. The symbols are:

I	V	X	L	C	D	M
1	5	10	50	100	500	1000

The character for 500, namely D, is a modified form of I⊃, CI⊃ is 1000, I⊃⊃ is 5000, CCI⊃⊃ is 10,000, and so on. Sometimes a stroke was placed over a number to indicate that its value was increased a thousand fold; thus $\overline{I} = 1000, \overline{V} = 5000, \overline{X} = 10,000$.

As the Roman notation was adopted throughout Europe, and was almost exclusively employed during twelve or thirteen centuries, and is still for certain purposes (to distinguish chapter from verse, volume from page, &c.) current everywhere, it is expedient to state the rules to be observed in reading any number expressed in their manner.

(1) If to the right of any number another number is written which is equal to or less than the first, the value of the first must be increased by that of the second. Thus

II	VI	XII	LV	DC	MDCLXV
2	6	12	55	600	1665

(2) If to the left of any number another number is written which is less than the first, the value of the first must be diminished by that of the second. Thus

IV	IX	XL	CD
4	9	40	400

(8) If a number is written between two others which are greater than it, it must be subtracted from the one on the right of it. Thus

XIV	XIX	LIX	CXL	MCM
14	19	59	140	1900

As regards the invention of the nine digits and the cipher, with the application to them of the principle of local value, it is not possible to speak with certainty. It is now, however, an accepted opinion that it is to the Hindoos we must ascribe this momentous improvement in arithmetical notation, but we have no evidence to enable us to say when the improvement was first made. Before the end of the ninth century the Hindoo figures were known to the Arabs, and before the end of the tenth they were in general use among them. By the eleventh century they had been introduced into Spain by the Moors, and they were known in Italy at the beginning of the thirteenth century. It has been conjectured that the commercial intercourse between Italy and the East would suffice to account for the introduction of these numerals; and it is certain that the first Italian who wrote about them (1202), Leonardo of Pisa, the son of Bonacci (Fibonacci), had travelled extensively in the East.

It is sometimes asserted that Gerbert, who was born at Aurillac, in Auvergne, and who was afterwards promoted to the bishoprics of Rheims and Ravenna, and finally became Pope under the title of Sylvester II., introduced into France a knowledge of the Arabic numerals in the latter part of the tenth century, but this is rather improbable. It is known that in early life Gerbert studied among the Saracens, and he is said to have written extensively on arithmetic and geometry.

When or how the Arabic notation came into England it is impossible to say with any approach to certainty. One of the modes in which persons who could read obtained a knowledge of it was from the ecclesiastical calendars, which were widely distributed in the fourteenth and fifteenth centuries.

After the introduction of the Hindoo numerals for the expression of integers, the next great improvement in arithmetical notation was the invention of decimal fractions. From the time of Ptolemy, and probably also before his time, it had been customary to divide the circle into 360 degrees ($\mu o \hat{\imath} \rho a \iota$). Each of these degrees was divided into 60 equal parts called primes, each prime into 60 equal parts called seconds, each second into 60 equal parts called thirds, and so on. Our names, minutes and seconds, whether applied to angular magnitude or to time, are shortened forms of the expressions first minute parts (*partes minutae primae*) and second minute parts (*partes minutae secundae*). The notation adopted for degrees was a stroke written above the number of them and accents, ' " ''', &c., for the different orders of sexagesimals.

The first indubitable appearance of decimal fractions occurs in the year 1525, in the extraction of a square root. Orontius Finaeus, a professor of mathematics in Paris, wishing to approximate to the square root of 10, affixes to it six ciphers, extracts the root in the usual way, and obtains the number 3162. Then taking 162 he multiplies it by 60, getting 9720, whence 9 primes are obtained by cutting off the three right-hand digits. Again, $720 \times 60 = 43,200$, whence 43 seconds; lastly, $200 \times 60 = 12,000$, whence 12 thirds. According to our mode of working this would stand—

$$3 \cdot 162$$
$$60$$
$$\overline{9 \cdot 720}$$
$$60$$
$$\overline{43 \cdot 200}$$
$$60$$
$$\overline{12 \cdot 000}$$

Thus $\sqrt{10} = 3\ 9'\ 43''\ 12'''$. Though Finaeus expresses the root sexagesimally, yet he expressly states that in 3162 the 3 denotes units, the 1 one-tenth of a unit, the 6 six-tenths of one-tenth of a unit, the 2 two-tenths of one-tenth of one-tenth of a unit. This is the germ of the doctrine of decimal fractions. The most notable development of it is found in Stevin's *Arithmetic*, which was published in 1585 in French. It contained a small treatise, *La Disme*, "by the which we can operate with whole numbers without fractions." This is not quite the modern view, namely, that by extension of the notation for integers, integers and fractions can be treated by the same rules, but it comes near to it. The number which we write 27·847 Stevin writes 27(0) 8(1) 4(2) 7(3), or when using it in operation $\underset{(0)\ (1)\ (2)\ (3)}{27\ 8\ 4\ 7}$. The following are other notations for decimal fractions which occur in books subsequent to Stevin's time :

$27 \mid \overset{1\ 2\ 3}{847}$		$27\quad 8'\ 4''\ 7'''$
$27\quad 847'''$		$27\quad 847^{(3)}$
$27 \mid 847$ thirds		$27\quad {\cdot}8{\cdot}4{\cdot}7$
$27\quad \underline{847}$		$27 \mid \underline{847}$

The question of who introduced the point or comma to separate the integers from the fractions has been discussed by De Morgan, and he does not admit the claim that has been made by Peacock for Napier, the inventor of logarithms. Whether or not Napier habitually used the comma, there is at any rate one instance where it occurs in his *Rabdologia*, which was published in 1617; he gives a quotient as 1993,273 or 1993,2′ 7″ 3‴. This simplification of the notation for decimal fractions, obvious enough as it seems, did not become common till the middle of the seventeenth century.

It was only about a century ago that decimals were applied to metrological reform. The tables of the measures for length, area, capacity, weight in use in France were very irregular, and the French National Assembly in 1790 resolved to create a new system of measures, the sub-divisions of which should harmonise with the decimal system of numbers. The commission of scientific men to whom this reform was entrusted selected as a basis a length which should be the ten-millionth part of the distance between the North Pole and the Equator. This distance they called a *metre*, and to express the multiples of it they used as prefixes the Greek words, somewhat modified, for 10, 100, 1000 (deca-, hecto-, kilo-) ; to express the sub-multiples they used the Latin words for 10, 100, 1000 (deci-, centi-, milli-) in the sense of $\frac{1}{10}$, $\frac{1}{100}$, $\frac{1}{1000}$. The standards or units for the other tables are derived from the metre, and hold a definite and easily remembered relation to it, and their multiples and sub-multiples are expressed by the same prefixes. Thus the unit for measuring capacity or volume being the litre, and that for measuring weight being the gram, it is known at once that a hectolitre = 100 litres, a centilitre = ·01 litre, a kilogram = 1000 grams, a milligram = ·001 gram. The process of reduction therefore from one measure down to or up to another of the same kind consists in nothing more than changing the position of a decimal point.

This is not the place in which to discuss the advantages or the disadvantages of the Metric System, but after the exposition which has been made of how a tolerably uniform system of numeration and a completely uniform system of notation have been gradually built up among civilised nations, it may be worth while to see what improvement awaits them in the distant future.

Herbert Spencer, in a pamphlet[1] entitled "Against the Metric System," proposes as the radix of numeration the number 12. He says, " This process of counting by groups and compound groups, tied together by names, is equally practicable with other groups than 10. We may form our numerical system by taking a group of 12, then 12 groups

---

[1] Published by Williams & Norgate, 1896.

of 12, then 12 of these compound groups; and so on as before. . . . It needs only a small alteration in our method of numbering to make calculation by groups of 12 exactly similar to calculation by groups of 10; yielding just the same facilities as those now supposed to belong only to decimals. . . . To prevent confusion different names and different symbols would be needed for the digits, and to acquire familiarity with these, and with the resulting multiplication-table, would of course be troublesome: perhaps not more troublesome, however, than learning the present system of numeration and calculation as carried on in another language." Spencer states that he thinks this system will not be adopted for generations. " But it is not an unreasonable belief that further intellectual progress may bring the conviction that since a better system would facilitate both the thoughts and actions of men, and in so far diminish the friction of life throughout the future, the task of establishing it should be undertaken."

The crazy attempt of certain Frenchmen during their first Revolution to reform the Calendar of the world has been derided by every nationality, the French themselves included, but the Frenchmen's task (it was carried on for more than twelve years) was simplicity and sanity itself compared to this proposal to change the radix of numeration.

CHAPTER II

ANCIENT SYSTEMS OF ACCOUNTING

BABYLONIAN AND ASSYRIAN—EGYPTIAN—JEWISH—GRECIAN
—ROMAN—UNDER THE EMPEROR CHARLEMAGNE

THE development of social life and especially the formation
of states or sovereignties levying any form of taxation
necessitated, in addition to a knowledge of numbers, a power
of holding count and reckoning. In this we find the origin
of the science of accounting. It antedated the stating of
accounts as we understand them,—since that could not take
place until some monetary standard had been adopted in
which the items composing an account could be expressed
in terms of equality.

In the earliest of such states some kind of organisation
must have been necessary to collect and account for the
public revenues, and an inquiry into the methods of accounting in use among peoples of antiquity, and the arrangements
for administering state property, may be of interest before
we enter upon the investigation of the history of accounts
proper.

The nineteenth century added enormously to our knowledge of ancient nations. At the beginning of that century,
history may almost be said to have begun with the Greeks
and Romans. Now we can look back on civilised communities existing more than 5000 years before Christ.

The Chaldæan-Babylonian Empire is said to have been
the first regularly organised government in the world. As
far back as 4500 B.C. civilisation in Babylonia had already
reached a high point, pre-supposing unknown ages of pre-

vious development. Babylon was from the remotest antiquity one of the chief commercial centres of the East.[1]

So great was its influence that Babylonian became the
language of commercial and political influence throughout
the whole civilised world.[2]

Among the most notable evidence of the wonderful
civilisation of Babylonia is the monument discovered at
Susa, on which is inscribed the code of laws promulgated
by Hammurabi—a contemporary of Abraham, supposed to
be Amraphel of Genesis — who reigned in Babylon from
2285 to 2242 B.C. This code contains a number of enactments dealing with commerce. Thus—

"(104.) If the merchant has given to the agent corn, wool,
oil, or any sort of goods to traffic with, the agent shall
write down the price and hand over to the merchant; the
agent shall take a sealed memorandum of the price which
he shall give to the merchant.

"(105.) If an agent has forgotten and has not taken a
sealed memorandum of the money he has given to the
merchant, money that is not sealed for, he shall not put
in his accounts."[3]

A large number of business records has come down to
us from the period beginning about 2600 B.C., dealing with
sales, letting, hiring, money-lending, partnership, &c. The
medium employed by the scribe in preparing these records
was clay, an abundant supply of which was ready at
hand. He wrote with a stylus on a small slab, sufficiently
moist to receive an impression easily, and sufficiently firm
to prevent the impression from becoming blurred or effaced,
and then he made the record permanent by baking or sun-
drying the slab.

Among these tablets are the records of two banking and
money-lending firms, The Sons of Egibi of Babylon and
Marashu Sons of Nippur. The firm of Egibi carried on

---

[1] "History of Babylonia and Assyria," Rogers, i. 386.
[2] Nippur, Peters, ii. 259.   [3] Johns's Translation.

business from an unknown period to about the fourth century before Christ. "The tablets recording their transactions vary in size from three quarters of an inch by half an inch to nine inches by twelve. They are usually covered with writing on both sides, and sometimes on the edges as well. Many contain no date, and these, on examination, prove to be either rough memoranda, lists of objects or produce, or letters. The more important transactions were re-copied on larger tablets with great care and elaboration of details. These larger tablets usually contain impressions from cylinder seals, and nailmarks, which were considered to be a man's natural seal." [1]

A room at Nippur, excavated by the Expedition of the University of Pennsylvania, contained 730 tablets recording the transactions of Marashu Sons, who flourished in the times of Artaxerxes I. (464–424 B.C.), and Darius II. (423–405 B.C.), in whose reigns the documents are dated. [2] Other tablets indicate the existence of similarly important trading firms as far back as 2700 B.C. [3]

The provinces of this vast empire were administered by satraps or governors, one of whose principal duties was to receive the tribute in money or in kind, for which purpose each was assisted by a superintendent of the revenue, under whom were numerous officials. The business of the central administration and of the provinces was carried out by the scribes, who seem to have combined the functions of the barrister, the attorney, and the accountant of the present day. A carefully prepared register served as a state record of the titles to estates, and also as a basis for the imposition of taxes. [4] The system of storehouses for the custody of the taxes paid in kind seems to have been similar to that of Egypt, to which we shall presently refer.

[1] "Records of the Past," XI. 89.
[2] "The Babylonian Expedition of the University of Pennsylvania," Series A., Vol. IX. 13.
[3] "Babylonians and Assyrians," Sayce, 161.
[4] "Ancient History of the East," Lenormant, i. 424.

The offerings to the gods were treated by the priests, says Maspero, as articles of commerce. "We have to look upon the temple and the industrial establishment of the rich citizens as factories. We have a number of certificates of delivery which show how the raw materials were delivered into the establishments, and how the finished products were delivered from them. These indicate how long the labourers worked, and what wages they received."[1] From the temple archives of the sun god have been derived "a great mass of tablets, which, after the fashion of commercial book-keeping, record the temple revenues in money and other commodities, the expenses in salaries, wages, &c., and the investment and employment of the temple property in loans, real estate, rents, &c."[2]

Much information as to business methods is derived from these ancient tablets, but we have not succeeded in finding evidence that any of them can, strictly speaking, be described as accounts; and Dr. Budge of the British Museum, in courteous response to our inquiry, informs us that he knows of none. He says: "There is no reason for thinking that they (the Babylonians and Assyrians) managed their money affairs as we do. There are many contract tablets known, and hundreds of records of commercial transactions, but I know of none which could be considered as accounts in the modern sense of the word."

The valley of the Nile boasts of a civilisation only less ancient than that of Mesopotamia. According to Manetho, who wrote in the days of Ptolemy Philadelphus, the dynasties of the Egyptian kings go back to 5004 B.C. The pictures on the walls of Memphite tombs of the fourth and fifth dynasties show large square-sailed barks floating on the Nile "employed in a commerce which everything proves to have been most extensive."[3]

[1] "A Sketch of Babylonian Society," Peiser (Smithsonian Institution Report, 1898).
[2] "Discoveries in Mesopotamia," Delitzsch (Smithsonian Institution Report, 1900).
[3] "Ancient History of the East," Lenormant, i. 208.

In ancient Egypt, as elsewhere in early times, the use of money was unknown, and the fiscal receipts and payments of Pharaoh were in kind. " If the tax were received in oxen, they were led to pasturage, or at times, when a murrain threatened to destroy them, to the slaughter-house and the currier; if it were in corn, it was bolted, ground to flour, and made into bread and pastry; if it were in stuffs, it was washed, ironed, and folded to be retailed as garments or in the piece. The royal treasury partook of the character of the farm, the warehouse, and the manufactory." [1] This system necessitated a large number of storehouses, every class of goods having one or more allotted to it,—and for the security and management of these, troops of porters, accountants, directors, &c., were employed. In addition to the staff of officials in the royal city, similar officials administered affairs in the provinces, forwarding the least perishable part of the provincial dues to the central treasury, and using the remainder on the spot in paying workmen's wages, and for the needs of the Administration. The scribe, as in Babylonia, was the mainspring of the administrative machinery. His qualifications consisted in a knowledge of reading, writing, arithmetic, and elementary book-keeping, and some proficiency in wording the administrative formulas. Beginning in one of the lowest offices of the administration, he might, and often did, work his way to the top, exercising a kind of vice-regency over half of Egypt. [2]

The " house of silver of the treasury," or central finance department, employed numerous officials, the " superintendent," " deputy-superintendent," and the " scribes of the house of silver," all under the control of a lord high treasurer, " the governor of all that exists, or that does not exist," under whom there was also a " treasurer of the God." [3] The nome, or district, was a diminutive copy of the state, having its treasury and storehouses, with similar officials. The territory

---

[1] " Dawn of Civilisation," Maspero.   [2] Ibid.
[3] " Life in Ancient Egypt," Erman.

belonging to each town and district was frequently surveyed. The surveyors recorded in their books the name of each estate, the name of the proprietor, those of the owners of adjoining lands, and the area and nature of the ground. This information enabled the scribes to regulate the assessment of the land tax.[1]

The Egyptian scribe prepared his accounts on papyrus with a calamus. "Numerous documents," says Erman, " have come down to us, showing how the accounts were kept in the department of the 'house of silver,' and in similar departments ; the translation of these is however extremely difficult, owing to the number of unknown words and the abbreviations they contain. These documents show exactly how much was received, from whom and when it came in, and the details of how it was used. This minute care is not only taken in the case of large amounts, but even the smallest quantities of corn or dates are conscientiously entered."[2] The pictures in the old tombs testify that the scribes were present on all occasions —whether the corn is measured out, or the cattle are led past. " They squat on the ground, with the deed box or the case for the papyrus rolls by them, a pen in reserve behind the ear, and the strip of papyrus on which they are writing in their hands."[3]

Nothing was given out of the treasury without a written order. Peculation on the part of the workmen was provided against by the records of one official checking those of another. When the corn was brought to the storehouses each sack was filled in the sight of the overseer and noted down, and when the sacks were carried to the roof of the storehouse and emptied through the receiving opening the scribe stationed there recorded the number received.[4] The system in operation is shown in the accompanying illustration, which is taken from the pictures in the tomb of Chnemhôtep, and which the publishers of " Life in Ancient Egypt " have kindly all ved us to reproduce.

[1] " Dawn of Civilisation," Maspero.   [2] " Life in Ancient Egypt," Erman, 112.
[3] Ibid.   [4] Ibid. 95.

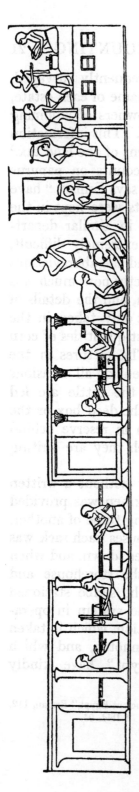

HISTORY OF ACCOUNTING

Some interesting accounts belonging to the end of the second or to the early part of the first century before Christ have quite recently been found in a strange resting-place—the mummies of crocodiles.[1] From the editors of these accounts we learn that in one of them the receipts for each day are given, then follow the payments, which are subtracted from the receipts, the balance being carried to the next day. The payments are of a very varied description, including payments for food of all kinds, and other personal expenses, such as baths, writing-material, doctors' and barbers' fees, &c. Another account deals with the rents of a farm during three successive years, and throws light on the system of rotation of crops; while a third is the account of a dining-club, giving the cost per head exclusive of wine, which is reckoned separately, as are also bread and garlands. These accounts are in Greek. There are numerous mistakes in arithmetic, which is not

[1] See the "Tebtunis Papyri." Edited by Grenfell, Hunt, and Smyly. The crocodile-mummy as a source of manuscripts was accidentally discovered by the editors of this collection of Papyri in 1900 at Ûmm el Baragât (the ancient Tebtunis) in the south of the Fayûm. When excavating in the large Ptolemaic necropolis adjoining the town one of the workmen employed, disgusted at finding a row of crocodiles where he expected sarcophagi, broke one of them in pieces and disclosed the surprising fact that the creature was wrapped in sheets of papyrus. The ordinary process employed in the mummification was to stuff the mummy with reeds and sticks, which were covered with layers of cloth. When papyrus was used, sheets of this material were wrapped once or several times round the mummy inside the cloth, and a roll or two would frequently be inserted in the throat or other cavities.

surprising in view of the notation. A summation is shown thus: /ρπε (*i.e.* 185).[1]

Other ancient peoples among whom, though history gives us little information on the subject, it may safely be assumed that methods of accounting were more or less developed, were the Persians, whose provincial tribute was collected by satraps, accounting to the monarch ; the Phœnicians, including the Carthaginians, with their extensive commerce and their colonies ; and the Rhodians, with their navigation laws, which were adopted by the Romans. In the case of the Israelites, the Bible furnishes us with a number of references to matters of accounting ;[2] but after the Egyptian the next nation of whose methods of accounting we have any real information is the Grecian.

The public economy of the Athenians shows a highly developed system of accounting.[3] The administration was in the hands of the Senate, under whom were numerous boards and officials. All regular impost duties were let to farmers, under the supervision of the Poletæ, a board of ten to which each tribe contributed one member. The property of the temples was let by the directors of sacred possessions ; that of the tribes and burghs was let by themselves through their own agent. The proportion of justice-fees and fines effeiring to the State was transferred by the presidents of the court of justice to officers called exactors, the proportion allotted to any god being paid to the treasurers of the proper temple.

There were officers for the determination of the contributions to the extraordinary property tax, and officers who fixed the rate of the tributes of the allies. Certain persons

---

[1] *Vide ante,* page 9.

[2] *E.g.* The elaborate reckonings under the Mosaic law ; the arrangements made by Jehoash for the receipt of the temple offerings, " even the money of every one that passed the account," and their disbursement by the king's scribe and the high priest in repairing the temple ; the parable of the talents ; the parable of the unjust steward, &c.

[3] Our information with regard to the accounting of the Greeks is derived from the English translation of Boeckh's " Public Economy of Athens."

were also employed as collectors.   The subordinate officers delivered up the revenues to others, who either distributed them for the public service or kept them for security.   Lists of those indebted to the State were kept by government receivers (*apodectæ*).   These officials received and entered the money paid in, and, with the Senate, they assigned it to the separate offices.

The most important of the offices of finance was that of Treasurer or Manager of the Public Revenue.   Aristides, Lysias, and Lycurgus may be mentioned as having held this office.   Like every other officer, the Treasurer of the Public Revenue was subject to the restraint of legal checks and of the will of the people.   He appears to have occupied a similar position to that of a modern Chancellor of the Exchequer, superintending the whole revenue and expenditure.

In addition to innumerable treasurers (of the goddess, of the tribes and burghs, of the generals, &c.), there were secretaries or clerks, and also subordinate or private secretaries. The entering of the receipts and payments, and the respective purposes to which the monies were assigned, the noting of acknowledgments of payment, and the passing of the accounts, came within the department of the secretary or clerk.   There was a checking-clerk of the Senate for money received, a checking clerk of the highest authority for disbursements, and there were a number of subordinate checking-clerks.

The public accounts being kept by the clerks, and controlled by the checking-clerks, it was possible to make the scrutiny which was entered into at the expiration of every office.   Every one who had had any share in the government or administration, from the Senate downwards, was subject to this scrutiny.   "No person who had not rendered his account could go abroad, consecrate his property to a god, or even dedicate a sacred offering; nor could he make a will, or be adopted from one family into another."   According to Aristotle, the officials whose business it was to examine the accounts of public officers were called in some places ἔυθυνοι, in

others, λογισταί, ἐξετασταί, or συνηγοροι. The difference between
the duties of the euthuni and the logistæ is not well known,
but it is thought that the euthuni were assistants to the
logistæ.

While there was no lack of well-conceived and strict
regulations, the spirit of the administration in Greece was
bad. All officers of finance were sworn to administer without peculation the money entrusted to them; "but if in
Greece," says Polybius, "the State entrusted to any one
only a talent, and if it had ten checking-clerks, and as
many seals and twice as many witnesses, it could not ensure
his honesty."

To ensure publicity the accounts of public officials were
engraved on stone and exposed in public. Some of these
accounts still exist, and specimens of them are among the
Elgin Marbles in the British Museum.

We give as an illustration a photographic reproduction
of one of them, No. XXIII, which is a slab of white marble,
height 1 ft. 10 in., breadth 1 ft. 2¾ in.

We are indebted to Mr. Cecil Smith, Director of the
Department of Greek and Roman antiquities in the British
Museum, for the following transcript and translation, and he
has also very kindly furnished us with the valuable notes
on the subject which are added on pages 27 and 28. The
parts enclosed in square brackets are restoration.

['Αθηναῖοι ἀνήλωσαν ἐπὶ Χαρίου ἄρχοντος καὶ ἐπὶ τῆς βουλῆς ᾗ . . .]
ἴδης πρῶτος ἐγραμμάτευε· ταμίαι ἱερῶν χρημάτων
[τῆς 'Αθηναίας, Λεωχάρης . . . . . . καὶ ξυνάρχοντες, οἷς Τελέα]ς
Τελενίκου Περγασῆθεν ἐγραμμάτευε, παρέδοσαν στρ-
[α]τηγοῖς Τηλεφόνῳ [. . . . . 'Ελληνοταμίᾳ καὶ]
παρέδρῳ Φερεκλείδη Πειραιεῖ, ψηφισαμένου τοῦ δήμ-
[ου] τὴν ἄδειαν, ἐπὶ τῆς Αἰαντίδος τρί[της πρυτανευούσης . . . . . .]
ἐρ[ᾳ] τῆς πρυτανείας ꓷΤΧΧΧⲦΗΗΗⲂΛΛΛΛⲦⲦ ΙΙΙΙⲤ τε καὶ χρυσίου
5 Κυζικηνοῦ ΗΗΛΛΛΛⲦϹϹϹ · τιμὴ τούτων γί[γ]ν[εται] . . . . . .
ϹϹϹϹϹϹϹ
'Ελληνοταμίαις καὶ παρέδροις ἐδανείσα[μεν . . . . . .] 'Αριστοκράτει

Εὐωνυμεῖ καὶ ξυνάρχουσι, ⊢ΤΤΤΤ, οὗτοι δ-
ὲ ἔδοσαν Ἀθλοθέταις ἐς Παναθήναια, Ἀμέμπτῳ [. . . . . . καὶ] ξυνάρχουσι,
ἐπὶ τῆς Ἐρεχθηΐδος δευτέρας πρυτανευούση-
ς, εἰκοστῇ ἡμέρᾳ τῆς πρυτανείας.
Ἐπὶ τῆς Κεκροπίδος τετάρτης πρυτανευούσης [ἕκτῃ ἡμέρᾳ τ]ῆς
πρυτανείας, Ἑλληνοταμίαις καὶ παρέδροις Ἀριστοκρ-

10 άτει Εὐωνυμεῖ καὶ ξυνάρχουσι, στρατιώταις ε . . . . . . ΛΛ
Ἐπὶ τῆς Ἀντιοχίδος ὀγδόης πρυτανευούσης δεκ[άτῃ ἡμέρᾳ τῆς]
πρυτανείας, Ἑλληνοταμίαις καὶ παρέδροις Ἀριστοκρ[ά-]
τει Εὐωνυμεῖ καὶ ξυνάρχουσι στρατιώταις ἐμ Μ . . . . . .
Ἐπὶ τῆς Ἀντιοχίδος ὀγδόης πρυτανευούσης τρίτ[ῃ καὶ δεκάτῃ τῆς πρυ-]
τανείας, Ἑλληνοταμίαις καὶ παρέδροις Ἀριστοκρ[άτ-]
ει Εὐωνυμεῖ καὶ ξυνάρχουσι, ⊦⊦⊦. οὗτοι δ᾽ ἔδοσαν [τῇ ἐν

15 Σικελίᾳ στ]ρατιᾷ.
Ἐπὶ τῆς Ἀντιοχίδος, ὀγδόης πρυτανευούσης, εἰκοσ[τῇ ἡμέρᾳ τῆς πρ-]
υτανείας, Ἑλληνοταμίαις καὶ παρέδροις Ἀριστοκρ[ά-]
τει Εὐωνυμεῖ καὶ ξυνάρχουσι, ἐς τὰ[ς] ναῦς τὰς ἐς Σι[κελίαν
διακομιούσας] τὰ χρή[μ]ατα, ΤΤΤΤΧΧ.
Ἐπὶ τῆς Ἀντιοχίδος ὀγδόης πρυτανευούσης δευτέ[ρᾳ καὶ εἰκοστῇ ἡμέρᾳ τῆς
πρυτα]νείας, Ἑλληνοταμίᾳ καὶ παρέδρῳ Φιλομή[λῳ Μ-]
αραθωνίῳ, καὶ στρατηγῷ ἐν τῷ Θερμαίῳ κόλπῳ . . . . . .
[Τῇ] αὐτῇ ἡμέρᾳ Ἑλληνοταμίᾳ κ[αὶ παρέ-]
δρῳ Φιλομήλῳ Μαραθωνίῳ καὶ στρατηγῷ ἐν Ε . . . . . .

20 Κεφάλαιον ἀνα[λώματος τ]οῦ ἐπὶ τ[ῆς]
ἀρχῆς ⊦⊦⊦⊓⊢ΤΤΤ . . .

Translation

Expenditure of the Athenians in the Archonship of Charias and
during the session of the Boule in which . . . ides was the first Secretary. The treasurers of the sacred funds of Athena, Leochares . . . and
his colleagues, with Teleas son of Telenikos of Pergase as secretary,
disbursed to the generals Telephonos . . . the Hellenotamias and his
assessor Pherekleides of Peiraeus, the demos having voted their sanction
in the third prytany, that of Aeantis, on the —— day of the prytany;
eleven talents three thousand seven hundred and ninety-seven drachmas,
four and a half obols; and of Kyzikene gold two hundred and fifty-five
staters; valued at . . .

ACCOUNT OF DISBURSEMENTS OF THE ATHENIAN STATE, 418 B.C. TO 415 B.C.
(size of original 1 foot 10 inches by 1 foot 2¾ inches)

British Museum—Greek Inscription No. 23

To the Hellenotamiai and assessors we lent . . . to Aristokrates of Euonymia and their colleagues nine talents, and these gave to the Athlothetæ (Games-Committee) for the Panathenaia, viz. Amemptos and his fellow officials in the second prytany—that of Erechtheis—on the 20th day of the prytany. In the fourth prytany, that of Kekropis, on the 6th day of the prytany, to the Hellenotamiai and assessors Aristokrates of Euonymia and his colleagues, for troops. . . . In the eighth prytany—that of Antiochis—on the 10th day of the prytany, to the Hellenotamiai and assessors Aristokrates of Euonymia and his colleagues for the troops in M. . . .

In the eighth prytany—that of Antiochis—on the 13th day of the prytany, to the Hellenotamiai and assessors, Aristokrates of Euonymia and his colleagues, three hundred talents; and they paid for the campaign in Sicily.

In the eighth prytany—that of Antiochis—on the 20th day of the prytany, to the Hellenotamiai and assessors Aristokrates of Euonymia and his colleagues for the ships which were to transport the funds to Sicily we paid four talents and two thousand drachmas. In the eighth prytany—that of Antiochis—on the 22nd day of the prytany to the Hellenotamias and assessor, Philomelos of Marathon, and to the general (commanding) in the Thermæan gulf. . . . On the same day to the Helleno-tamias and assessor Philomelos of Marathon, also to the general in E——.

Total of expenditure during our office three hundred and fifty-three talents. . . .

This is one of a series of inscriptions which record the disbursements of the Athenian state, and when complete formed part of a large stone giving the account by the Treasurers of Athena of the expenditure of a quadriennium, from Ol. 90·3 (B.C. 418) to Ol. 91·2 (B.C. 415). The date is identified by the mention of the Archon Charias; and this part of the document refers to the last year of the quadriennium. The portion in the British Museum is here completed in the cursive text from supplementary fragments which are in Athens; these supplementary portions are en-closed within square brackets.

The Parthenon, from the moment of its completion in B.C. 438, served as the principal storehouse of the sacred treasure. This treasure included not only the ἀναθήματα—

the valuables dedicated to the goddess—but all the property accruing to her from sacred lands and other sources, and even such part of the national treasure as was not required for current expenses came under this category. It was administered by a board of ten ταμίαι, chosen by lot yearly, one from each tribe, from among the most wealthy. The accounts were rendered annually, but only inscribed on a marble *stele* on the occasion of the Greater Panathenaic festival, which recurred every four years. Whenever a question arose of entrenching for state purposes on the balance of the national treasure it was necessary (as we see from l. 3) that the sanction, or rather indemnification (ἄδεια), should first be obtained from the popular assembly.

In l. 5 it is supposed by Canon Hicks, the editor of this inscription, that the seven sigmas written below the other figures are intended as the correction of a mistake made either by the treasurers or the lapidary; and that the letters at the end of this line are the beginning of δι' ἀν[ομολογήματος; if so, the meaning would be, that the value of these sums was paid over by means of a bill-transaction, the generals in Sicily having drawn a bill on the Athenian treasury; τίμη may represent the value of the bill at the current rate of exchange.

In l. 14 is recorded the payment of three hundred talents of silver; this transaction is probably alluded to by Thucydides (vi. 94) and Diodorus (xiii. 7), who state that in the winter of B.C. 415-414 the Athenian general Nikias, in command of the Sicilian expedition, sent a trireme to Athens asking for money and cavalry: and in the following spring the cavalry were sent, together with three hundred talents of silver. The money was required, says Thucydides, as τροφὴν τῇ στρατιᾷ, and it will be noticed that this expression coincides with the entry in our inscription. In l. 18 the general referred to is probably Euetion, who, according to Thucydides (vii. 9), at the end of the summer of B.C. 414 made a fruitless attempt to recover Amphipolis.

The Romans possessed the genius of administration as well as of jurisprudence. Their system of financial administration, which began with the simple arrangements required under the Kings and the Republic, developed into the elaborate and complicated organisation of the enormous Empire.[1]

In order to obtain a clear view of the subject it is necessary to look at it in three divisions: (1) under the Kings and the Republic; (2) under the earlier Empire; and (3) under the later Empire, that is to say, from the time of Diocletian.

In the original constitution of Rome there was no regular direct taxation nor was there any direct regular state expenditure. The state gave no recompense for service in the army or for public service generally: so far as there was such recompense at all, it was given to the person who performed the service by the district concerned in it, or by the person who could not or would not perform the service himself. The king managed the finances—how far he was restricted by use and wont in the administration of public property is not now known. The receipts consisted chiefly of port dues, income from domain lands, cattle fines and confiscations, and the gains of war. A special tax was sometimes imposed, but was repaid if circumstances permitted.[2]

It is under the Republic that we first see the idea of a treasury of the Roman people, governed by the senate, administered by the consuls, and managed by the quæstors. These were the first elements of the financial organisation, created for a municipality, which developed with the growing requirements of the state, until we see it under the Empire spreading like a network over the greater part of the known world.

The system of recording the state accounting in Rome was based on the system practised in private life from very early times. The father of the Roman family entered in a

[1] Except where otherwise stated, our information with regard to the Romans is directly derived from Monsieur Humbert's elaborate work *Essai sur les Finances et la Comptabilité Publique chez les Romains.*
[2] "History of Rome," Mommsen, I. 79.

sort of waste book (*adversaria*) all the receipts and payments
of his household. He posted these monthly to a carefully
kept register of receipts and payments (*codex accepti et depensi*), in which an entry, made with the consent of the
debtor, was considered as a good ground of civil obligation.
Bankers, of whom there were many at Rome, and merchants,
used similar registers down to the time of Justinian. Bankers
appear also to have kept a third kind of register, called the
book of accounts (*rationes, liber rationum*), probably arranged
in alphabetical order, in which an account was kept for each
customer, a page being allotted for the debits and a page
for the credits. The accounts were balanced at certain
agreed-on times, the banker being bound to render an account,
and to produce, if required, an extract of the account before
the prætor. The fidelity of the bankers was placed under
the supervision of the præfect of the town, and, in the provinces, of the governor. When the balance of the account
was at the credit of the customer, the banker had to pay
the amount to the customer unless he was authorised anew
to retain it. Sometimes the Roman citizen paid his creditors
in cash, kept usually by a cashier, who was a slave; but
more frequently the father of a rich family paid by means
of a sort of cheque on his banker.

From the earliest times the Romans recognised the
essential distinction between the person who imposes taxes
and authorises expenditure and the person who is responsible for the actual receipt and payment. Under the Republic,
legislative control over the public revenue and expenditure
was in the hands of the senate. Subordinate to the senate,
the consuls first were entrusted with the power of ordering payments, having to account to the senate for their
intromissions, but in 443 B.C. this power was taken from
them and given to the censors, who thereafter became the
real ministers of finance. The general administration of
the domain of the state was one of the principal functions
of the censors, who also let the farming of the taxes to

publicans in the presence of the quæstors of the treasury, and to whom credits were voted in the quinquennial budget of the senate. All receipts and payments having been ordered or authorised by the magistrates, the actual receipt and payment was the special work of the *quæstores ærarii*. There were originally two of these officials, then the number was increased to four, and, under Sulla, to twenty. The two town quæstors had charge of the keys of the public treasury (*ærarium Saturni*), and even of the reserve fund (*ærarium sanctius*), the latter of which could only be used in virtue of a special vote of the senate, followed by an order of the magistrates. They had offices, with numerous assistants, in the Temple of Saturn. There were also quæstors of the army and navy, appointed to each commander by the comitia, having charge of the military and naval receipts and payments, and, later on, provincial quæstors attached to the proconsuls, who managed the local tribute and provincial expenditure; all of whom had to account to the town quæstors at the central treasury, their directors and correspondents.

The scribes of the treasury under the orders of the quæstors recorded the transactions in *tabulæ publicæ*, a species of journal analogous to the *adversaria* of the father of the Roman family. A monthly register was also kept, resembling the *codex accepti et depensi*, in which the receipts and payments were entered separately and regularly, with particulars of the dates, the names of the persons paying or receiving, the nature of the transaction, and the balance of each account at the end of the month. There was also a register of debts (*calendarium*), and there were special registers for the current accounts between the treasury and the military cashiers, who exchanged letters of credit with the quæstors of the provinces.

All expenditure had to be legally authorised and regularly ordered by a competent magistrate, and could only be discharged by the production of the formal order, supported by documents tending to guarantee the existence and liquidity of the debt, the title of the creditor, and the execution of the work indicated by the order. The identity of the magistrate ordering payment and of the creditor, had, if necessary, to be attested by witnesses.

The quæstors on demitting office rendered an account to their successors of the state of the funds and of the condition of the registers, and they also submitted accounts of their administration to the senate, the meetings of which body they attended for the purpose of advising regarding the credits asked for by the magistrates, and financial business generally, and in which in later years they had seats. The accounts of the sub-quæstors were also submitted to the senate, as well as to the central quæstors.

These various regulations rendered fraud very difficult, in Rome at all events, their observance being under the supervision not only of the senate, but of the censors, consuls, and each member of the college of quæstors. Every illegal act could be easily nipped in the bud, or at least the offender could be prosecuted by the tribunes. From the sixth century of Rome, however, financial abuses crept in. The wars of conquest, along with the establishment of provinces, led to the increase of the public resources and needs, to the long duration of the magistrates' terms of office, to the abuse of proconsular authority, and finally to disorder and even anarchy in the whole government. The organisation of Rome, suitable for a municipality, was ill-adapted to the requirements of a great state. The governors, all-powerful outside the precincts of the city, and exempt from all local supervision, respected as little the rights of the treasury as the feeble guarantees of the provincial constitution. The generals, not content with enriching themselves at the expense of the enemy, adopted also in their turn independent and almost kingly state. Several laws were passed to repress abuses in financial matters—the Calpurnian law in 149 B.C., the Cornelian law of Sulla and the Julian law of Augustus—but they

had but little effect. Salutary regulations were ineffective
owing to the absence of a judicial control powerful enough
to repress the abuses of financial administration in the hands
of an unscrupulous aristocracy, or to apply a remedy to the
vices of the too-municipal organisation, or to the excesses of
the sovereignty directly exercised by the factious and corrupt
comitia.

With the Empire, in spite of the official maintenance of
the national sovereignty, public government assumed a dual
form, that of the senate and that of the emperor. The
provinces and the magistratures were divided into senatorial
and imperial; the treasury, into the treasury of the people,
that of the emperor, and that of the army; and officials, rules,
and responsibilities were multiplied. While republican forms
were at first retained, all authority became concentrated more
and more in the hands of the emperor, until the last trace
of representative government disappeared with the rights of
the senate over the treasury and the right of consent to the
imposition of taxes in the name of the Roman people.

At first Augustus endeavoured to maintain the unity of
the public treasury; but the necessities of a standing army
gave rise to the establishment of a military treasury, and the
increasing charges of the imperial government led to the
establishment of a treasury of the emperor. The *ærarium
populi* or *Saturni* was taken as the model of the new creations,
but it was reduced to a part only of its former resources,
and its jurisdiction was restricted abroad within the borders of
the senatorial domain. Instead of the two town quæstors
elected by the comitia, who were often young and inexperienced politicians, two præfects were elected by the senate
from among the members of the rank of ex-prætors, under
the title of *prætores ærarii* or *ad ærarium*. Later, election
by vote not appearing to be the best method of appointing
the chiefs of the treasury, Claudius restored the office to the
quæstors, but chosen from among the college of quæstors
by the emperor, under the title of *quæstores ærarii Saturni*.

A further change was made under Nero, who in 56 A.D. confided the office to two senators of prætorian rank, who took the title of *præfecti ærarii Saturni*. Finally, under Diadumenus a *rationalis* or *procurator* was put at the head of the præfects of the treasury.

A sort of budget of expenditure was drawn up by the emperor. It was accompanied by statements of the fiscal cash at the beginning and end of the year, of the annual produce of the farm of the indirect taxes, of the amount of the tribute, and of the poll tax of the provinces. The whole formed a statement called *rationarum* or *breviarium imperii*.

In the early days of the Empire the power to order or authorise the expenditure included in the senatorial budget continued to belong to the censors, and failing them, usually to the consuls. These magistrates exercised this prerogative only within the limits of the quinquennial budget or the credits specially voted by the senate, and they acted under the control of the emperor. Special curators were gradually substituted for these magistrates. The expenditure of the military treasury, of the crown lands, and of the emperor's treasury, was directly controlled by the emperor through his officials. Under Hadrian, the knight invested with the department of the finances received the title of *procurator a rationibus* with the rank of *perfectissimus*. There was also created, probably under Marcus Aurelius, a sub-director under the name of *procurator summarum rationum*. The finance minister in the third century received the name of *rationalis*, which title was extended later by custom to the fiscal procurators of the provinces. The staff of the minister of finance consisted of a great number of officials whose titles have been preserved to us by inscriptions, which do not, however, inform us of their respective functions.

The central accounting office was called *tabularium*, where the work, under a superintendent, was carried on by the book-keepers or *tabularii*, the *approximi* and the assistants, the latter being often slaves.

The quæstors in the senatorial provinces, subordinate to and correspondents of the central treasury, preserved their former functions with respect to the goods and rights falling to that treasury, and the subordinate officials corresponded to those of the central treasury. In the third century they were replaced by imperial governors of the provinces (*procuratores* or *rationales Cæsaris*).

The accountants of the military treasury were originally similar to those of the public treasury, but under Hadrian the collection was entrusted to a special administration with a central treasury at Rome, and with offices also in the provinces.

With regard to the administration of the private property of the prince and of that of the fisc, comprised at first under the name of *patrimonium privatum*, originally freedmen and even slaves fulfilled at Rome the duties of cashiers. There were fiscal *procuratores*, and a chief of the office of *tabularii*. There was a department of public works and a special treasury in connection with the *patrimonium* with cashiers and their assistants. The inscriptions do not furnish any trace of a central administration or a treasury at Rome for the fisc before the reign of Claudius. The free funds proceeding from the governors of the provinces were deposited in certain temples at the disposal of the director of the fisc.

The governors of the provinces had numerous officials under them. They had often a sub-director, accountants or book-keepers, mostly freedmen, and superintended by a chief of the office, and cashiers, who were mostly slaves. The funds not employed in local expenses were capitalised or sent to Rome. In fact, besides the central treasury of the province, there were district treasuries, independent of the stations of publicans placed under the supervision and control of the governors of Augustus.

After the time of Claudius, a *procurator patrimonii* administered at Rome the domain of the emperor, having a staff of calculators, book-keepers, and messengers. In the second century we find superintendents of the patrimony, having complete offices and a special treasury with cashiers. Under Septimius Severus a greater separation was made between the fisc and the *Res privata*, the latter being administered at Rome by a *procurator Rei privatæ*, and in the provinces by special *procuratores*.

The communal accounting was on much the same lines as that of the old public treasury. The verification of all the necessary deeds was confided to the chiefs of the scribes of the treasury. There were a large number of these scribes, of whom Horace was one.

All the innumerable officials—the quæstors, prætors, or præfects of the public treasury, the proconsuls of the senatorial provinces, the provincial quæstors, &c.—had to render accounts of their intromissions to the senate, to the emperor, or to their superior officials, as the case might be. The administrative control was, however, far from complete or permanent, and in spite of severe penalties bribery and corruption flourished. During the Empire, the great principle of separating the power to order payment from the power to handle money disappeared, with disastrous results.

Under Diocletian the government was divided into four centres of administration, or præfectures, having each its prætorian præfect, its vicar, its army, and its finances. Diocletian multiplied and subdivided the provinces, and arranged them in twelve dioceses. The three classes of governors, the proconsuls, the consuls, and rectors or presidents, were placed under the supervision of the vicar of the diocese, of the prætorian præfect, and of the emperor. The provincial administration was centralised under the prætorian præfect, and was under a powerfully organised *régime*. The reforms begun by Diocletian were continued and completed by Constantine. The minister of the public treasury received the extraordinary title of count of the sacred largesses (*comes sacrarum largitionum*), "with the intention perhaps," says Gibbon, "of inculcating that every

payment flowed from the voluntary bounty of the monarch;"
while the minister of the domain of the emperor was styled
comes rei privatæ.   The three treasuries were now the public
treasury (*ærarium sacrum* or *sacræ largitiones*), the crown
treasury (*ærarium privatum* or *privatæ largitiones*), and
the treasury of the prætorian præfect (*arca præfecturæ*).   The
ærarium sacrum seems to have corresponded very much to
the old *ærarium Saturni*, but it was no longer under the
control of the senate.   It received in general all that arose
from public contributions in gold or in money, and the crown
treasury in general all the other revenue except the tribute
in kind, which went to the treasury of the præfect for the
requirements of the army.

The emperor having fixed the amount to be raised by
each prætorian præfect, the præfect issued an order for his
præfecture, and divided the required amount among the
various dioceses.   The vicar in his turn divided the amount
allocated to his diocese among the provinces therein, and
lastly the rector divided the amount allocated to his province
between the cities and districts.   The amount allotted to
each of the rectors was divided by the number of taxable
units, thus giving the portion payable by each owner.   The
chief decurions of a city had to prepare, by means of the
director of the archives and of the local accountant (*tabularius*
or *logographus*), the principal assessment roll, which was sent
to the rector for approval.   The latter examined the roll by
his director of contributions (*numerarius*), and returned it as
approved to be published and sent to the receiver for the
purpose of collecting the contributions, and a copy of it was
sent to the *exactores* to recover contributions in arrear.   The
contributors had to pay to the local receiver or cashier of the
tribute in exchange for a receipt delivered to them by the
annotator of the receiver, the contribution being recorded by
the local accountant and noted on the margin of the roll.
Thereafter, the competent decurion had the receipts transferred to the treasury of the receiver-general of the province

attached to the director-general of the finances of the governor.
Thus the records of the local accountant acted as a check on
the transactions and records of the receiver of the city. In like
manner, the records of the director of the provincial finances
checked the transactions of the local accountants, and showed
to what extent they and the *exactores* had accomplished the
work of recovering the contributions. They served also to
check the accounts of the receipts of the chief receiver-general.
The receiver-general of the province had to send the money
received, under the seal of the central accountant, to the
treasurer of the public treasury intimating to him its despatch.
On his part, the governor had to send by his accountant
to the same official a statement of the rolls for the four
months to enable him to check the amounts which had been
sent to him, and if necessary direct the *palatini* against any
governor who was negligent or in arrear. Thus the collection
in each province was thoroughly organised and controlled.
Moreover, the public treasurer had a staff of inspectors for
the purpose of controlling the accounts of the receiver-
general and of the accountant both of the province and of
the city.

It is unnecessary to describe the arrangements for the
recovery of the other income, which were similar in character,
or to give the names of the host of employees—those administering the tribute in kind, flowing into the treasury of
the prætorian præfect, and those under the direction of the
count of the crown treasury. The indirect taxes were still
let to publicans.

The central organisation was no less elaborate than that
throughout the provinces. The count of the public treasury
had an office divided into ten departments, and twelve under
Justinian, of which eight were occupied with the accounting.
The count of the treasury corresponded with the counts of
the largesses in the dioceses, one of whom was in each diocese,
with the governors or *rationales*, one of whom administered
several provinces, and with the *procuratores* of the manufac-

tures, the accounts of all of whom were submitted to him. The minister of the domain of the crown also had a large central office, divided into four departments, for the examination of the accounts of his numerous agents.

The fundamental distinction between the official authorising expenditure and the official responsible for the actual payment, which was so clearly recognised under the Republic and in the earlier days of the Empire, but which was departed from later, was re-established at least in the provincial administration, as is shown by the words: *qui aurum largitionale susceperunt, nihil cum arcæ ratiociniis habere commune.* Moreover, every accounting official had to render an account of his administration to his superior official, the chief minister accounting to the emperor. All this elaborate machinery with its carefully devised checks and counter-checks signally failed, however, to attain its object, lack of efficient control rendering nugatory the most skilfully devised arrangements.

After the fall of the Western Empire (dating that event from the election of Odoacer as Patrician in Italy), while elaborate methods of accounting were continued in the Eastern Empire, as we have seen, Roman accounting traditions were continued for a time in Italy by Odoacer, the Scyrrian, and Theodoric, the Ostrogoth, and in later years in the ecclesiastical organisation. The Pope we know possessed enormous revenues, and was at the head of a large administrative body, having an *arcarius,* or treasurer, a *sacellarius,* or cashier, and a *protoscriniarius,* who, an Italian writer [1] informs us, was at the head of a staff of officials similar to that of the eastern emperor, and who had to·be an accountant. In the year 1001 we find also that there was a high official on the papal staff called *logotheta,* whose duties latterly were those of an accountant (*ratiocinator*).[2] But with Italy a prey to barbarian invasions and internal struggles little information regarding matters of accounting

---

[1] Vincenzo Campi, *Il Ragioniere,* p. 64.   [2] Ibid.

can be looked for there until we reach the times of the communes and the maritime republics.

Before leaving the dark ages, however, we may pause for a moment to refer to the enlightened arrangements established by Charlemagne in the Frankish Empire, which are especially remarkable in view of the barbarism prevailing elsewhere. An ordinance of that emperor of the year 812 contains elaborate instructions for the management of the imperial estates. It prescribes that accounts of income and expenditure shall be kept and rendered. Every *judex* (the *judices* were stewards on the *villæ* or estates of the emperor) was required to report yearly at Christmas separately, distinctly, and in order, what he had out of his administration — rents, duties, fines, farm produce, &c. " In all the foregoing, let it not seem harsh to our *judices* that we require these accounts, for we wish that they, in like manner, count with their subordinates, without offence." [1]

[1] "Scotland in the Middle Ages," Innes, 329.

CHAPTER III

EARLY FORMS OF ACCOUNTS

ENGLISH EXCHEQUER—PIPE ROLLS—SCOTTISH EXCHEQUER—
SCOTTISH BURGH ACCOUNTS AUDITED IN EXCHEQUER—
HOUSEHOLD ACCOUNTS OF ELEANOR, COUNTESS OF LEI-
CESTER—ACCOUNTS OF THE EXECUTORS OF THE CONSORT
OF EDWARD I. ; OF THE ROYAL WARDROBE ; OF ENGLISH
MANORS—EVOLUTION OF THE MONEY COLUMN—ACCOUNTS
OF THE CITY OF LONDON ; OF THE LIVERY COMPANIES OF
LONDON—CHARGE AND DISCHARGE FORM—ACCOUNTS OF
THE LORD HIGH TREASURER OF SCOTLAND—ACCOUNTS OF
THE CITIES OF ABERDEEN, EDINBURGH, GLASGOW, DUBLIN
—ARABIC NUMERALS—ACCOUNTS OF THE HOUSEHOLD EX-
PENSES OF THE PRINCESS ELIZABETH ; OF THE CHURCH-
WARDENS OF LUDLOW — THANE OF CAWDOR — KING'S
COLLEGE, ABERDEEN—MERCHANTS' HOUSE OF GLASGOW
—BURGH OF STIRLING—SCOTTISH FORFEITED ESTATES.

IN Great Britain the earliest systems of accounting of which
we have any record are those of the Exchequers[1] of England
and Scotland, and the oldest account which has been preserved is the English Pipe Roll of the year 1130–1131.
Some authorities maintain that the English royal revenue
was audited as far back as the reigns of the first two Norman
kings, but the establishment of the English Exchequer (or
Scaccarium) is usually assigned to the reign of Henry I (1100–
1135). The basis of the accounting was the Domesday Book,

---

[1] Authorities : ENGLISH EXCHEQUER—*Dialogus de Scaccario*, edited by Hughes,
Crump, and Johnson ; Hall's "Antiquities of the Exchequer." SCOTTISH EXCHEQUER
—*Rotuli Scaccarii Regum Scotorum*, edited by Stuart and Burnett ; *Compota Thesaur-
ariorum Regum Scotorum*, edited by Dickson.

which contained the unalterable record of the demesnes from which most of the royal revenue was derived. Supplementary to this were records of the liabilities of the military tenants of the crown, and statements of the royal farms payable by the sheriffs in every county. From these records the Treasurer's great roll (known as the Pipe Roll) was prepared annually, showing all the debts to the crown answerable at the Exchequer, and in which was entered the accounting with each sheriff. Receipt and Issue Rolls were kept by two Remembrancers, recording the amounts paid into the Receipt and issued thence day by day. The great roll was compiled from the dictation of the Treasurer, a second roll was written out by the Chancellor's clerk, and in the early days of the Exchequer a third roll was kept by a special representative of the king.

From the official records a summons was issued half-yearly, at Easter and Michaelmas, to each sheriff requiring him to attend at the Exchequer on a specified day to account for the revenue from his farm or county. At Easter the sheriff made a payment to account in cash to a required amount, and received a tally therefor. The tally, as is well known, was a narrow shaft of wood on which notches were cut representing pounds, shillings, and pence, and a superscription setting forth the object and nature of the tally. The tally was then split in two, so that each portion showed the amount recorded on the original stick, the two pieces being fitted together again at the final accounting. At Michaelmas the sheriff had again to attend, and on this occasion he had to account for the whole year's charge. This he settled partly by production of his tally, partly by production of vouchers for authorised expenditure, and the balance in specie or cash. The accounting was settled on the famous Exchequer-table. The table was covered with a russet cloth which was marked in squares by intersecting lines, probably with chalk, the columns of which represented money columns, the column farthest to the right of the calculator being for pence, the next for shillings, the next for pounds, then scores, hundreds, and thousands of pounds.

The sheriff having duly appeared, the various sums for which he had to account were read out from the great roll. As each item was announced the calculator arranged specie or counters representing the amount thereof in the appropriate columns on the side of the table farthest from him. Below these he then similarly arranged the sheriff's various credits, subtracted the one set from the other and brought out the balance, if any. The tallies produced by the sheriff were carefully compared with the foils in the Exchequer — the discovery of any flaw being immediately followed by the consignment to prison of the fraudulent sheriff.

The earliest existing Pipe Roll belongs to the reign of Henry I., of the year 1130–1131, and an almost unbroken series extends from the twelfth to the nineteenth century. In form the old Pipe Roll can best be described as a narrative of receipts and expenditure, rather than an account in the modern sense. The following translation (in which Arabic numerals have been substituted for the original Roman) of a Pipe Roll of the first year of Richard I., given in the *Growth of English Industry and Commerce*, shows the form.[1]

Nicholas the son of Robert renders account of the ferm of Cambridge-shire and Huntingdonshire.

In the treasury £241.5.3 blank.

And for customary charity for the Knights Templars, 2 marks. And for the canons of Huntingdon 40/-.

And for customary payments in Cambridgeshire: to Radolf of Muntfort 30/5. And to Gervase the clerk 60/10 of the charity which was William's the son of Walter's by the King's letter.

And in Huntingdonshire to Alan Cornieins 30/5. And to the steward of the vineyard 60/10. And for the cost of the vineyard 20/- for this year.

And for lands granted in Cambridgeshire to Roger of Sanford 40/- by tale in Bercheia. And to Peter Picot 100/- in Wilbraham. And

---

[1] Facsimiles of the Pipe Roll and of the Receipt Roll can be seen in the works of Mr. Hubert Hall, F.S.A., of H.M. Public Record Office.

to Richard of Clare and Henry of Kemeseke £20 blank in Fordham.   And to Esweillard of Seissuns £10 by tale in Cumberton.   And in the Burgh of Cambridge £60 blank for which account is to be made separately.   And to Hugh of Malalnet £15 by tale in Wilbraham by Letter of Ranulf de Glanville by the King's command: and to the same £7.10 from the same income by a Letter of the same.

And for the cost of carrying the treasure of Galfrid bishop of Ely from Cambridge to London 25/6.   And for the cost of bringing the same bishop's wine from Cambridge to Selveston 10/5.   And for the payment of John . . . and his horses and his birds 3/11.   And he is quit.

The burghers of Cambridge owe £60 blank of the ferm of the town of Cambridge for this year: and £180 blank for the four years past, and £30 blank for the half of the ferm of the year before that.

Total £270 blank which is £276.15/- by tale, according to the combustion of vi denarii because they had paid in the treasury.

The same burghers render account of the said debt.   In the treasury £196.7/10. by tale.

Remitted by Royal Letter to these burghers £80.7/2 by tale, which they had paid in the treasury for holding their own town *in capite* from the king: about which town the king has now done his pleasure.   And they are quit.

The same burghers render account of 4/2 for some trifling matters found in the new additions to the township of the same Burgh.

They have paid into the Treasury,
                                    And are quit.

. . . of Huntingdon render account for 40/- for their Gild.

They have paid into the Treasury,
                                    And are quit.

In Scotland, the *Camera*, or Royal Treasure-chamber, afterwards commonly known as the Chekker, presided over by the *Camerarius* or Great Chamberlain, dates from the reign of David I. (1124–1153).   The table covered with chequered cloth was in use in Scotland as in England, and in all probability the system of reckoning employed was similar, but the fiscal systems of the two countries were by no means identical. The use of tallies does not appear to have been adopted in Scotland; for after the Union of the Kingdoms, when, among other English innovations, a cargo of birch fagots arrived in Edinburgh for use as tallies in the Exchequer it excited ridicule among the citizens.[1]

The Chamberlain of Scotland was both the receiver and disburser of the Crown revenue. The Crown rents, feudal casualties, &c., were collected by the sheriffs and *ballivi ad extra*,[2] and the burghal fermes and great customs by the magistrates and custumars of the royal burghs. These various officials made disbursements in their respective localities in virtue of royal precepts, the net revenue only being paid to the Chamberlain. All these officials, including the Chamberlain, had their accounts audited in Exchequer, usually every year, by Lords Auditors appointed by the Crown to hear the accounts and grant acquittance thereon. These audited accounts were engrossed on parchment rolls, generally in an abbreviated form. The existing series of these rolls goes back to 1326. The basis of territorial imposts was the old extent, or survey, which was a valuation of the temporal lands of the country.

The time and place of the sitting of the auditors having been arranged, intimation was made to the various officials entrusted with the collection of revenue requiring them to attend in Exchequer on an appointed day to render their accounts.

The accounts of the sheriffs contain the receipts from the crown lands, casualties, fines, &c., and the expenses of the king and royal family when resident within the sheriffdom, expenditure on royal castles and manors, for the defence of the country, &c., &c., and the amounts paid to the chamberlain and officers of the household for the king's use.

An approximately complete series of the burgh accounts

---

[1] Hill Burton's "History of Scotland," VIII. 209.

[2] As distinguished from *ballivi burgorum*, and describing all the King's administrative officers outside the burghs.

audited in Exchequer begins in 1327. These accounts are of two different classes—the one rendered by the provosts, bailies, or farmers of the burghs, the other by the custumars. Originally officers appointed by the King collected the rent payable by each burgher as a Crown vassal, the fines imposed in the courts of the royal burghs, and the burghal toll or *parva custuma*. From about the beginning of the fourteenth century the burgesses got short leases from the Chamberlain, under which they acquired a right to the rents, &c., paying a specific sum to the King.

These old Exchequer Rolls are of great interest to the student of history, recording as they do payments connected with such events as the building of Tarbert Castle by Robert Bruce, the illness and death of Bruce, and the capture of Edinburgh Castle in 1342.

We give in an illustration facsimiles of the engrossments of the accounts (1) of the magistrates and (2) of the custumars of the burgh of Stirling audited in Exchequer at Dumbarton on 25th January 1327–1328, and the following are transcripts and translations, the former taken from the "Exchequer Rolls of Scotland," edited by Stuart and Burnett, and the latter from "Charters and Other Documents relating to The Royal Burgh of Stirling, A.D. 1124–1705," printed for the Provost, Magistrates, and Council of the Burgh, 15 and 16.

(1) *Account of the Magistrates*

Striuelyn.

"Compotum Mauricii Hunter et Fynlai sutoris, prepositorum burgi de Striuelyn, redditum apud Dunbretan xxv° die Januarii, anno gracie supradicto, de firmis dicti burgi de duobus terminis huius compoti. Iidem onerant se de xxxvj ħi., receptis per firmas dicti burgi de anno huius compoti. De quibus, pro superexpensis suis factis in compoto suo precedenti, xl š. j đ. et oƀ. Et in feodis abbatum de Cambuskyneth et Dunfermelyn, hospitalis de Striuelyn

ACCOUNTS OF THE BURGH OF STIRLING, AUDITED 25th JANUARY, 1327–1328 (width of original 11½ inches)

From the Scottish Exchequer Rolls

et hospitalis de Torphichin, per tempus compoti, xxiij łi.
v ŝ. iiij đ. Et Fratribus Predicatoribus de Striuelyn, ex
elemosina regis annua, x łi. Et pro constructione cuiusdam
domus pro coquina ad opus regis, liij ŝ. iiij đ. Et in
diuersis cariagiis per tempus compoti, xxvj ŝ. et viij đ.
Summa huius expense, xxxix łi. v ŝ. v đ. et oɓ. Et sic
superexpendunt lxv ŝ. v đ. et oɓ. Iidem petunt allocacionem de xl ŝ. pro multura de Cragorth subtracta de molen-
dino de Striuelyn, que est in manu Reginaldi More, super
quo consulatur rex, qui sibi postmodum allocantur. Et Consulator
sic superexpendunt cv ŝ. v đ. et oɓ. De quibus, sibi solu- rex.
untur per allocacionem sibi factam in compoto custumariorum
de Striuelin, de alia parte rotuli, l ŝ. et v đ. Et sic super- Superexpendunt de claro lv ŝ. et oɓ." expendunt.

"Account of Maurice Hunter and Fynlay Sutor, bailies of
the burgh of Strivelyn, given up at Dunbretan on the
twenty-fifth day of January, in the year of grace above
mentioned, of the fermes of the said burgh for the two terms
of this account. They charge themselves with £36 received on
account of the fermes of the said burgh for the year of their
account. Whereof, for their superexpenses made in their preceding account 40s. 1d. halfpenny. And in duties to the abbot
of Cambuskyneth and Dunfermelyn, the hospital of Strivelyn
and the hospital of Torphichen, during the time of the
account, £23, 5s. 4d. And to the Friars Preachers of
Strivelyn of the yearly alms of the king, £10. And for
the building of a certain house for a kitchen for the use
of the king, 53s. 4d. And in sundry carriages during the
time of the account, 26s. 8d. Sum of this outlay, £39, 5s. 5d.
and a halfpenny. And thus they superexpended 65s. 5d.
and a halfpenny. They ask also allowance of 40s. for the
multures of Cragorth abstracted from the mill of Stirling,
which is in the hand of Reginald More, on which let the
king be consulted, which is afterwards allowed to them.
And thus they superexpended 105s. 5d. and a halfpenny.
Whereof, paid to them by allowance made to them in the

account of the custumars of Strivelin on the other side of the roll 50s. and 5d. And thus obviously they super-expended 55s. and a halfpenny."

(2) *Account of the Custumars*

Striuelyn. "Compotum custumariorum burgi de Striuelyn, redditum apud Dunbretan xxv⁰ die Januarii, anno gracie supradicto, de receptis et expensis dicte custume, ab vltimo die Februarii anno gracie xxvi, vsque in diem presentis compoti. Iidem onerant se de lj s̃. et viij d̃. receptis per custumam sex saccorum et quinque petrarum lane, et nouem dacrarum coriorum, per tempus compoti. De quibus, in seruicio collectorum, xv d̃. Et debent l s̃. et v d̃. qui assignantur prepositis burgi de Striuelyn et alia parte rotuli, in partem superexpensarum suarum. Et sic eque hic."

"Account of the custumars of the burgh of Strivelyn, given up at Dunbretan on the twenty-fifth day of January, in the year of grace above mentioned, of the receipts and outlays of the said custom, from the last day of February, in the year of grace [1326] till the day of the present account. They charge themselves with 51s. 8d. received for the custom of six sacks and five stones of wool and nine dacres of hides during the time of the account. Whereof, for service of the collectors, 15d. And they owe 50s. and 5d., which are assigned to the bailies of the burgh of Strivelyn on the other side of the roll in part of their superexpenses. And thus this is equal."

The beneficial influence exerted on the advancement of accounting in Great Britain by the elaborate systems of accounts for the royal finances employed at the Exchequers must have been great and far-reaching. "Agriculture," says Dr. Cunningham, "was much the most important industry in England, but so far as we know landowners did not attempt to keep accurate accounts in the eleventh century, and it is not till the thirteenth century that the practice became general. The organisation of the Exchequer was not only a reform in the management of royal finance, for it also gave an example of a mode of keeping accounts which was gradually copied by corporations and individuals for their own private affairs."[1] In these circumstances it is not surprising that we have no specimens of private accounts in Great Britain of earlier date than the thirteenth century.

The Household Roll of Eleanor, Countess of Leicester, of the year 1265 (*Rotulus Hospitii Dominæ Alianoræ Comitissæ Leicestriæ, Anno Regni Henrici Regis Angliæ Tertii Quadragesimo-nono*),[2] is said to be the earliest existing account of an English subject. This account, which is, of course, in Latin, with Roman numerals, is in form similar to the Exchequer accounts, each entry following the preceding entry without any intervening space, and thus forming paragraphs, at the end of each of which the total amount of the entries in the paragraph is stated. On the back of the skin, however, where are entered certain personal or miscellaneous expenses incurred during, or about, the period comprised in the entries on the face of the skin, the individual amounts are carried to the margin in a sort of elementary money column, but the narrative is not kept clear of the marginal space occupied by the money column. Neither are the pounds arranged perpendicularly under the pounds, the shillings under the shillings, nor the pence under the pence, the amount being in every case carried to the extreme edge of the skin. Notwithstanding these deficiencies, the accounts endorsed on the back of this roll give clear indications of the conception of a money column.

Of this period also we have three rolls containing the accounts of the executors of the will of Eleanor, Consort of Edward I., who died in 1290 (*Liberationes factæ per Exe-*

[1] "Growth of English Industry and Commerce," Cunningham, I. 217.
[2] "Manners and Household Expenses of England in the Thirteenth and Fifteenth Centuries," Roxburghe Club.

cutores Dominæ Alianoræ Consortis Edwardi Regis Angliæ Primi.)[1] In form this account is similar to those endorsed on the back of the Household Roll of the Countess of Leicester. The expenditure is divided into periods of time, the total amount for each period being given, thus—

Summa totalis hujus termini, M.DCCCC. iiii[li]. xviii[s]. v[d]. ob.[2]

and the sum total at the end of the roll—

Summa summarum totius hujus rotuli, } M[le]. M[le]. M[le]. DCCC. xxiii[li]. xvi[s]. i[d]. OB.[2] Q[a].[3]

But the best thirteenth-century account which we have seen is the account of the Royal Wardrobe (*Liber Quotidianus Contrarotulatoris Garderobæ*)[4] of 1299–1300, a specimen page of which we reproduce.

The department of the Wardrobe was one of the royal treasuries for the receipt of the revenues of the Crown, out of which naval and military, as well as civil and domestic expenses were met. The author of *Fleta*, who is supposed to have written his work on the laws of England early in the fourteenth century, gives the following minute description of the office of treasurer of the King's Wardrobe, presenting an interesting picture of the elaborate accounting in use in the royal household, which was also practised on a smaller scale in the households of great families :—

"To him is committed the care of the expenses of the King and his family, who, together with a clerk, associated with him as a comptroller, shall keep a record of what belongs to their office. He shall keep the King's money, jewels, gifts, and private receipts, and shall make a separate roll thereof, which shall be returned annually into the Exchequer. And, in another roll, which shall be examined by the steward, treasurer, and comptroller, he shall enter the daily expenses (*expensa quotidiana*); also necessary expenses, in which the buying of horses, carriages, and many other articles, shall be comprised; also gifts, alms, and oblations;

---

[1] "Manners and Household Expenses of England in the Thirteenth and Fifteenth Centuries," Roxburghe Club.
[2] Ob. or OB.=obolus, or halfpenny.   [3] Q[a].=quadrans, or farthing.
[4] Printed by the Society of Antiquaries, London, 1787.

PORTION OF THE ACCOUNT OF THE ROYAL WARDROBE, 1299–1300 (reduced).

wages of knights and archers; messengers, foreign fees, presents or accommodations; also the expenses of the wardrobe, in which the buying of cloth, furs, wax, spices, linen, and such like, shall be comprised; also of jewels, foreign expenses, ambassadors, falconers. The treasurer ought also to convene every night the steward of the household, the chamberlain, comptroller, and his clerk; the marshall of the hall and the usher, and knights serjeants of the marshall; the ushers of the hall and of the chamber; the purveyors of the table; the butler, pantryman, baker, and the clerks of those offices, who were accountable for the expenses of diet, *viz.* of bread, wine, and ale; fish, cups, salt, fruits, cheese, and such like; also the master cooks, the larderer, poultryman, scullery, or saucery-man, salter, and clerk of the kitchen, who were necessary to give an account of what passed in their respective offices; also the almoner, the doorkeeper, the serjeant for the care of the sumpters and carriages; the clerk of the marshalsea, who should answer for the expenses of hay and corn, litter, shoeing of horses, harness or trappings for horses and carriages, and the wages of serjeants, esquires, clerks, and boys; and it was his duty to know those who were newly admitted to the wages of the King, and those who went out of duty; and to withhold the wages of such as were absent without the King's special licence, or were not in the King's service, &c."

In the account under notice, of the year 1299–1300, the various receipts of the treasurer are given, those from the Exchequer, and from the various branches of the revenue of the Crown receivable at the department of the Wardrobe. Then follow the payments under headings,—charitable donations of the King and his family, necessaries bought for the household, victuals and stores, wages of archers, sergeants-at-arms, &c. As will be seen from the specimen given, the total amount of a series of entries is not stated in the middle of the page, as in most accounts of even later date, but is carried to the margin of the page, and the narrative is not run into the marginal column. The total amount of the receipts is entered at the foot of the money column, as is also the total of each class of payments, and the amount of the whole expenditure is stated at the close. The balance, however, is not shown. Every page of the account is corrected and approved by the controller.

Of the same period, but in marked distinction to the last account in the matter of form, is an account of the expenses of John of Brabant and Thomas and Henry of Lancaster of the year 1292-1293.[1] Its form is of the most elementary description, in paragraphs, without a money column, having the amount of each paragraph stated at the foot of the paragraph.

The thirteenth century shows a wonderfully complete system of accounting in England in connection with manors. From the "Growth of English Industry and Commerce," we learn that the *Extenta* or survey of the manor contained an account of the whole condition of the estate, the buildings belonging to it, the fields and stock on the domain, the pasturage, the amount of wood and the profits of the waste, the mills, fisheries, and so forth. It also enumerated the free tenants and stated the terms of their tenure; the villans and cottagers, and their services, as well as the patronage and other incidental rights belonging to the manor. It enabled the landowner to see at once what his revenue in each year ought to be or what item had fallen short. The *Inventory* enumerated the pigs and the poultry, as well as the kitchen and dairy utensils, and the furniture of the hall. These two documents together recorded both the estimated annual value, and the actual condition of the whole live and dead stock on the estate, together with all the pecuniary rights which the lord enjoyed—that is to say, his whole assets. The annual revenue from the estate was recorded in the accounts (*compotus*). There are two interesting forms of bailiff's accounts in the Cambridge University Library, with brief remarks on the way in which they should be kept. "One, which dates from the time of Edward I., has special reference to the audit; it is intended to help the lord to understand the accounts presented, and tells him to insist on seeing all the tallies and letters of quittance produced. The other is meant to assist the bailiff in writing the accounts, and tells him in what order the various items should be entered; it gives him a choice of

[1] Camden Society Publications.

two alternative modes of entering the horses; and the copyist confesses that by a stupid blunder he has entered the heifers in the wrong place. It also points out that certain headings should be inscribed in the margin; and of course concludes with the form of quittance by which the accounts were passed."[1] A treatise of the thirteenth century on estate-management lays down, *inter alia*, the method to be pursued in drawing up the account. At the beginning comes a statement of the bailiff's arrears from past years; then the receipts are to be entered, rents of assize and other things which yield money, and the total is to be given; next comes the outlay in money on materials and all necessaries not found on the estate, and the payment of all work which could be neither begged nor commanded.[2]

It will have been noted from the accounts which have been described that it was not until nearly the end of the thirteenth century that any signs appear of attention being given to the art of stating accounts. Up to that time accounts had been written out in primitive form of narrative. But towards the close of the century it had apparently been found that advantage was to be derived from grouping transactions of like nature and showing the summation of each group, and also that it greatly assisted the ready apprehension of the account if the sums of money were invariably entered on the right hand margin of the page. This was further improved upon by reserving this space for figures only, but the benefit of separate money columns for the different monetary values had not yet been realised, so far as we have evidence to show.

When we come to the fourteenth and fifteenth centuries we find more numerous specimens of accounts and evidence of greater skill in accounting. The earliest existing account of the City of London is of the year 1334; and interesting series of accounts of the Livery Companies of London and of the

---

[1] "Growth of English Industry and Commerce," Cunningham, I. 220.
[2] Ibid. 224.

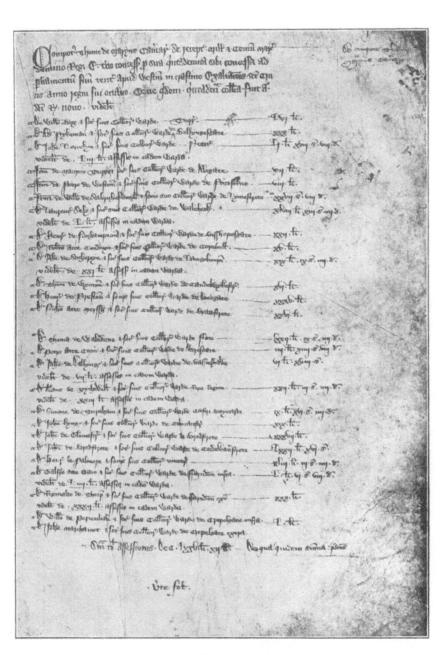

ACCOUNT OF THE CHAMBERLAIN OF THE CITY OF LONDON, 1334
(size of original 13¾ inches by 9¼ inches)

Scottish burghs also begin in the fourteenth century. Of this period, also, we have a series of account rolls of the Priory of Finchale in the County of Durham,[1] beginning in 1354, which are in the primitive form of most early accounts in Latin, the entries being in paragraphs without any money column. They convey full information, however, stating the amount of the balance at the beginning, the arrears brought forward, the total receipts, the total payments, and the arrears and the balance in hand at the close, if any.

The accompanying illustration is a facsimile of a portion of the earliest existing account of the City of London, the following translation of which is given in the "Calendar of Letter-Books of the City of London," Sharpe, Vol. F. 8.

The Account of Thomas de Maryns, the Chamberlain, of the receipt of 1100 marks granted to King Edward III. for a fifteenth at his Parliament held at Westminster the morrow of the Exaltation of H. Cross [14 Sept.], the eighth year of his reign [A.D. 1334], which fifteenth was collected in the ninth year, viz.:—

Of William Box and his fellows, collectors of Tower Ward, £56.

Of Adam Pykeman, &c., of the Ward of Billyngesgate, . £30.

Of John Lovekyn, &c., of the Ward of Bridge, . . £51 18s. 8d. viz., of £53 assessed in the said Ward.

Of Maurice Turgis, &c., of the Ward of Alegate, . . £7.

Of Peter de Westone, &c., of the Ward of Portsokne, . £8.

Of William de Sabrichesworth, &c., of the Ward of Lymestrete, ... 27s. 8d.

Of Laurence Sely, &c., of the Ward of Walebroke, . £48 13s. 4d. viz., of £50 assessed in the said Ward.

Of Henry de Norhamptone, &c., of the Ward of Bisshopesgate, £22.

Of Robert atte Conduyt, &c., of the Ward of Cornhull, . £15.

Of John de Sothereye, &c., of the Ward of Langebourne, £19 9s. 4d. viz., of £21 assessed.

Of Thomas de Wynton, &c., of the Ward of Candelwykestrete, £16.

Of Henry de Prestone, &c., of the Ward of Douegate, . £35.

Of Nicholas atte Mersshe, &c., of the Ward of Bradestrete, . £26.

Of Thomas de Waledene, &c., of the Ward of Chepe, £72 9s. 4d.

---

[1] Surtees Society Publications.

Of Peter atte Corner, &c., of the Ward of Aldresgate,   £4 14s. 8d.

Of John de Dallynge, &c., of the Ward of Bassieshawe,   . £6 18s.
  viz., of £7 assessed.

Of Alan de Tychewell, &c., of the Ward of Queenhithe,   £22 3s. 4d.
  viz., of £23 assessed.

Of Simon de Turnham, &c., of the Ward of Castle Baynard, £9 16s. 4d.

Of John Kyng, &c. of the Ward of Colmanstrete,   .   .   £19.

Of John de Gloucestre, &c., of the Ward of Bredstrete,   .   £37.

Of John de Bredstrete, &c., of the Ward of Cordewanerstrete, £72 16s.

Of Henry le Palmere, &c., of Vintry, ...   £43 3s. 4d.

Of Geoffrey atte Gate,&c.,of the Ward of Farndone Within, £50 6s. 8d.
  viz., of £54 assessed.

Of Reginald de Thorpe, &c., of the Ward of Farndone Without, £30.
  viz., of £32 assessed.

Of William de Pertenhale, &c., of the Ward of Crepelgate
  Within, and of John Marchaunt, &c., of the Ward of
  Crepelgate Without, ...   £50.

Sum total of assessment, £775 12s.

The City accounts of this period were kept, some in Latin
and some in Norman-French, with Roman numerals; and an
elementary money column was used.

The Livery Companies of London trace their origin from
the early associations termed gilds, which were either ecclesiastical or secular. The steel-yard merchants of London were
a branch of, or rather gave existence to, the Hanseatic League,
which was a commercial confederacy first formed on the east
shores of the Baltic in the eighth century to protect their
trade from the piratical incursions of the Normans, and who
thence derived their name of Easterlings. They are known
to have settled in England before the year 967.[1]

These Livery Companies in the height of their power
exercised great influence on public affairs, and gave life to
trade and commerce. Their wealth and enterprise contributed greatly to the prosperity of the nation. All the old
court books of the Companies are in Norman-French, sometimes intermixed with abbreviated Latin, or the old English

---

[1] " History of the Twelve Great Companies of London," Herbert.

of Chaucer's day. In the reign of Henry V. these languages gave place to English.[1]

The Worshipful Company of Grocers of the City of London claims to be the oldest of the Twelve Great Companies. In its early accounts, if the printed copies are reliable, the sums of money are carried out clear of the narrative as in a modern money column. The columns are not added up on each page, but the total is stated at the foot of the account, thus—

Sm^{to} de les achates & de les costages
xxij lb. iv s. iii d.

An account of 1401 is headed—

En le nom de Dieu & sa douce mere, lundy le **xxix.** jo^r de mars, l'an du Grace m, cccc, j, & l'an du Roy Henry Quarte, puisse la conqueste tierce.

An account of 1435 is rather more elaborate, and is in English. The payment side is headed: "The Paiement and Discharge of Thomas Catworthe and John Godyn" (the Wardens). It is in the form of an account of receipts and payments. In the case of most of the payments it is stated by which Warden they were made—"be the handys of Thomas Catworthe," or "be the handys of John Godyn." In many cases the item in the money column was partly paid by each, the amount for which each was responsible being stated in the entry. The total amount disbursed by each is shown at the close, thus—

	lb.	s.	d.
Sm^{to} pd. be Thomas Catworthe			
lxxvij lb. xix s. iiij d.	Sm^{to}		
Sm_{to} pd. be John Godyn	iiii c. **xxix**	ii	x
iii^c li lb. iii s. vi d.			

The early accounts of the other companies are very similar, being simple statements of receipts and payments, some in

[1] "History of the Twelve Great Companies of London," Herbert.

English and some in Norman-French with Roman numerals. The series of accounts of The Worshipful Company of Carpenters begins in 1438, that of The Worshipful Company of Pewterers, called "Audit Books," begins in 1451, "yoven and deliuered up" by the Master and Wardens to the Master and Wardens of the succeeding year, the former being described as the "seyd Accomptants."

A form of account still held in much favour in Scotland is the "Account of Charge and Discharge." In this account the accountant "charges" himself with the estate entrusted to him, including the whole revenues thereof during the period of his accounting, and "discharges" himself of the monies lawfully expended or paid over by him as well as of the estate and uncollected revenues at the close of the period. The earliest examples of this form of account which we find, apart from the accounts of the Priory of Finchale already referred to, which, though recording the information found in an account of charge and discharge, can scarcely be said to be stated in that form, are those of the Lord High Treasurer of Scotland.

In Scotland in 1424 James I., with the view probably of reducing the influence of the Great Chamberlain, appointed two new officials, the Comptroller and the Treasurer, to whom was assigned the chief portion of the functions in regard to the Exchequer formerly exercised by the Chamberlain. The accounts of the Treasurer appear to have been audited at irregular intervals, generally of two years or more. Preparatory to the audit, the accounts for the period were framed from the various books containing the current accounts. A considerable series of these audited accounts is still preserved, beginning fifty years after the institution of the office of Lord Treasurer. These accounts are of much interest, showing a very great advance in form as compared with the accounts we have hitherto been considering. The Account of John, Bishop of Glasgow, for the period from 4th August 1473 to 1st December 1474, is the earliest of the accounts of the Lord Treasurer now extant. It is headed—

Compt of a reuerennd fader in God Johnne bischope of Glasgow, Thesaurare to oure Souerane Lorde, of the office of Thesaurary, maide at Edinburgh the first day of the moneth of Decembre in the ȝere of God J^m iiij^c lxxiiij ȝeris, of all his ressatis and expensis made in the saide office, fra the ferd day of the moneth of August, the ȝere of God etc. lxxiij ȝeris inclusiue, to the saide first day of Decembre alsa inclusiue, befor richt reuerendis, mychti and noble lordis of oure sade Souerane Lordis counsale, be his hienes specialie deput and ordanit thairto, for the hering and resaving of the saide compt in his name, that is to say, Andro lorde Avandaile Chauncellare, Colin erle of Ergill lorde Lorne and Cambell Master of houshald, reuerendis faderis in God Thomas and Williame, of Abirdene and Orknaa bischoppis, a venerable fader in God Archibald abbot of Halirudehous, a noble and mychti lorde Dauid erle of Craufurde lorde Lindesay, Master Williame Scheues archdene of Sanctandros the Secretare, Master Alexander of Murray, Schir Richarde Robysone and Schir Dauid Luthirdale channounis of Murray, Abirdene and Dunblane, and Master Alexander Inglis subdene of Dunkeld.

The account is, as we have said, in charge and discharge form, beginning with "Composicionis sen the Comptaris last Compt," which are all detailed, thus—

Imprimis the comptare chargis him with a composicione made with George of Moncrefe for the mariage of the are of Trestrame Makgorty : composicio, . . xl ℔.

Item componit with Patrik of Maxvale for the resignacione of a hundreth schilling worth of land callyt the Stanly, lyand within the schirefdome of Renfrew . vj ℔. xiij š. iiij đ.

The next heading is "Composiciones facte in Drumfres in vltimo Itinere Justiciarii tento ibidem, viz. xxiiij° die mensis Octobris, anno Domini etc. lxxiij°"—each county being under a separate heading; and then are stated "The Chargis of the last Jakkere" (Exchequer). The summation of each page is entered at the foot of the page, but the amount is not carried forward. The "Sum totale of all the charge befor writtin" is, however, duly recorded at the end of the charge. The discharge side opens with what the Treasurer takes credit for in respect of "his superexpensis of his last compt as schewit in the fute of it." Then follow branches or headings for—"Expensis for the Kingis Persoune"; "Thingis tane be the Thesaurar at the Kingis command, vj^{to} Septembris, fra Dauid Quhitehed and Johnne of Fawsidis wife, chamlotis for his persone and deliuerit ay to Andro Balfour as he askit, as his buke of ressat beris, for the quhilk he sal ansuer to the compt"; "Thingis tane be Androw Balfoure fra Thom of ȝare at the Kingis commande, for the quhilkis the said Andro sal ansuer at the compt"; "Thingis tane for the Quenis Persone"; and so on. In the discharge, in addition to the summation of each page, the total of each class of expenses is given, as "Summa totalis harum expensarum Regine." The account closes with the "Sum totale of all the expensis befor wirtin, with the superexpensis of his last compt," and the balance is shown thereafter, thus: "And sua is the Comptare superexpendit."

We have already mentioned that from about the beginning of the fourteenth century the practice was adopted of granting short leases to the Scottish burghs of the rents, issues of court, and petty customs in consideration of a specific sum paid to the Crown. In the records of the burghs beginning at the close of the fourteenth century we find many interesting references to the burgh accounts of these revenues and to the audit conducted by the burgesses themselves. If we reflect that this period, following the growth in the prosperity of the Scottish burghs which had distinguished the thirteenth century, was one of arrested industrial development, it is surprising to find how much care and thoroughness was bestowed on municipal accounting and auditing. The form of the earlier accounts is indeed very elementary, but so far as their knowledge went the burgesses took care that accounts should be regularly prepared and duly audited.

The accounts of the city of Aberdeen begin in 1398. The

first account is in Latin, the form is elementary, and the figures are not carried to the margin of the page. When we come to 1453, Latin is giving place to the vernacular—the entry, "*Item, domino abbati de Arbrothat in vino, iis. viiid.*," being immediately succeeded by "Item, for mendyng of the bryg at the grene ende in all costis, 1 lib. iis. vid."

The earliest existing account of the City of Edinburgh is for the year from Michaelmas 1552 to Michaelmas 1553. This " Compt " of the City Treasurer, which is in the vernacular, is an excellently prepared account in charge and discharge form. The " compter chargis him " with the various customs, rents, &c., receivable, and states the " summa of the hale charge." Then follows the discharge, divided into " the counter's discharge ordinar "; " the counter's discharge be preceptis " (or acts of the town council), which is subdivided into months ; " the counter's discharge extraordinar "; the total under each heading being stated, thus " Summa of the haill extraordinar," &c. ; then follow " The expensis maid on the New Well at the townis command," and " The expensis maid be Alexander Park, thesaurer, on the schoir of Leyth, on the stane-work of the bulwark, maid at command of the provest, baillies and counsale," the summa of each oulk—*i.e.* week—being stated under the latter headings as well as the total of the headings. The discharge concludes with certain items which the Treasurer has been unable to recover, such as—

Item, the counter is to be dischargit of vj[li] for sex flesche stoks[1] of the personis following, quhairof thre stands waist, ane uthir occupiit be Andersoun, ane puir man, and the occupiars of the uthir twa past to France to the weris and left thair stokkis waist; summa. . . vj[li]

The " Summa of the hale discharge " is then given, and the difference between the charge and the discharge. " And sua restis, twa hundreth thre scoir ten punds v[s] ij[d]."

The accounts both of the Town Treasurer and of the Dean

[1] Wooden blocks on which the butchers prepared the flesh.

of Guild are preserved in almost unbroken series from 1552 down to the present time.   The form in which they are prepared, as we have endeavoured to show in regard to the earliest one, is excellent.   They are beautifully written, and contain very few erasures or alterations.   The figures are carried out to the margin of the page from the earliest period. Roman numerals are used until 1673, and in that year, in addition to the adoption of Arabic figures, a further improvement is introduced in the form of a regular money column. Up to the year 1720 the summation of each page was not carried forward either to the succeeding page or to the end of the account, but from 1720 the summation of each page is " transported " to the following page, and an abstract is given at the end of the account.

Many of the entries in these sixteenth-century accounts are very quaint, and throw light on the conditions then prevailing in Edinburgh.   A few of those recording the expenses incurred in the administration of the rough justice of the time, which are arranged under the " discharge extraordinar," may be quoted—

Item, the   day of   1554, for takin of ane greit gebet
    furth of the nether tolbuith and beiring of it to the
    hecht of the Dow Crag, to haif hangit hommill Jok on,
    and down bringing of it agane to Sanct Paullis Wark. .   xij^d
Item, for cords to bynd and hang him with,   .   .   .   viij^d
Item, the feird day of Fabruar 1554, for cordis to bind
    Nicoll Ramsay quhill he wes hedit, ...   vj^d
Item, thesamyn day, for cords to hang the man that brint
    Lord James' cornis, ...   viij^d
Item, the xxviij of Junij 1555, for cords to bynd Katharen
    Martine quhen scho wes brint on the cheke, .   .   .   v^d
Item, the vj day of July 1555, for cords to bynd and hang
    the foure Inglismen at Leyth and Newhevin,   .   .   iij^s
Item, the xiij day of Julij 1555, for towis to bind the fallow
    that wes skurgit and his lug nallit to the trone, .   .   iiij^d
Item, for cords to hang and bind uthir vj Inglismen peratts
    on the gallows of the Borrow Mure, ...   iiij^s

Item, the viij day of October, cords to hang and bynd ane
    theif and skurge ane uther theif, ... x^d

Item, the xvj day of October 1555, for cords to bynd and
    mak ane lang ledder to James Wod quha wes hedit,   . xij^d

Item, for ane cart to cary the fallow that brak his leg furth
    of the tolbuyth throw the town, quhen he wes scurgit,   . $iiij^s$

Item, for towis to him, ... $xiiij^d$

It will have been observed that all the accounts we have
hitherto been considering are stated in Roman numerals;
and it is not until we reach the close of the fifteenth
century that we find evidence of the use in accounts in this
country of the so-called Arabic notation. The earliest instance which is preserved of the use of Arabic cipher is,
we believe, to be found in a twelfth century MS. in the
Biblioteca Palatina, Vienna, placed by Theodor Sickel as of
the year 1143, which contains that cipher on every page.
According to a correspondent in Venice "the introduction
of Arabic cipher into Italy was a slow process, opposed
even by law. The whole sentiment of humanism was
against it, and for long that cipher was limited to journals
of expenditure, and to the accounts of small merchants;
finding its way only late into the ledger, and later still
into public accounts. Even in the fifteenth century Roman
numeration was considered the proper form for anything
of the nature of official or public accounts. Arabic cipher
was actually known as the 'vulgar cipher.'" In this country
the use of Roman numerals in accounts does not appear to
have been common until the seventeenth century. Andrew
Halyburton, whose "Ledger,"[1] preserved in Edinburgh, embraces the period from 1492 to 1503, uses Arabic numerals
for the most part, though with occasional reversions to
Roman, but, no doubt from his residence in the Netherlands, he was in advance of his countrymen in this respect.
The transition from the one notation to the other was still
in progress in the seventeenth century, as is shown in the

[1] Published under the direction of the Lord Clerk Register of Scotland, 1867.

" Compt Buik of David Wedderburne, Merchant of Dundee," [1] extending from 1587–1630. Wedderburne uses both notations in the most impartial manner. Sometimes the figures in the narrative of an entry are in Roman notation, while those carried to the margin of the page are in Arabic, or *vice versâ;* or both sets of figures are in the same notation; or a sum of money is stated partly in the one notation and partly in the other. The city of Aberdeen began to adopt the improved notation in 1605, the Pewterers Company in 1615, the City of Edinburgh in 1673, and the City of London in 1685.

The account of the Treasurer of Glasgow for 1573–1574 is also in charge and discharge form.[2] The charge consists of the total amounts of revenue receivable from the various sources, while the discharge is a detailed statement of payments in chronological order, without any attempt at arrangement under separate headings, followed by the items for which the treasurer was entitled to be discharged as outstanding at the close of the account, such as duties in arrear. In the first half of the seventeenth century Arabic figures were used occasionally by the Treasurer of Glasgow in the same account in which Roman figures were chiefly employed, and sometimes a sum of money was expressed partly in the one notation and partly in the other, thus: xviij li. 3s. 4d. The transition is shown in the account of 1649–1650, but after 1652–1653 the use of Roman figures ceases.

The Corporation of Dublin were evidently desirous that the City Accounts should be properly kept. In 1576 they awarded a certain George Russell £3 Irish " for and in consideration of his pains taken and to be taken in closing the Accounts of this City." [3] And in 1607 they passed the following resolution with regard to arrears " for the most parte desperate," and the " surveying of the accoumptes " :—

---

[1] Scottish History Society Publications, 1898.
[2] Scottish Burgh Records Society Publications.
[3] "Calendar of Ancient Records of Dublin," Gilbert, II. 114.

1607–1608. Third Friday after 25th December 1607.

Laws, orders, and constitutions:—(1) Whereas the commons made humble petycion unto this assemblye, shewing that wheras the booke of this cittie accoumptes is muche pestered with arrearadges of old and newe debtes, and that for the most parte desperate, and therefore required that a course might be laid downe that all such desperate debtes mighte be quite dashte out, and the sperat arrearadges givin in chardge to some sufficient person, whoe shall have allowance for gettinge in the same, and be accoumptable for them to this cittie; it is therfore agreed by the aucthority of this assemblye, that Mr. Maior, Mr. John Forster, Mr. Fraunces Tailor, Mr. John Shelton, Mr. Roberte Ball, and Mr. John Cusake, alderman, and Mr. Nicholas Stephins, or any fower of them, shalbe commissioners to surveye the accoumptes, and to take such order therin as they shall thincke best for the good of this cittie, and the same to be executed before Easter nexte.[1]

Of the sixteenth century, we have an interesting account recording the household expenses of the Princess Elizabeth during her residence at Hatfield in 1551–1552.[2] In form it shows a considerable improvement on earlier accounts, particularly as regards the discharge side. It is in English, Roman numerals being used, and is headed—

The House of the Right Excellent Prynces
The Ladie Elizabeth Her Grace.
Thaccumpte of Thom's Parry, Esquyer,

Coaferor to the righte excellent Princesse the Ladie Elizabeth her grace, the Kinges Majesties moste honorable sister, aswell of all and singler somes of Redie money to him deliuered by her graces owne handes, and all other her graces Officers, with all somes of money by him receaved of Forren Receiptes. As also the payment and disbursing of the same, unto her graces handes or otherwise, for the provision of her graces Householde and expences of the same. From the first daie of October. . . .

"The said Mr. Parrye is charged with certen somes of money by him receaved and to him payd," which are arranged under the following heads: "The remayne with the prest of the laste yere"; "By thandes of my Ladies grace"; and "By

---

[1] "Calendar of Ancient Records of Dublin," Gilbert, II. 488.
[2] Camden Society Publications.

thandes of diuerse persons for forren receptes." No money column is used in the charge side, the entries forming a continuous narrative. The summation of each branch is stated at the foot of the branch, and the "Some Totall of all the Receptes" is given, with an abstract recapitulating the total of each branch. On the discharge side are arranged the payments made for the various departments of the household, thus—

There is to be deducted suche somes of mony as the said Master Parrye hathe disburced for the provic'on and expences of the Householde within Thoffices of

> The Bakehouse and Pantrye.
> The Buttrye and Sellor.
> The Stable.
> &c. &c.

On this side of the account a money column is employed, the sums of money being carried out to the margin, and each branch is summed separately—not merely a statement of what the total of each amounts to as in the charge side. The totals of the branches are not, however, added together on the face of the account, but the total amount of the payments is stated at the close. After the payments is the following:—

There remayneth in sondrie proviçons the furst day of October, Anno Sexto Regis predicti, as by a boke of parcelles therof made at large appereth; As well with certen money delyvered to diverse persons in prest for the provicion of the Housholde, who have not yet accompted for the same; As also for redie money delyvered to the coaffers, M^l. viij^c. lij. ƚi. ij. š. viij. đ. dɪ̃ q^a iij^{tia} pars q^a," the particulars whereof are detailed below: "In proviçon," with the amounts in the "Bakehouse," "Buttrie and Cellar," &c.; "In prest," with the names of the debtors and the amount due by each; and "In redie mony"—the last of which amounting to "one thousande five hundred seven poundes one halfe pennye halfe farthing and the third parte of a farthing, the said Mr. Parrie hathe delyvered to her graces owne handes upon the determinaçon of this his accompte.

The account is completed by the following summary :—

And so thexpences of the House doe amounte unto for this yere to the some of iij M. ix C. xxxviij ℔. xviij ẛ. vij đ.

There is to be deducted for the hides, felles, and intrales of the cattall provided, with certen vendiĉons, as before in the charge appereth, CC vij. ℔. iij ẛ. viij đ. oƀ.

And so there is clerely expended iij M. vij C. xxvj. ℔. xiiij ẛ. xđ. oƀ., videlĩt, In

> The House—Mᴵ. Mᴵ. viij C. l. ℔. xvj s. ix đ.
> The Chamber—viij C. lxxv. ℔. xviij ẛ. j. đ. oƀ.

The account is adorned with an illuminated commencement, and five pen-and-ink drawings, forming capital initial letters. It is signed on every folio by Elizabeth and by Sir Walter Bucler, the chamberlain to the princess.

Of this period also we have the accounts of the Churchwardens of the town of Ludlow in Shropshire, extending from 1540 to the close of the reign of Queen Elizabeth.[1] The account of the year 1540 begins with the payments, headed thus—

> Reparaĉons done by Richard Longforde and Willyam Lacon, wardens of the pareshe churche off Ludlowe, anno Henrici octavi xxvijᵗᵒ, anno Domini 1540.

The payments are detailed item by item, without dates or arrangement into classes, the amounts being carried to the margin clear of the narrative, thus—

> Item, payd unto Thomas Smyth for a barre of yryn weynge vj. li. and for the workemanshype of the same . . ix d

The use of the money column, however, does not seem to have been fully understood, as the column is not summed, but the total is recorded in the centre of the page, thus—

> Summa totalis, iij li. x s. j d.

---

[1] Camden Society Publications.

Then follow the " Reseyttes of the churche the same yeare," the total of which is stated as iij li. iiij s. ix d.

> And so the churche rest in ther dette .   .   .   .   **v s. iiij d.**
> Wherof the be deductide for wesshinge of the churche
>   clothes. . . . . **iij s. iiij d.**
> And so the parishe ys indettede to them .   .   .   **ij s.**

The municipal authorities appear to have exercised supervision over ecclesiastical affairs; and the following certificate is appended to the account, which shows the settlement of the balance so far as the one warden was concerned, leaving him to settle with his fellow·warden :—

> *Die Lunæ, videlicet* xvj° *die mensis Februarii anno regni regis Henrici octavi* xxxj°, *coram Johanne Taylor et Johanne Lokyer ballivis domini regis villæ de Ludlow.*

At whiche day it ys orderede and agreede be the seid baylifes that the forseid Richarde Langforde ffrom hensfourth shalle pesably have, occupie, and enjoye the pewe or sette in the churche late in the tenure of Alice Lane decessede, ffor whiche pewe the seide baylifes have awardede that the seide Richarde Langforde shalle content and paye to the churche wardeyns, over the ij s. wherin the churche upon hys account restith in hys debtt, the some of vj s. viij d. stervinge, whiche ys payde the seide day and yere, &c. quinte.   ffinis.

The record of the Western journey of the Laird of Cawdor, made in 1591, furnishes us with a specimen of a Scottish private account of the same century.[1] The account, which is headed " Alexander Campbell the Lard of Calder his Pursmaisteris Compt," contains details of the personal and travelling expenses of the Laird; the last item, completing the journey on returning to Edinburgh, being—

> 6 day of November being Satterday in Edinburgh.
> Item giffen to Michell Libertoun for poling your heid .   . **vj s. viij d.**

---

[1] " Sketches of Early Scotch History," Innes.

A summary of the whole is shown thus—

This compt was maid in Edinburgh the vij day of November 1591 yeiris.

Summa of Alexander Campbellis resait . . xiij^{xx} xij lib. ij s.
Summa debursit of the foirsaid sowme of resait xij^{xx} xvij lib. iij s.
Sua restis on Alexander . . . . xij lib. vi s. x d.[1]

The account is signed by "Jane Lauder," the widow of the murdered Laird.

The series of accounts of King's College, Aberdeen, of this period are in charge and discharge form. The accounts of the Endowments, &c., begin in 1641. The general accounts of the College, beginning in 1658, are well framed. There is "The first part of the Silver Compt containing the Charge," divided into "Sectio 1^a," "Sectio 2^a," &c., the "Summa of the Charge" being shown. Then "Charge Extraordinar"—"Summa of the Bill of Rights at Michaelmas." Then follows "The second part of the Silver Compt containing the Discharge," "Sectio 1^a. Discharge Ordinar," "Sectio 2^a," &c., with the "Suma sumarum of the haill Discharge Ordinar." Then "Sectio 4^a of the Discharge containing the Extraordinar Deburs ements and Incident Charges fra Michaelmas 1658 to Michaelmas 1659."

The accounts of the Merchants' House of Glasgow beginning in 1660–1661 are well-framed accounts in charge and discharge form. An earlier account, of 1624, has been preserved, but it is almost illegible. The account of 1660–1661 is titled: "Charg and Intromissioune and Discharg and Exoneratioune by Ordinar and Extraordinar depursements off John Louk, with the Comoun goods belonging to the Merchants hospitall in Glasgow, from November, 1660 to November, 1661." It shows in the charge the amounts due to the House in bonds, &c., the balance due by the previous

[1] This appears to be an example of the vigesimal system, or counting by scores, (see *ante*, page 7), but in any case the arithmetic seems to be at fault.

collector, and the revenue; and in the discharge the amounts
in bonds, &c., at the close of the period, the interest, &c.,
in arrear, the expenditure, and the balance in the collector's
hands at the close.   In 1715 it was ordered " that ye method
of keeping of ye books be altered, and the books be kept for
ye future in ye regular way of debite and credite."   A regular
set of account books was accordingly begun in sterling money,
the first entry in the journal recording the assets beginning
" In the name of God, Amen." [1]

A volume of " Instructions for the Collectors and other
Officers Employ'd in Her Majesties Customs, &c., in the
North-Part of Great-Britain," published in 1707, shows
careful and accurate accounting in the collection of customs.
A monthly abstract in columnar form is prescribed, and ela-
borate instructions are given for its preparation.

In 1720 improvements in the system of accounting were
introduced in the burgh of Stirling.   In that year—

The magistrats and toune councill of the said burgh being conveined,
and considering that by the annual accompts of the toune and hospitalls
the condition and state thereof is not so plainly obvious, and being
resolved the same be sett in clear light that it may appeare yearly
what the debit and credit of the toune and hospitalls may be, they
recommend to the extrordinare auditores to cause forme ane book by
way of abstract for doing thereof after such method, and to imploy
such persone as they shall thinke fitte for that end; and the said book
to be ballanced at each Michaelmasse that the circumstances of both
may yearly appeare.

Again in 1741 it is recorded—

The councill considering that the method wherein the publick accompts of the town and Cowans Hospitall have been framed for some time
past, by the accomptants not charging themselves with any principall
sumes or annualrents except as to these bonds whereof they have paid
annualrent for that year, renders it quitt impracticable to discover the

---

[1] " View of the Merchants House of Glasgow."

real state of the town or hospitall from the accounts themselves or such abstracts as can be made from them, and which may be of dangerous consequence unless suitably and timeously remeded, the councill therefore enjoin, order, and appoint the severall accomptants in all time coming, either for the town, Cowans Hospitall, Nether Hospitall, and Allan's mortification, that in making up their severall accompts for the future they do charge themselves with the haill principall sumes and annual-rents due thereon to the term of the bonds preceeding the making of the accompts, and that they discharge themselves likeways with the principall sumes and annualrents that may be then unpaid of every particular principall sume, so that the haill principall sumes, with what annualrent is due on each of them, may distinctly appear from the face of the accompts; and the councill do appoint the town clerk for the future to make up regular abstracts of the severall accompts within fourteen days of their being fitted, so that they may be ready for booking so soon as the time is elapsed which these accompts are obliged to lye in his hands to be inspected by every burges that has a mind; and furder the councill declare that the foresaid accompts shall not be approven of in councill till once the foresaid abstract be booked.

It is thus apparent that the Town Council of Stirling appreciated the value of the charge and discharge form of account.

In the eighteenth century also we find a further advance has been made in the form of accounts. The troublous times in Scotland of "The Fifteen" and "The Forty-five," and the subsequent proceedings against the Jacobite landowners, have left us numerous accounts, which are preserved in the General Register House, Edinburgh, many of which would serve as excellent models for the use of present-day accountants. There are both the accounts of the Receiver-General on the Forfeited Estates, and the accounts of the numerous factors on the estates. The Receiver-General's account, beginning in 1718, contains the receipts and payments connected with the estates, arranged under the names of the estates. No distinction is made between the rents and the prices for which the estates were sold, both being recorded under the names of the estates to which they apply. It is interesting to come on the entries under the heading " Rob Roy," as—

Cash Received from M^r· John Graham of Kilearn as the Ballance of an Acco^t· setled with him of his Intromissions w^t· the rents of the Estate of Robert Campbell alias McGrigor commonly call^d· Rob Roy Attainted for the crop and year 1717 as p^r· precept of the Comm^{rs}· of Enquiry the 5th of July 1718, & Receipt 29th· Novem^r· 1718 .   .   .   .   .   £22 6s. 11d.

The Exchequer does not appear to have made anything out of Rob Roy's estate after meeting the debts thereover. Rob Roy's estate was not unusual in that respect, however, for while the charge of the Receiver-General's first account amounts to £295,926 14s. 9$\frac{8}{12}$d., only £27,735 3s. was paid into the Exchequer at Westminster—a balance of £1210 7s. 9$\frac{1}{3}$d. being handed over to the succeeding Receiver-General.

The accounts of the factors on the estates—especially those forfeited in 1745—are excellent examples of well-framed accounts of charge and discharge. The factor charges himself with the arrears outstanding at the close of the preceding account, the rents of the period covered by the account, "as they are contained in the Judicial Survey of the Estate," feu-duties, and other receipts, and discharges himself with the payments, arranged under appropriate headings, and with the arrears outstanding at the close, the free rents being paid to the Receiver-General. The accounting in connection with the forfeited estates gave employment to some of the early professional accountants of Edinburgh, to whom remits were made by the Court.

Having now traced the development of the form of accounts from the earliest primitive narrative through its various stages—the grouping of items, the introduction of the money column, and the discarding of antiquated notation and language—to the shapes with which we are familiar in the present day, and having reached the period when the professional accountant appears upon the scene, we may safely leave the subject, knowing that from that time there was no lack of skill and ingenuity applied to the drawing up of accounts best adapted to the particular circumstances of each case, and calculated to show in the clearest and simplest manner the nature and effect of the transactions which had taken place.

CHAPTER IV

HISTORY OF AUDITING

CHECKS IN USE AMONG ANCIENT PEOPLES—EXCHEQUER AUDIT-
ING—AUDITING OF THE ACCOUNTS OF ENGLISH MANORS—
MUNICIPALITIES—LIVERY COMPANIES OF LONDON—PRIVATE
INDIVIDUALS—PAROCHIAL AUTHORITIES.

THE origin of auditing goes back to times scarcely less remote
than that of accounting. Whenever the advance of civilisation brought about the necessity of one man being entrusted
to some extent with the property of another the advisability of
some kind of check upon the fidelity of the former would become
apparent. As we have seen,[1] the ancient Egyptians imposed
such a check by arranging that the fiscal receipts should be
recorded separately by two officials. In later times, the
Greeks instituted a system of checking public accounts by
means of checking-clerks,[2] every public official having his accounts scrutinised at the expiry of his term of office. The
Romans too, as early as the time of the Republic, recognised
the salutary distinction between the official who authorises or
orders revenue and expenditure and the official who has the
duty of handling cash; and they developed an elaborate system
of checks and counter-checks among the various financial
officials.[3] In Italy in the Middle Ages the transactions of a
cashier appear to have been checked by means of a separate
record of them kept by a notary.

The same system of check by means of separate records was
also employed in the accounting of the English Exchequer
and of the Royal Wardrobe. At the Exchequer the great
roll was compiled from the dictation of the Treasurer, a

---

[1] *Ante,* page 21.   [2] *Ante,* page 24.   [3] *Ante,* page 30, *et seq.*

74

second roll was written out by the Chancellor's clerk, and in the early days of the Exchequer a third roll was kept by a special representative of the king. These rolls were independently kept records which had to agree in every respect, every leaf and page of the one corresponding to the leaves and pages of the other; thus ensuring a complete check at the close of the year. At the audit, every discrepancy between the rolls was adjusted and settled, "pb^t," *probatum*, being added to the item as finally adjusted. Two of the similar rolls kept for the Wardrobe are thus described: "They correspond, as required by the rule derived from the Exchequer, leaf to leaf, page to page, almost line to line. The "probatum," the mark of audit, has been affixed to the sum of every page, and to the sum of every leaf on its second page, and in some cases, where the sum has been apparently corrected by a second audit, a second mark is affixed to the finally stated sum. The rolls are neither a copy of the other, but separately kept Accounts for the year, brought on the expiration of the year into agreement in the manner described."[1]

In addition to this system of check on the Exchequer officials, the method of accounting with the sheriffs, which we have already described,[2] was a carefully conducted audit in the modern sense of the word. This audit insured that the crown revenue was duly accounted for by the sheriff, and provided for the examination of vouchers for all his expenditure.

In the early days of the Exchequer the accounts, or some of them, appear to have been audited either by some of the justices or barons or by clerks or others to whom the duty was delegated. Later, there were special officials called *Auditores Compotorum Scaccarii*.[3] From the reign of Henry III. the officer in charge of the receipt and issue rolls was called the clerk of the pells, and the intromissions of this official were checked by the auditor of the Receipt, who

---

[1] *Archæologia*, xlviii. 282.   [2] *Ante*, page 42.
[3] "History of the Exchequer," Madox.

76 HISTORY OF ACCOUNTING

recorded the receipts and issues in duplicate. There were
also auditors of foreign accounts—"foreign" revenue being
revenue from every source not included in the Pipe Roll.

In Scotland, the accounts of the Exchequer officials who
collected and disbursed the Crown revenue, including those
of the Chamberlain, were audited in Exchequer, usually every
year, by certain Lords Auditors appointed by the Crown to
hear the accounts and grant acquittance thereon.[1] The audit
was by no means a formality. Charges were frequently
disallowed for reasons which are explained, as being insuf-
ficiently vouched, &c. Thus, of the sum of £640 charged
in the Chamberlain's accounts of 1337 and 1340 for stores
for Lochleven, £60 was disallowed, after the vouchers had
been called for, as having been already charged in a previous
account.

The thirteenth century supplies us with references to
auditors and auditing both in Italy and in England. Early
in the century we find an auditor employed to revise (or
audit) the account books of the commune of Pisa.[2] The
English Statute 13 Edward I. c. 11 (A.D. 1285), "Concerning
servants, bailliffs, Chamberlains, and all manner of Receivers,
which are bound to yield Accompt," provides "That when
the Masters of such Servants do assign Auditors (auditores)
to take their Accompt, and they be found in arrearages upon
the Accompt, all Things allowed which ought to be allowed,
their Bodies shall be arrested, and by the Testimony of the
Auditors of the same Accompt, shall be sent or delivered
unto the next Gaol of the King's in those Parts . . ." In
the thirteenth century too, as we have seen,[3] the accounts
of landed estates were carefully audited. A thirteenth century
treatise on estate-management in French, named *Seneschaucie*,
by an unknown author, recommends that the lord of the manor
ought to command that the accounts be heard every year

---

[1] An Act of James VI. of 1596 "anent custumes," ordains "the saidis custumaris
to mak compt thairof yeirlie to the lordis auditouris of the chekker."
[2] *Infra*, page 176.   [3] *Ante*, page 53.

at each manor. The auditors ought to be faithful and prudent, knowing their business. The seneschal ought to be joined with the auditors, but subordinate as having to answer to the auditors on the account for his doings, just as another. " It is not necessary," continues the author of the treatise, " so to speak to the auditors (*acunturs*) about making audit because of their office, for they ought to be so prudent, and so faithful, and so knowing in their business, that they have no need of other teaching about things connected with the account."[1]

The accounts of the executors of the will of Eleanor, Consort of Edward I., who died in 1290, appear to have been audited, the word *probatur* being written in many instances after the total expenditure for a stated period. And in these accounts also, we find the entry : *In expensis auditorum compotorum de terris Reginæ, senescallorum et ballivorum, post mortem Reginæ, apud Londoniam.*

The records of the City of London[2] show that the accounts of the Chamberlain were audited in the time of Edward I., though when the audit was first instituted we do not know. In 1298 the Mayor, Aldermen, Sheriffs, and certain others were appointed auditors; and a little later—in 1310— " Six good men of the City were elected in the presence of the whole Commonalty." In 1311 in the list of officials elected officers of the City we find a " Comptroller against (*versus*) the Chamberlain," as well as a number of auditors, "to audit and determine the accounts of divers Chamberlains and other officers of the Commonalty for the time past."

The following extract from the records of the City of Dublin, of the year 1316, shows that accounts were audited in Ireland at that time. "Tallages (*i.e.* taxes) and imposts to be collected under supervision of four or six good men duly sworn, and accounts to be rendered of receipts and payments before the commonalty or their auditors."[3] This

---

[1] "Walter of Henley's Husbandry, &c.," Lamond, 105, 107, and 109.
[2] "Calendar of Letter Books of the City of London," Sharpe.
[3] "Calendar of Ancient Records of Dublin," Gilbert, I. 133. The above is translated from the Norman-French of the original.

is also shown by a charter granted by Edward III. to the borough of Kinsale, dated 7th January 1333, in which it is stated : " The Corporation to have the custom of all customable goods to go to the repair of their walls, a proper Account thereof to be rendered yearly before two burgesses, or before the Earl of Desmond.[1] In 1456, the appointment of auditors of the accounts of the city of Dublin is thus recorded—

That hyt was ordenyt and estabelyt, the ferd Fryday next aftyr the fest of Synt Michell the Archangell, the yer of King Henry the Syxt, the XXXV. (1456), by autoryte of the sayd semble that ther schold be from that tym forward two Audytores assignet upon the tresowrerys saud cytte, to hyr har acownt yerly, thar ys to sayn, as for thys yer Thomas Barby and Arlanton Usher.[2]

From the fourteenth century onwards we have ample evidence that the advisability of having accounts audited was widely recognised. In England the decisive share of the Commons in the bestowal of money grants had become since the reign of Edward III. an admitted principle. " The rule of insisting on a proper audit of accounts was a corollary from the practice of appropriating the supplies to particular purposes. It was one which was scarcely worth contesting. In 1406 the Commons, who objected to making a grant until the accounts of the last grant were audited, were told by Henry that "kings do not render accounts ;" but the boast was a vain one; the accounts were in 1407 laid before the Commons without being asked for ; and the victory so secured was never again formally contested." [3]

Many interesting references to auditing are supplied by the existing records of the Livery Companies of London and of the burghs of Scotland, to the accounts of which we have referred in the last chapter. The *Remembrances* of the meeting of the Worshipful Company of Grocers of the City of

[1] " History of Cork" (Reprint), Smith, 204.
[2] "Calendar of Ancient Records of Dublin," Gilbert, I. 292.
[3] Stubbs' " Constitutional History of England," III. 274.

London of 21st May 1346, state that after the feast, " and
the cloth taken away," the money and valuables of the
Fraternity were delivered to the newly elected Wardens " in
the presence of William Grantham, William Hanapstede,
Thomas Freland, and John de Bromsford, who were chosen
by all the Company to superintend the accounts and the
delivery of the aforesaid Wardens." This procedure was gone
through annually, the details of the funds handed over being
entered in the Wardens' accounts.[1]

The accounts, or " Audit Books," of The Worshipful
Company of Pewterers of the City of London were audited
by members of the Craft.[2]

The Book of Ordinances of 1564 contains the following
" Order for yᵉ audytors ":—

Also it is agreed that there shalbe foure Awdytours Chosen euery
yeare to awdit the Crafte accompte and they to parvse it and search
it that it be parfect. And also to accompt it Correct it and allowe
it So that they make an ende of the awdet therof between Mighelmas
and Christmas yearely and if defaute be made of ffenishinge thereof
before Christmas yearely euery one of the saide Awdytours shall paye
to the Crafte boxe vj s. viij d. a pece.

The auditors " parvsed and searched " the accounts to
some purpose. In 1465–1466 they refused to certify the
accounts of the year because the balance of the preceding
year had not been included. In 1547–1548 the following
items were disallowed:—

Jtm spent at the Ale howse by the Hall Amonge the
wardens & dyuers of the company yᵉ xxvij daye July . iij d.
Jtm the therde daye of August spent at yᵉ ale howse . . ij d.
Jtm spent at an ale howse at yelde Hall when mʳ Curteyes
prentyce was made free . . . . . . iij d.

---

[1] "Some Account of the Worshipful Company of Grocers of the City of London,"
Heath.
[2] "History of the Pewterers' Company," Welch.

The accounts of 1560 do not meet with the auditors'
approval, the Wardens having charged themselves with an
insufficient amount. It is recorded—

ℳ^d that this accompt was awdyt the xxij daye of Decemℏr in Anno
Dñi 1560 and in the therd yere of the Raigne of o^r Soveraigne lady
Quene Elyzabethe, by us Wiℏm Baker, Wiℏm Mills, Nicholas Turℏ And
Richard Scot. So that we fynde by the neclygence of m^r Hustwayte,
Nicholas Crostwayte and John Gery warden theise pcells following.

Jn p^rmis the whole Receipts to lytle cast by   .   .   .   xij d.
Jtm where it is acustome that every weding that is kept in
   the hall ought to paye iij s. iiij d. we fynd to lytle by .   xvj d.

The above sums were duly accounted for in the next
account.

Again, in 1573–1574, the auditors took exception to certain payments, and referred the decision of the matter to
the Court of the Company, and the latter disallowed two
of the items.

In the accounts of 1574–1575 occur the following quaint
entries consecutively:—

Jtem receyued, of John God, for his abuse, & greate radge, had and
   vsed, to Richarde Parke, his Jorneyman at an vndue howre,
   of the nighte, ...   v s.
Jtem receyued, of the same Richarde Parke, for his contempteous
   vsadge, in strikinge, his saide maister, & for takinge further
   wages, of him, then by the lawes, of this realme, he oughte,
   to doo, ...   v s.
Jtem paide vnto the Beadle, that deade is, for his quarters wages,
   due at Michaelmas laste, ...   xx s.

To this account is appended the following docquet:—

We, thincke it not reasonable, that these Accomptantℯ, be allowed,
that two Shillingℯ, wch they saie, was loste, by an Angell, taken of
John God, & his man, by waie of ffyne, ...   ij s.
ℳor, that any allowaunce, shalbe made them, for the some of xx s.
wch they saie, was spent, by Thomas Hawkℯ, and Roberte Newes, in
Jorneyinge, to ypswitche, vnles, the companie thinck, of it otherwise,
for to what ende, that Jorney was made, or of any proffyte, that came
of it, we knowe nothinge, as yet, ...   xx^{tl} s.

Though the auditors were liable to be fined 6s. 8d. each, as we have seen, if the audit were not completed in due time, they themselves had power to fine the highest officials. In 1581 it is recorded:—

> **Jfm** we (the auditors) fynd the mr and wardens mr nogaye master mr Chawner & mr wood for brech of cartayne ordynaunces in ther tyme the matter being put vnto vs to determyne we order that ech one of them shall paye or geue vnto the house xx s. a pece that is to saye thre poundes or the valew of thre poundes in any thyng as they shall thynke betwyxt thys and the fest St. John baptyst next comyng or els iij li of money.

To the Lords Auditors in Scotland, in addition to the auditing of the accounts of the various officials who collected and disbursed the Crown revenue, was confided the duty of auditing the accounts of the intromissions of the magistrates with the common good of the burghs. An Act of James V. of 1535 (Parliament 4, cap. 26) ordains the provost, bailies, and aldermen to account yearly in the Exchequer for their administration of the common good. The provost, bailies, and aldermen had to give public notice fifteen days before the audit that their accounts were to be examined, in order that any one who cared to do so might inspect the accounts and take exception to them. An earlier Act, of the year 1491, had provided for a yearly "inquisition" into the expenditure of the common good. In addition to this central audit of the accounts of the common good, the burgesses themselves in many of the burghs audited the accounts of the burgh treasurer.

In Peebles the audit was held before the provost, council, and inhabitants of the burgh after warning by "proclamatioun to cum and heir thair thesaurare to mak his compt as vse is." The records refer to the "awdytouris" under date 17th November 1457, when the "cont" of the burgh of Pebillis was made. Again, in 1458, the names of the auditors (eight in number "with other mony") are given, and we are told that "all thingis contyt that suld be contyt and alowit that suld be lowyt"—a comprehensive, but rather vague certificate.

In Lanark, also, the rentmaster, or treasurer, apparently read his account to the auditors, but here the auditors wrote out a certificate in which they detailed every item of expenditure which they passed as correct. Thus in 1488 the certificate states: "The cownt of William Foster, rentmaister, herd of twa termys in the yer bigane, that ar to say Martynmes and Witsonday in the tym of his yer, the xij day of the moneth of Junij, the yer of Gode a thousande four hundreth lxxxviij yeris, be thir auditouris thairto sworn, that ar to say, Thomas Weir, John Mowat, Thomas Lokart, Andro Williamsoun, and John Smyth. The quhilkis auditouris fyndis the rentell in the said yer with the fut of the rest of the last cownt xxxiij li. xiij s.

"The auditouris allowys thir sommys underwrittin." (Here follow the items in detail).

The following docquet is appended to a fragment of the account of George Aczinson, rentmaster, of the year 1490:—

The auditouris fyndis that George Aczinson sall stand under the cownt of the breid irnis,[1] and se at thai be done sufficiantly, as he that has gevin it in cownt and nocht done, and allowit till him be the said auditouris, the quhilk som is xxvj s. iij d.; item, x s. gevin be the said George to John Symson for the fluring of the tulbuth and nocht done; and the werk done be Fasternevin, or ellis lay in the som to the rent maister.

The said auditouris fyndis of the rest of ix lib. x s. iij d., the quhilk remanyt in Thom Weiris handis; in his yer of rent maisterschip, allowyt till him, gewin to Stene Lokart at the command of the town, iiij lib.; and sa restis the said Thomas awand to the town, v lib. x s. iij d.

The said auditouris fyndis in George Merser hand of the tolbuth silver, xij d., the day of his cownt.

In Stirling the audit was originally carried out by the provost, bailies, and council. In 1528–1529 it is recorded that: " Duncan Patonsoun offerit the compt of wmquhill David Crag, thesawrar to this gud toune, and the buk tharof, to Johen Ackyne and Allexander Watsoun to be in thar keipin on to the tyme that the saidis coumptis war

---

[1] Bread irons, *i.e.* stamps for bread.

futtit befoir the saidis provest, baillies and counsall, of the said burgh." Later, the council appointed auditors from among the burgesses. Thus, in 1554, "the said William (the treasurer) comptis being maid and hard be certane auditouris, comburgessis of the said burgh, chosin and admittit tharto, he restis awing apone the fute of his saidis comptis to the community foirsaid the sowme of thre hundreth lix li. xix s. x d. . . ."; and in 1562 "The counsall has namit Johne Lecheman (and six others) to be auditouris of the townis comptis for this instant yeir."

The accounts of the city of Edinburgh were regularly audited and docqueted. The present degenerate race of auditors will learn with some astonishment that their predecessors "hard" the accounts on one occasion at "vj houris in the morning." The audit appears to have been carried out in a careful and thorough manner. Under date 28 May 1535 it is recorded: "The quhilk day, it is diuisit and ordanit that thir auditouris of compts abouewrittin begynand resaif the compts of this towne, in the first Robert Henrysouns compt and fute the samyn, and thairafter William Adamesouns compt, and syne the compt of the calsay and taxt, and swa furth ay and quhill the compts of the towne be compleitly endit." In 1576 some of the auditors refused to sign the accounts on the ground that they contained "certane soumes debursit at the conventioun of burrois to quhilk they wer nocht privye." The auditors were chosen by the provost, bailies, and council—after 1583 equally from the merchants and craftsmen. The following is a copy of the docquet appended to the earliest existing account of the Treasurer, for the year 1552–1553 :—

Apud Edinburgh, Secundo Martij, Anno Jm vᶜ quinquagesimo tertio.

[At Edinburgh, the second of March, in the year 1553.]

The quhilk day, the auditors of comptis underwrittin hes deligentlie vesyit the compt foirsaid and fund, the charge and discharge being seine, hard and understand, that the compter restis awing to the towne the sowme of twa hundreth lxx^{li} v^s ij^d *de claro* of his haill comptis; and als ordains in the nixt yeir Robert Grahame, new thesaurer, be chargit herewith; and als with the silver of the tymmer extending to xliij^{li} xvj^s quhilk he bocht to the towne in the moneth of July the yeir of God J^m v^c lj yers to the bulwerk, and thairefter allowit and dischargit to him in his comptis the samyn yere, he beand thesaurer, and intromettit with be the said Robert and sauld be him to his awin utilite agane.

Maister JOHNE PRESTOUN, baillie.
WILLIAM LAWSON, balze.
WILLIAM MUIRHEID, baillie.
DUNCANE LEVINGSTOUN, baillie.

WILLIAM HAMMYLTOUN, provest.
WILZEM CRAIK.
Mr JAMES LINDESAY.
JOHNE SYM, with my hand.

Item, I fynd in Robert. Grahame's compt, nixt thesaurer, that he charges him with the sowme of twa hundreth thre score ten^{li} v^s ij^d resavit be him fra the said Alexander Park, and siclik charges him with the xliij^{li} xv^s [xvj^s] for the tymmer above writtin in the samyn compt; and sua hes Alexander Park payit this rest.

[*Equidem.*]
GUTHRE. [1]

The records of Lanark of 1552–1553 contain the following report of the audit :—

Compotum Pattryk Makmoran, Robart Young, James Hetoun, and Watte Wikkitschaw :—The count of Patryk Makmoran, hard apon the xxix day of Janauar in the yer of God ane thousand fyf hundreth and lij yeris, hard be thir audyturis underwrytten, that is to say, David Walkar, David Brentoun, James Hetoun, Allexander Hammyltoun, James Grub, George Forrest, Robert Yowng, Watte Wikkitschaw, Wylyem Fokkart, and Wylyem Allexander, sworn and admitit tharto be the toun to alow that suld be allouit, defas that suld be defassit, fand that the rentell in the said Patrykis yeir of rentmastyrchip extendit to xx li. vj s. viij d. and the soum of his defasans extendit to xxj li. viij s. iiij d., sa restit the toun awand to the said Patryk Makmoran xxij s. iiij d., and vj s. viij d. that the audyturis dranc; and sa the said Patryk syk eque wyth the toun in his yeir of rentmasterchip.

Memorandum, apone the said day abone wryttin, the audyturis hard the fut of Robart Youngis count, James Hetoun count, and Watte Wikkitschawis count, and fand the saidis personis syk eque wyth the toun in

---

[1] Alexander Guthrie was the Town Clerk.

thair yeris of rentmasterschip, sa that James Hetoun had payit to the lard of Blakwod viij pundis quhylk the toun was awand to hym and allouyt in the said James count be the said audyturis, he getant the toun ane dyscharge at the lard of Blakwod of the said soum, and sa syk eque.

It is satisfactory to find that the creature comforts of the auditors were not overlooked. It will be noticed in the above quoted report that the auditors "dranc" 6s. 8d., and the "compt of the land malleis" of 1568–1569 contains the entry: "Item, xs. gevin to the audetouris in drink."

The auditors were not to be trifled with, as the following resolution, of date 1683, shows:—

Baillie Inglis being wairnit and callit for this day to give in his accounts and not compearing, orders that betwixt and Fryday he compeire before his former auditors and count; and alse Thomas Stodhart upon oath produce his registres and haill papers that he hes quhich appertenis to the brugh; otherwayes both of them are ordered to be taken to prissone.

The auditors of the Guildry of the City of Aberdeen report in their docquet appended to the accounts of 1586–1587: "Futit, calculat and endit by the Auditors;" and another docquet bears: "Heard, seen, considerit, calculat and allowit by the Auditors." The auditors appear to have received even better treatment than their Lanark brethren, as an entry records a payment for "Wine and Spicerie given to the Auditors." As further proof of the good cheer enjoyed by auditors in past times, reference may be made to "audit ale" still brewed at certain colleges of the English universities, which was originally for use at the feast held on the day when the college accounts were audited.

In the list of English Exchequer officials in the reign of Queen Elizabeth, of the year 1593, we find mention of five auditors, each of whom received fees amounting to £10, the Lord High Treasurer receiving £368 and his robes, and the Chancellor of the Exchequer £113 6s. 8d. and his livery.

The demands made on the accounting officers by the Lords

Auditors in Scotland, and the penalty incurred by failure to comply therewith, are shown in the following extract from the Exchequer minutes :—

Apud Halyruidhous, septimo Septembris, anno 1580.—
The quhilk day the lordis auditouris of the chekker ordanis the provest, baillies of Dundee, makaris of the baillie comptis of the said burgh, to compeir personalie befoir thame the day to be affixit in the nixt chekker be the preceptis to be dirrect thairupoun, and thair bring and exhibit with thame the said day to be prefixt be the said preceptis the perfyte comptis of thair commoun guidis, and siclyke of the annuellis and Freris landis disponit to thame be the kingis grace for sustentatioun of the hospitallis and pure of this instant yeir, 1580, and of the yeir nixt heireftir, 1581, to be sene and considerit be the saidis lordis auditouris ; under the pane of rebellioun and putting of thame to the horne,[1] with certificatioun to thame, and thay failye, the said day to be affixt, as said is, being bipast, ordanis letteris to be direct to denunce thame our soverane lordis rebellis, and put thame to the horne.[1]

The Scots Acts of Parliament of this period also contain references to the auditing of the national accounts. Thus, Acts of James VI. of 1593 and 1598 provide for the appointment of commissioners for auditing the accounts of the Collector-General. Later, in the reign of Charles I., (Act of 1640), power was given to a committee of the Estates to call the collectors and others to account, and to "appoynt auditoures for heiring and receiveing" the accounts thereof.

The Worshipful Company of Carpenters[2] furnishes yet another example (and more might be given) of careful auditing, from the fifteenth century onwards. Every year at the Court of the Company held in September, a committee consisting of the "old Master and Wardens" and some others was appointed to examine workmen's and tradesmen's accounts,

---

[1] " Put to the horne," *i.e.* proclaimed an outlaw for contempt of the King's authority, &c., which proclamation, made by a King's messenger, was preceded by three blasts of a horn.

[2] " An Historical Account of the Worshipful Company of Carpenters," Jupp.

and to "the new Master and Wardens and as many as would attend" was delegated the duty of auditing the accounts of the retiring Warden, and upon their report and the payment of the balance, if any, the retiring Warden's bond was returned to him. The Master and Wardens were not allowed "to sitt at the table with the other assistants untill the auditors have putt their hands to the accompt." A special gathering was held on the audit day, on which the work of the audit was not allowed to interfere with the more serious business of dining. In 1671, before the audit was completed, "as the day was farre spent and the dinner approached," business was postponed to the following day. In 1602 a question having arisen as to whether the accounts had been properly audited, it was declared that they had been fully examined "and allowed of for good," and a fine of £5 was imposed on any one who should animadvert upon them as though things had not been "orderlye and duely performed." In spite of all precautions, however, abuses crept in. At the audit day in 1673 (on which day only a "frugal dinner" was ordered) the auditors reported—

That they found many exorbitant expenses in dinners & reparacons, with divers frivolous and extravagant expenses both at home and abroad, as well upon publique meetings & courts, as in private with old masters and others, and that severall sumes of money were given to the poore over and above their pencons on the qter eves & on hydaies without any order of Court whereby the stock of this Company is unnecessarily wasted & the Company run further in debt & little likehood of getting out unlesse a speedy retrenchment be or some other remedy or redresse found out. And for that purpose they therefore represented the matter to the consideration of this Court; whereupon this Court after some debate in yᵉ premisses doth think fitt and so order upon vote That no more superfluous money be given to the poore on the qter day eves besides their pencons nor any other money in charity then or othertimes without order of Court or unlesse already ordered and settled. Item that no publique Auditt dinner from this day forward exceed xvˡⁱ. Item that noe dinner at the eleccon of Lord Maior on

Michas day & of Sheriffs & on Midsomer day doe from henceforth exceed 50ˢ each day. Item that no dinner on the Lord Maiors day upon his swearing at Westminster doe from henceforth exceed xxvˡⁱ. Item that noe dinner upon any ordinary or private monthly court day doe from henceforth exceed xlˢ a time. Item that the dinner and the expenses on each Court day exceed not xxˢ a time.

In 1769 an " Auditt Room" was ordered to be "built of brick and arched over, the better to secure the Company's writings and plate from fire."

The accounts of the Merchants' House of Glasgow, the earliest of which now existing is of the year 1624, seem to have been regularly audited, and are mostly certified by the Clerk of the House as having been found correct and duly vouched. An audit of private accounts in England about this time is shown by the Household Books of Lord William Howard of Naworth Castle,[1] covering the period from 1612 to 1640. The total of every branch of the receipts and of the payments, as well as the total amounts of the receipts and payments, is certified thus: "Ex. per Tho. Clay, Auditor." The epitaph of an auditor of such accounts may be seen inscribed on a tomb in the parish church of Chesham, Buckinghamshire, which is as follows:—

Here lyeth part of Richard Bowle who faithfully served divers great lordes as auditor on Earth but above all hee prepared himselfe to give up his account to the Lord of Heaven, and now hath his *quietvs est*, and rests from his torments and labors. He was a lover of God's ministers, a father of God's poore, a help to all God's people, and beleeves that his flesh, which with the Sovle was long tormented, shall with the same Sovle be æternally glorified.
He died the 16th of December 1626 and of his age 77.

The accounts of the City of London were, as we have seen, audited from the time of Edward I. The following is a copy of the certificate appended by the auditors to the accounts of the year 1633:—

---

[1] Surtees Society Publications.

And so it is found by the said Auditors that this Accomptant oweth the Maior, and coïalty and Citizens of this Citty upon both the said Accompts . . . . viij^m ix^c lxxxij^{li} xv s̃ x^d iij q^a.

NICHOLAS RAYNTON, Maior
GEORGE WHITMORE
MARTIN LUMLEY
ROB. PARKHURST
RICHD BLADWELL
SAMUEL ARMITAGE
WILLIAM COKAYNE
EDWARD DICHFIELD

In the same century the auditors of the accounts of the Treasurer of Glasgow, of the year 1659–1660, report: "Whilk compt befor wryttin, charge and discharge therin conteined, being of befor at lenth hard, red, sein and considered, calculat and laid, was allowed and approvine in everie heid and article therof."

In Stirling in 1695 steps were taken to make the audit more independent and effective by enacting "that neither provosts nor bailies should be auditors of the accounts, but that, in addition to the ordinary number of auditors chosen by the town council, two merchants should be chosen by the guildry and two tradesmen by the incorporated trades; that the auditors should have the exclusive power to approve or reject the accounts as they see cause; that the burgesses should be entitled to inspect the accounts and state objections during the auditing; and that members of council should, at their election, be sworn to observe these rules in all time coming."[1]

In King's College, Aberdeen, from 1695, the Mortification accounts are certified by the College authorities in the following cautious manner: "Approved the foresaid Accompts in all the Heads and Articles thereof (errors and mistakes always excepted)."

During the period which we have just considered, namely,

---

[1] "Extracts from the Records of The Royal Burgh of Stirling."

from the fourteenth to the seventeenth century, auditing, or "revising accounts," was also in operation in Italy, as will be seen in a subsequent chapter on Early Italian Accountants.

By the year 1702 the office of Auditor of the Receipt of the Exchequer appears to have risen in importance, and was then held by Lord Halifax. The record of the proceedings connected with the ceremony of the installation of the Lord High Treasurer in the Black Book of the Exchequer, under date 11th May 1702, informs us that the Treasurer, having received his staff of office from Queen Anne, came, about ten in the morning, "to the house of Lord Halifax, the Auditor of the Receipt of the Exchequer, where he was attended with many Earls, Barons, Privy Councillors, the King's Attorney and Solicitor, and other persons of quality ; they being assembled in the two great rooms were treated with chocolate, &c., by the said Lord Halifax." In the narrative of the subsequent proceedings it is stated that the great keys of the Treasury were presented to the Treasurer by the Auditor, and handed back again to the latter; and that his Lordship, attended by the Barons of the Exchequer, Dukes, Earls, &c., went into the Auditors', Pells', and Tellers' offices, and viewed the cash in the last.

In the eighteenth century the whole system of auditing the national accounts had become little better than a farce. When Pitt became Chancellor of the Exchequer the audit was ostensibly performed by two officers, called "Auditors of Imprest," who "each had in some years of the war received as much as £16,000, but their office had become a sinecure ; its duties were wholly performed by clerks, who confined themselves to ascertaining that the accounts were rightly added, but without any attempt at a real investigation. Every kind of fraud and collusion could grow up under such a system, and there appears to have been also little or no check upon the fees, perquisites, and gratuities given to persons in official situations."[1] Among the many measures carried by

[1] Lecky's "England in the Eighteenth Century," V. 30.

Pitt for the purifying of administration was one abolishing the office of "Auditors of Imprest," and appointing a board of five commissioners with the largest and most stringent powers of auditing the public accounts of every department.[1]

To the eighteenth century, also, belongs the last series of audited accounts to which we shall refer, namely, the accounts of the factors on the estates forfeited in consequence of the Jacobite risings of "The 'Fifteen" and "The 'Forty-five." These accounts were sworn to by the factors, and were examined and passed at the Exchequer. The docquet usually appearing on the accounts of "The 'Fifteen" is: "This Accompt being this   day   of   17   examined, settled and aggreed to is signed by the Commissioners and the Accomptant, and the Ballance ordered to be payed into the Exchequer by the Commissioners precept of this date being for the sume of   pounds   shillings and   pence sterling." The majority of the accounts of "The 'Forty-five" bear only the short certificate:

"Ex^d p. D. Moncreiffe, Aud^r.
Ex^d p. Alex^r Dougall, Accompt^t."

When the Poor Rate was first established in England the accounts of the overseers were merely submitted to the vestry of the parish for approval. An Act of Elizabeth imposed on Justices of the Peace the duty of examining these accounts. This examination, which degenerated into a mere formality, though subsequently modified, was not abolished until 1834, when auditors were appointed to audit the accounts of each Union and of the parishes comprised in it. This system in its turn gave place in 1879 to the system of audit by officials of the Local Government Board. In Scotland, while the accounts of many parishes were regularly audited, a compulsory audit of the accounts of parochial boards, which then became parish councils, was only introduced so recently

[1] Lecky's "England in the Eighteenth Century," V. 32.

as 1894.[1] The accounts of the Scottish burghs, as we have seen, have for long been subjected to audit. In 1822 it was enacted[2] that accounts of royal burghs certified by the provost should be annually deposited with the town-clerk, to remain for thirty days open to inspection and complaint to the Exchequer. An effective audit of burgh accounts was introduced by the Town Councils (Scotland) Act, 1900,[3] and the appointment of burgh auditors is now, with the exception of the five largest burghs, in the hands of the Secretary for Scotland. In Ireland, the official system of audit was introduced in 1838. The first Irish poor law statute,[4] of that year, provided for the appointment of auditors to audit the accounts of all persons liable to account under the Act. The powers and duties of these auditors are now regulated by the Local Government (Ireland) Act, 1902.[5]

Although auditing and auditors, as we have seen, date from a remote period, the professional auditor comes into being in comparatively modern times. The development of auditing in the nineteenth century, following on the construction of railways, and the establishment and growth of insurance companies, banking companies, and other joint-stock concerns, falls to be dealt with in a subsequent chapter.[6]

---

[1] 57 and 58 Vict. c. 58.   [2] 3 Geo. IV. c. 91.   [3] 63 and 64 Vict. c. 49.
[4] 1 and 2 Vict. c. 56.   [5] 2 Edward VII. c. 38.   [6] *Infra*, page 314.

CHAPTER V

HISTORY OF BOOK-KEEPING

THE OLDEST PRESERVED ACCOUNT-BOOK—OTHER EARLY AC-
COUNT-BOOKS OF THE THIRTEENTH AND FOURTEENTH
CENTURIES—THE DEVELOPMENT OF BOOK-KEEPING—THE
EARLIEST INSTANCES OF DOUBLE-ENTRY — THE FIRST
PRINTED TREATISE ON BOOK-KEEPING—DESCRIPTION OF
THE WORK OF PACIOLO—THE INFLUENCE OF PACIOLO ON
SUBSEQUENT AUTHORS — THE EARLIEST TREATISES IN
GERMAN, DUTCH, ENGLISH, FRENCH, AND SPANISH.

BOOK-KEEPING, rightly regarded, is simply a specialised form
of the art of keeping accounts. It is neither a discovery of
science, nor the inspiration of a happy moment, but the
outcome of continued efforts to meet the necessities of trade
as they gradually developed. One by one the successive
steps in the evolution of account-books were achieved till
finally it was realised that the transactions of a business in
their entirety form a homogeneous whole which is capable
of being marshalled in the framework of a system. When
this was discovered there originated what is known as " double-
entry," which may be said to form the basis of all systems
of book-keeping worthy of the name.

The written records of account-keeping applied to trade
fortunately go back to a date which is earlier than even the
most rudimentary book-keeping. We are thus enabled to
trace the development of this branch of the science of Accounting through all its stages. A book is extant which was
kept by a Florentine banker in 1211, and it proves that
book-keeping, in the only sense in which the word can be
used, was then unknown. The man who made the entries

was evidently highly efficient for his day. His technical methods are out of all comparison superior to those observed in books of a very much later date, but his account-book exhibits a mere series of detached memoranda. There are spaces on the various pages set aside for different clients, but all connection between these accounts is lacking. Moreover, the transactions of the bank, apart from dealings with its clients, are not recorded at all, so that the exposition of the affairs of the business is most incomplete.[1] Such was the art at its best at the commencement of the thirteenth century. We find that it had not advanced beyond a stage which is still that of account-keeping and not book-keeping. Books at this date contained nothing more than a series of unconnected jottings relating to those portions of business in which it would have been unwise to rely on memory alone. There was no provision for anything except personal accounts, the means for detecting omissions and errors were absent, and balancing was unknown.

Next to this oldest account-book of 1211 a considerable number of so-called ledgers are preserved from the period 1300–1400. They show methods and technique greatly inferior to those of the Florentine banker, and they illustrate further the primitive beginnings of book-keeping. The memoranda we find there, for they can be described by no other name, are obviously intended to serve only as aids to the memory in retaining the details of numerous transactions. When an important piece of business is concluded, the original agreements are copied in full, as in a modern sederunt-book, the principals sometimes signing the record, or a notary public adding his endorsation.[2] Entries, moreover, relating to sales and purchases, are mixed up with jottings of household expenses, and in one or two

---

[1] The book is described by Professor Sieveking in some valuable researches on the history of book-keeping which he contributed to *Schmoller's Jahrbuch für Gesetzgebung, &c.* (75th year, 4th Issue). The articles are entitled *Aus venetianischen Handelsbüchern*.

[2] Sieveking, *loc. cit.*, pages 302 and 303.

cases, even, the character of account-book so completely merges in that of memorandum-book that a few pages are set apart for a family chronicle.[1] Characteristics such as these are universal in the books of this time. Italy, which is the birthplace of modern commerce, furnishes some of the earliest examples, and the South of France, which had intimate relations with that country, shows at least one instance of an extremely interesting book which will afterwards be referred to. German books are also extant, especially from the Baltic regions where the Hanseatic League had its settlements. Nothing can be more primitive than these Teutonic records—indeed, Dr. Jäger, a learned authority on everything relating to accounts, dismisses them with the remark that from the point of view of book-keeping they are beneath criticism.[2] It is purely by accident that the oldest German account-book has come down to us. It was kept by two brothers between 1329 and 1360, and when one of them, who was burgomaster of Lübeck, became involved in a political intrigue and was brought to trial, the book was confiscated. It lay unknown in the archives of the Court of Justice until the other day, when it was discovered and duly reprinted under the direction of a competent editor.[3] The nature of the book-keeping may be gathered from the single fact that the entries are all made by the owner himself without assistance from clerks. The ledger is really a note-book. Business transactions are mixed up with household matters, and whole years pass without a single entry being made. Other German books are of the same nature.[4] None of them contains anything

---

[1] This is the case in books kept by Guido di Filippo di Ghidone dell' Antella in 1290 ; by the firm of Peruzzi in 1308–1336 ; and by Stephen Maignow, a goldsmith of Constance, in 1480–1500.   [2] *Altes und Neues aus der Buchaltung,* page 2.

[3] *Das Handlungsbuch von Hermann und Johann Wittenborg* (Mollwo, Leipzig, 1901).

[4] Other German account-books belonging to the fourteenth century which have been reprinted are : Johann Klingenberg (1331–1336) and Vicko von Geldersen (1367–1377). For further information see the list of old commercial books given at the commencement of Sieveking's articles ; also Mollwo, *loc. cit.* (Vorwort) ; and B. Zieger, *Die Kaufmännischen Bildungsstätten, &c., vom Ausgange des Mittelalters bis ins 18te Jahrhundert,* page 3.

which can properly be described as book-keeping.[1] A facti-
tious interest attaches to the books kept by the family of
Fugger at Augsburg between 1413–1426. The Fuggers became celebrated as the Rothschilds of early finance and their
descendants at the present day hold princely rank in Austria.
It was asserted a century ago by an early German writer
on book-keeping[2] that these old ledgers were kept by double-
entry. Although it has long been disproved, this statement
is frequently repeated. From specimens of the books which
have been published it is clear that the Augsburg ledgers
are simply memorandum-books of the contemporary German
type.[3] In our own country, unfortunately, no old account-
books have yet been published.[4]

A decided advance can be traced in the books of a
French firm, the Frères Bonis of Montauban, which were
kept during the years 1345 and 1359. At the latter date
this firm used its books to obtain a review of its position
and made up a list of its debtors and creditors. The money
owing to them was 678 lib. 7s. 8d.; that due by them was
551 lib. 2s. 10d.[5] But further particulars of the result of
their trading the books could not furnish. Still, a beginning
was made. As soon as a set of books was no longer
regarded as a mere repository for detached notes, to be
produced at a settlement between creditors, the evolution
of systematic book-keeping had commenced. From this
period onwards we begin to trace progress. The circum-

---

[1] Besides the authority of Dr. Jäger already quoted, see Zieger, *loc. cit.*, page 3.

[2] Gerhard Buse, *Das Ganze der Handlung* (Erfurt, 1804).

[3] Dr. Arnold Lindwurm, *Handelsbetriebslehre* (Stuttgart, 1869). See Dr. Jäger's comments in his *Beiträge, &c.* page ix. ; *Lucas Pacioli, &c.* page 146 ; and *Drei Skizzen, &c.* page 6.

[4] The ledger of Andrew Halyburton (1492–1503) belongs to a later period than that which we are now considering, but it may be chronicled here, for it is the only early "ledger" in our language which has been reprinted. Halyburton was "Conservator of the Privileges of the Scotch Nation in the Netherlands," an important office under the Scottish Crown, with duties not unlike those of a Consul. The book-keeping extends to nothing but personal accounts and is of a very primitive description.

[5] Sieveking, *loc. cit.*, page 303 n.

stances which brought about this development were mainly two. The first, and by far the most important, has been pointed out by Professor Sieveking. He characterises the transition from chaos to order by remarking that no advance was made as long as the account-books were intended solely for the private information of the trader. As soon, however, as accounts had to be prepared for submission to others, there appear signs of improvement. Banks, as we have already seen, had the most perfect methods of account-keeping, and naturally so, for they had to keep records of how they stood with each customer. But the requirements of banker and client were satisfied by the keeping of personal accounts. Partners in a business, on the other hand, required a record of the entire course of trading so as to apportion profits, and it is in this necessity that we find the prime motive for creating a system of book-keeping. But if the extension in the scale of commercial enterprises and the consequent impetus which was given to the formation of partnerships and joint adventures, led to improvements in book-keeping, the mere growth in the volume of transactions itself must also have led men to ponder on some orderly method for recording their dealings. In early days we find that a few pages sufficed for chronicling the business of a life-time. Now numerous books were required which were distinguished by letters, numbers, crosses, or colour of binding. An Italian firm of merchants named Peruzzi, for instance, opened eleven new books in 1339 : five white, two black, and one red, orange, yellow, and green respectively.[1] With such a mass of entries, and the endless possibility of error they imply, the discovery of some device for classifying the accounts and proving their accuracy would become a pressing necessity.

The first steps in the development of systematic book-keeping were very gradual. The methods practised by the banks contained certain rudiments of what may be called

---

[1] Sieveking, loc. cit., p. 308.

" cross-entries," and we find that these were slowly extended to commercial accounts. In the case of the banks the device arose naturally. Owing to the difficulty and risk of making payments in specie a large part of a banker's business consisted, then as now, in acting as intermediary in settling accounts. Merchants deposited money so as to be able to make payments by means of orders and to receive orders. The bank merely made a transfer in its books debiting one client and crediting another. Entries of this description arose from the nature of things and are very old. We already meet traces of them in the accounts of the Florentine banker of 1211. Applied to mercantile accounting the idea proved a fruitful one, for it led to the formation of "nominal accounts." There are books preserved from the year 1297 belonging to Rinerio and Baldo Fini, in which accounts were opened not only for persons, but for things, and the two classes were debited and credited *vice versa* in regular fashion.[1] Thus the idea of making transfers, together with the practice of using the books for making up a state of affairs, as already noticed in the case of the Freres Bonis, proved to be the first suggestion of systematic book-keeping. In detail the accounts were still imperfect to the utmost degree. The entries were more like narratives than postings. Individual accounts were often kept open for very long periods; thus an account in the books of the Freres Bonis opens on the 19th of December 1345, and goes on without intermission to the 11th December 1358. Debits and credits, also, were by no means always separated, but often placed one below the other as they occurred.[2] Finally there was no attempt made at a general balance, for in some cases the accounts were not even kept in the same monetary unit.[3] But for those book-keepers who desired to adopt improved methods the lines of development were indicated. Less than fifty years

---

[1] Sieveking, *loc. cit.*, p. 306.

[2] Ibid. p. 309. An account from the year 1289 is preserved, kept by Ser Cepperello Diotainti, a tax-collector of Philip the Fair. In this the debits, or *Recepta*, a replaced opposite the credits, or *Expensa et Liberationes*. But this is exceptional.

[3] Sieveking, *loc. cit.*, p. 308.

from the date when Rinerio and Baldo Fini opened their nominal accounts, a complete system of double-entry had made its appearance.

Double-entry is first met with in Genoa in the year 1340 in the accounts of the stewards to the local authority. The date when it actually commenced cannot be determined, but the period may be narrowed down within certain limits. The stewards' books of 1340 show a complete system of double-entry. The books immediately preceding were destroyed by a fire which occurred in 1339 and no books exist of an earlier date than 1278. These earlier books show not the faintest trace of double-entry. The following extracts will illustrate the nature of the entries in the ledger of 1340 [1] :—

Massaria Communis Janue de MCCCXXXX

MCCCXXXX die vigesima sexta augusti. Jacobus de Bonicha debet nobis pro Anthonio de Marinis valent nobis in isto in LXI

lib. xxxxviiii s. iiii

Item die quinta Septembris pro Marzocho Pinello valent nobis in isto die in LXXXXII

lib. xii s. x

Item MCCCXXXXI die sexta martij pro alia sua ratione valent nobis in alio cartulario novo de XXXXI in Cartis C

lib. s. xvi

Summa lib. LXII s. X

MCCCXXXX die vigesima sexta augusti. Recepimus in ratione expense Comunis Janue valent nobis in isto in CCXXXI et sunt pro expensis factis per ipsum Jacobum in exercitu Taxarolii in trabuchis et aliis necessariis pro comuni Janue et hoc de mandato domini Ducis et sui consilii scripto manu Lanfranci de Valle notarii MCCCXXXX die decima-nova augusti

lib. LXII s. X

An account called "Pepper Account" throws further light on the system of double-entry adopted in this ledger. The account is debited with expenses, credited with receipts,

[1] Taken from *Storia della Ragioneria Italiana*, by Guiseppe Brambilla, Milan, 1901.

while the balance is transferred to profit and loss, as the following specimens show:—

MCCCXXXX die VII marcij
Piper centenaria LXXX debent nobis pro Venciguerra Imperiali valent nobis in VIIII et sunt pro libris XXIIII sol V. pro centenario
lib. MDCCCCXXXX

On the same date there is the following credit entry:—

Recepimus in pipere centenaria LXXX pro libris XXIIII sol V. ianuinorum pro centenario valent nobis in XXXXIIII
lib. MDCCCCXXXX

On the credit-side there are further—

Item die VII novembris in dampno centenariorum LXXXIV et lib. XII
1/10 dicti piperis in ratione proventuum in isto in XXXVII
lib. CXXXXVIIII s. XII

Besides the books of the local authority of Genoa we have the records of a bank in that town going back to 1408, and these also are kept by double-entry. From the opening entries it has been supposed that a similar system of book-keeping had been used by the bank for some time.[1] An indefatigable antiquarian has subjected himself to the labour of finding out whether these old books balance. He has discovered that the total credits of 54,295 lib. 14s. do not agree with the total debits by an amount of 10s. 7d. This error he looked for and found to be due to the omission of a posting of like amount.[2]

Next in antiquity to those of Genoa are books preserved in Venice. They are of particular interest because they belong to traders, not bankers, or stewards of local authorities. These books are kept with most remarkable care and neatness, and the "Method of Venice," which afterwards became so celebrated, was evidently already beginning to be built up. The gradual development of the

[1] Sieveking, p. 310.   [2] Ibid.

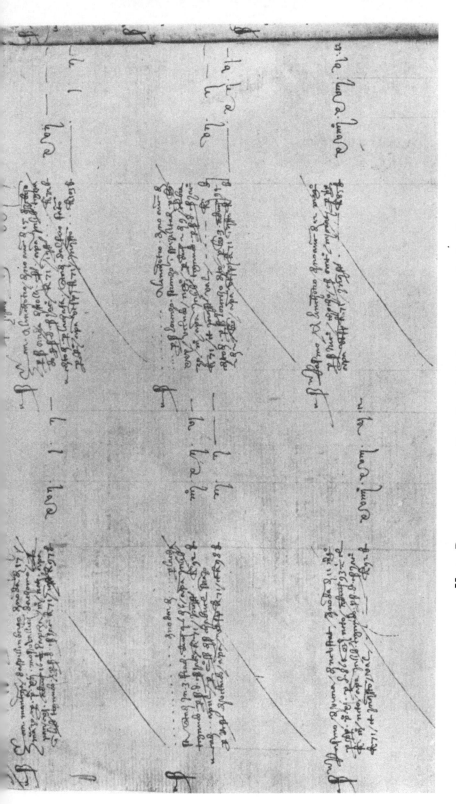

UPPER PORTION OF PAGE 98 OF SORANZO'S LEDGER, 1422 (reduced)

In the State Archives of Venice

art can be traced in two ledgers of the firm of Donado
Soranzo and Brothers, merchants.   Of the older ledger only
a fragment is preserved, bearing dates 1410 to 1416.   The
later book is complete and was evidently commenced before its predecessor was discontinued.   It covers the period
1406–1484.   In the first-mentioned ledger there is a very
accurate system of double-entry, but only up to a certain
point.   Every debit has its corresponding credit, and the "goods
accounts" are closed with a balance of profit or loss.   The
idea, however, of combining the items of profit and loss and
transferring them to Capital Account had not yet been adopted.
In short, the system stops at a sort of trial balance stage.
The second ledger, which commences in 1406, is complete.
It has a Profit and Loss Account and Capital Account.

The photographic reproductions of portions of two pages
of this ledger, which, by the courtesy of the custodians of the
State Archives of Venice we are able to give, illustrate both
personal and impersonal accounts, and contain a reference to
the Profit and Loss Account.   The money is stated in *lire,*
soldi, and *denari.*   What the fourth column containing Arabic
figures represents is not quite clear.   It is suggested that it
was used for *denari piccoli* as distinguished from *denari grossi.*

The following are transcripts and translations of the
accounts reproduced, for which we are also indebted to the
authorities of the Archives and a correspondent in Venice :—

Page 98

+ Jesus Mcccc° xxij j

„ Ser Ian mantegan da
 spilimbergo deno
 dar di 17 marzo per
 pᵃ (pezza ?) xij mosto
 vallieri da chomo Et
 per pani xi, a duc.
 16¼ la peza, m°.,
 nete. apar in libro
 tegnudo per ser d.
 e ser jac° K. 71,
 in questo   K. 97 £xvij   i   ij —

+ Jesus Mcccc° xxij j

„ ser Ian alinchontro deno
 auer dj 15 dezem-
 brio, per ser Andrea
 di priollj, R° apar In
 libro tegnudo per ser
 d. e ser jac° K. 71,
 in questo   K. 72 £xvij   — — —
„ e dito dj per la chasa,
 contadi dal suo fator
 per R° apar ut supra
 K. 71, In questo
              K. 103 £—   i   ij —

„ ser . . . . . . deno
dar dj . . . per lac-
hasa, contadj in 3
fiade, duc. 46 grossi
6 apar in libro teg-
nudo per ser d. e
ser jacᵒ, K. 71, In
questo   K. 92 £iiij   xij vj —
„ e adj . . . april, per
cᵒ ss. (conto supra
scritto?) de ser chab-
riel soranzo per resto
de veludo, apar ut
supra K. 71 et K. 98 £iij   ij — —

„ ser . . . . . . a linch-
rontro deno auer di
. . . per ser Lorenzo
soranzo in spizilitade
per braza (?) xxx,
veludo negro per
duc. 2 gr. 9 el brazo,
mᵒ, apar in libro
tegnudo per ser d. e
ser Jacᵒ K. 71, et in
questo, val K.⎫ £vijⱼ   ij — —
e dito dj per ser⎪
lorenzo dito per⎪
brazo 3 a duc. 2 ⎬94
gr. 2 il brazo (?)⎪
apar ut supra, K.⎪
71, in questo K.⎭ £— xij vj —

„ ser Rasmo de viena, de
neustat, deno dar,
dj 11 magio per
piper pᵒ xj per L. 86
onze (?) 1ª, neto a
duc. 93⅓ el K. (Kan-
taro?), mᵒ neto, apar
in libro tegnudo per
ser d. e ser jacᵒ K.
71, et In questo,
val   K. 92 £xviiij xviij vj 12

„ ser Rasmo a linchontro
deno auer di 12
magio per ser Nicolo
chocho e ser antonio
miorati per piper
apar ut supra K. 71,
In questo   K. 85 £xxiiij xxiij vj 12

Translation

+ Jesus Mccccᵒ xxij j

Mr. John Mantegan of
Spilimbergo *Dr.* on
17ᵗʰ March for 12
parcels of *mosto val-
lieri* of Como and
for 11 webs of cloth
at 16½ ducats the
web—amount net, as
entered in the book
kept for Mr. D. and
Mr. James, page 71,
in this book page 97 £xvii   i   ii —

+ Jesus Mccccᵒ xxij j

Mr. John per contra
Cr. on the 15ᵗʰ
December, per Mr.
Andrew di Priuli, on
account of monies
received, as entered
in the book kept for
Mr. D. and Mr.
James at page 71, in
this book   page 72 £xvii — — —
and at same date, for
moneys deposited by
his factor, as appears
as above at page
71, in this book
page 103 £—   i   ii —

Mr. . . . . . . *Dr.* on the . . . per the firm, advanced on 3 occasions, 46 ducats 6 grossi as entered in the book kept for Mr. D. and Mr. James page 71, in this book   page 92 £iiii   xii vi — and on . . . of April, on above-mentioned account of Mr. Gabriel Soranzo, for the remainder of velvet, as entered as above on page 71 and page   98 £iii   ii — —

Mr. . . . . . . per contra *Cr.* on the . . . by Mr. Lorenzo Soranzo on his special account for 30 braccia of black velvet at 2 ducats 9 grossi the braccio. Amount as entered in the book kept for Mr. D. and Mr. James at page 71, and in this book at   page 94 £vii   ii — — and on the same day by said Mr. Lorenzo for 3 braccia at 2 ducats 2 grossi the braccio as entered as above at page 71, in this book at page 94 £—   xviii — —

Mr. Rasmo de Viena of Neustadt *Dr.* on 11th May for 11 parcels of pepper, weight 86 pounds . . . ounces net at 93⅓ ducats per cantaro(?). Amount net, as entered in the book kept for Mr. D. and Mr. James at page 71, and in this book   page 92 £xviiii xviij vi 12

Mr. Rasmo *Cr.* per contra on the 12th May per Mr. Nicholas Cocco and Mr. Anthony Miorati for pepper, as entered as above page 71, in this book   page 85 £xviiii xviij vi 12

Page 100

+ Jesus Mcccc° xxij j

,, Fuine che aspeta per ½ a ser Lucha donado laltra ½ per chaxa nostra deno dar di 8 luio / per ser Iullian loredan, per fuine / 184 / in le qual fo martori. 9 a s. 22½ l'una mᵃ apar In libro tegnudo per ser d. a ser jacomo Karte 77 in questo val   K. 99 £iij   xxij — —

+ Jesus Mcccc° xxij j

,, Fuine, a lincontro deno auer di 7 luio 1423 per ser lucha donado per la ½ de le contra scritte che labudj linuerno pasado mᵃ/ apar ut supra K. 77 et in questo val, che son fuine / 92 / K. 89 £ij   iij viiij 16

„ e dito e per la chaxa
per dazio a la tolla
apar ut supra, K.
77 In questo, val
K. 103 £—   iij ij —

„ e dito de per la chasa
per far conzar le
dite / a s. 2 luna / m⁹/
apar ut supra K. 77
In questo   K. 103 £—   vij v —

„ e dito de per ser Iulian
loredan per fuine,
c°/m⁹/apar ut supra,
K. 77 In questo val
K. 99 £iij   — — —

„ ser Nichollo e jacomo
di priolli fo de miser
constantin, deno dar
dj ulltimo lujo per
ser andrea di priolli,
R° (resto ?) apar in
libro tegnudo per
ser d. e ser Iuane,
K. 78, in questo
K. 72 £—   xv x 7

„ e dito di per ser
Lorenzo soranzo / I
qual I aduse duc
23 scharsi / apar ut
supra, K. 78, in
questo   K. 100 £ij   vj — —

„ e dito di per la chaxa
per   in p° i° 331
che piero condusse
di qua tocha per
la so ½ apar ut supra
K. 78 in questo
val   K. 72 £—   vj iij —

„ e di . . . per ser
Nicolo e Jachomo,
medemi per saldo de⁻
questo val   K. 123 £ — — — v —
3 / 8 / 6 / 7

„ e dito, per ser piero
soranzo per la monta
de ¼ de le dite fo 46,
apar ut supra K. 72,
in questo.   K. 94 £j   j x 24

„ e dito dj per la C° ss.
ser d. soranzo per
lalltro ¼ che fo foine,
46 / apar ut supra K.
77, in questo K. 91 £i   i x 24
tollti per vetor.

„ ser Nichollo e jacomo
di priolli deno auer
di 3 Zugno per 331
Ci [Cellidi (?)] e
piper (?) p° 1° per lo
trato neto de quellj
i tocha per la sua ½,
apar ot supra, K. 78.
K. 95 £iij   iij v 2

„ e dito per vtelle e
dano per fito de 1°
magazen apar ut su-
pra K. 78 in questo
K. 86 £—   v i 5

3 / 8 / 6 / 7

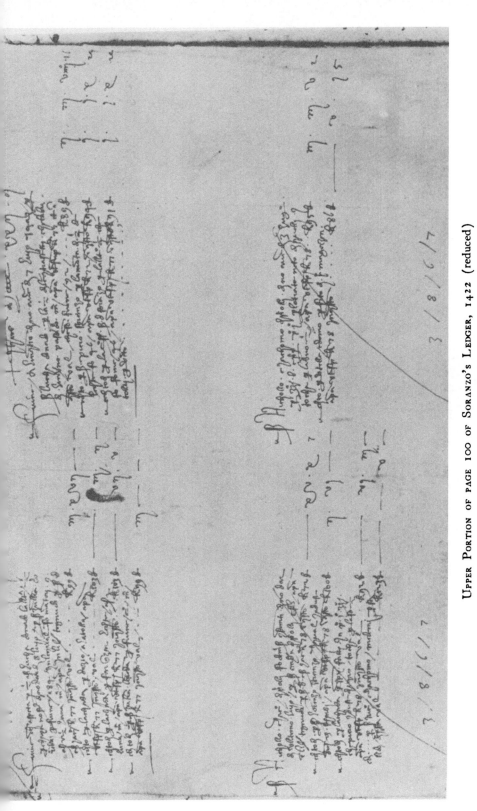

UPPER PORTION OF PAGE 100 OF SORANZO'S LEDGER, 1422 (reduced)

In the State Archives of Venice

Translation

+ Jesus Mcccc° **xxij** i

Pole-cat skins which belong half to Mr Lucha Donado, the other half to our firm, *D^r* on 8th July, per Mr Julian Loredan for 184 skins, among which were 9 marten skins, at 22½ soldi each—amount as entered in the book kept for Mr D. and Mr James at page 77, in this book   page 99 £iii   xvii — —

The same to our firm for the duty at the Custom House, entered as above, page 77, in this book
      page 103 £—   iii   ii —

The same to our firm, for tanning said skins, at 2 soldi each, amount entered as above, page 77, in this book
      page 103 £—   vii   v —

The same per Mr Julian Loredan for pole-cat skins, amount entered as above, page 77, in this book
      page 99 £iii   —   — —

Messrs. Nicholas and James Priuli, sons of the late Mr Constantine, D^r on the last day of July, per Mr Andrew de Priuli, balance as entered in the book kept for Mr D. and Mr John, page 78, in this book
      page 72 £—   xv   x   7

+ Jesus Mcccc° **xxij** ii

Pole-cat skins, per contra *C^r* the 7th July 1423, per Mr Lucha Donado, for half of the said skins which he received this winter past—amount entered as above, page 77, & in this book, 92 skins   page 89 £ii   iii   viii 16

Same, per Mr Piero Soranzo, for the value of a quarter of said skins, 46 skins, entered as above, page 72, in this book   page 94 £i   i   x 24

Same date for the above mentioned account, Mr D. Soranzo for the other quarter, that is 46 skins, entered, as above, page 77, in this book   page 91 £i   i   x 24
Taken by Victor

Messrs. Nicholas & James Priuli *C^r* 3rd June, for 331 parcels of pepper, for their half share, entered as above, page 78,   page 95 £iii   iii   v 2

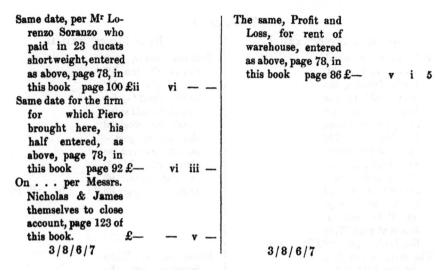

Same date, per Mᵣ Lorenzo Soranzo who paid in 23 ducats short weight, entered as above, page 78, in this book page 100 £ii	vi — —	The same, Profit and Loss, for rent of warehouse, entered as above, page 78, in this book page 86 £—	v i 5
Same date for the firm for which Piero brought here, his half entered, as above, page 78, in this book page 92 £—	vi iii —		
On . . . per Messrs. Nicholas & James themselves to close account, page 123 of this book. £—	— v —		
3/8/6/7		3/8/6/7	

While a few specially well-kept books prove that the art of book-keeping was pretty fully developed by the commencement of the fifteenth century, it must not be supposed that a high standard was attained all round. The incomplete system which went no further than the trial-balance stage was in very general use and was imported from Venice into Florence.[1] And even in the best books there was a most marked deficiency in one department, which in modern times is almost the accepted standard by which we judge book-keeping—namely, the power of balancing, *i.e.* proving the equality of debits and credits. It would be too much to say that balancing was unknown, but it was extremely rare. The fact seems to have been that the merchant regarded his book-keeping by double-entry as a guarantee of the formal completeness of his posting, and trusted to careful "comparisons" for the detection of errors. An interesting light is thrown on the position of book-keeping in these days by an incident in the family of Soranzo, whose two ledgers have been referred to. The brothers had kept house together, but terminated the arrangement in 1434 and made a mutual accounting. Disputes arose, and the case was taken into court. In

---

[1] Sieveking, p. 312.

these legal proceedings reference is made to wills and inventories, but the books of the firm are hardly brought into the case at all. Yet we know that they were excellently kept. Another instance worth noting occurs in connection with another great merchant-house of Venice. One Andrea Barbarigo kept a ledger between 1440 and 1449, and in this whole period there is not a single attempt at balancing. His son Nicolo kept another ledger from 1456 to 1482, and he, at least, makes an annual calculation of profit. But a balance he only made once, in 1482, when the book was full. This practice of not making a general balance till the ledger was completed continued to be widespread till the seventeenth century. It is beyond all question that although about this time we find a high development in the theory and principles of book-keeping, we fail to discover a recognition of its many practical advantages. To bring the position of affairs home to us we must bear in mind that the ledger was kept in Roman numerals. It might be supposed that much of the futility of the book-keeping of the day was due to this cumbrous system of notation. But the difficulty of balancing with the old cyphers was only a question of degree. The Goods Accounts were regularly closed off, and to treat every other account in the ledger in the same manner would certainly have been possible had it been thought advisable. The true position seems rather to be that the continued adherence to Roman figures is simply an additional proof that the mediæval merchant did not realise all the convenience his double-entry could afford. He had discovered in a system of cross-entries a fairly serviceable means of satisfying himself that all his transactions were entered in his ledger, and there, for the time being, he stopped. Roman figures he retained because they prevented fraudulent changes in his postings.[1] One old ledger only is written in Arabic

[1] In 1299 we find the guild of bill-changers of Florence forbidding the use of the "new" figures, while as late as 1520 the municipality of Freiburg refused to accept entries as legal proof of debt unless they were made in Roman figures or written out in words.

figures, that of Jacob Badoer (1436–1439), and it was kept at Constantinople—that is to say, in the East, the birth-place of the new cyphers. What was sometimes done was to give the particulars in both figures, and here Germany, which in general was very backward in book-keeping, so far led the way that it placed the Arabic figures in the money-column and the Roman ones in the text. Italy still retained the old numerals in the money-columns.

Such was the general position of the art of book-keeping when, in 1494, at Venice, the first treatise on the subject was given to the world.[1] The author was one of the most celebrated mathematicians of his day, Luca Paciolo—Latinised Lucas Patiolus—and he had become familiar with the problems of commerce through acting as resident tutor to the sons of one of the merchant princes of the Republic.[2] Paciolo describes himself as " Brother Luke of the borough of San Sepolcro, of the order of St. Francis, and of sacred theology a humble professor.[3] The purpose of the work was not in the first place to give instruction in book-keeping, but to summarise the existing knowledge of mathematics. It is therefore entitled " Everything about Arithmetic, Geometry, and Proportion " (*Summa de Arithmetica, Geometria, Proportioni et Proportionalita*), and is divided into two parts, one dealing with arithmetic, the other with geometry. Having given directions for making numerical calculations

[1] In a book entitled *Manuele di Storia del commercio*, by G. Boccardo, Book II. chap. 2, § 101 (cited in the *Elenco cronologico*, 4th ed., 1889, page 7), there occurs the following passage : " Three merchants of Florence, Pegoletti, Uzzano, and Davanzati, have left the earliest treatises on commerce. The first two have given with wonderful method and order various instructions about merchandise, coins, weights and measures, and about the use and keeping of books." Karl Peter Kheil, in Prague, a diligent investigator of the history of book-keeping, states that he has read through these books and found no trace of the alleged reference to book-keeping. (*Über einige ältere Bearbeitungen des Buchhaltungs-tractates von Luca Pacioli*, page 1 n.).

[2] Antonio de Rompiasi by name. A mistake in the spelling of this name has become widely adopted through a printer's error in the 1523 edition of Paciolo, where we read " Ropiansi."

[3] In the original : "*Frater Lucas de Burgo sancti Sepulchri Ordinis minorum, Et sacre theologie humilis professor.*" San Sepolcro is a little town in Tuscany. Paciolo was born there about 1445.

TITLE PAGE OF PACIOLO—1523 edition (size of original 11½ inches by 8 inches)

and having devoted particular attention to the difficulties involved in counting-house work by the chaotic state of the coinage of the period, Paciolo brings the arithmetical part of the work to a close by adding the treatise on book-keeping. It is introduced with the following apology: "In order that the honourable subjects of the most gracious Duke of Urbino may have complete instructions in the ordering of business, I have decided to go beyond the proposed scope of this work and add this most necessary treatise."

The dissertation on book-keeping is composed of thirty-six chapters, and is entitled "Of Reckonings and Writings" (*De computis et scripturis*). Paciolo makes no claim to offer any original contribution to the art of book-keeping. He states explicitly that he will follow "the method of Venice," which in his opinion is to be recommended in preference to others. At the same time there can be little doubt that in his exposition the subject gained immeasurably in clearness. The author most fully answered that first requirement of the good teacher: the understanding of the subject himself. Paciolo's command of detail is astonishing, and in taking the trouble to acquire this knowledge he cannot but have contributed towards carrying the somewhat vague ideas of merchants and their book-keepers to a logical conclusion. It is well worth while to enter somewhat fully into this first printed treatise on book-keeping.[1] Not only is it extremely interesting, but the original can be intelligible only to a few.[2] The points on which Paciolo's book-keeping

[1] Paciolo's is the first *printed* treatise on book-keeping. In 1573, at Venice, a book by Benedetto Cotrugli was published with the title *Della mercatura et del mercante perfetto*. It is said to have existed in MS. as early as 1463. This book contains a short chapter on book-keeping, showing that the writer was familiar with double-entry, which, as we know, was first practised more than a century earlier. If the statement as to the age of the original composition is correct, Cotrugli would be the first known *writer* on book-keeping, and his work, however rudimentary, may have circulated in MS., as old works did even after the invention of printing.

[2] It is written in contemporary Italian, and the printing is full of contractions. While having the original before him, the present writer has relied on a German translation by Dr. Jäger (*Lucas Paccioli und Simon Stevin*. Stuttgart).

Distinctio nona. Tractatus .xi°. De scripturis

Commo se debiano saldare tutte le partite del quaderno vechio: e i chi: e per che e de la su ma summarum del dare e delauere ultimo scontro del bilancio.   ca°.34

Del modo e ordie a saper tenere le scripture menute cõmo sõno scripti de mano elke familia ri polize: pcessi: sentẽtie e altri istrumẽti e del registro de le lettere iportãti.   ca°.35

Epilogo o uero sũmaria recolta de tutto el psente tractato: acio con breue substãtia se ha bia mandare a memozia le cose dette.   ca°.36

Distinctio.nona.Tractatus.xi°.pticularis de cõputis z scripturis.

De quelle cose che sõno necessarie al uero mercatante: e de lordine a sape bẽ tenere vn q̃ derno cõ suo giornale i vinegia e anche p ognaltro luogo.   Capitolo primo.

A reuerenti subditi de.U.D.S.Magnanimo.D. acio a pieno de tutto lordine mercantesco habino el bisogno: delberai.(oltre le cose dinanze i q̃sta nfa opa ditte) ancora particular tractate grandemẽte necessario cõpillare. E in q̃sto solo lo iserto: p che a ogni loro occurrẽça el psente libro li possa seruire. Si del mo do a conti e scripture: cõmo de ragioni. E per esso intendo dar li norma sufficiente e bastante in tenere ordinatamente tutti lo conti e libri. Pero che.(cõmo si sa)tre cose maxime sõno opoz tune: a chi uole con debita diligẽtia mercantare. De le q̃li la potis sima e la pecunia numerata e ogni altra faculta su stantiale. Iu xta illud phy vnũ aliquid necessariorũ e substantia. Sẽça el cu suffragio mal si po el manegio traficante exercitare. Auẽga che molti gia nudi cõ bona fede cõmençando: de grã facẽde habio fatto. E mediante lo credite fedelmẽte seruato i magne richeççe sìeno peruenuti. Che asai p ytalia discurrẽdo nabiame cognosciuti. E piu gia nele grã republiche non si poteua dire: che la fede del bon mercata te. E a quella si fermaua loz giuramento: dicẽdo. A la fe de real mercatante. E cio nõ deue sere admiratione: cõciosia che i la fede catolicamẽte ognuno si salui: e sẽça lei sia ipossibile piacere a dio.   La secõda cosa che si recerca al debito trafico: sie che sia buon ragioneri: pmpto cõputista. E p questo cõsequire.(disopra cõmo se ueduto)dal pricipio alasine: ha uemo iducto regole e canoni a ciascuna opatione requisiti. In modo che da se: ogni diligẽ te lectoze. tutto potra iprendere. E chi di questa pte non fosse bene armato: la seguẽte in ua no li serebbe.   La.3 ª.e vltima cosa opoztuna sie: che cõ bello ordie tutte sue facẽde debita mẽte dispõga: acio con breuita: possa de ciascũa hauer notitia: quanto aloz debito e anch credito: che circa altro non satẽde el trafico. E q̃sta pte fra laltre e aloro utilissima: che i lo facẽde altramẽte regerse: seria ipossibile: sẽça debito ordine de scripture. E sẽça alcũ reposo lor mẽte sempe staria in gran trauagli. E po acio con laltre q̃sta possino hauere. el psẽte tr ctato ordiai. Nel q̃le se da el mõ a tutte sozti de scripture: a ca°.p ca°. pcedẽdo. E bẽ che n si possa cusi apõto tutto el bisogno scriuere. Nõ dimeno p q̃l che se dira. El pegrino igeg̃ q̃lũcaltro laplicara.   E seruaremo i esso el mõ de vinegia: q̃le certamẽte fra gli altri e molt da cõmẽdare. E mediante q̃illo i ogni altro se porra guidare. E q̃sto diuideremo i.2.pti p cipali. Luna chiamaremo iuẽtario. E laltra dispõne. E p°.de luna: e poi de laltra successiu mẽte se dira scdo lordie i la pposta tauola contenuto. Per la q̃l facilmente el lectoze porra occurẽtie trouare secondo el numero de suoi capitoli e carti.

Chi cõ lo debito ordie che saspecta uol sap bẽ tenere vn q̃derno cõ lo suo giorn le a q̃l che qui se dira con diligẽtia stia a tẽto. E acio bẽ siintẽda el pcesso idurre mo i cãpo vno che mo dinouo comẽçi a traficare cõmo p ordie deba procede nel tenere soi conti e scripure: acioche sucitamẽte ogni cosa possi ritrouare post al suo luogo p che nõ asettandole cose debitamẽte a li suoi luoghi uerebbe i grandissimi tr

differs from modern practice will be found to be broadly
four: there is no separation in the books of primary entry;
all entries, with exception of transfers and closing entries,
are journalised; the profit and loss account is written up
in a distinctive way; and stock is not treated in the
modern fashion. These peculiarities, however, are far from
being due to a defective grasp of the principles of book-
keeping. On the contrary, they were the most convenient
and probably the only practicable methods in the circumstances of the time. Much of the interest of an examination
of the old treatise *De Computis* lies in tracing how much
of our modern practice is new, how much is old. It is
remarkable how many of our present methods are described
in the quaintest language by this monk of four hundred
years ago.

The object of book-keeping is stated by Paciolo in precise
terms: to give the trader without delay information as to
his assets and liabilities. In giving directions how to proceed he begins with showing how to open a new set of
books. The first step, he explains, is to make a complete
inventory of one's possessions and of one's liabilities. This
inventory, he observes, must not be made at different dates,
but on one and the same day. Having completed the inventory, the merchant is advised to keep three books, which
Paciolo calls Memorial, Journal, and Quaderno, *i.e.* ledger.
The Memorial and Journal require some explanation. The
Memorial is best described as a general book of primary
entry. In it everything is entered as it occurs: sales, purchases, and every other transaction. The use of this book
becomes apparent on a consideration of the confused state
of the coinage which in these days served as circulating
medium. We must remember that in the Middle Ages there
was no such thing as uniformity in monetary systems. Each
petty state, even each important town, had its mint, and if
we include token coins, there was money in circulation which,
it has been said, was readily accepted in one street while

it was looked at with suspicion in the other. Add to this the fact that much of the coinage was debased and clipped, and it becomes evident that the book-keeping of the period was of necessity seriously affected by such a state of affairs. The first important duty of the book-keeper was to convert each item in the Memorial to the monetary unit in which his accounts were kept. Having made his calculation, he transcribed the entry into the Journal, arranging it at the same time as a cross-entry of debit and credit. Such is the historical origin of the Journal as a posting medium. We see that in the early days of book-keeping it was altogether out of the question to post direct from the books of primary entry. It says little for the originality of subsequent generations that centuries should have elapsed before it was recognised that a book prescribed as essential by the old masters, and rightly so, had under altered conditions ceased to be useful and become only cumbersome. As regards the use of a single book for all primary entries, we find that, as late as 1796, Edward Jones in his "English Book-keeping" advised such a book, and discountenanced even a separate cash-book.

The old form of Journal had only one column, which was not summed; nor would there have been any particular object in doing so. The entries themselves, as prescribed by Paciolo, are absolutely faultless. There is not yet the grouping together of kindred items, which now saves so much clerical labour, but under a state of affairs when each entry necessitated an arithmetical calculation, it was probably more convenient to write up the items *seriatim*. Apart from these superficial details, however, the entries were just as we make them to-day. Paciolo begins with the items of the Inventory and opens his books. He takes cash on hand, and debits Cash Account and credits Capital. Incidentally he observes that the balance on Cash Account must always appear as a debtor. Should it ever work out as a creditor, a mistake must have arisen, which should immediately be looked for. Each successive item in Inventory and Memorial is then taken and "journalised." As an example a short account may be given of the instructions for making entries relating to a Joint Adventure. Each partner is to be credited with the money or goods he contributes, and the Adventure debited. The sales and expenses, such as freights, &c., are to be entered up in the regular manner, and the accounts closed by dividing the proceeds according to the terms of the agreement.

Before passing to the peculiarities of early book-keeping as exemplified in the ledger of Paciolo, a few technical details may be mentioned which have been preserved till recent times. After each Journal-entry, Paciolo mentions that it is customary to rule a line across the page; he also notes that in the Journal the date should be placed in the middle of the page and not at the side, as in the ledger. No satisfactory reason can be given for doing either of these things, yet they have been retained through centuries. Again, as auditors know who see many styles of book-keeping, there is a habit in use among members of a certain school of indicating posting by scoring the item through with a vertical line. Let them not hastily put this down to slovenliness or ignorance. It is a practice of remote ancestors handed down with reverent piety. Paciolo knows of it, although he hastens to add that a " tick " will serve every purpose. Even down to details like posting-folios the old monk was conversant with the methods of book-keepers. He carefully mentions the best method of recording these clearly, and his instructions were followed minutely as long as one-columned journals were in use. The debit and credit folios were placed one above the other in form of a fraction, and two centuries later this habit prevailed as far as remote Scotland, as the reader will see if he refers to the illustration given later on from the Journal of the ill-fated Darien Company.

The ledger is treated by Paciolo with equal excellence

and in the same detail as the Journal. But first a point is referred to, which the author regarded as highly important and worthy of a separate chapter. This is the "alphabet," or index to the ledger. The system described is very elaborate, for it consists of an ordinary alphabetical index with sub-divisions under each letter for the second letter in the name. It may be noted that at this time persons were indexed according to their Christian names. Edward Jones, for instance, would have been entered under E, sub-division D. Paciolo then passes to the ledger. As ruled books were not provided ready made, instructions are given for arranging the money and date columns.[1] These are identical with those we now use, and they have also a division for posting-folios on the left of the money-column. A curious practice occurs in regard to posting-folios, which gives additional weight to the observation already made that the mediæval merchant laid the chief emphasis on obtaining an assurance that every entry was doubly posted, rather than trusting to a regular balance of his books. The folios entered as references in the ledger are not the pages of the journal, but the number of the ledger-folios where the counterpart of each debit and credit was to be found. Thus the entry crediting a customer with payment of his account would have as reference the folio of the cash account where the receipt was debited. We find this practice still in use in the books of the Darien Company. So much importance was attached to these cross-references, that when Paciolo later on gives directions for making a "comparison" of the books, he tells that after checking the debit, the credit should be at once looked up. Regarding the balancing of the books, Paciolo's directions presume that the balance takes place when a new ledger is commenced.

Among the ledger-accounts themselves the most distinctive is the Profit and Loss Account. Owing to the conditions of the trading of the period no accounts were kept showing in aggregate all sales and purchases. Instead

[1] The books of the Darien Company, kept between 1696 and 1707, are ruled by hand.

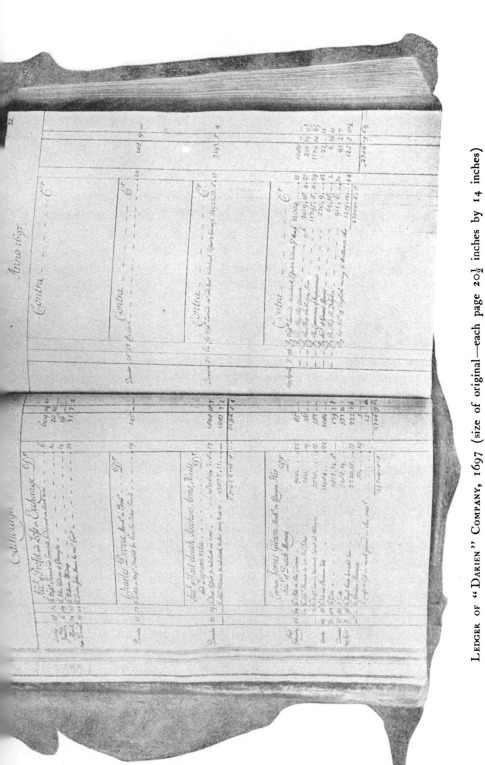

LEDGER of "DARIEN" COMPANY, 1697 (size of original—each page 20½ inches by 14 inches)

In the Advocates' Library, Edinburgh

there were separate accounts for each particular consignment of goods. Partly this arose from the miscellaneous nature of the articles in which each merchant traded. Commerce had not yet become sufficiently lucrative to permit of specialisation, and to earn a living a man had to deal in everything.[1] Thus we find one and the same merchant sending on a "journey to Venice" an assortment of goods from which the following items may be taken as typical: linen, furs, iron kettles, altar candlesticks, brass work, and 728 dozen of thimbles. To have kept a general goods account would have served no purpose. Further, it must be borne in mind that the defective means of communication and the insecurity of transit made each undertaking appear in the light of a special venture. Delivery of goods to a neighbouring town took the form of a military expedition to ward off bandits. A "journey" down the Rhine or the Danube was of the same kind. Each robber-castle levied toll. Even sea-borne commerce was in the highest degree precarious. We find, for instance, that the cost of insuring a cargo of wool between London and Pisa was from 12 to 15 per cent.[2] Freight, tolls, tariffs, and other charges so far increased the price that English wool was sometimes sold in Florence at twelve times its original value.[3] These circumstances brought it about that a merchant's transactions did not appear to him as a continuous process of trading, but as a succession of individual ventures. His book-keeping reflected this state of affairs, and we accordingly find separate accounts for each undertaking. Expenses also, such as freight and so on, were not grouped together in one account, but carefully apportioned to each venture wherever possible.[4]

[1] Schultze, *Geschichte des mittelalterlichen Handels.*
[2] Pagnini, *Della Decima.*   [3] Doren, *Florentiner Wolltuchindustrie.*
[4] Petty expenses were entered in a special account, and Paciolo gives his usual careful direction as to the expenses which it is not worth while to specially apportion. As an instance he cites the wages paid to porters for unloading a ship and carrying the goods to the merchant's warehouse. No attempt should be made, he says, to divide this expense over the several items of the cargo.

When each of these various transactions which we have called "ventures" came to an end, the account relating to it was squared off and the balance transferred to Profit and Loss. It may be noted in passing that these entries and all others of the same nature were made directly in the ledger and not by means of the Journal. That book bore in no respect its modern character of a place for recording closing entries, but served exclusively as a medium for arranging the rough jottings in the "Memorial" and the items recorded in the "Inventory." Profit and Loss was thus not written up at the end of the year, but posted periodically as each enterprise came to a conclusion. To a large extent this method of dealing with profit explains why book-keepers at this time did not take stock or balance at regular periods. The absence of a general goods account showing aggregate sales and purchases reduced the importance of stock-taking. Ventures which were completed appeared duly in the profit and loss account; enterprises, on the other hand, which were in course of being settled, simply occurred as balances in the list of assets. This practice, which in the circumstances of the time was the most convenient that could have been adopted, would greatly diminish the necessity for yearly general balances. Where profits were ascertained piece-meal a balance would only be required for detecting errors in clerical labour, and this contingency was carefully guarded against.

Paciolo's description of the process of balancing the ledger stipulates, as has already been remarked, that a new book is commenced at the same time. Before commencing operations a careful "comparison" of the books is to be made. The instructions that are given may be reproduced as a specimen of the author's style. They may also be of value to any young accountant who may chance to read this page. What he now regards as the most tedious portion of his labours may hereafter to his mind become invested with some of the glamour of an immemorial usage.

The "comparison" of books is thus described four hundred years ago by the Franciscan monk, and for the sake of its quaint interest we will reproduce the passage as it appears in an English translation of Paciolo which was published in 1543.[1] "And for the more expedition and cleerness yee shall keepe this order, which is, that yee take and assigne one of your fellowes to helpe you. For it were much labour and over tedious to one alone to examin all that which belongeth unto this acte. Wherefore for the more speede first deliver unto your fellow the Journall and holde yourselfe the Leager. Then request your fellow that hath the Journall to begin with the first parcell of the said Journall, and that he tell you the name and the thing and in what leafe of the Leager it standeth, in Debitor or Creditor, so that you may perceive to what leafe he sendeth you. And when you have found the parcell, by the shewing of him that hath the Journall, then marke and make a token in the said Leager in the same parcell with a pricke upon the pound, thus, lib. • or some other signe, so it be no blemish in the book; that done say to him that hath the Journall, that he also make a pricke or signe of your concordance. And beware that none of you without consent of the other marke any parcell, by reason whereof might grow grievous labours to reforme the correction again of the same. For the parcells discreetly perused and so marked testifyeth a due examination. . . .

"Then proceede ye forth in your worke by and by, and by examining your Journal and Leager together, of all the parcells both Debitors and Creditors, by the which doing thoroughly examined ye shall perceive and find if that your said Leager be perfectly governed and compiled or not. And note you also that every one parcell in your Journal must for the concordance have two prickes because it ought to accorde with two parcells in the Leager, one in *dare*, the

[1] By Hugh Oldcastle. See *infra*, p. 126.

othere in *habere*.[1] Then these bookes thus truely and thoroughly examined, if there remain any superfluous parcells not pricked in the Leager, then it presupposeth an error in the Leager." Paciolo then explains how these errors in the ledger may arise, and how they are to be corrected. False postings are to be cancelled by a cross-entry, and entries omitted are to be filled in with an explanation why they appear out of order of their date. He also points out that some items will occur in the ledger which are not to be found in the journal. These are the balances on the debit and credit which have been transferred, and they must be looked up according to their folios and verified. " And then," concludes the old monk in the words of his translator, "this acception so discussed, if that your two books the Journall and Leager together well and truly examined, as aforesaid, agree both like in their marking or pricking, then that testifyeth your foresaid two bookes have been discreetly governed and kept : and by this work and provision is your Leager sufficiently rectifyed to the making of your ballance, as afterwarde shall be shewed." This description of a "comparison" is a good instance of Paciolo's knowledge of the usages of book-keeping down to the minutest detail. The celebrated mathematician who had visited all the great courts of Europe must have compared books himself. How else could he describe the operation so faithfully ? Let the youthful accountant take his great predecessor's advice to heart and let him make sure that items are never marked off in one book and not in the other, " by reason whereof grow grievous labours to reforme the correction again of the same."

Having completed his directions for making a comparison, Paciolo gives instructions for opening the new ledger. All accounts representing assets and liabilities are to be squared off and their balances transferred to the new book. Accounts relating to freights, carriages, household expenditure,[2] interest

---

[1] *Dare et habere* = Debit and credit.

[2] Household expenditure was carried to Profit and Loss Account till a very late period. Legacies received, on the other hand, were credited to Capital Account.

and rents received, &c., are to be transferred to Profit and Loss Account. It is correctly explained that a credit balance on this account represents a profit, while a balance on the opposite side indicates a loss, " from which," says Paciolo, " may God preserve every man who proves himself a true Christian." The balance on Profit and Loss Account is then carried to Capital Account, and thereafter this Account is also balanced and carried to the new ledger. The author is careful to add that each account when it is entered in the new ledger should be noted with its folio in the "alphabet" or index. As a check on the accuracy of the work it is interesting to note that it is not the balances in the new ledger that are taken down, but the totals of debit and credit sides in the old ledger.[1] Should the two grand totals not agree, then Paciolo can only suggest that the book-keeper should set to work " with such talent as God has given him."

To briefly review the position of book-keeping at the close of the fifteenth century as reflected in the work of Paciolo we may say that in the technicalities of balancing there was still much to learn, but that in all other departments the "method of Venice" was developed to a state which exactly met the requirements of the period. In none of the respects in which it differs from modern practice can it be said that the later improvements would have recommended themselves to a merchant of these days. When so excellent a system, therefore, was described with the methodical clearness and mastery of detail which Paciolo commanded, it was natural that the treatise should become a standard. And this is exactly what happened. The history of book-keeping during the next century consists of little else than registering the progress of the *De Computis* through the various countries of Europe. But before the work of Paciolo could attain its full usefulness, an improvement had to be made in the method

---

[1] This operation, it will be observed, is hardly a proper trial balance with totals. When a page was carried forward it was squared and the balance transferred. Paciolo's end totals were thus comparatively meaningless figures.

of giving instructions in book-keeping. Paciolo uses no examples, and without the assistance of these the art can hardly be acquired by a novice. Paciolo addresses himself to experts, but a demand had arisen for a school-book. It is an interesting feature of the beginnings of modern commerce that it gave rise to institutions which we may describe as "commercial academies." The schools of the time, few as they were, devoted their energies to the classical learning which had been revived by the Renaissance. They prepared for the learned professions. To provide for the requirements of intending merchants private enterprise had to step in. We consequently find schools establishing themselves where the new science of arithmetic was the principal item in the "prospectus."[1]   In these schools book-keeping was taught.

The next oldest treatise on the art published at Venice in 1525 would probably be more useful in a class-room than the *De Computis*. Its author is Giovanni Antonio Tagliente, and the work is a modest little pamphlet of twenty-four unnumbered leaves. But it marks this important improvement from the point of view of teaching that it gives examples. The advance made by Tagliente was very soon followed up and improved on. In 1534 Domenico Manzoni, a teacher of arithmetic and book-keeping in Venice, published his *Quaderno doppio col suo giornale secondo il costume di Venetia*, which became so popular that it went through seven editions.[2]   The work illustrates fully the importance of Paciolo's treatise. It is divided into two parts, and the first, which gives the theoretical exposition of the subject, is to all intents and purposes a mere transcription of the *De Computis*. The material is slightly re-arranged and some chapters are transposed, but in other respects the two books are identical.[3]

[1] A very interesting historical account of "Commercial Academies" is given by Zieger in *Die Kaufmännischen Bildungsstätten, &c., vom Ausgange des Mittelalters bis ins, 18te Jahrhundert*. See also Sieveking.

[2] Kheil, *Bearbeitungen von Luca Pacioli*, p. 3 n.

[3] Kheil, *Über einige ältere Bearbeitungen des Buchhaltungs-tractates von Luca Pacioli*. Kheil also cites numerous Italian authorities in support of the results of his investigations (*loc. cit.*, p. 3).

1540 Adi ultimo Febraro.

94 ℞ Pro & danno // A doni uarij, per danno feguido, tratto in refto, per faldo di quello ℞ 1   ual ℔
— 4 4 / 3 0

Di faldar la partida de li doni, ponendo il refto di quelli in pro & danno.   ℞ 2 ℔   ℞

95 ℞ Pro & danno // A Spefe de uiuer di cafa, per piu fpefe fatte, come in effe appar, per faldo di quelle ℞ 1 ℔ 548 ℔ 20 ℞ 14   ual ℔
— 4 4 / 3 1

Di faldar le fpefe di veftir in ditto pro & danno.   15 ℔ 9 ℞ 8 ℞ 14

96 ℞ Fitti della poffeßion da Moidn. // A Pro & danno per fitto di quella per l'anno prefente, finira de Luio 1541, per faldo de quelli ℞ 45 ℔   ual ℔
— 3 4 / 4 4

Di faldar li fiiti della poffeffion, in pro & danno.   4 ℔ 10 ℞   ℞

97 ℞ Pro & danno // A Spefe diuerfe per piu fpefe fatte l'anno prefente, come in effe appar, per faldo fuo ℞ 399 ℞ 12 ℞   ual ℔
— 4 4 / 3 3

Di faldar le fpefe diuerfe, in ditto pro & danno.   33 ℔ 19 ℞   ℞

98 ℞ Pro & danno // A Spefe de falariadi in monte, per piu fpefe fatte l'anno prefente, come in effe appar, per faldo di quelle ℞ 48 ℞ 12 ℞   ual ℔
— 4 4 / 4 0

Di faldar le fpefe de falariadi, in ditto pro & danno.   4 ℔ 17 ℞   ℞

199 ℞ Pro de zeccha in monte // A Pro & danno, per uti lita feguida, come in quello appar, per faldo fuo, ℞ 150 ℞   ℞   ual ℔
— 4 0 / 4 4

Di faldar in pro de zeccha, in lo ditto pro & danno.   15 ℔   ℞   ℞

100 ℞ Pro et danno // A Cauedal de mi Aluife Vallareffo, per utilita feguida de l'anno 1540, tratto in refto, per faldo di quello ℞ 900 ℞ 22 ℞ 17   ual ℔
— 4 4 / 3 3

Di faldar poi il pro & danno nel tuo cauedal, per vltima conclufione.   90 ℔ 1 ℞ 10 ℞ 17

Fine dil prefente Giornale, tenuto per mi Aluife Va
lareffo, per conto d'ogni traffico, & negotio à me oc
corfo, da di primo Marzo 1540, fin adi ultimo Febraro del ditto milleximo, nelqual ordinatamente de
giorno in giorno, ho fcritto di mia mano, ne
in effo piu intendo fcriuere, per hauer
quello conclufo & faldato in
12 partide, lequal ho
reportate nel li-
bro nouo fe
gnato
A

Manzoni's second part is original and admirable. It gives an example of a representative journal and ledger which is compiled with care and thoroughness. The journal extends to twenty folios and the ledger to forty-six folios. The system of book-keeping described is in every essential detail the same as Paciolo's. A slight innovation is to give a reference in the ledger to the journal by means of consecutive numbers attached to each journal-entry. Another change, and this time a step in the line of advance, is to use the journal for transfers. Thus, 4844 pounds of sugar were purchased on 15th March 1540 and sold on 2nd April. A special account had been opened, and on the day of sale the balance of profit was transferred to Profit and Loss Account by means of the following journal-entry:—

$57 \frac{9}{13}$ Zucchari ditti ‖ A Pro & Danno
per utile sequido di quelli   2 lbs : 8s : 3d : 20p.

" lbs. " &c., refers, of course, to money; 57 represents the consecutive number in the journal; folio 9 refers to Sugar Account in the Ledger; folio 13 to Profit and Loss Account. Apart from this extended use of the journal, Manzoni makes no advance on his predecessor. He gives no trial balance, but he remarks that, in his opinion, the ledger should be balanced at the end of every one, two, three, or four years. The stock difficulty he shirks by assuming that there are no unsold goods on hand.

Paciolo's treatise, incorporated without mention of his name in Manzoni's *Quaderno doppio*, soon made its progress through the commercial world, aided no doubt by the examples which the copyist had added. Germany alone can point to two early authors on book-keeping who wrote uninfluenced by Italian teaching. When historians of their own country refer to these old worthies, they treat them with very scant respect. Certainly the first of them, Heinrich Schreiber, a native of Erfurt, who Latinised his name as Henricus Grammateus, deserves no praise beyond that of being the first German who conceived the idea of writing about book-keeping. He was an arithmetic-master in Vienna and according to his preface composed his treatise in 1518. It was printed in Erfurt in 1523 under the title *Rechenbüchlin künstlich, behend und gewiss auff alle Kauff-manschafft gericht*. The part dealing with book-keeping is very brief, and so confused and bad that it proves the arithmetic-master's knowledge to have been very perfunctory. Three books are kept, a journal, a sales and purchases book,[1] and a ledger.[2] The postings are of the simplest description, and at the end the following directions are given for "proving" the books: "Add together the sums due to you and the stock on hand, and from these deduct what you owe to others; there will remain the sum of profit, and that is correct." This passage has been taken to indicate that Schreiber describes "single-entry." But an account of sales and purchases is strictly speaking alien to this system; besides, capital is not mentioned. It seems better, on the whole, not to trouble to find out the arithmetic-master's intentions, for it is extremely improbable that he himself knew much about what he was professing to teach.[3]

More successful is the attempt made by the next German author, Johann Gottlieb,[4] a merchant of Nuremberg who published his treatise in 1531. This man had the advantage of practical knowledge of his subject, and whatever may be thought of the merits of his system, his explanation is certainly clear. The method he describes is probably the same as that which Schreiber vainly endeavoured to express. Briefly stated,

---

[1] The word used is "Kaps," which Dr. Jäger conjectures to be derived from *caput*, head, the ledger being still in Germany called "head-book" (*Hauptbuch*). The most serviceable translation is the above, although it is not really a book, but only a few leaves set aside in the ledger. [2] Literally, "debt-book" (*Schuldbuch*).

[3] Kheil, *Über einige ältere Bearbeitungen des Buchhaltungs-tractates von Luca Pacioli*, p. 74. An earlier book of Schreiber's, *Behend und Künstlich Rechnung nach der Regel und welhisch practic*, contains only arithmetic. The above notes on this author are taken from Jäger's *Beiträge*, p. 234 *et seq.*, and from Kheil's *Bearbeitungen von Pacioli*, who both consulted an edition of Schreiber which appeared in 1572.

[4] The name is sometimes spelt Gotlieb.

it is a perfect system of double-entry, adapted, it is true, to the very simplest requirements. The same three books are pre-scribed,[1] and the journal commences with the capital put into the business which is in cash. The specimen postings given are only twenty-five in number, but they amply illustrate the simple transactions, which consist solely of sales, purchases, and cash payments and receipts. There is no reference to expenses of any kind. The "sales and purchases book" is kept as follows: Each purchase is debited, and opposite it the sales of that particular lot of goods are credited. Stock on hand at the time of balancing is also credited, and the balance is noted as profit. The various items of profit are added up and noted at the close of the "book," with the explanation: "By this amount I have become richer through this trade. To God be the thanks and praise." The balance-sheet is sufficiently short to be given in full:—

Of ready money .	2229 fl.	10ss.	3h.
„ debts .	20	...	...
„ goods (stock).	16	...	...
These riches and balances make together .	2265	10	3

To close this account there is everything which I owe in this trade, viz.—

Me Gotlieb my capital	2000 fl.	...ss.	...h.
Other creditors .	44	16	...
Makes together .	2044	16	...
One side compared with the other shows a surplus of net profit .	220	14	3
	2265	10	3

It may be noted that the profit of 220fl. 14ss. 3h. agrees with the sum brought out on the "sales and purchases book."

---

[1] The curious word "Kaps" is not used by Gottlieb, but instead "Goods-book" (Güterbuch). Here again it is not really a book, but a ledger account.

There is no profit and loss account, for there are no expenses. Assuming that the demands of German commerce were met by so very primitive a style of book-keeping, one must admit Gottlieb's treatise to be excellent. It certainly does not sin against the canon of simplicity. In passing, we may record that both Schreiber and Gottlieb use Arabic figures in the ledger columns. Gottlieb, also, is the first author to treat stock properly.

With Schreiber and Gottlieb we leave the native German book-keepers, and enter the period when Italian influence becomes dominant, not in Germany only, but also in all other countries of commercial importance. Book-keeping, in fact, becomes international. Down to the minutest details we find identically the same methods prevailing among book-keepers whether they hail from Venice, Nuremberg, Antwerp, or London. Journal-entries are everywhere numbered consecutively, posting-folios in the ledger refer to the link between debit and credit, and no book is opened or closed without some religious formulary, however perfunctory. The friar of San Sepolcro set the fashion in this matter, so much so that taking his book up at random one might imagine one was reading a breviary rather than a commercial treatise. He tells his readers to post their journal and to hear mass, or he stops short in the middle of some explanation of bills of exchange to inculcate the giving of alms. Never on any account, he warns us, must a new book be commenced without the glorious sign of the cross, "before which every enemy flees and the powers of Evil deservedly tremble." And so throughout Europe when a new book was opened it was *Laus Deo* the 1st of January, or *Jesus Maria* the 1st of January, or at the very least ✠ the 1st of January. This uniformity in certain characteristic practices of the time was partly due to the fact that young men who intended to become merchants went to Italy, there to acquire a knowledge of commerce which was not to be obtained in the same degree elsewhere.

As early as 1488 we read of a Nuremberg trader who sent one of his apprentices to Venice, giving him the parting advice "to rise early in the morning and first to hear mass, after that to attend the class of a master of arithmetic and then to make his way to the German House on the Rialto."[1] But before long those who stayed at home were furnished with the means of acquiring a knowledge of Italian commercial practice. Simultaneously in England, Holland, and France, and a few years later in Germany, thére appeared translations of the works of the Italian masters.

The treatise which introduced Italian book-keeping into England is the earliest work on the subject in our language of which we have a record. It is a translation of Paciolo, and was produced in 1543 by Hugh Oldcastle, a teacher of arithmetic and book-keeping in London. Unfortunately no copy of this oldest English treatise on book-keeping is known to exist.[2] We can form an opinion of it only by a reprint which was issued in 1588 by John Mellis, also a schoolmaster in London. Mellis is perfectly frank in disavowing any claim to originality. He tells us in his preface that for thirty years he had beside him, "for his own private knowledge and furtherance," a little volume on book-keeping which is "a iewell so commmodious" that he decided to republish it. "And knowe ye for certaine," he continues, "that I presume ne usurpe not to set forth this worke of mine owne labour and industrie, for truely I am but a renuer and reviver of an auncient old copie printed here in London the 14th of August 1543, then collected, published,

---

[1] Zieger, op. cit., p. 9.

[2] B. F. Foster, a writer on book-keeping and a collector of old works on the subject, may possibly have seen a copy of Oldcastle (see "Origin and Progress of Book-keeping," London, 1852). At the commencement of his preface he almost states in so many words that he had seen the book, but later on, when he refers to John Mellis, who acknowledges himself to be a mere reprinter of Oldcastle's treatise, Mr. Foster says that Mellis's book would "appear to be simply a reprint of Old-castle." Had the two books been before him, Mr. Foster would surely have used a more definite expression. His statement that he had seen Oldcastle possibly means only that he had seen Mellis's reprint.

made and set forth by one Hugh Oldcastle, Scholemaster, who as appeareth then taught Arithmetike and this booke in Saint Ollaves parish in Marke lane." Mellis himself enlarged the book, "bewtified and enlarged it," to use his own words, but he preserved the form of the original, for when he came to the conclusion of what we can identify as the work of Paciolo he printed the word " Finis," adding " here endeth my Authour, and for the better and plainer understanding and practice of these rules, I have hereunto added a little Inventorie, Journal, and Leager, as followeth : with a briefe Treatise of Arithmetick all together." That Oldcastle was a translator becomes perfectly obvious when we compare the reprint with the *De Computis*. The headings of the first fourteen chapters are identical in both cases, except that Oldcastle omits the seventh chapter, in which Paciolo refers to the practice of having commercial books certified by notaries, a custom unknown in England. The succeeding chapters in Paciolo relate to banking, and these, of course, Oldcastle also omits, as banks had not yet been established in this country. Altogether eleven chapters of the original are left out. Several passages are also somewhat condensed, but in other respects the translation is literal.[1]

In the same year 1543 which saw the publication of the first English work on book-keeping, there also appeared what is the earliest known Dutch book on the subject. It is the work of Jan Ympyn Christoffels, a merchant of Antwerp, and is entitled *Nieuwe Instructie Ende bewijs der lo-effelijcker Consten des Rekenboecks ende Rekeninghe te houdene nae die Italiaensche maniere, &c.*[2] Of the personality of Jan Ympyn,

---

[1] It is literal to the point of inaccuracy, as near the end of Chapter XIV. a reference to an *earlier* chapter is stated as to Chapter XV. (!). This is the number of the chapter in the original, but Oldcastle has overlooked the fact that by his omissions the chapter has become No. XIII. in his translation.

[2] The following description of the *Nieuwe Instructie* is taken from the account of the book given by Kheil in his *Über einige ältere Bearbeitungen des Buchhaltungs-tractates von Luca Pacioli.*

as he was commonly called, we know very little. He did not live to see his book through the press, and all the details that can be gathered regarding him are the references contained in a short notice, which his widow prefixed to the work on its publication. We find that Ympyn had travelled much in Spain, Portugal, and Italy, and that for twelve years he lived at Venice. This long residence in itself indicates the source of his knowledge of book-keeping, and he places the matter beyond doubt by stating himself that his book is a translation from the Italian. " I made the acquaintance," says Ympyn, " of a man of good reputation, Jehan Paulo de Biancy, who has worked more [in book-keeping] than all others. Through his labours one can comprehend and learn the said science, if one only studies the following book and applies oneself to it. This treatise I have procured and acquired from the above-mentioned Jehan Paulo de Biancy and translated." A blundering reference to other Italian authors is also given by Ympyn, which is worth mentioning on account of the curious error to which it seems to have given rise. " Several celebrated personages," says Ympyn, " have written about the noble art and science of book-keeping, as Brother Lucas de Bargo & sancty sepulchry of the order of St. Francis, who has written of book-keeping in his *Somma de Arithmetica and Geometria.*" This ridiculous perversion of Paciolo's name, with omission of the " & sancty sepulchry," made its way into England, and in this abbreviated and completely meaningless form has become perpetuated there. In most of the scant notes on the history of book-keeping in our language, we may read of a certain " Lucas de Bargo," who is confidently stated to have been the first writer on the art. Of Biancy, nothing is known,[1] but on examining Ympyn's translation,

---

[1] The obscurity is increased by variants of the spelling of the name. The *Nieuwe Instructie* was translated into French and English, and in each of the three editions the reading is different (Biańci, Bianchi, and Briancy). He is said to have been connected with Perugia, but Kheil's inquiries there resulted in nothing, and no such name was found occurring in any local archives.

it becomes clear that the treatise he took as his model was simply Paciolo's *De Computis.*

The first part of the book is identical with the corresponding part of the *Quaderno doppio,* which in its turn was a transcription of the *De Computis.* The second part of the book is taken up with examples of journal and ledger, and these are said to be excellent both as regards form and accounting, although in general they closely follow Manzoni. One important advance is made, namely, the introduction of the modern trial balance. It will indicate how slavishly the first portion of the book was copied, that the description of balancing which we find there is the cumbrous mode detailed by Paciolo. In the example, however, the method is adopted which we use at the present day. Stock, also, is treated properly in the example, and though this is not the first time that we meet the practice, the system is much better than Gottlieb's. A separate account is opened and debited with " Remainders of goods which are over at the conclusion of this book." The amounts agree with the sums credited to the various goods accounts before striking profit. The entries relating to stock are not journalised, but goods accounts which had come to a close during the course of trading have their balances transferred to Profit and Loss Account by journal-entries. In other respects there is no advance on Manzoni. Periodical balances are still of irregular occurrence, for the merchant is told to take stock every year, or at the end of two, three, or four years. Roman figures, it is noteworthy, are still used in the ledger, and other details are also copied. The paraphernalia of piety become almost obtrusive in this book. At the commencement of the journal, for instance, the following prayer is entered : " May God our merciful Saviour vouchsafe me Grace to make a profit and preserve me from all bad fortune." When the balance on Profit and Loss Account eventually comes out on the right side, the acknowledgments to the Giver are not omitted. Right across the book there is written in large letters : " Honour and praise to the Almighty God, who has granted me these things."

Ympyn's book was translated both into French and English. The French translation appeared in 1543, the same year as the original edition, and it forms the first work on book-keeping in that language. The English version did not appear till 1547. It had completely fallen out of notice, and was lately discovered in a very interesting manner. Dr. Hugo Balg wrote a description of an anonymous English work which had been found in the library of the Nicolai-Gymnasium at Reval, in Russia.[1] The title was as follows : "A notable and very excellente woorke, expressyng and declaryng the maner & forme how to kepe a boke of ac- comptes or reconynges, &c. Translated with greate diligence out of the Italian toung into Dutche and out of Dutche into Frenche, and now out of Frenche into Englishe" (London, 1547). From the title and from extracts given by Dr. Balg, Kheil was able to identify this anonymous work as a hitherto unknown English translation of Ympyn.[2]

The introduction of Italian book-keeping into Germany was made in 1549 by a treatise published in Nuremberg under the title of *Zwifach Buchhalten.* It is a translation of Manzoni's *Quaderno doppio,* but the author, Wolffgang Schweicker, who was living in Venice at the time of publi- cation, makes no reference or other acknowledgment to his original. The book calls for no special remark, except per- haps that the examples are executed very carelessly, so that the apparent balance is the result of a "cook."[3] One of the most interesting points about the *Zwifach Buchhalten* is the preface composed by the printer, Johann Petrejus, and addressed to the "dear, kindly reader." Petrejus incidentally remarks that while only two books are described as necessary

[1] *Zeitschrift für Buchhaltung,* April 1893.
[2] *Op. cit.,* p. 66.
[3] Kheil points this out. He has taken the trouble to work through a number of old works on book-keeping to find out how far they are copies of Paciolo. *Über einige ältere Bearbeitungen, &c.,* p. 120.

(journal and ledger), it is sometimes found convenient to make sub-divisions in the ledger. Thus the Cash Account may be placed in a ledger of its own—the modern cash-book, of course, which is nothing but a ledger account bound up separately, as a recent writer has remarked. The debts which arise through buying and selling may also be placed in special ledgers—our debtors' and creditors' ledgers. We cannot leave this intelligent old printer without giving him his due for having produced the typographically most beautiful book on book-keeping which has ever been printed. Indeed, great beauty of printing characterises the German books as a whole. Paciolo is a dignified tome, and some of the early Dutch and even some of the English authors have their work embodied in handsome volumes. But the best German books are works of art. It seems as if the love of art for its own sake, which distinguished the German craftsman of the sixteenth century, made it impossible for him to produce in an ugly shape even so utilitarian a thing as a treatise on book-keeping.

It is a curious fact that Spain, at this time the most important country in Europe, should be found to lag behind its neighbours in the knowledge of book-keeping.[1] No doubt we have here reflected that absence of enterprise in the regions of legitimate commerce which made Spain's wealth and power so transitory. The earliest Spanish treatise— excluding an arithmetical work by Gaspar de Texada published in 1545—appeared in 1565, and not only in date but in merit it falls short of the achievements of other countries. The author's name is Antich Rocha, and like so many of his contemporaries he is a translator. But far from having copied the great writers of Venice, Rocha knew of nothing

---

[1] The claim, once put forward on behalf of Spain, that double-entry had originated in that country does not bear investigation. The evidence was partly drawn from collateral circumstances, such as the early acquaintance of Spain with Arabic numerals and with paper, partly from the alleged existence of clauses in early statutes which make double-entry compulsory for merchants. No such clauses have been discovered by subsequent research, and the early use of paper, &c., proves nothing in point. See Kheil, *Valentin Menher und Antich Rocha.*

better than to introduce his countrymen to the work of an obscure German schoolmaster, Valentin Menher, whc had produced a treatise which is very far from showing a com-

PRACTICQVE

POVR BRIEVEMENT

apprendre à Ciffrer, & tenir Liure
de Comptes, auec la Regle de
Cofs, & Geometrie.

PAR M. V. MENHER ALLEMAN.

A ANVERS, l'An M. D. LXV.
Auec priuilege du Roy pour.4.ans.

petent knowledge of book-keeping. Menher was born at Kempten in Bavaria and later migrated to Antwerp, where he taught mathematics and book-keeping. His works are written in French. The first is dated 1550,[1] and shows its

---

[1] The second part of this same book (dealing with Algebra) is dated 1556.

author's German origin so clearly that it prescribes the
" Sales and Purchase Book " which we meet with in
Schreiber and Gottlieb.   Improvements are introduced in
later editions, but they are not sufficient to bring Menher's
teaching to anything like the level of excellence attained
by students of Italian book-keeping.

CHAPTER VI

HISTORY OF BOOK-KEEPING—(*Continued*)

GRADUAL IMPROVEMENTS UPON THE EARLY ITALIAN METHODS —PETRI—PIETRA—PASSCHIER-GOESSENS—SIMON STEVIN— THE SCHOOL - MASTER AUTHORS — ENGLISH AUTHORS: IN THE SIXTEENTH AND SEVENTEENTH CENTURIES—PEELE, MELLIS, CARPENTER, DAFFORNE — THE FIRST SCOTTISH AUTHOR—EXERCISE BOOKS OF GEORGE WATSON—BOOKS OF THE DARIEN SCHEME—"JONES' ENGLISH SYSTEM OF BOOK-KEEPING"—MODERN DEVELOPMENTS

THE knowledge of book-keeping had now spread to all the countries of commercial importance, and the form in which it had established itself was so clearly adapted to the contemporary conditions of commerce that there was little immediate call for improvement. But even in the sixteenth century books issued from the press which indicated the directions in which the next advance would be made. Nicolaus Petri published an excellent treatise at Amsterdam in 1588 which went through four editions. It deals with arithmetic and geometry as well as with book-keeping, and treats the subject succinctly and well. The improvements in the matter of stock-taking and of making a periodical trial - balance are incorporated, and the satisfaction which the mercantile community must have derived from the latter invention is clearly indicated by the terms of the ascription which appropriately closes the ledger: "Thus is this my book balanced and compared, wherefor to the almighty and eternal God be all praise, honour and glory. Amen." Besides adopting the work of his predecessors, Petri intro-

TITLE PAGE OF PETRI—1605 edition (same size as original)

From Copy in the Edinburgh Chartered Accountants' Library

duces for the first time two important departures from the older methods, although it is not possible to say that he himself inaugurated them. For one thing he no longer journalises all transactions *seriatim*, but occasionally groups the kindred items. The arrangement is not carried through consistently, but it is noteworthy as the first hint of a device by which a great saving of clerical labour is effected. Next Petri takes a step towards the separation of the books of primary entry. He introduces an "Expenses Book" (bearing the interesting title of *Oncost-boec*) and at the end of every month he transfers the total to cash account by means of the journal. This is an advance on the "cash-ledger" mentioned by Schweiker, or rather by Schweiker's printer, for Petri's book is truly one of *primary* entry, which is written up directly without the intervention of the journal.

Another interesting author of the sixteenth century is Don Angelo Pietra, a monk of Genoa, who adapted commercial book-keeping to the requirements of monasteries. His book was published at Mantua in 1586 and was inscribed to the Congregation of Cassino.[1] Pietra was cellarer of his monastery and took charge of its business affairs. He shows a thorough knowledge of mercantile accounting, and his book is chiefly remarkable for the completeness of the stock-taking which he introduces. Not only is a list made of the contents of cellars and magazines, but the difficult question of striking the profit of a farm is correctly treated. A value is placed on the growing crops, and the expenditure on seeds and manure for next year's harvest is carefully calculated.

Germany also in this century produced one more good writer in Passchier-Goessens.[2] He was a Huguenot refugee from Belgium, and had made his home in Hamburg, where

---

[1] Monte Cassino was one of the most important of the Benedictine Congregations in Italy.

[2] *Buchhalten fein Kurz zusamen gefasst*, &c., Hamburg, 1594. The book is very carefully printed.

he taught writing, arithmetic, book-keeping, and the French language. In some respects Goessens is distinctly old-fashioned. His journal has the cumbersome consecutive numbers of Manzoni, and there is no grouping of entries. Further, the method of closing and re-opening the accounts at the time of balancing is unduly complicated. Goessens' merit lies in the absolute clearness of his instructions and in the admirable arrangement of his ledger. The accounts in the ledger up to this time are very clumsy. There are no separate headings, and the titles are placed at the commencement of each line, or at least indicated by constant repetition of " ditto." Goessens introduces the modern practice of placing a heading at the top of the folio, and in general makes a marked improvement in the direction of clearness and simplicity.

At the close of the sixteenth and the commencement of the seventeenth century there stands a figure which fitly represents the transition from the old order to the new in book-keeping. Simon Stevin ranks with Paciolo in this respect that he is a man of general learning who has not thought it beneath his dignity to compose a treatise on book-keeping. Stevin was born at Bruges in 1548, and at an early age was placed by his parents in a mercantile office in Antwerp. He did not remain in this employment long, although we are not told why he abandoned it. After a protracted course of foreign travel he returned home and entered the public service. Here he had a prosperous career, holding successively the offices of Surveyor of Taxes at Bruges, Quarter-master General, and Chief Inspector of Public Works. He died at the Hague in 1620. Stevin's fame rests on his discoveries in dynamics and hydrostatics, which make him rank as one of the founders of modern engineering. One of his practical inventions was a form of lock for canals, while his treatise on fortification was long a standard. Also in mathematics he did important work, and was the first to make use of decimal fractions, although the way had here been prepared by the discoveries of

TITLE PAGE OF PASSCHIER GOESSENS, 1594 (size of original 12 inches by 8 inches)

others. Stevin acted as tutor to Moritz of Nassau, Prince of Orange, and in later years became his intimate friend. In public life he was closely identified with the Protestant party, so much so that, when in 1845 a proposal was made to erect a statue at Bruges to his memory, a Catholic agitation was got up in the House of Representatives to cancel the project. A clerical editor also expunged his name from a Dutch dictionary of biography, where in earlier editions he had been included.[1]

The occasion for writing his book, which he entitled *Hypomnemata Mathematica* (mathematical traditions), was the course of instruction Stevin gave to the prince. The scope of the two great volumes is to treat of mathematics, and only Part II. of the second volume deals with book-keeping. The second volume was written in Latin by Stevin himself and published in 1605;[2] the first volume did not appear till three years later. It had been composed in Dutch and was given for translation to Willebrord Snell, professor of mathematics at Leyden.[3] Stevin gives his treatise on book-keeping the high-sounding designation *De Apologistica Principum Ratocinio Italico*, which may be rendered: Account-keeping for Princes after the Italian manner. The work is dedicated to Maximilian Bethune, Duke of Sully, who ranks with Colbert as a reorganiser of the finances of France. The author argues that double-entry should be applied to public accounts, for, says he, "merchants are better informed than princes of the state of their affairs and are less defrauded by those in their employment." As an introduction to his proposed reform of public accounts he then gives an exposition of ordinary mercantile book-keeping, which he fully explains and illustrates. The ex-

[1] The above facts are taken from the *Nouvelle Biographie Général*, vol. 24.

[2] So it is stated, but there would seem to have been a French edition of the book-keeping dated 1602 (see Morgan's "Arithmetical Books," p. 104) and a Dutch edition dated 1604.

[3] On the title-page the name is contracted "Wil. Sn." The authority for the identification is the *Nouvelle Biogr. Général*.

amples of journal and ledger are in many ways excellent. The journal-entries are systematically grouped, and wherever practicable only the totals are shown in the ledger. For instance, as an opening entry we find "Sundry Assets" made debtor to capital, and capital made creditor to "Sundry Liabilities." The wording of the entry is as follows :—

> Diversa nomina debet per sortem me Theodori Rosae 2667£, 9s. 8d.
>   Cum enim dicto die opum mearum statum et aestimationem
>   instituissem, inventi sunt in parata pecunia, mercibus, et
>   creditis : primo Cassa in parata pecunia 880£, &c.
> Sors mea Theodori Rosae debit per varios creditores, &c. [1]

Other interesting features are the journalising of cash in daily totals and the journalising of petty expenses and private outlays in monthly totals. In the ledger, again, we find the profit and loss account written up at the end of the year and not at the close of each piece of business as in older writers. But while Stevin in these respects shows an advance towards modern practice, he falls short of his predecessors in other points. Closing entries are not put through the journal, and Ympyn's trial-balance is unknown to him. Further, Stevin makes a mistake in accounting when he credits a legacy of £1000 to profit and loss.[2] He carries household expenses to the same account, but in this he conforms to the general practice of the time. In spite, however, of these few defects, Stevin was a very competent book-keeper. His examples are clear, and cover a wide range of transactions.

After dealing with mercantile accounts the author turns to "Book-keeping for Princes" proper, and it cannot be said that here he achieves a success. The fault lay with the subject, for while double-entry may be serviceable where the state administers domains or engages in commercial enterprises, the system

---

[1] Translated : Sundry Assets Dr. to Capital of me Theod. Rosa 2667£, 9s. 8d. When, namely, on said day I instituted an accounting and valuation of my goods, there were found in ready money, goods and debts : firstly Cash in ready money, &c.

[2] Manzoni correctly credited a legacy to capital.

is altogether unsuited for the simple transactions connected with the collection and spending of taxes, which can be tabulated clearly with much less expenditure of labour. Stevin acknowledges this himself by implication. He makes great preparations for the elaboration of detail, but he never comes to the point. Contrary to his practice in the case of mercantile accounts, he gives no examples in his " Book-keeping for Princes," so that there are no means of judging how his system would work out. Indeed, most of his space is taken up with long strings of the names of suggested accounts. There are accounts in the names of governors of towns and provinces, of the principal officers of state and of the household (*thesaurarius stabuli, thesaurarius venationis*), and even accounts for the princely kitchen (*culinariae dispensatio*), followed by accounts for warlike materials (*dispensatio bellicorum apparatuum*). But all these lead to nothing. The modern reader will find little to interest him, unless he becomes amused by the author's gallant attempts to preserve the dignity of the Latin language. Nothing will serve Stevin but to take the few terms of Roman accounting which are known, and apply them to modern book-keeping. He devotes a chapter to proving that the ancients knew double-entry and asserts that *tabulae accepti et expensi* signifies ledger. Literally translated it simply means tablets of receipts and payments, but Stevin consistently renders ledger with *codex accepti et expensi*. These attempts to use nothing but genuine Latin sometimes lead the author into obscurity and even absurdity. There is an important account for a functionary described as *thesaurarius aedilis*, but what sort of a Dutchman is meant thereby we inquire in vain. Another and more humble individual is also designated by a truly imperial title, but here Stevin thought it better to sacrifice dignity to precision, for he adds in brackets the ridiculous explanation (*vulgo* een Cassier). Encountering in the course of his exposition such purely Gothic inventions as treacle and gun-powder, Cicero is eventually thrown to the winds, and words adopted such as *syrupus* and *pulvis bombardicus*. The climax is reached in the account for munitions of war. Lances and swords are fitly rendered by *hastae* and *enses*, but the most unmitigated dog-Latin has to be requisitioned when the author comes to enumerate that important mediæval engine the blunderbuss. In general one wonders how many readers Stevin had in his day. Yet Jäger, who took much interest in the book-keeping of states and public bodies, asserts that a marked improvement set in after the publication of the *Hypomnemata Mathematica*.

Stevin's immediate successors are small folk. One and all they are either schoolmasters, or quacks who think that they have invented a new system. Of the quacks a single example will suffice. In 1610 Nicolaus Wolff, who describes himself as citizen of Nuremberg, published a book[1] which was to supersede all previous treatises on book-keeping. He explains in his preface that he had been engaged as a clerk "almost since his youth," and that he had been greatly valued by his employers. This one can readily believe, for nothing could be neater than the arrangement of his books, to which the printer by type and spacing has done full justice. Wolff's journal also is quite the best encountered so far, for the entries are most systematically grouped. But the difficulty begins with that curious German tradition the "sales and purchases book." The device is quite superfluous, but even an old author like Gottlieb was able to get satisfactory results in spite of it. Wolff is less fortunate. At first one imagines all is going well, for the balances on the "sales and purchases book" are neatly journalised and transferred to an account in the ledger. The result is gross profit, and the account ought to form the basis of a profit and loss account. Instead of this sundry debtors are neatly journalised and transferred to this

---

[1] *Kurtze doch gründliche und aigentliche beschreibung eines ordentlichen rechten Buchhaltens,* &c.

new account, then sundry creditors are neatly journalised and treated in the same way, till in the end the account squares. There is no calculation of profit, and capital account is lost in a congeries of journal totals. The books then finish. Appended there are five separate tabular statements for "proving" the posting, and for making up profit. There is a first proof of the books, a second proof of the books, a closing balance with six columns, another with two columns, and then yet another for bringing out the results. They are all exceedingly neat-looking, they must be very difficult to draw up correctly, and it is claimed for them that they come to the same in the end as Italian book-keeping. Wolff is typical of his class. Since the year 1610 many would-be improvers of Italian double-entry have come forward, and their works all bear a strong family resemblance. They all lose themselves in a mass of detail, while in their broad features their systems are nothing but the most ordinary double-entry. We who live in the twentieth century may say that experience has established two principles in the development of book-keeping. The simple rule, that all the various phases of a business will be exhibited if every transaction is entered as debit and credit, is fundamental and cannot be improved. That is the first principle. In working out the details of double-entry there is endless scope for ingenuity, but as all mechanical labour is associated with a persistent liability to make errors, the scheme adopted should attain the maximum of simplicity which is compatible with the requirements of the case. Common sense must act as a constant drag on inventiveness. That is the second principle. Few and far between are the improvements which conform to these canons.

The schoolmasters, who for the greater part make up the list of authors on book-keeping in the seventeenth and eighteenth centuries, seldom risked being inventive. Indeed, if we may believe the testimony of one of their number, they rather erred in the opposite direction. "The teacher," says an old German schoolmaster-author, "must not place before his pupils old, threadbare examples of book-keeping, which perhaps have come down to him from his grandfather and grandmother. He must not keep the children working for year and day at such stuff, or at his own *praeconceptas opiniones*. But he must diligently read the works of celebrated authors . . . and first learn himself what he professes to teach." The treatises on book-keeping which attained celebrity in their own day are very numerous, but for tracing the development of the science they offer very few points indeed. Book-keeping had long passed out of the experimental stage, and it was in the daily experience of the counting-house that improvements were made, not in the closet of the theorist. Schoolmasters who had to acquire their knowledge by reading "celebrated authors" could not be expected to originate anything new.

Italian authors of this period may be passed over in a survey of the history of book-keeping. Their country, once in the van of commercial progress, had fallen behind. It is in the German Hanse towns—to judge by treatises which have come down to us—that the best book-keeping was now found. A work by Georg Nicolaus Schurtz,[1] is not only an excellent book within its limits, but it gives colour to the presumption that printed books no longer reflected the best practices of the time. Schurtz gives his instructions by examples of the three time-honoured books, the Memorial, the Journal, and the Ledger, but he mentions in his preface that in many counting-houses the following are used with great success: Secret book (*i.e.* Private Ledger), Cash book, Petty cash book, Cash sales book, Balance book, Goods received book, Bill book, Copy letter book, Goods sold book, Copy accounts rendered book. Here we see what a distance separates the schoolmasters' instruction from the merchants' practice. Schurtz details all the material for his example in the Memorial, classifies it in the Journal, and posts the Ledger

---

[1] *Nutzbare Richtschnur der löblichen Kauffmannschaft*, Nuremberg, 1695.

For teaching beginners no better method could be devised. But the counting-house no longer uses the clumsy Memorial, for the above list shows a complete separation in the books of primary entry. Schurtz naturally could not adopt all these for teaching his scholars. In the matter of balancing this old author is equally interesting. We have nowhere yet found a reference which would lead us to conclude that regular periodical balances were made, but in the pages of Schurtz we encounter the system complete. He has quarterly balances[1] of his ledger, the details of which are duly recorded. In addition to these trial-balances Schurtz gives complete journal postings for closing entries, and a final balance after these items have been entered. In every detail his examples are excellent. One more particular may perhaps be referred to, and that is the practice of paying a round sum periodically to the petty cashier instead of passing petty outlays themselves through the cash-book, either singly or in total. Household expenses, we may also note in passing, are still debited to profit and loss account.

For us English, the Dutch authors of this period possess particular interest, because Holland was the training school not only of many of our own writers, but of our merchants. The treatise which seems to have been most thought of at the time is the work of Hendrick Waninghen and Joannes Buingha. Both were schoolmasters in Amsterdam, Buingha succeeding his master Waninghen in his school and also publishing a new edition of his work.[2] The exposition of book-keeping is perfectly competent, though there is not the least advance on the later writers of the preceding century. But these old Dutchmen are very quaint. Stevin had introduced a kind of Platonic dialogue into

[1] Owing probably to a printer's error the periods are not equal. The books open on 1st March and the balances are taken at the end of June, September, December, and February.

[2] *Tresoor vant Italiaens Boeck-houden*, published by Waninghen in 1615, and re-edited by Buingha in 1639.

his *Hypomnemata Mathematica,* and the device was much
copied by later writers.   In the "Treasury of Italian Book-
keeping" a special feature is made of it, and the title-page
explains that in the book there will be found one hundred
beautiful problems and five hundred clear questions with their
answers.   Such a large number of "posers" naturally taxed the
invention of the author, so he had recourse to the ingenious
expedient of a "Daily Examination" among his imaginary
scholars, which enabled him to repeat himself without being
put out of countenance.   The sanction of proverbial wisdom
is given to the device by Buingha, who quotes an Italian
saying—

> "L'uso è Padre della sapienza
>   &c la Memoria è la Madre."

The feeling that they had really nothing new to say
about book-keeping found expression among these old schoolmasters in the practice of republishing other men's books.
A charming justification for such a proceeding is given by
one B. H. Geestevelt, Book-keeper, who reprinted a treatise
entitled "The Flaming Torch of Italy's Book-keeping," by a
certain David Kock.[1]   Everything, Geestevelt philosophises
in his preface, has a beginning and an end.   The world itself
had a beginning (*vide* Gen. i. 1); and it will have an end
(*vide* Matt. xiii. 29).   Writers of Books have shared the same
fate; they come and they go.   "Among heathen, for instance,
there is Aristotle, Seneca, and Plato; among moderns there
are the following authors on book-keeping: Hercules Cordes,
Henricus Grammateus, Valentyn Mehear, Fusterus, Juan
Impijn, Nicolaes Petri, Martinus Wenseslaus, Sebastian
Comerfelt, Bartholomeus Cloot, Hendrich Wannigen, Buinga,
Coutereel, van der Schuyre, the great and praiseworthy Neuli-
gern, Sybrant Hansen Cardinael, and in Germany Achatius
Hagar and Otto and Henricus Weselon."   With this universal
ruin about him, and "state itself confounded to decay," the
worthy Geestevelt hastens to do his little towards keeping

---

[1] Amsterdam, 1658.

DE
LUCHTENDE
FACKEL
VAN HET
ITALIAENS
BOECKHOUDEN,

Verdeelt in drie Deelen,

Vraeghs-wijse voor-gestelt, ende beantwoort,

DOOR

DAVID KOCK van Enckhuysen.

Maer nu op nieuw van verscheyde oude stellingen gesuyvert, ende
na den rechten stijl, ende beste *Methode* der hedendaeghse voorname Kooplieden
gedirigeert, soo als de selve op hun *Cantores* tegenwoordigh gebruyckelick,
oock met *differente* nieuwe *Annotatien* ende andere dingen verrijckt,
noyt voor desen soodanigh gedruckt, alles gepractiseert
ende in 't Licht gebracht door

B. H. Geestevelt Boeckhouder.

t'AMSTERDAM,

Gedruckt by de Weduwe van Theunis Jacobsz, Boeckverkoopster op 't Water/
in de Loots-Man/ Anno 1658.

alive the sacred flame. To this end he republishes Kock. It must have been the title of the " Flaming Torch " that attracted him, for in itself the book has nothing which deserves the preference it received. It is one of the few absolutely worthless treatises on book-keeping which have come down to us. As a rule the old schoolmasters, though commonplace and tedious, are sound.

France on the whole has played a very small part in the development of book-keeping, possibly owing to the fact, mentioned by Dr. Jäger,[1] that at an early date the legislature of that country saw fit to make an attempt to check fraud by issuing stringent laws regulating the methods of keeping accounts. The necessity of conforming to these requirements naturally hampered improvement, so that, for tracing the historical progress of the art of book-keeping, it has deprived French treatises of a great deal of interest. An excellent example of the fostering care extended to commerce and its pertinents is given in a French work on book-keeping, *Methode pour bien dresser toutes sortes de comptes à parties doubles*, by Claude Irson (1687). The intimate connection between book-keeping and the Courts of Law is brought out in this book, while the treatise itself was prepared at the order of Colbert, the great minister of Louis XIV. who wasted his life in fruitless endeavours to render the extravagance of his master innocuous by developing the resources of France through trade and industry. It is probably not generally known that the solicitude of this statesman for the welfare of commerce extended down to details like book-keeping. Irson is described as *Juré teneur de Livres, nommé par sa Majesté, pour l'Ordre et l'examen; la Verification et Liquidation de toutes sortes de Comptes.* Colbert, we are told, had frequently employed him, and had, in fact, made him his protégé. It strikes us as an exaggeration when Irson says in his dedication that the greatest thing Colbert had done for the finances of France was the regulation of the national

[1] *Drei Skizzen zur Buchhaltung.*

book-keeping. There was, however, possibly an element of truth in the statement. When Colbert became minister 52 million livres were absorbed in collecting 84 millions of revenue. Under his administration 27 millions only were spent in collecting 104 millions. Book-keeping may have played a small part in achieving this result.

Irson's work is a scholarly production, commencing with a short historical introduction. The text of the instructions is brief and pointed, and the examples are very full and detailed. There is, however, no improvement in method and also no particular defect which it would be of interest to chronicle. A valuable part of the work is the portion which deals with former writers on book-keeping. Irson first gives a list of all the authors he knows who have referred to the subject, mostly lawyers whose treatises deal with the statutory enactments passed for the regulation of accounts. Then follows a list of authors who have described methods of keeping books. Irson closes his notice with the remark: "*J'ay beaucoup de veneration pour ceux qui m'ont precedé, ils ont beaucoup fait; mais ils n'ont pas atteint les Colomnes d'Hercules, il reste encore beaucoup à faire.*"

We have now mentioned many foreign authors of note in the history of early book-keeping, and we may return to the story of the art in our own country.

In England, as far as we know, Italian book-keeping had been introduced in 1543 by Hugh Oldcastle's translation of Paciolo. Ten years later there appeared an original English treatise of much more than ordinary merit. This is James Peele's "Maner & fourme how to kepe a perfecte reconyng after the order of the most worthie and notable accompte of Debitour and Creditour," published in London in 1553. A second book, considerably enlarged, and entitled "The pathe-way to perfectness in the accomptes of Debitour & Creditour," was brought out by Peele in 1569. It is only natural that Peele should be largely indebted to his Italian predecessors, through whose agency a competent method of book-keeping had so recently been brought to England. Peele freely acknowledges this, for he writes in his dedication: " I have done my goodwill and followed the most easie and best waye that I perceive amongst marchantes, even the trade (as I thinke) that is used in Venice and in other places for their great occupiying, very notable." Similarly he says in his preface to the work of 1569: "It is probable enough that this order is both ancient and famous; and doubtless grounded altogether upon reason, for time out of mind it hath been and is frequented by divers nations and chiefly by such as have been and be the most ancient and famous merchants." These frank admissions are, however, no prelude to the mere plagiarising from foreign authors which we have met in Oldcastle and Mellis. Peele reminds one of Paciolo in many of the details of his work, such as the directions for ruling columns in the ledger, for making a comparison of the books and for balancing, but this merely shows that his instructions are very complete, for there is no scope for wide differences in describing these operations. Peele had no doubt learned book-keeping from the Italian masters, but he had thoroughly grasped the subject himself, and produced an original treatise for the use of English readers. The matter dealt with in the last chapter of his first book is not found in the Italian writers. This chapter describes " What is to be done of a master that is minded to keep the quaterne" (*i.e.* ledger, from *quaderno*) "in his own custody by reason whereof his substance may be kept secret, except unto himself or his account keeper." Peele adds examples to this book, and although these are not complete in the copy preserved in the British Museum, the only one known to exist, there is sufficient left to prove that the author dealt properly with Profit and Loss and Capital Account, and generally taught a good system of book-keeping. The "patheway to perfectness " of 1569 gives most elaborate and excellent examples.

Peele describes himself on the title-page of his second work as " citizen and salter of London, Clercke of Christes

Hospitall, practizer and teacher of the same," that is, of the " accomptes of Debitour and Creditour." In addition to these varied accomplishments, Peele possessed a decided literary bent. His book gains considerably in value by being written in good nervous English, and not content with prose, the author every now and again aspires "to build the lofty rhyme." The introduction into the mysteries of Debitour and Creditour is profusely garnished with tributes to the poetic Muse, of which the following lines may serve as a specimen :—

> " As lacke of science causeth povertie
> And dooth abate man's estimation
> So learnyng doth brynge to prosperitie
> Such as of goods have small possession
> Then must we counte hym ware, discreet & wyse
> Whyle tyme doth serve, can tyme so well reteyne
> That in good tyme hym tymely can advyse
> Tyme well to spende and tourne it to his gayne
> For tyme well spent to gayne and not to waste
> The gayne will byde, though tyme doth passe and runne.
> But all to late, yf tyme shall ones bee paste
> For tyme ones loste, can not agayne be wonne."

This " curse of rhyme" descended to Peele's progeny, and blossomed out in his son George, who might have had a distinguished career had the excellent precepts of his father for the attainment of "prosperitie" been as potent in forming his character as the hereditary tendency to write verses. George Peele showed signs of promise as a scholar at Oxford, but after coming into collision with the college authorities, he cast himself on the mercy of the world in London, and wrote for the stage. Some contemporary fame attended his early career as a play-wright, but in the end he was cut off by debauchery.

Next to Peele in antiquity is John Mellis, already mentioned as the reprinter of Oldcastle. The title-page of his little volume is reproduced from the copy in the possession of the Institute of Chartered Accountants in England and

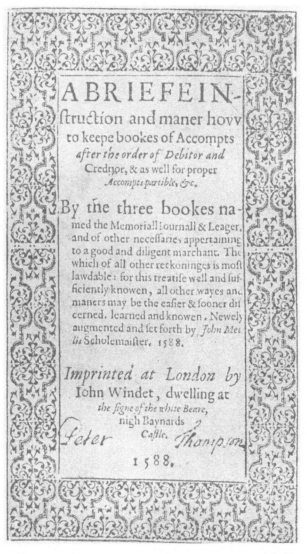

A BRIEFE IN-
struction and maner hovv
to keepe bookes of Accompts
after the order of Debitor and
Creditor, & as well for proper
Accompts partible, &c.

By the three bookes na-
med the Memoriall Iournall & Leager,
and of other necessaries appertaining
to a good and diligent marchant. The
which of all other reckoninges is most
lawdable: for this treatise well and sufficiently knowen, all other wayes and
maners may be the easier & sooner dis-
cerned, learned and knowen. Newely
augmented and set forth by *John Mel-*
lis Scholemaister. 1588.

Imprinted at London by
Iohn Windet, dwelling at
the signe of the white Beare,
nigh Baynards
Castle.

Peter Thompson

1588.

TITLE PAGE OF MELLIS, 1588 (same size as original)

From Copy in the possession of the Institute of Chartered Accountants
in England and Wales

Wales. Mellis added a few examples to the original treatise, but these possess small value.

Passing to the seventeenth century, we find that the first English contribution to the literature of book-keeping is a chapter on merchants' accounts in Malynes' *Consuetudo, vel lex Mercatoria*, published in 1622. It calls for no special remark, and in a later edition of the book was superseded by Dafforne's Book-keeping, which made its first appearance as a companion to this compendium. Of Dafforne more will be said hereafter. The next writer we encounter is I. Carpenter, "Gent.," as he styles himself on his title-page. He was one of the servants of the East India Company, and dedicated his book to its Governor as a token of gratitude for having been taken into the Company's employment. Carpenter explains that the composition is only partly his own. There was presented to him by accident, he says, "this small treatise (being partly a collection of the vertuous labour and worke of some well experienced practitioner in the Art of keeping Merchants' bookes of Accounts; and partly mine owne paines, by adding what I thought fit, and did conduce to the perfecting of this worke) not unworthy your worship's countenance, to which I humbly recommend the same for patronage." What share the writer had in the treatise which he after all published in his own name, it is not easy to determine. He compares himself with the "Lunary Orb and other inferior Planets of the Celestial spheres who receive their splendour from a more glorious Orb." But he would evidently have us believe that his reflected glory was by no means inconsiderable, for there is a ring of conscious merit about the conclusion of the dedication: "Your worship's faithfull and not unprofitable servant." Nor can we be certain as to the book from which Carpenter borrowed. All that can be determined is that it must have been anonymous, for he clearly indicates that he did not know the author. He says of his treatise that there might be some other man who "may challenge to be a chiefe or a part Author thereof . . . but I send it not out as absolutely mine own worke, nor do I go about hereby to detract from the due merit of him, whosoever he be, that hath so well deserved in framing the chiefe ground-worke thereof." It is, however, permissible to hazard a conjecture regarding the unknown author. The " chief ground-work" of the book, as Carpenter calls it, is unquestionably Manzoni's *Quaderno doppio*. Besides this, there are traces of Dutch work, particularly in the use of Ympyn's form of trial-balance. It may be, therefore, that what Carpenter gives us is an adaptation of the anonymous English translation of the *Nieuwe Instructie*. Ympyn's work, as we know, was a professed translation of an Italian source, which has been found to contain a fairly literal copy of Manzoni. If this supposition is correct,[1] Carpenter has considerably abbreviated his original, particularly in the examples, and further his " paines," of which he tells us, have by no means " conduced to the perfecting of this worke," for it is inferior in many ways to the original.

Two-thirds of Carpenter's book are taken up with a general explanation of the principles of book-keeping, and this is distinctly the best part of the work, although probably the least original. The remaining third of the book is devoted to practical examples, and these show that English book-keeping at this period was not in a very advanced state.

Carpenter gives the following list of necessary books: Cash book, Charges book, Household expenses book, Receipt book, Copy book for letters, Remembrance book, Invoice book, Memorial, Journal, and Ledger. This seems at first sight to imply a considerable subdivision in the books of primary entry, but such is not the case. Carpenter is emphatic in

---

[1] It is a supposition which is not easily verified, as the only known copy of the translation of Ympyn is not accessible. Dafforne asserts that Carpenter is simply a copyist of Waninghen, but a comparison of the two books does not bear this out.

his instructions that *every* transaction should be entered in the
Memorial, and from thence pass through the Journal to the
Ledger. Invoice book and even cash book, therefore, do not
rank much higher than the remembrance book and copy book
of letters, for they serve simply as memorandum books unconnected with the actual system of accounting. Carpenter's
journal is very primitive. Each entry is numbered consecutively, and there is no grouping of items. Even the
details of the inventory are journalised one by one, and
laboriously entered in the various accounts. Regarding the
other points arising on the journal little can be said, as
the variety of transactions exemplified by the author is very
limited. Of twenty-one payments appearing in the cash-account, for example, no fewer than eleven relate to the trader's
private drawings. In several instances the instructions given
in the text are not followed out in the specimen books.
For instance, the author lays down the sound rule that no
entry should be made in the ledger without being recorded
in the journal,[1] and yet when we come to the journal we
find, for one thing, that not a single closing entry is passed
through it. Carpenter's ledger, also, is not without serious
blemishes. In the case of bills no entry is made in any
book when a bill is drawn or accepted (and most of the
personal accounts are settled by bill). If, however, at the
time of balancing, the account is still open, it is squared
by entering the bill, which in the trial balance appears as
a sum due to or by the book-keeper. Sometimes, in such
cases, the bill is not even entered in the ledger. In various
minor matters errors are made. The owner of the business
is supposed to have a house styled " My Mansion House in
Cheapside." Rents received for a stable are credited to this
property account instead of to profit and loss, which is
the proper place for them under the old-fashioned system of
book-keeping, which makes no separation between private
and business affairs. The old authors all credit profit and

---

[1] We nowadays would, of course, add, " or in some book of primary entry."

loss with income received from extraneous sources, and debit it with household expenditure.

A gift of "household stuff" is credited by Carpenter to a wrong account, although in the text of the instructions Manzoni's remarks about the way of posting such gifts are faithfully reproduced. The balance of profit, finally, is not carried to capital account, although in the text it is stated that this ought to be done. All these are appreciable defects in this treatise, but it must not be supposed that England was necessarily behind other countries. In the Hanseatic Museum at Bergen some books are preserved dating from the year 1725 which show even less proficiency than might be assumed to be possessed by a student of Carpenter.[1] The transactions relate to the traffic in fish and supplies of various kinds, such as salt, brandy, &c., and even personal accounts are only balanced off roughly by noting the difference at debit or credit of the customer. It is quite obvious that the most primitive methods were in use even in establishments connected with so important a body as the Hanse League.

A much higher standard of book-keeping is found in Dafforne's "Merchant's Mirrour," published in London in 1636.[2] Dafforne seems to have been an arithmetic master, for he describes himself as "Accomptant and Teacher of the same." He states that he had lived for many years in Amsterdam, and he also tells us that the object of his book is to familiarise his countrymen with the methods of book-keeping practised in Holland. The book-keeping used by merchants in London he sweepingly ascribes to "Disdain-

---

[1] These books were kindly sent for examination by the Curators of the Museum.

[2] The book is bound up with an edition of Malynes' *Consuetudo vel lex Mercatoria* published in that year. The full title is: "The Merchants' Mirrour: or, Directions for the Perfect Ordering and Keeping of his Accounts. Framed by way of Debitor and Creditor, after the (so-tearmed) Italian manner: containing 250 rare Questions with their Answers, &c. Compiled by Richard Dafforne, of Northampton, Accomptant and Teacher of the same, after an exquisite Method in the English and Dutch language."

worthy, wilfull Ignorance." The same sentiment is implied
in his far from complimentary dedication to the five Companies of Merchant Adventurers: "Richard Dafforne so
wisheth your Understandings' Illumination in your Terres-
trial Talents' Administration that with comfort you may
hear the joyful sentence of your twice commended Service,
Matt. xxv. 21:—

> "'Well done, thou good and faithfull Servant true,
> Thou hast been good and faithfull over things a few,' &c."

Indeed, according to Dafforne, English book-keeping was
in a bad way. It was on the "importunate solicitation" of
numerous friends that he left Holland "to pitch the Tent
of his abode in London." "I then (after some rest)," he
goes on, "set my course into several Stationers' shops, there
gazing about me . . . to view what the Labourious Artist
had acted or divulged in Print for the assistance of Mer-
chandizing." But "as a Skipper anchoring upon an unknown
Isle, presently perceiveth those parts not to be inhabited,"
so Dafforne found the stationers' shops devoid of treatises on
book-keeping. Had there been a demand, he argues, there
would have been a supply. He instances foreign authors:
"Forestain, John Impen, Coot, Meunher, Savonne, Nicholas
Pietersen, Neutergem, Marten van den Dyck, Hoorbeck,
van Damme, Wencelaus, Coutereels, Simon Stevin, John
Willemson, Waninghen, Passhier Goossen, and others."
These writers must have found "many Science-lovers that
affected this Art, by whose allurements they were induced
to set Pen to Paper, endeavouring with their best gifts to
satisfy the desire of these Art-desirers." Merchants in the
Low Countries, we are told, "are generally enamoured of
this Art," while in England, "alas, the small love that a
great part of our merchants bear to this science, daunteth
the Pen of Industry in our Teachers." Dafforne suggests
that perhaps "Dame Nature with her Co-adjutor Industry
hath bestowed her Benevolence more sparingly upon our

Nation than upon others." But he puts the insinuation aside, for, says he, when Englishmen go abroad, they learn book-keeping "exquisitely." The mention of Englishmen going to foreign countries suggests a new reason to the ingenious author why a native treatise should appear. He fears grave dangers may ensue from sending our youth among foreigners:—

> "They being then at Rome
> Will do as there is done."

"Against which preposterous poyson," exclaims the Accomptant and teacher of the same, "I have emboldened my self to prepare this Antidote, being by Nature obliged to offer up part of the Widow's Mite of my Knowledge unto the Land of my Breaths-first Drawing."

In spite of his egregious style Dafforne produced quite a competent work on book-keeping. His form is somewhat clumsy, for he adopts dialogue as his medium of instruction and extends the process to no less than 250 "rare questions and their answers." But the book-keeping, if difficult to separate from the padding introduced by the "labourious artist," is good. Dafforne's methods are similar to those of Waninghen and Buingha. He also frequently refers to Simon Stevin, but he does not adopt the grouping of journal-entries practised by the latter, for each item is treated *seriatim*. In other respects, however, the journal is well kept, and closing entries are systematically passed through it. To stock on hand at the close of the books Dafforne has no reference, as the style of business he illustrates in his examples is that of an agent who sells goods on commission. But in some examples which he appends as additional practice for the learner, it appears that stock is treated in the customary and correct manner. Dafforne makes no mention of separate books of first entry and uses, besides an Inventory, the old-fashioned trio of Memorial, Journal, and Ledger. A noteworthy point in his Ledger

is an index on the "vowel" principle. We find it here
for the first time. The book closes with examples of arithmetic. Dafforne was succeeded by John Collins, and Abraham
Liset, Gent., who both gave their instructions perfectly
competently, but not in a manner which calls for particular
notice. Towards the close of this century we find the first
Scottish treatise on book-keeping, written by Robert Colinson,
and published in Edinburgh in 1683. There was no particular merit at this period in producing a good work on
book-keeping, so that it would be out of place to bestow
special praise on Colinson. This, however, may be said of
him, that he seems to have been familiar with the best practices of his day. His journal is grouped, so that the labour
of entering details in the ledger is saved, and the closing
entries are systematically carried out. In the matter of books
of first entry Colinson is no better than his contemporaries.
All his transactions are detailed in the Memorial (called
"Waste Book,)" and his "Specie, or Cash Book," and
"Invoyce Book," are simply supplementary memorandum
books. The "Specie or Cash Book," indeed, was a necessary
primary record in Scotland as it formerly was in Italy,
for in addition to the national coinage, which was very
bad, there were large quantities of foreign money in circulation, particularly English and Dutch. A pleasing feature
about Colinson's treatise is the sensible style in which it is
written. Instead of fulminating against the "Disdain-worthy
wilfull Ignorance," of his countrymen, or even comparing
himself to "the Lunar Orb and other minor Planets," Colinson
sets out the advantages of book-keeping in a calm, business-
like manner. One of his remarks is particularly interesting,
as it confirms by contemporary practical experience the
supposition advanced by Sieveking. The German professor,
as has been mentioned, originates the theory that improvements in book-keeping date from the time when business
came to be conducted by partnership, so that a mutual accounting between the proprietors became necessary. Colin-

son's observations fully substantiate this view. One of the chief advantages of book-keeping, he says, will arise in cases where the enterprise is carried on with joint capital. Commercial undertakings are often on too large a scale for one man to provide the whole means for carrying them on, "so men are oblidged to joyn in Partnership, which often blowes up with great discord, if they have not a true form to satisfie the Concerned what has become of their Stock."

To this same period, but a little earlier than the publica-cation of Colinson, belongs a record of an old Scots worthy, George Watson, one of our early accountants. When young Scotsmen of these days wished to prepare for a commercial life they had to go abroad to get the necessary training, and George Watson, we find, went to Holland. There he attended the school of a "teacher of mathematics and book-keeping," and by a fortunate chance the copy books he worked in are preserved.[1] This is not the place to expatiate on the quaint interest of these old manuscripts, but we may reproduce an extract from some "Nots and directions wherby to keep Merchants Accompts" which Watson copied out in one of his books. The notes, forty-eight in number, relate to various points of book-keeping, some elementary, others more advanced. The following are the "directions" whereby to make a balance and trial balance: "When ye wowld make a balance ye most even all yowr accompts of wares carying the remainer to the nixt voyde leaff and the gain to profitt and lose the like ye shall doe for voyadges and accompts partible (*i.e.* joint-venture accounts) then even the accompt off profitt and losse and cary the foot theroff to stoke the neat stock cary to balance in the C^r syde wherto carry all your C^n which is yowr fwll charge and set on yowr D^r syde your ready money wares and debtes then If the on syde of the balance agree with the other yowr accompt is even for all maters being ended ye may ballance up yowr books and if ye finde any desperat

---

[1] Now in the custody of the Edinburgh Merchants' Company.

debts ye may bear them to the D^r syde of profitt and losse. As also for the gaine of yowr comodities bear them to C^r syde of profitt and loose then take in the neat rest of each particular accompt and bear all D^m to the D^r syde but if ye find that either D^r or C^r syde excead then prick over the leadger from the Jwrnall parcells and se whether or no each D^r answereth each C^r which if ye find answerable in each digree your ballance cannot faill yo by which yow may see the certain statte of yowr book."

No treatise which appeared either in England or Scotland during the seventeenth century possesses outstanding merit, but there is every reason for believing that here also the printed books of instruction lagged behind the practices of the counting-house. A most valuable example of practical book-keeping between 1696 and 1707 is preserved in the ledgers and other books of the Darien Scheme, "The Company of Scotland trading to Africa and the Indies," which are to be found in the Advocates' Library, Edinburgh. In their external features these old books are in exact accordance with the methods made familiar to us in the school-masters' lesson-books. The journals have one column which is not summed, and posting-folios are noted one above the other like a fraction. The ledgers have cross references for every debit and credit, and the amounts are carried forward to a new page by balancing instead of transferring totals.[1] Every care also is taken to avoid possible tampering with the entries. If the writing does not reach to the end of the line, the space, be it ever so small, is carefully ruled out. No blank pages are left in the ledger for long accounts, and as a result the cash account, for instance, is transferred till one gets tired of following it. The clerk who kept the books might have been Paciolo himself. But while these superficial characteristics are faithfully reproduced, we find evidence of a thorough grasp of the more intricate problems of book-keeping, which have no place in the treatises of mere

---

[1] In a few cases, however, totals are "transported."

teachers.   The treatment of subscribed capital will serve as an
example.   The journal-entries are as follows :—

> Sundry Persons their Accompt Currant Debitor to Stock of the
> Company of Scotland trading to Africa and the Indies £ – – – for
> so much this day Subscribed by Them.
>   Cash Debitor to Sundry Persons their Accompt Currant £– – –
> for so much Payd by them.
>   Acct. of Discount Dr. To Cash £– – – for so much Payd the
> underwritten Persons as Discount (at 12 per cent.) of the Money they
> advanc'd befor this Day.
>   Sundry Persons Their Accompt of Debts Standing out, Debitor
> to Dito their Accompt Currant £– – – For so much They Rest
> for the ¾ of Their Subscriptions, They having Pay'd the First ¼ the
> 26th of February last.

The various calls, the interest paid, and the transfers, can
all be traced with perfect clearness.   There appear to have
been three departments distinguished in the books : the Stock
or Capital, the Trading, and the Banking departments.   Each
had a ledger which balanced in itself, the cash-account being
transcribed in full.   There is also a general cash-book showing
the balance on hand, which was very large, for the Bank of
Scotland had only just been formed, and no use seems to have
been made of such facilities as it provided.   The ledgers had
separate indices—" alphabets," as they were called—and the
larger ones were kept on the " vowel principle."   Scroll books
were kept to a large extent.   We find even scroll journals
and scroll ledgers.   A stock-book showing the receipt and
disposal of the numerous articles purchased and sent out by
the company is noteworthy for the accurate manner in which
it was kept and balanced with stock on hand.   It could not
be improved at the present day.   But as a contrast to the
careful balancing of this stock-book, it is necessary to note
that there is no record of a balance of the account books
themselves.

It is a curious experience to go through a set of ancient
books.   One can picture the old-world clerks in their peri-

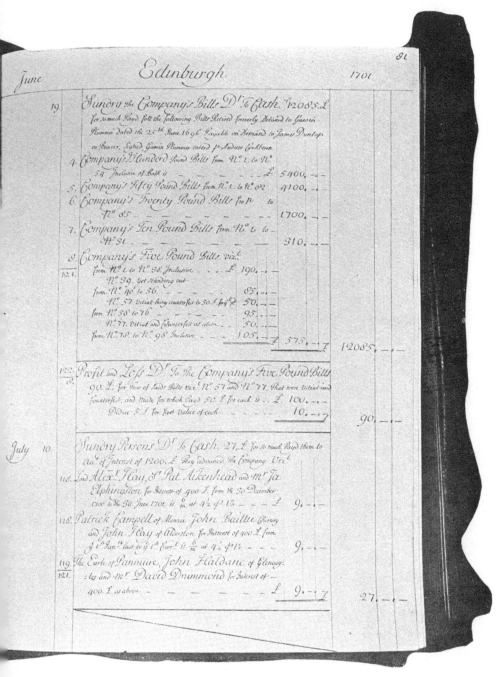

PAGE OF JOURNAL OF "DARIEN" COMPANY, 1701 (size of original 17¾ inches by 12⅞ inches)

In the Advocates' Library, Edinburgh

wigs and knee-breeches writing up journal and ledger with a deliberation as archaic as their quill-pens. Little thought was there in those days of time-saving. Their entries are circumstantial far beyond what was necessary, and the writing is drawn like copper-plate. The traditions of the old school long held their ground. When the Darien Company had been dead and gone for a century gentle Charles Lamb pored over his ledgers in the South Sea House. A famous essay describes his leave-taking. He bids them farewell with their fantastic flourishes and their pious invocations of the deity. Two clerks of the modern degenerate days, he says, could scarce lift these ponderous tomes. And they inshrine in their sumptuous bindings and lattice-work of parchment "his works"—more MSS. in folio than ever Aquinas left, and full as useful!

The eighteenth century is not marked by improvements in the art of book-keeping, but at its close there appeared a work which is the most widely-known book on the subject in the English language. The history of book-keeping in England does not possess the interest which in Italy is created by the personality of Paciolo, or in Holland by that of Simon Stevin, but Edward Thomas Jones, accomptant in Bristol, certainly succeeded in arresting attention far beyond the bounds of his own country. He devised what he called a new system of book-keeping, and launched it forth as a death-blow to the Italian method under no less pretentious a title than the following: "Jones' English System of Book-keeping by Single or Double Entry, in which it is impossible for an error of the most trifling amount to be passed unnoticed. Calculated effectually to prevent the evils attendant on the methods so long established and adapted to every species of trade. Secured to the Inventor by the King's Royal Letters Patent, Bristol, 1796."

Had Jones left his invention to take its chance on its merits, his name would now be unknown. Having, however, all the instinct of his countrymen for business, he managed to make a small fortune by his book, over and above the reputation he secured. This happy consummation was attained by a most brilliant piece of advertising. Before publication Jones issued a prospectus of his work, adding testimonials which he succeeded in securing from all kinds of well-known people, like Peel and the Governor of the Bank of England. In this prospectus the book was offered for subscription at a guinea a copy. The invention was to be patented, but the guinea fee would include a special Licence to the subscriber, empowering him to put the new invention into practice in his own book-keeping. The idea was a glorious success, and the happy inventor secured thousands upon thousands of subscriptions. His "Address to the Trading and Commercial World" was indeed a work of art. Jones commences with an attack on Italian book-keeping. He makes the observation, which is perfectly well founded, that double-entry is a mere mechanical device for securing systematic posting, and affords no guarantee whatever that each individual account is correct. This criticism, which is a commonplace, Jones takes as an occasion for issuing a warning against the dangers of double-entry. He contemptuously quotes the maxim: "For every debit there must be a credit, and for every credit there must be a debit." "Alas!" he cries; "Alas! how few consider that if this *must* be the case, this the rule to go by, nothing is more easy than to make a set of books wear the appearance of correctness, which at the same time is *full of errors*, or of *false entries*, made on purpose to deceive!" (The italics are in all cases those of Jones.) A vivid picture is then drawn of the facilities double-entry gives to a swindler and of his absolute security from detection. Double-entry is "capable of being converted into a cloak for the vilest statements that designing ingenuity can fabricate. A man may defraud his partner, or a book-keeper his employer, if he be so disposed, without ever being detected. . . . By this method of keeping accounts ingenious men have it in their power to make a profitable concern appear a losing one, so as to incline their partners to withdraw from the trade ; or they may make a losing concern appear profitable, so as to influence some other person to take their situation ; or, if they be minded, they may deceive their partners by false statements *until not a shilling* be left in the trade or until they become insolvent! In the course of my practice I have seen the books of several partnerships in which this had been done."

But to hold the door wide open to fraud is not the only defect of double-entry. It is, further, only with the utmost difficulty that books kept by that system can ever be balanced. Months are spent, Jones tells us, in ineffectual endeavours to balance books, while in other cases which have come under his own observation, books have been kept for fifteen and twenty years and never balanced, "although great pains were taken to keep them correct." And what if the balance does work out correctly, what if debits and credits do agree? "A partner or book-keeper may have short-debited or over-credited his own or some other account in the ledger, and have altered some nominal account on the contra side to make the books appear correct."

So defective a system of course calls for reform, and Jones tells us that he "determined never to give the matter up till he had completed such a system as would, to a certainty, counteract those alarming Evils." His labours were arduous, but he is very modest about them. "I do not mean," he assures us, "to arrogate to myself any exclusive or superior intelligence to other men." He only takes credit for having worked harder. "The labours of an Accomptant occasion him, in general, gladly to devote his leisure moments to relaxation rather than study." But Jones scorned delights and lived laborious days. "More than five years were spent in wearisome and fruitless endeavours. From strong prejudices I had in favour of the method by Double Entry, I attempted to lay my plan on that foundation ; but my pursuit only tended fully to convince me that the basis of it was fixed on erroneous principles; I was obliged to begin on new and untried ground." Having abandoned the trammels of double-entry, his progress was rapid. "I soon established a foundation on which I could build with safety." The only delay was caused by the height to which the inventor aspired. "The difficulty was to form my plan so that no material objection might be raised to the structure, while its conveniences and advantages should claim universal admiration. In this also, I flatter myself that I have been successful."

Before divulging the secret of his invention Jones himself summarised its advantages: "My system is perfectly simple and concise." "It requires *less labour* than any system now in use." "It is impossible for an error of the *most trifling* amount to be passed unnoticed." The books may be balanced "*every month* or *oftener* without the *least inconvenience;* with the satisfaction, when balanced, of the Accounts being *correct* to an *absolute certainty*." "It is *impossible* to produce a false Statement from Books kept after this plan, that will not be immediately detected." "The Books may be balanced in *two or three hours;* and in no Compting-house in the Kingdom need it be procrastinated to a *second* day:—and although it be done with so much dispatch, yet, such certain accuracy attends the process, that IF A LEDGER CONSIST OF A THOUSAND FOLIOS WITH TEN OR MORE ACCOUNTS ON EACH IT IS IMPOSSIBLE TO TAKE OFF THE BALANCES OF ONE FOLIO WRONG; and when the balances of all the accounts in the ledger are taken off, the work is finished, nor needs in the *least* examination." Should any over-anxious person think it desirable to compare the books in the old-fashioned way, then in books kept on Jones' plan "the posting of *one thousand* entries may be easily examined in an *hour* by one *person*, without the *least assistance*, or the *possibility* of *passing unnoticed* an error of the most *trifling* amount." "An invention more *extensively useful*, more *advantageous* to the commercial and trading interests of these Kingdoms . . . never yet made its appearance."

One more objection had yet to be met before the invention could be given to the public. Riots were taking place all over England in consequence of the introduction of labour-saving machinery. Starving hand - loom weavers and miserable spinners had seen themselves cast adrift by the invention of the power loom and the Jenny. Would not the employment of book-keepers be taken from them and civil war become imminent through the introduction of "the most extensively useful invention which had ever made its appearance?" "Were such the truth," says Jones, "perhaps I might, in favour of a general good, justify a partial evil. But the fact is not so, as the effect will prove. The office of book-keeper is still the same; its duties are relieved only from that which renders it an irksome task."

The ground was now prepared, the subscribers had paid, and the Invention was made known to the licence-holders. Briefly stated it was as follows: Instead of two columns in the ledger, make ten; in all essential points proceed as directed by Paciolo. That is "Jones' English Book-keeping" in a nut-shell. A specimen of the cash - account in the ledger will illustrate the method of using the ten columns. Posting columns cannot be reproduced for want of space, but the reader will be interested to know that there were eight of them—one to each quarterly column on debit and credit—making, that is to say, eighteen columns in all for every account in the ledger.

Let the reader picture to himself such a ledger in practice! Instead of the two dozen or so items which in the specimen make up the total cash transactions for four months, let him fill this maze of columns with the thousands of entries which would occur even in a moderate sized concern. Let him repeat the same process on all the other pages of the ledger, and then let him imagine the state of mind of the unfortunate subscriber who was solemnly licensed to put this epoch-

July 1-Sep. 30	Oct. 1-Dec. 31	Dr.	ABRAHAM BOLD, Cashier	Cr.	Jan. 1-Mar. 31	Apl. 1-June 30	July 1-Sep.
			Jan. Cash received this month . . 3100 . . 2929 10 0 Balance	Jan. Cash paid this month . . 770 10	Jan. 1 750 2 20 10	Apl. 1 . . 15 23 400 27 175 29 400	
			Feb. Cash received this month . . 127 2464 0 0 Balance	Feb. Do. 2 10	Feb. 2 2 10		
			Mar. Cash received this month . . 395 7 1997 17 0 Balance	Mar. Do. 851 10	Mar. 1 1 10 27 850		
			Apl. Cash received this month . . 385 17 6 1407 19 6 Balance	Apl. Do. 975 15			

SPECIMEN PAGE OF A LEDGER ACCOUNT (CASH) IN JONES'S ENGLISH SYSTEM OF BOOK-KEEPING making invention into practice ! In the index to the ledger Jones introduced a curious device. Every account was to be furnished with a special mark or letter, and this sign was to be noted in the index along with the folio. Should the arithmetical agreement of debits and credits be proved by a trial-balance, Jones suggested that the labour of comparison, usually undertaken to verify the posting to each account, might be lessened if the posting mark in the day-book were gone over with the ledger-index, without looking up the actual ledger-account. Apart from the fact that Jones had stated that with his invention comparison would be superfluous, this abridged method he suggests is obviously unsatisfactory. A careless clerk might very well mark the right folio in the day-book and yet enter the amount on a wrong folio in the ledger. A dishonest clerk would make false entries with impunity if he knew that comparison would be restricted to the ledger-index. Finally the special marks or letters are quite unnecessary for carrying out Jones' idea. It would be as easy to compare the name of the account and the folio, as the name of the account and the mark.[1]

[1] The detailed particulars of what Jones himself conceived to be the characteristic portions of his "invention," may be gathered from the terms of the specification of his patent. (See Dodsley's *Annual Register*, 1796, vol. xxxviii. p. 445.) Summarised they are as follows :—

The books required are a Day-book, a Journal, an Alphabet, and a Ledger.

Day-book to have a debit, and a credit, and a total column. Also two columns on either side (four in all) for the letter (*i.e.* mark) distinguishing the account in the Ledger.

Alphabet to contain name of each Ledger Account, the letter (*i.e.* mark) annexed to it, and the folio.

Ledger to have 3, 4, 5, 7, &c., columns.

All entries (including cash) to be written into the Day-book.

Side columns in Ledger to be used for the entries of each month, and monthly total to be carried to centre column.

Each month's totals in Ledger can be balanced.

To check Ledger postings, compare the letters (*i.e.* marks) in the Day-book with the Alphabet.

In taking down Ledger balances see that the differences between the totals of debits and credits on each page agree with the differences between the balances on each page.

It will be observed that Jones' specification deals exclusively with details as to methods and does not so much as refer to general principles.

Besides the ledger Jones advised that no other book should be kept except the old Italian "Memorial" (called by him Journal or Day-book) in which every transaction whatsoever should be entered as it occurred. He discountenanced even a separate cash-book, as the ledger account|for cash would give all the necessary information. Jones also strongly recommended—although not as an integral part| of his invention —that only personal accounts should be kept in the ledger. An account for calculating profit could be kept in a sort of sales-book.

How the claims Jones had put forward were to be realised, he did not stop to explain. He had stated that he had invented something different in principle from double-entry, that his system would save labour, that mistakes would be detected on the surface, and, chief of all, that it would be an absolute impossibility to post items to wrong accounts, so that comparison would become practically a work of supererogation. He leaves the reader, or more correctly, the subscriber, to judge for himself whether these statements in his prospectus were true, or whether he had not simply reproduced the ordinary well-known principles of book-keeping buried beneath the most cumbersome system of columnar ledger which is ever likely to be conceived.

Yet Jones had made some provision against complaints from his subscribers. Before the book appeared he himself tells us that opprobrious epithets like "take in" had been applied to his scheme, and that the subscription list had been characterised as a way of "begging." His indignation as a man and as an inventor is very great. He points to the integrity of Peel and of the Governor of the Bank who had signed his testimonial. "They," he says, "convinced that an improvement in the art of book-keeping was much wanted, *readily* and *liberally* stept forward to give the work their sanction ; crushing thereby the *unmanly reflections* of *illiberal men* whose conduct implies that they had a *sinister end in view*." His opponents, he hints, are probably disreputable characters, and he advises their friends to be on their guard. "The intention of the man who opposes it ought to be *suspected*, and his conduct undergo a *minute investigation* by those with whom he is connected." "May shame burn their cheeks and cause them to *bury* their opposition in oblivion." For a moment he cools down when he reflects that the invention is yet unpublished and unknown. "Let me request those persons," he says, "who have unthinkingly and, of course, too hastily. condemned this method of book-keeping which they have not seen . . . to reflect on the subject and weigh the matter well." "Then will the English System of Book-keeping rise to its proper level, and the men who continue to oppose it be left in a *sullen minority—dark* as the *principles* in which they have grounded their opposition." Jones also will rise triumphant, for he feels justly that after the statements he has made and the money he has collected, criticism involves his personal honour. "I am risking," he says, "my reputation as a man, and my credit as an accomptant, in what I have thus offered to the notice of the world: in which if there be a possibility of failure, both are totally involved." Jones, in fact, occupies in Book-keeping the place which Macpherson with his "Ossian" fills in Literature. Both prove what success can be achieved by unblushing impudence. The reputation Jones achieved was tremendous. His book is known all over Europe. It has been translated into German, Italian, and French—and foreigners to this day, when they refer to English book-keeping, assume that we have no books except a ledger and a memorial, and that the former has ten columns. At home his fame was equally great. Even James Mill thought it worth his while to point out errors in this remarkable treatise. *Habent sua fata libelli.*

With Edward Jones' much noised treatise we enter the era of modern book-keeping. Entirely unfruitful as the book was in itself, it indirectly exerted a great influence on the development of the art. The very circumstances of its pub-

lication aroused a widespread interest in the subject which
had never existed before. The calmest critic, who in course
of the day's work had seen fit to differ from the inventor's
assertions, found himself assailed with a torrent of personal
abuse, which very naturally stimulated his desire to subject
the author's pretensions to the most searching examination.
The principles of book-keeping were studied once more from
the foundation, and the process could not be otherwise than
salutary, for the salient feature of the whole controversy
was after all the fact that a virulent attack had been delivered on double-entry, without in reality altering its principles by one jot or one tittle. The complete failure of Jones'
"English Book-keeping" has established double-entry once
and for all as the only method of recording commercial
transactions with completeness. But apart from this fundamental theory the teaching of the old masters soon became
antiquated. The minute investigation which the practice of
book-keeping underwent at the hands of Jones' critics tended
to show that there is practically no limit to the alterations
in detail which may be introduced in the matter of tabu-
lating and posting accounts. A religious adherence to archaic
conventionalities ceased to be the test of a good book-
keeper. The very words "after the Italian manner" fell
out of the terminology of the trade.

To trace in detail each modern development of commercial book-keeping hardly comes within the scope of this
history, nor would it be possible to do so in its limit of
space. It must suffice to generally indicate the lines of
improvement. Boundless as the opportunities for change in
book-keeping may be in themselves, their scope is more or
less rigidly confined. The advances made in modern practice
have all tended towards one or other of two objects: to lessen
clerical labour, or to increase the clearness of the books as
statistical records. The first step in the elimination of useless
repetition of entries was the abandonment of the Journal
as a posting medium. Once supreme and second in import-

ance only to the ledger, the journal had with reforms in national coinage become one of the least necessary of books. Other improvements followed which are now incorporated in the daily routine of most large counting-houses : balancing by totals, self-balancing ledgers, columnar cash-books and day-books, and many other useful devices and checks. Great Britain on the whole has led the way in these matters. On the Continent legislative enactments have kept book-keepers in leading-strings and led to the perpetuation of methods which our merchants would consider unsatisfactory. But in spite of these trammels changes are taking place even in these countries. In Italy, particularly, historical research has stimulated an interest in book-keeping, and led to much fresh thought being devoted to the subject. The most original development is a system of accounting which has been called " Logismography," and is based on a theory propounded by the late Joseph Cerboni, Accountant-General to the Italian Government. It is out of the question to enter into a discussion of this new development of book-keeping, round which an extensive literature has grown up, but the leading idea may be briefly indicated. According to Cerboni we must distinguish two groups of accounts connected with every business: An account relating to the Proprietor of the business, and an account relating to his debtors and creditors—the latter being styled " Agency Account," for sake of a short descriptive title. Within these two main collective accounts there are, of course, an indefinite number of sub-accounts. But the net debit or credit of the Proprietor's account will only vary through losses or gains being made, while the shiftings of the objects forming the capital of the business (*e.g.* transfers from one " agent " to another) neither modifies the Proprietor's account, nor the collective Agency account. Each entry is distinguished according to whether it brings about one or other of these results. Those which produce changes in the sub-accounts without altering the principal accounts are termed " integral "; those which bring about an adjustment in the principal accounts (losses or gains) are termed " differential." Cerboni therefore recognises four classes of accounts : Accounts integral to the Proprietor, or integral to the Agency; Accounts differential to the Proprietor or differential to the Agency. In this framework the book-keeping is arranged, and it is claimed for the system that while it yields nothing in accuracy to ordinary double-entry, it makes the most minute sub-division possible, thus enabling the book-keeper to exhibit with ease all the various phases of a large undertaking. Historically the chief interest of Logismography lies in the fact that it unreservedly accepts the groundwork of double-entry, while in other respects it is the most uncompromising break with the past which book-keeping has yet experienced. To hazard a prophecy as to the various changes which the future may have in store for the craft would be futile. Has not an American arisen who throws the ledger—the " Great Book " of his fathers—to the winds and substitutes a drawer full of loose sheets ? But there is one assertion which even in this age of change may be made with confidence. Luca Paciolo enunciated principles which have stood the test of time and use and will regulate book-keeping for all ages. " For every debit there must be a credit " will be our axiom, let us otherwise keep our ledger according to whatever arrangement may suit our requirements.

PART II

HISTORY OF ACCOUNTANTS

CHAPTER I

EARLY ITALIAN ACCOUNTANTS

IN THE COMMUNES AND MARITIME REPUBLICS—FIRST ASSO-
CIATION OF ACCOUNTANTS AT VENICE—QUALIFICATIONS
FOR ADMISSION—ASSOCIATION AT MILAN—SCALE OF
CHARGES PRESCRIBED—ACADEMY AT BOLOGNA—VICISSI-
TUDES OF THE OLD ASSOCIATIONS—LAWS RELATING TO
ACCOUNTANTS

As it is in Italy that we find the earliest development of accounts and book-keeping, so also it is in that country that we
come on the first traces of professional accountants. The history of accounting and accountants in Italy is an extremely
interesting study, and it has been investigated with much
zeal by the Italians themselves. A number of books on the
subject have been published, to an examination of which we
are chiefly indebted for the information given in this chapter.[1]

In an earlier chapter we have described the elaborate state
accounting organisation of the Romans, and though this, no
doubt, fell to pieces with the ruin of the Roman empire, its
influence appears to a large extent to have remained and
beneficially affected the Italian national habits and predi-
lections.

With the organisation of the cities of Italy as free and
independent communes, and with the rise of the prosperous
maritime republics, we have evidence of renewed attention

---

[1] *Storia della Ragioneria Italiana*, Brambilla ; *La Professione del Ragioniere*, Massa ;
Storia della Ragioneria Italiana, Bariola ; *Il Ragioniere*, Campi ; *Storia del Collegio dei
Ragionieri di Milano*, Cantoni ; and others. Some passages in this chapter have
already appeared in an article on the subject in *The Accountants' Magazine* by the
present writer.

173

being paid to matters of accounting and of the existence of accountants. A maritime law of the eleventh century enjoins the public scribe of the commune to render an account of the goods in the ships, of those received and sold or bought; and the statutes of the communes contain numerous rules as to how books should be kept. At Milan in 1225 we find the chief magistrate undertaking to render accounts every four months. Among the municipal officials there were a treasurer, a collector, and a keeper of the depot in which the goods of the city were collected. Two treasuries were kept, one for current funds and another for a reserve fund, and no payment could be made without an order signed by a magistrate, the financial control being in the hands of the municipal council. Florence in 1299 prescribed the methods of keeping bank accounts.

An account-book of the receipts and payments of Pope Nicolas III., which extends from 1st May 1279 to 1st March 1280, is described as a sort of journal of cash transactions. It is interesting as an example of the system, which appears to have been common, of checking a cashier's transactions by means of a separate record kept by a notary. After the last entry the cashier, having noted the balance, adds, "and thus it is also in accordance with the book of our notary." Of the same period is also a MS. which records the expenses of the Chamber of the Commune of Florence from 7th August to 80th September 1303: "*Hic est liber sive quaternus exituum et expensarum factorum et factarum per dictos Camerarios infrascriptis hominibus et personis, et infrascriptis de causis,*" the entries in which are made in chronological order without any distinction of headings.

In Genoa, from the beginning of the fourteenth century, it was ordained: that books should be kept similar to those of bankers; that the folios should be numbered; that no erasure should be made or blank space left; that corrections should be marked in a special column to be carried forward at the end into the column used for rectifying the results; that the books should be renewed every year; and that a journal, a ledger, and an inventory should be kept, as well as books for the entry of expenses, for entries in suspense, &c.

Although in a census of the liberal professions made in the thirteenth century in Milan no mention is made of accountants, possibly because they were included among mathematicians, as early as the year 831 a deed entered into between the Abbot of St. Ambrose of Milan and a certain Giovanni Donnolo is signed by one who calls himself an accountant: *Signum manus Garefrit Rationatori, qui ipsis rebus mensuravit, et estimavit.* Further, we meet with accountants at Milan in 1164, where the vestry of the cathedral, the ducal court, and the commune each employed an accountant, as is shown by a general register of taxable land compiled in that year. Again, at Milan in 1387, at a meeting of the commission for the building of the cathedral, mention is made of the appointment of an accountant and reviser, or auditor, of accounts; and in 1394 a certain Giovanni Scanzi was elected *Ragionato* of the commune of Milan. Chapter 115 of the statutes of Milan of 1396 is entitled *De Rationatore communis et ejus officio,* which attributes to the accountant the most important administrative functions in public affairs. In 1463 we meet with a certain Julius Vimercato, Accountant-General to the Chamber of Magistrates, called *Domini Mag. Intratorum,* and in the public administration there were *Rationatores ad papiri, ad expensœ conficiens et ad cartam.* In 1484 a nobleman, Giovanni Longone, was accountant to the Duke Gian Galeazzo Maria Visconti, to whom the duke as a reward for his important services granted the right to transmit to his descendants the office of accountant to the city of Milan. In the next century we find that the accounts of the commune of Milan, of the hospital, and of the vestry of the cathedral, were checked by accountants; and in 1593, when the new Bank of St. Ambrose was founded, the management was entrusted to an accountant. That the accountants of that time were held in high esteem is evidenced by the fact that in the settlement of accounts those authenticated by accountants were accepted as decisive by the parties.

In Venice, accountants flourished from very early times; and the senate recognised it *esse summopere necessarium habere unum fidelem practicum et exercitatum Rationatorem.* The examiners of accounts received a percentage on the amount of the mistakes and frauds which they discovered.

At Pisa, the famous Leonardo Fibonacci, the author of mathematical works dated 1202, 1220, and 1250, was employed to revise or audit the accounts of the commune at a fee of twenty pounds' weight of denarii, as is shown by the following inscription recording the official resolution, which is still preserved at Pisa [1]:—

Considerantes . nostre . civitatis . et . civium . honorem . atque . profectum . qui . eis . tam . per . doctrinam . quam . per . sedula . obsequia . discreti . et . sapientis . viri . magistri . leonardi . bigolli . in . abbacandis . estimationibus . et . rationibus . civitatis . eiusque . officialium . et . aliis . quoties . expedit . conferuntur . ut . eidem . leonardo . merito . dilectionis . et . gratie . atque . scientie . sue . prerogativa . in . recompensatione . laboris . sui . quem . substinet . in . audiendis . et . consolidandis . estimationibus . et . rationibus . supradictis . a . comuni . et . camerariis . publicis . de . comuni . et . pro . comuni . mercede . sive . salario . suo . annis . singulis . libre . XX . denariorum . et . amisceria . consueta . dari . debeant . ipseque . pisano . comuni . et . eius . officialibus . in . abbacatione . de . cetero . more . solito . servat . presenti . constitutione . firmamus.

In Florence, about 1250, guardians of the estates of pupils were called *Ragionieri dei pupilli,* and in that commune in the fifteenth century there were regular administrative and accounting arrangements, with systematic book-keeping, indispensable corollaries to the numerous industries that flourished there. The Venetian plan of payment by results was introduced in Florence in 1555.

---

[1] Quoted by Bariola in *Storia della Ragioneria Italiana,* 52. It will be noticed that Leonardo is referred to by the sobriquet of *Bigolli,* that is, *Bigollone,* or simpleton, given to him, says Libri in his *Histoire des Sciences Mathématiques en Italie* (vol. ii. page 25), "probably because the study of the sciences completely absorbed him, and prevented him from devoting himself to commerce, the favourite occupation of his fellow-citizens."

The first association of accountants of which we find any record, the *Collegio dei Raxonati*, was founded in Venice in 1581. Only Venetian citizens who had resided in the town for five consecutive years, who were not engaged in any mechanical art, and who had not suffered any legal punishment, could at first be admitted to membership; but in 1596 it was decreed that strangers might be admitted if they had been resident in Venice for fifteen consecutive years. By the year 1669, the influence of the college had become so powerful that no one could exercise the functions of an accountant, in connection with either public administration or the law, unless he were a member of the college. The controllers and revisers of the accounts watched over the register of members with power to exclude the incapable and the unworthy. Whoever intended to follow the profession of an accountant, having obtained from a magistrate a certificate of his fitness for admission, had to serve in the office of a public accountant an apprenticeship of six years, usually from the ages of eighteen to twenty-four, the latter being the age at which membership could be obtained. Before submitting to examination the candidate had to obtain a further declaration by a magistrate that he possessed the legal requirements. He then presented himself before the commission of examiners with this declaration, and with a certificate by the accountant with whom he had served his apprenticeship, as a proof that he had the required capacity. The commission was composed of forty-five persons, of whom thirty were accountants. Two-thirds of the commission having decided that the candidate should be admitted to the examination, he was required to draw by lot two of the questions prepared, and in order to pass he had to receive the approval of two-thirds of the commissioners. Thereafter he had to submit to a similar examination before the controllers of accounts and five learned merchants. If he obtained three-fourths of the votes of that body he was granted a certificate for admission to the college.

At Milan also, from the sixteenth century, the accountant occupied important public positions and enjoyed special privileges. In 1609, 1654, and 1685, the accountants of Milan contemplated the establishment of a professional tariff, but, the time not being yet ripe, the matter was delayed. Later, the need of a college being felt, one was established in 1739, received the approval of the Senate in 1741, and was opened in 1745. It decreed that only its members should be legally recognised, and the statute of 1744 laid down the rules for admission. These required a knowledge of economics, commerce, and public affairs; a complete knowledge of Latin and arithmetic, a five years' apprenticeship, the attainment of 25 years of age, and an examination in the science of accounting. The position of the college at Milan was different from that at Venice—the latter having been established under the protection of the State, while the former was a private institution. So unwilling was the government at Milan to have the college interfering in State affairs, that when, in 1748, the government was asked to appoint to public offices only accountants whose proficiency was attested by the college, the request was refused. The application was renewed in subsequent years, and was finally granted, but was so little given effect to that another application was necessary. Although it did not readily comply with this request, the government understood the advantage of a scale of charges for accountants, and a scale was established in 1742, applicable to all accountants, whether members of the college or not. In this scale the work of an accountant was divided into two classes:—

(a) Material—namely, ordinary arithmetical accounts, various calculations and transactions in double-entry.

(b) Intellectual—namely, the work of reconciling complicated accounts, or checking part of them by admitting those that are admissible and excluding those that have to be gone over again in respect of the various documents and justifications.

For the material work the fee was 14 lire for every diet of six hours; and for the intellectual there was in addition one per cent. on the greater amount either of debit or credit, not, however, to exceed 1200 imperial lire. For every regular and formal sitting the allowance was 7 lire if in town, 14 lire, with food and travelling expenses, if out of town. There were also fees for writings. This scale was considerably altered in subsequent years. In the event of a dispute arising as to the time occupied, the matter was first laid before the heads of the college, and thereafter before the magistrates. It was compulsory to use the legal tariff, an accountant not doing so being debarred from practising. The college at Milan aroused jealousy on account of its privileges and was suppressed; it was re-established in 1799, and again suppressed shortly after.

In 1813 the private academy of the *Logismofili* was established in Bologna, with the object of furthering practical and theoretical studies cognate to the profession. It had various vicissitudes. It prospered until 1818; its meetings ceased in 1822; it reformed its statute in 1829–1830; recommenced its work after the prohibition of its meetings had ceased in 1858, and is again a prosperous Institution bearing the name of the *Accademia di Ragionieri*, but with functions which, it would appear, are chiefly scientific.

With the political events of the time of Napoleon the old professional *régime* was partly changed; but the ordinance of 3rd November 1805 "for rendering capable of practising the profession of public accountant in the Kingdom of Italy," was nothing new; it merely re-enacted, with some modifications, the laws already in force. The officials who administered the laws were the same; and the examination of applicants, the keeping of registers, and the power of removal for faults or incapacity, continued as before.

Previous to the unification of Italy, conditions similar to those prevailing in Venice and Milan prevailed also in the majority of the States; the State laws providing that no one could practise as an accountant unless he were a member of a recognised association. Thus, in the Sardinian States, accounting work was confined to the Royal Liquidators, of whom there was a fixed number which could not be exceeded.

The developments which have taken place subsequent to the unification of Italy fall to be dealt with in a later chapter.

CHAPTER II

SCOTLAND — BEFORE THE CHARTERS

THE ORIGIN OF THE PROFESSION IN EDINBURGH—EARLY
ASSOCIATION WITH LEGAL PROFESSION—SOME PROMINENT
ACCOUNTANTS OF THE EIGHTEENTH CENTURY—ANECDOTES
OF JAMES BALFOUR—THE FOUNDERS OF THE SCOTTISH LIFE
ASSURANCE SOCIETIES—LETTER OF SIR WALTER SCOTT
RELATING TO THE PROFESSION—EARLY GLASGOW AC-
COUNTANTS—LARGE BANKRUPTCIES IN LATTER PART OF
EIGHTEENTH CENTURY—ACCOUNTANT FIRMS THEN ESTAB-
LISHED—AN EARLY STATEMENT OF THE SCOPE OF THE PRO-
FESSION IN GLASGOW—EARLY ACCOUNTANTS IN ABERDEEN,
DUNDEE, ETC.

IT is not unfitting that when we come to deal with the modern
profession of accountant, Scotland should occupy the place
of priority. It is there that the Chartered Accountant originated, and in Scotland we find the oldest existing societies
of public accountants. We are not unmindful of the claims
of Italy, to which country we are indebted for so much in
connection with the profession, but however important a position accountants occupied there during the seventeenth and
eighteenth centuries, their influence undoubtedly diminished
thereafter, and the old Gilds and Colleges became either
dormant or extinct. It may also be said with justice that in
no country in the world is the profession of accountant so
highly developed or so important relative to other professions
as in Scotland.

In tracing the growth of the profession in Scotland as elsewhere one meets with many difficulties. In Edinburgh it was

for long associated with the profession of law, so that we frequently find the designation of Writer applied in one place to the same individual who is in another designed Accountant. There are several instances of members of the Society of Writers to the Signet, the leading Solicitors' Society in Scotland, practising as accountants. Moreover, until comparatively recent times much accountants' work was done in solicitors' offices. Again, to a certain extent in Edinburgh, but to a greater extent in the more commercial city of Glasgow, the designation of accountant was, in early times, confounded with that of merchant, a term of much wider significance then than now.

Another difficulty arises from the inclusion in lists of accountants of the names of gentlemen who were well entitled to that designation, but who are found on enquiry to have been either entirely employed as officials by some institution, or to have been rather teachers of book-keeping and accounts than practitioners. The Darien Company, formed in 1696, had three accountants in its employment, and the various banks which were formed soon thereafter had their accountants. The Board of Excise, which, notwithstanding the union with England, continued to be a separate department in Scotland until 1834, seems to have been in the eighteenth century an important nursery of accountants, many of whom, although designed Accountants to the Excise, appear to have been at liberty to carry on independent practice.

The compilation of the lists of those who have practised the profession in Scotland, which are given as an appendix to this volume, has therefore, in regard to the earlier period embraced, been a matter of no little difficulty. The name of no one has been included as to whom there were not reasonable grounds for believing that he was in public practice, but the exercise of this censorship may have brought about the unwitting exclusion of some who were well entitled to recognition.

The first *Directory* of Edinburgh was published in 1778,

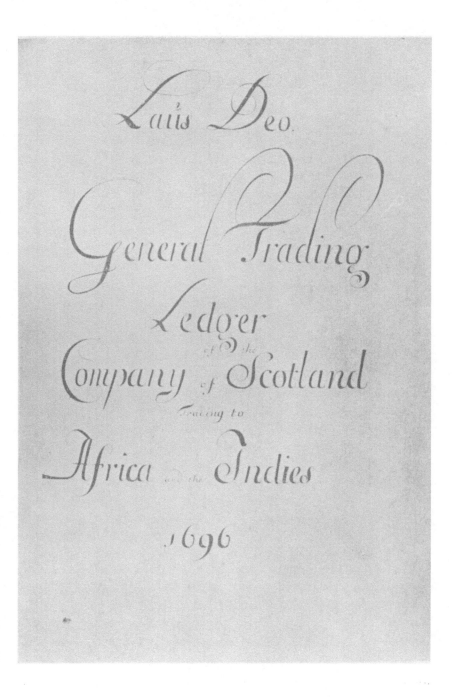

TITLE PAGE OF LEDGER OF THE "DARIEN" COMPANY, 1696
(size of original 20½ inches by 14 inches)
In the Advocates' Library, Edinburgh

and the series has been continued to the present day, although at the first one issue was sometimes made to serve for two or three years.   The *Directory* of 1773 contains the names of seven persons in Edinburgh who are designed accountants, but the lists in this first issue were admittedly incomplete. In the volume for the following year there are found the names of fourteen persons described as accountants.   The earliest separate list of accountants in Edinburgh which has been found is contained in *The British Almanack and Universal Scots Register* for 1805, and there are seventeen individuals included there.   In Glasgow the first *Directory* appeared in 1783, and it contained the names of six accountants.   In the issue for 1807 the number had risen to ten.   From these dates it is possible to give a complete list of those designing themselves accountants, but prior thereto it is only from miscellaneous sources that information can be obtained.

The first professional accountant in Scotland of whom we have been able to discover any trace is George Watson, who founded George Watson's Hospital, from which charitable foundation have sprung two of the largest and most efficient educational institutions of Edinburgh, as well as, in association with Daniel Stewart's Hospital, the Chair of Commercial and Political Economy and Mercantile Law in Edinburgh University.   George Watson was born in Edinburgh in 1645, the son of a merchant there.   His grandfather "and others their predecessors, were likewise merchants of good account and substance in the place."   His father dying early, George Watson was cast upon the care of his aunt, Elizabeth Watson, Lady Curryhill, and after he was bred at schools and had served an apprenticeship to a merchant she sent him abroad to Holland "for his further improvement in merchandising and particularly for his learning book-keeping, which then was a very rare accomplishment."   George Watson's exercise-books in writing, arithmetic, and book-keeping are still preserved.[1]

[1] See Part I. Chapter VI. p. 156.

On his return to Scotland in 1676 he was taken into the service of Sir James Dick of Prestonfield, sometime Provost of Edinburgh, who was then a merchant of great business, as his accomptant and cashier. Lady Curryhill having provided her nephew with a "little stock" of his own, Sir James Dick allowed him to negotiate bills for himself, and to carry on his own separate trade and business.

He continued "in that station for about 20 years, and having obtained from Sir James a very ample discharge, acknowledging his faithful service, he left his family in the year 1696.

"He was so much reputed for his book-keeping and distinct stating of accounts, that he was employed by several corporations and public societies; and particularly he was chosen accomptant to the Bank of Scotland when it was first erected, and was employed as cashier for receiving the town of Edinburgh's impost on ale for many years, and was also for some years appointed Treasurer for the Merchant Maiden Hospital, and was Treasurer for the Society erected for the Propagation of Christian Knowledge in Scotland, immediately after Sir Hugh Cunningham of Bonington, sometime Provost of Edinburgh, from 4th January 1711 to 26th March 1723, when he demitted some days before his death; and in all these stations he acquitted himself with a great deal of integrity, faithfulness, and diligence, as appears from the several discharges he had from these corporations.

"These were not stations by which he could have any gain, his service therein being most partly gratis, for the public use and advantage. But he did not neglect his own private business while he had these public trusts. His inclination led him chiefly to factory business, and dealing in bills of exchange with correspondents, particularly at London; and the greatest part of his fortune he made in that sort of business. And in all these affairs he had a particular faculty of keeping things very distinct, so that he cleared very fairly, and without any contest, with all those he dealt with."

Laus Deo in Rotterdam

Balance Debet

1674			L	β	d
20 October	A: Cassa	1	1412	5	—
dito	A: Rogge voor Lasten 18	2	210	—	
dito	A: Lemmael voor Stucken 3	3	15	12	6
dito	A: Jacob Jansz Fortuyn	3	1200	—	
dito	A: Jaques de Colonalr	4	101	10	—
dito	A: Armosynen voor Stuck 6	6	169	8	
dito	A: Damasten voor Stucken 5	8	178	—	
dito	A: Gillis Hoofman tot Hamb: myn reeck: Courant		33		
dito	A: Michiel Pieterz syn reeckeninge by my en de Compagnie op Weest Indien	20	22	10	
	A: Capitael van de Compagnie op Weest Indien	20	87	10	
dito	A: Derck Teulenck	22	178	10	—
dito	A: Scheeps part genamt St Jacob	23	82	—	
dito	A: Bartholomeus Beerekman	24	53	5	6
	Somma		3735	11	—

Laus Deo in Rotterdam

Balance Credd

1674			L	β	d
20 October	Pr Capitael	2	2911	17	10
dito	Pr Pieter Backer tot Alckmaer	8	173	6	8
dito	Pr Arent van Buyl	11	168	13	
dito	Pr Gillis Hoofman tot Ham syn reeck courant	14	110	—	2
dito	Pr Michiel Pieters syn reeckeninge by my en de Compagnie op Weest Indien	20	37	10	—
dito	Pr Capitael van de Compagnie op Weest Indien	20	52	10	
dito	Pr Isack Sollemans	22	175	—	
dito	Pr Regnier Reael	24	166	13	4
	Somma		3735	11	—

TRIAL BALANCE FROM GEORGE WATSON'S EXERCISE BOOK, 1674 (reduced)

In the possession of the Edinburgh Merchant Company

" Mr. Watson, never having been married, . . . he soon came, by his own great diligence and frugality, to have a tolerable stock of his own," though " when his riches increased he also increased his charities to the indigent, but in such a way as little noise was made about them; which, besides what he gave at other times, he ordinarily distributed at the balancing of his books."

" He did own that he had gained his fortune amongst the Merchants of Edinburgh, and being resolved to make some charitable foundation, he thought it reasonable to provide for the maintenance and education of the children of decayed merchants, especially of those of the Company of Merchants of the City of Edinburgh, where he was born and bred, and among whom he had made his fortune; and likewise because that he was descended of those who were for so many generations of the order and calling of Merchants in Edinburgh, and that he was so nearly related to several of the same employment.

" And having been successful in the improvement of his fortune by the help of his education in Accompting and Bookkeeping, he did particularly recommend that care should be taken that the children of the said Hospital should be educated in these arts : and also reflecting on the small stock his aunt gave him to begin his business withal, and how useful it was to him, he recommended that some provision of that kind should be made in favour of the boys of this Hospital."

He died on 3rd April 1723.

The foregoing particulars have been derived from a memoir of George Watson written in 1725. His portrait, painted by William Aikman, an eminent Scottish portrait painter of that time, adorns the Hall of the Edinburgh Merchant Company, and is reproduced as the frontispiece to this volume. His countenance expresses his kindly qualities, and his account-books show his exact and careful habits.

The next important accountant in Edinburgh of whom we find record is Alexander Chalmers, Accomptant, and latterly Accountant-General, to the Board of Excise. Mr. Chalmers also held the position of Accountant to the City of Edinburgh from 1717 to 1759. When the Church of Scotland in 1744 established a Fund for the Widows and Orphans of its Ministers, Mr. Chalmers was employed to prepare a Table of Interest, and he also laid down a plan for the keeping of the general books of the Fund, and was associated with George Drummond, Esq., Lord Provost of Edinburgh, and the Rev. Mr. Matthew Stewart, Professor of Mathematics there, in an examination of the calculations upon which the contributions and benefits were founded, which they certified to be "every way just and as well founded as the nature of the thing will admit." For making up the Table of Interest Mr. Chalmers was allowed £3 3s., and in 1748 "The Trustees considering the great Labour and Pains Mr. Alexander Chalmers has been at since commencement of the scheme, and particularly in Examination of the present Calculations, agreed that he have a Gratification of fifteen Guineas on that Account, and a copy of the said Calculations."

Mr. Chalmers died at Birmingham on 13th September 1760 while on a tour for his health.

A family of eminence as accountants in Edinburgh in the eighteenth century were the Farquharsons of Haughton in Aberdeenshire. The first of whom we hear much is Francis, who died about 1770. He is several times referred to in Sir William Forbes' "Memoirs of a Banking House," written in 1804. He was the friend and adviser of Sir William's father, and Sir William, in his Memoirs, makes frequent acknowledgment of the good guidance of Mr. Farquharson in reference to his own education and up-bringing. He was succeeded, both in his estate and business, by his nephew Alexander Ogilvie, who took the name of Farquharson. Of him Sir William, speaking of the year 1788, writes, "After revolving for a considerable time in my mind a subject to us so momentous" (the assumption of a new partner) "and consulting with my friend Mr. Farquharson, the accountant, to whose counsel I had been long accustomed to resort on every emergency, I fixed on Mr. Samuel Anderson, merchant in Edinburgh, as a gentleman who appeared to be well suited for us."

Alexander Farquharson seems to have carried on an important business as an accountant. Reports by him on some of the estates forfeited in consequence of the Jacobite risings are preserved in the General Register House, and lands belonging to Sir George Clerk of Penicuik were in 1782 conveyed by Sir George to Alexander Farquharson as Trustee for his creditors. He died in 1788, and was succeeded by his son Francis, of whom it is written he " was an intimate friend and adviser of the Gordon family, and on terms of a confidential character with both the Duke and Duchess during their estrangement; he acted as a mediator and arbiter in many of the disputes between them, and had the entire confidence of both parties." The Duchess referred to was Jane Maxwell, the famous Duchess, the patron of Burns and the friend of Pitt, a woman of extraordinary ability and force of character, of whom the first historical glimpse we have is careering down the High Street of Edinburgh on the back of a large sow, which her sister belaboured from behind. She wielded for a time great political and social influence, and could boast that she was the mother or mother-in-law of four Dukes. Her letters to Francis Farquharson, written in 1804 and 1805, which were privately printed in Glasgow in 1864, with an introduction by " J.W.G.," are highly characteristic of the lady.

About the middle of the eighteenth century it is recorded that Archibald Trotter, who had been a partner in the famous banking house of Coutts, Trotter, & Co., along with Sir William Forbes, tried to establish himself in business as an accountant, but with indifferent success. He apparently found more profitable employment in Glasgow in collecting a large number of the notes of one bank at the instance of another and rival concern, and presenting them for payment in specie all at one time, with the view, if possible, of bringing the bank to discredit. These tactics were met by the bank which was assailed paying over the specie in exchange for the notes in threepenny pieces, which the teller counted twice over in a very leisurely fashion. As a result of these proceedings litigation between the banks ensued, in which Trotter testified that he had on occasions to attend during business hours every day for more than a month before he could obtain full payment of the notes he presented.

Thomas Boswall, Accountant, Custom House Stairs, was Captain of the Honourable Company of Edinburgh Golfers in 1758 and died about 1778. James Balfour, Accomptant in Edinburgh, acted as Secretary of that ancient and distinguished Club for several years prior to his death in 1795. Of him many amusing anecdotes are told, and we quote the following from Dr. Robert Chambers' "Traditions of Edinburgh."

"One of the most notable jolly fellows of the last age was James Balfour, an accountant, usually called Singing Jamie Balfour, on account of his fascinating qualities as a vocalist. There used to be a portrait of him in the Leith Golf House, representing him in the act of commencing the favourite song of ' When I ha'e a Saxpence under my Thoom,' with the suitable attitude, and a merriness of countenance justifying the traditionary account of the man. Of Jacobite leanings, he is said to have sung 'The Wee German Lairdie'; 'Awa, Whigs, Awa'; and 'The Sow's Tail to Geordie,' with a degree of zest there was no resisting.

"Report speaks of this person as an amiable, upright, and able man ; so clever in business matters that he could do as much in one hour as another man in three; always eager to quench and arrest litigation rather than to promote it ; and consequently so much esteemed, professionally, that he could get business whenever he chose to undertake it, which, however, he only did when he felt himself in need of money. Nature had given him a robust constitution, which enabled him to see out three sets of boon-companions, but, after all, gave way before he reached sixty. His custom, when anxious to repair the effects of intemperance, was to wash his head and hands in cold water; this, it is said, made him quite cool and collected almost immediately. Pleasure being so predominant an object in his life, it was thought surprising that at his death he was found in possession of some little money.

"The powers of Balfour as a singer of Scotch songs of all kinds, tender and humorous, are declared to have been marvellous, and he had a happy gift of suiting them to occasions. Being a great peacemaker, he would often accomplish his purpose by introducing some ditty pat to the purpose, and thus dissolving all rancour in a hearty laugh. Like too many of our countrymen he had a contempt for foreign music. One evening, in a company where an Italian vocalist of eminence was present, he professed to give a song in the manner of that country. Forth came a ridiculous cantata to the tune of Aiken Drum, beginning, 'There was a Wife in Peebles,' which the wag executed with all the proper graces, shakes, and appoggiaturas, making his friends almost expire with suppressed laughter at the contrast between the style of singing and the ideas conveyed in the song. At the conclusion their mirth was doubled by the foreigner saying very simply, 'De music be very fine, but I no understand de words.'

"A lady, who lived in the Parliament Close, told a friend of mine that she was wakened from her sleep one summer morning by a noise as of singing, when, going to the window to learn what was the matter, guess her surprise at seeing Jamie Balfour and some of his boon-companions (evidently fresh from their wonted orgies) singing 'The King shall enjoy his own again,' on their knees, around King Charles's statue. One of Balfour's favourite haunts was a humble kind of tavern called Jenny Ha's, opposite to Queensberry House, where, it is said, Gay had boosed during his short stay in Edinburgh, and to which it was customary for gentlemen to adjourn from dinner-parties in order to indulge

in claret from the butt, free from the usual domestic re-
straints. Jamie's potations here were principally of what
was called cappie ale, that is, ale in little wooden bowls,
with wee thochts of brandy in it. But indeed no one could
be less exclusive than he as to liquors. When he heard a
bottle drawn in any house he happened to be in, and observed the cork to give an unusually smart report, he would
call out, 'Lassie, gi'e me a glass o' that,' as knowing that,
whatever it was, it must be good of its kind.

"Sir Walter Scott says, in one of his droll little missives
to his printer Ballantyne, 'When the press does not follow
me I get on slowly and ill, and put myself in mind of Jamie
Balfour, who could run when he could not stand still.' He
here alludes to a matter of fact, which the following anecdote
will illustrate: Jamie, in going home late from a debauch,
happened to tumble into the pit formed for the foundation of
a house in James's Square. A gentleman passing heard his
complaint, and going up to the spot was entreated by our hero
to help him out. 'What would be the use of helping you
out,' said the by-passer, 'when you could not stand though
you were out?' 'Very true, perhaps, yet if you help me up
I'll run you to the Tron Kirk for a bottle of claret.' Pleased
with his humour the gentleman placed him upon his feet,
when instantly he set off for the Tron Church at a pace
distancing all ordinary competition, and accordingly he won
the race, though at the conclusion he had to sit down on the
steps of the church, being quite unable to stand. After taking
a minute or two to recover his breath—'Well, another race
to Fortune's for another bottle of claret!' Off he went to
the tavern in question, in the Stamp-office Close, and this bet
he gained also. The claret, probably with continuations, was
discussed in Fortune's, and the end of the story is that Balfour
sent his new friend home in a chair, utterly done up, at an
early hour in the morning."

It may be mentioned that Jamie's burlesque, "There was a
Wife in Peebles," is still well known and sung in that locality.

JAMES BALFOUR

(c) 1735-1795

The Honourable Company of Golfers had Jamie's portrait painted for themselves by a distinguished member of the club, Sir Henry Raeburn. The following is Dr. John Brown's description of it: " Jamie Balfour in the act of singing ' When I hae a Saxpence under my Thoom'—you hear the refrain ' Toddlin' hame, toddlin' hame, round as a neep she cam' toddlin' hame.' Mr. Melville of Hanley, with whom have perished so many of the best Edinburgh stories, used to tell how he got this picture, which for many years hung and sang in his hospitable dining-room. It was bought at the selling-off of the effects of the old Leith Golf House by a drunken old caddy for 30s. Mr. Melville heard of this, went to the ancient creature, and got it for 40s. and two bottles of whisky. James Stuart of Dunearn offered him (Mr. Melville) £80 and two pipes of wine for it, but in vain. Sir David Wilkie coveted it also, and promised to pay for it by a picture of his own, but died before this was fulfilled." The portrait is now in the possession of Mrs. Babington, Mr. Melville's daughter, and with her kind permission and that of Mr. Elliot of Edinburgh, who published some years ago a collection of Raeburn's portraits, we are enabled to reproduce it here.

The following extracts from the Record Book of the Honourable Company of Edinburgh Golfers, relating to James Balfour, were printed in " Golf: A Royal and Ancient Game," edited by Robert Clark, F.R.S.E., London 1893 :—

November 14, 1795.

Mr. James Balfour, Secretary and Treasurer to the Society, having died on Tuesday, 20th October last, no Meeting has been held until the present, that has convened in consequence of the following Advertisement, which was repeated in all the Edinburgh Newspapers :—

" EDINBURGH GOLF CLUB

" A General Meeting of the Club is to be held, in Memory of their late worthy Secretary, in the Golf House, Leith, upon Saturday the 14th inst. The Members who mean to attend are requested to send their names to the Golf House on the Wednesday preceding. And it is expected they will appear in Mourning."

Accordingly appeared :—
Robert Allan, Esq., present Captain, in the Chair.
The Right Hon. Sir James Stirling, Bart., Lord Provost of the City of Edinburgh.
And 27 others. All dressed in mourning, agreeable to the Advertisement.
Immediately after Dinner the Captain gave the following Toasts :—

I. The Health of the Company.
> Then rising up slowly, which the Company also did, said—I well know you all feel with me on the melancholy cause of this meeting, and will join in dedicating this glass.

II. To the Memory of our Worthy and late departed Friend, Mr. James Balfour, whose benevolent and cheerful dispositions, and happy social powers, while they captivated all, particularly endeared him to his numerous friends.
> Being again seated, after a pause—

III. Comfort and Consolation to the Friends and Relatives of Mr. Balfour.

IV. May the Offices of this Society held by Mr. Balfour be agreeably supplied and attended to with that accuracy and precision for which he was peculiarly distinguished.
> During this solemnity, which was truly affecting, a profound silence was observed.
> The Captain then proceeded to general Toasts.

In the course of conversation it was early proposed by the Captain, and unanimously agreed to by the company, to have an Engraving of Mr. Balfour taken from the striking portrait or painting of him, the property of the Company, done by Mr. Raeburn,[1] to be executed by a first-rate artist; and for that purpose a Subscription Paper was opened under the following title :—

> " Subscribers for a print of Mr. James Balfour. The money paid to be accounted for by Mr. Robert Allan, present Captain of the Golf, agreeable to his initials."
> Proof, £1 1s.   Other Copy, 10s. 6d.

---

[1] In 1793, for which Raeburn got £31 10s.

The whole Company having subscribed, some for more copies than one, and for friends, the total was forty-five proof copies at one guinea each, and four other copies at 10s. 6d. each.

And for obtaining the work done in such way and manner as might be judged most eligible, the fullest powers were given to the following, named a Committee, viz:—

Capt. ROBERT ALLAN.	Mr. HENRY RAEBURN.
Sir JAMES STIRLING, Bart.	And six others.

David Russell was an eminent solicitor and accountant of those days, and he died in 1782. He was a Royal Archer and a member of the Musical Society of Edinburgh. David Herd, a well-known collector of Scottish Songs and Ballads, was his principal clerk and enjoyed his full confidence. Herd also carried on occasional business transactions for himself, undertook book-revising and copying, and saved money and time enough to be able to indulge in his literary and antiquarian propensities. He kept the accounts of the Cape Club, one of the famous convivial clubs of Edinburgh, and was a "Knight Companion of the Cape." He was born in Marykirk in October 1732. He became clerk to David Russell in the seventeen-sixties, and died in Edinburgh on 10th June 1810, unmarried.[1] He is one of those who was generally designated a Writer in contemporary publications.

David Russell was succeeded in business by his nephew Claud, who was a school-fellow of Sir Walter Scott, and is several times referred to in Lockhart's life of the great novelist. Claud Russell died in 1846, aged seventy-seven. There appears to have been another David Russell, accountant in Edinburgh, who died about 1799. He was Trustee for Mr. William Hay of Newhall, and in 1783 sold that estate to Mr. Robert Brown, advocate.

Another family of note as accountants in Edinburgh were the Keiths of Ravelston. William Keith, the son of Alexander Keith of Dunottar and Ravelston, was born in

---

[1] See introduction to "Songs from David Herd's Manuscripts," by Dr. Hans Hecht. Edinburgh, 1904.

1748 and died in 1803.   His wife was a sister of the mother of the child Marjorie Fleming, whose father, James Fleming, was an accountant in Kirkcaldy.   Mrs. Keith and Sir Walter Scott were friends and near neighbours, and we read in Dr. John Brown's inimitable sketch of Pet Marjorie how Scott when weary of work would call at Mrs. Keith's and carry off the quaint child in the neuk of his plaid to revel in her queer sayings and doings.   William Keith's business was continued by his elder brother, Alexander Keith, W.S., and by his son William, the founder of the firm of Keith, Christie, & Horne.

Of the other prominent accountants practising in Edinburgh before the date of the Charter mention may be made of John Buchan, who afterwards became Accomptant to the General Post-Office in Scotland and died in 1808 (he was the great-grandfather of a prominent London accountant of the present day, Mr. W. C. Jackson, F.C.A.); Mr. James Bruce, who, besides his general practice, was City Accountant to Edinburgh from 1796 to 1825; Mr. John Stuart, who carried on business from 1784 to 1836, and was a member of the Board of Trustees; and Mr. Charles Selkrig, who had one of the largest practices in Edinburgh from 1786 till his death in 1837.   A marble bust of this distinguished man by Laurence Macdonald, which is in the hall of the Society of Accountants in Edinburgh, was presented in 1864 by Mrs. Tod, the widow of John Robert Tod, W.S., who was a nephew of Mrs. Selkrig.   A photograph of the bust is given opposite this page. Mr. Selkrig acted as trustee on many large estates, the owners of which had got into difficulties, and his name is said to occur more frequently in the title-deeds of properties in Scotland than that of any other accountant.   He was on one occasion awarded what was then considered to be the largest fee ever earned by an accountant, something like £20,000.   His partner was Mr. Patrick Cockburn, who died in the same year.   Mr. Cockburn was the first Auditor of the Scottish Widows' Fund.   Mr. William Scott Moncrieff, of New Halls and Fossoway, was a leading Edinburgh accountant from

CHARLES SELKRIG
(c) 1760–1837

WILLIAM PAUL
1786–1848

JAMES BROWN
1786–1864

THOMAS MANSFIELD
1800–1868

1800 to 1846. His second son David and his fourth son John, who died in 1899, continued the business, which still exists as the firm of Scott Moncrieff, Thomson, & Shiells. Andrew Girvan was another leading accountant of the first half of the nineteenth century, and William Gallaway, whose portrait figures in Crombie's " Modern Athenians." Gallaway was a very tall man, an ardent volunteer, and he died in 1851 at the age of eighty. Adam Thomson, brother of the Rev. John Thomson of Duddingston, the well-known landscape painter, also practised as an accountant in Edinburgh from 1819 to 1848.

Others who may be mentioned are William Paul,—whose portrait is reproduced from a silhouette [1]—a partner of Lindsay Mackersy, and afterwards of William Moncreiff, in whose office quite an exceptional number of well-known men were trained, including William Thomas Thomson, John McKenzie, William Spens, and Patrick Brodie, all of whom became managers of leading Scottish banks or insurance companies.

The extensive and successful formation of life insurance companies in Scotland during the first half of the nineteenth century was largely organised by accountants. In those days there was no separate profession of actuary, and the accountant profession appears to have embraced practically all the actuarial skill of the period. We have seen how Alexander Chalmers was employed in connection with the formation of the Ministers' Widows' Fund, which was the first fund of the kind in Scotland, and preceded life assurance. It was followed in 1748 by that of the Excise, and it is a fair assumption that Mr. Chalmers, being Accountant of the Excise, had a good deal to do with its formation also. James Cleghorn, an eminent Edinburgh accountant of the early part of the nineteenth century, was responsible for the calculations on which the Fund for the members of the Faculty of Advocates and others of like nature were founded. He was author of a treatise on Widows' Funds published in

[1] See p. 194.

1833, and founder of the Scottish Provident Institution, though he died almost before it commenced business. The first four Managers of the Scottish Widows' Fund all commenced life as professional accountants, viz.: William Wotherspoon, John McKean, Samuel Raleigh, C.A., and John McKenzie. Its present Assistant-Secretary is a member of the Society of Accountants in Edinburgh. The Scottish Provident Institution has only had two Managers since the first year after its formation, both of them qualified accountants. At the present time the Manager, Secretary, and Assistant-Secretary are members of the Edinburgh C.A. Society. The first Manager of the Scottish Equitable was Robert Christie, and the second George Todd, both accountants. The Standard Insurance Company had for Managers James A. Cheyne and William Thomas Thomson, who both began life as accountants. Its present Manager and its London Manager are Edinburgh Chartered Accountants. William Low and Robert Rainie, both accountants, were respectively Manager and Secretary of the Life Association of Scotland, of which the present Manager is a C.A. George Mylne and David Maclagan, successive Managers of the Edinburgh Life Assurance Company, Archibald Borthwick, first Manager of the City of Glasgow Assurance Company, Robert Balfour, the Edinburgh Secretary thereof, H. D. Dickie, Secretary and afterwards Manager of the Caledonian Insurance Company, William Spens, the Manager of the Scottish Amicable, Holmes Ivory, the Manager of the Scottish National, and George Ramsay, the Manager of the Scottish Union, were all professional accountants.

This is a remarkable record, which could easily be augmented, and is a proof both of the actuarial knowledge possessed by Edinburgh accountants, and of the value of such a knowledge, which has all along been required as a condition of admission to the society.

In concluding this sketch of early Edinburgh accountants

no apology is necessary for quoting the following long extract from a letter of Sir Walter Scott, as showing the position occupied by the profession in that City in the early part of last century, and as a characteristic example of wise and kindly counsel, which is just as appropriate in the present day as when it was written.

The letter is dated 23rd July 1820, from Abbotsford, and is addressed to Thomas Scott, Esq., Paymaster, 70th Regiment, Sir Walter's brother :—

After my own sons, my most earnest and anxious wish will be, of course, for yours,—and with this view I have pondered well what you say on the subject of your Walter; and whatever line of life you may design him for, it is scarce possible but that I can be of considerable use to him. Before fixing, however, on a point so very important, I would have you consult the nature of the boy himself. I do not mean by this that you should ask his opinion, because at so early an age a well bred up child naturally takes up what is suggested to him by his parents; but I think you should consider, with as much impartiality as a parent can, his temper, disposition, and qualities of mind and body. It is not enough that you think there is an opening for him in one profession rather than another,—for it were better to sacrifice the fairest prospects of that kind than to put a boy into a line of life for which he is not calculated. If my nephew is steady, cautious, fond of a sedentary life and quiet pursuits, and at the same time a proficient in arithmetic, and with a disposition towards the prosecution of its highest branches, he cannot follow a better line than that of an accountant. It is highly respectable—and is one in which, with attention and skill, aided by such opportunities as I may be able to procure for him, he must ultimately succeed. I say ultimately—because the harvest is small and the labourers numerous in this as in other branches of our legal practice; and whoever is to dedicate himself to them, must look for a long and laborious tract of attention ere he reaches the reward of his labours. If I live, however, I will do all I can for him, and see him put under a proper person, taking his 'prentice fee, &c., upon myself. But if, which may possibly be the case, the lad has a decided turn for active life and adventure, is high-spirited, and impatient of long and dry labour, with some of those feelings not unlikely to result from having lived all his life in a camp or a barrack, do not deceive yourself, my dear brother—you will never make him an accountant; you will never be able to convert such a sword into a pruning-hook, merely because you think a pruning-hook the better thing of the two. In this supposed case, your authority and my recommendation might put him into an accountant's office; but it would be just to waste the earlier years of his life in idleness, with all the temptations to dissipation which idleness gives way to; and what sort of a place a writing-chamber is, you cannot but remember. So years might wear away, and at last the youth starts off from his profession, and becomes an adventurer too late in life, and with the disadvantage, perhaps, of offended friends and advanced age standing in the way of his future prospects.[1]

It may be of interest to add that young Walter was not placed in an accountant's office. In 1822 Scott, in writing to his own son who was in the Army, says of his nephew Walter—"The little fellow studies hard . . . if you do not take care he may be a General before you." He died a General in 1873.

Of early Glasgow accountants we have not much trace.

There was of course an "Accomptant" on the staff of each of the somewhat numerous banks of the period, but towards the latter end of the eighteenth century there were only a very few individuals styling themselves "Accomptants," and following the calling as a separate profession.

Unlike Edinburgh, where the business of accountant was associated with the legal profession, and where numerous matters of accounting arose in connection with the law courts, in Glasgow it had its origin as a distinctive calling in commercial circles, and it was not an uncommon thing for an individual to be designated "Merchant and Accomptant." It has to be noted that the designation "Merchant" was used somewhat generally in these early days. The general name of "Merchant" was applied to all Burgesses of Glasgow who were not comprehended by or included in the Trades rank.

A great commercial crisis visited Glasgow in 1777 as the result of the revolt in the previous year of the North American colonies, with which part of the world the trade of the city was closely identified.

---

[1] Lockhart's "Life of Scott," Vol. VI. p. 223.

Mr. Walter Ewing Maclae of Cathkin, who was designated in the earliest issues of the Glasgow *Directory* as "Merchant and Accountant," was, we are told, from the esteem and confidence in which he was held, employed to wind up some of the largest and most important of the bankruptcies which occurred in that unfortunate year.

Again, in 1798 an enormous number of bankruptcies occurred, including no less than twenty-six banking companies. Three Glasgow banks were among the failures, viz.: Thomsons' Bank, The Merchant Bank, and the Glasgow Arms Bank. It is recorded [1] that "The official Trustee for the creditors of this latter Bank (The Glasgow Arms Bank) was Walter Ewing Maclae—the well-known Merchant and Accountant." His son James Ewing, subsequently better known in the city than even his father, was then a young man in his father's office, and it is stated [1] that "the winding-up of the concern was conducted in a manner which fully justified the confidence reposed in these gentlemen, and added not a little to their own prosperity and good name. The 'Arms' eventually was enabled to meet all its liabilities and continue its business."

Mr. James Ewing became perhaps the best known public man in Glasgow during the first half of the nineteenth century. He filled the important offices of Lord Provost and Lord Dean of Guild, and was the first member of Parliament for the city under the Reform Bill.

Mr. Ewing, who in addition to the Estate of Cathkin, came into possession of the estate of Strathleven (by the title of which he became better known), had large West Indian possessions, and carried on an extensive and lucrative business —leaving accountancy to those who followed it as a distinct profession. The well-known firm of James Ewing & Co., founded by him, still exists, and holds a high position in the commercial life of Glasgow.

There are two firms of accountants still extant, the

[1] "Curiosities of Glasgow Citizenship," Stewart, 1881, p. 148.

origin of which can be traced back to the close of the
eighteenth century, viz.: Messrs. D. & A. Cuthbertson,
Provan, and Strong, and Messrs. Kerr, Andersons, and
Macleod.

Mr. William Cuthbertson—the father of Messrs. Donald
and Allan—was understood to combine the business of
accountant with that of a merchant from about the year
1787, in which year his office appears to have been situated
in Bell's Wynd. His sons were trained in his office. Donald,
the better known of the two, became his partner in 1810.
At his death in 1864, at the age of eighty-one, it was stated
in an article which appeared in the *Glasgow Herald* of the
day, that his father, William Cuthbertson, was believed to be
the man "who originated the profession of accountant (as
a separate calling, we presume) in this City."

Be that as it may, Mr. Donald Cuthbertson, LL.B., his
eldest son,[1] was a distinguished student both at the High
School and the University, and he retained throughout his
life a warm interest in these institutions. He served as a
Town Councillor and Magistrate of the City. He was one
of the first Directors and for many years Auditor of the
Scottish Amicable Life Assurance Society.

Of all his public employments he was identified most
with the Gartnavel Royal Asylum for Lunatics, which was
founded in 1810. From the commencement he took a deep
interest in its establishment and progress, and at its opening
in 1814 he was appointed Secretary and Treasurer, which
offices he held till his death in 1864.

The business originated, as above stated, by William
Cuthbertson, towards the end of the eighteenth century, is
still carried on at the beginning of the twentieth century
under the firm name above given, and the Secretary and
Treasurership of the Gartnavel Asylum is still held by one
of the partners.

Mr. James Kerr[2] began business as an accountant in

<hr>
[1] See portrait opposite.   [2] See portrait opposite.

DONALD CUTHBERTSON
1782–1864

JAMES KERR
1782–1842

JAMES McLELLAND
1799–1879

PETER WHITE
1810–1881

the year 1805. He was trained in the office of David Kay, who had been in practice, it is believed, for some time before the close of the eighteenth century, and it is probable that Mr. Kerr entered his service before the old century had expired. His son Henry was trained in his office, and in 1842 was assumed as a partner along with the late William Anderson, under the firm name of Kerrs & Anderson. The firm name has undergone numerous changes as partners have been assumed and as partners have died, but the name of Kerr, which connects it with the distant past, still continues to be the leading name in the present day firm of Kerr, Andersons, & Macleod. We have thus, in the names of Cuthbertson and Kerr, the accountant profession in Glasgow of the eighteenth century linked with that of the twentieth.

It may be of interest to quote here, as a very full compendium of the kind of work which a Glasgow accountant of the early part of last century professed to undertake, the list of duties which Mr. James McClelland (who will be afterwards referred to) attached to the circular, dated 12th March 1824, in which he announced that he had commenced business on his own account :—

Factor and trustee on sequestrated estates.

Trustee or factor for trustees of creditors acting under trust deeds.

Factor for trustees acting for the heirs of persons deceased.

Factor for gentlemen residing in the country for the management of heritable or other property.

Agent for houses in England and Scotland connected with bankruptcies in Glasgow.

The winding up of dissolved partnership concerns and the adjusting of partners' accounts.

The keeping and balancing of all account-books belonging to merchants, manufacturers, shopkeepers, &c.

The examining and adjusting of all disputed accounts and account-books.

The making up of statements, reports, and memorials on account-books or disputed accounts and claims for the purpose of laying before arbiters, courts, or counsel.

The looking after and recovering old debts and dividends from bankrupt estates.

And all other departments of the accountant business.

In Aberdeen and Dundee the profession of accountant was in early days a good deal associated with that of the local solicitor. No accountants appear as such in the Aberdeen *Directory* for 1825, but six names appear in the *Directory* for 1837 and eight in 1847. In Dundee the first public accountant appears in the *Directory* of 1829, and a " Writing-master and Accountant" appears in 1834. In the *Directory* for 1840 two gentlemen are designed "Writer & Accountant." When accountants were first separately classified in the Dundee *Directory* in 1845 twelve names are given, but five of these were accountants in banks, &c., leaving seven public accountants.

In 1820 William Kennedy (1758–1836), Advocate (as solicitors are designed in Aberdeen), made an elaborate report on the town's affairs. John Smith (1798–1884), Advocate, was designed accountant from 1831, and became the first President of the Aberdeen Society of Accountants when it was formed in 1867. Of the older Dundee accountants John Sturrock, Junr., began business about 1834, and gathered an extensive business both as Writer and Accountant. William Myles commenced practice as a Public Accountant in 1842, and was for many years the leading accountant in Dundee.

In Perth the first accountant of any standing was Mr. James Morison, who about 1827 founded the business of J. & R. Morison which is still carried on there. In Kirkcaldy James Fleming had a good business as an accountant about the end of the eighteenth century.[1]

Other eminent Scottish accountants of the early part of last century who lived to become members of the societies will be more appropriately referred to in the next chapter.

[1] See "The Story of Pet Marjorie," L. Macbean, 1903.

CHAPTER III

SCOTTISH CHARTERED ACCOUNTANTS

FORMATION OF THE EDINBURGH SOCIETY—INCORPORATION BY
ROYAL CHARTER—FORMATION OF THE GLASGOW INSTI-
TUTE AND INCORPORATION BY ROYAL CHARTER—EXA-
MINATION OF CANDIDATES—GENERAL EXAMINING BOARD
—ADOPTION OF PROFESSIONAL TITLE AND LETTERS C.A.—
INTEREST OF THE SOCIETIES IN PUBLIC AFFAIRS—LEGIS-
LATION FOR ACCOUNTANTS—LECTURES—PUBLICATIONS—
MEMBERSHIP—QUALIFICATIONS FOR ADMISSION—HALL
AND LIBRARY OF THE EDINBURGH SOCIETY—EVENING
CLASSES—ENDOWMENT AND ANNUITY FUND—THE AC-
COUNTANTS' COMPANY VOLUNTEER BRIGADE—STUDENTS'
SOCIETY—DECEASED PRESIDENTS—HALL AND LIBRARY OF
THE GLASGOW INSTITUTE—CLASSES—STUDENTS' SOCIETY
—SOCIAL FUNCTIONS—DECEASED PRESIDENTS—SHARE IN
VOLUNTEER MOVEMENT—INCORPORATION OF ABERDEEN
SOCIETY—STUDENTS' SOCIETY—WIDOWS' FUND

THE first step towards the formation of a Society of
Accountants in Edinburgh was taken on 17th January 1853,
when Mr. Alexander Weir Robertson, as arranged with one
or two of his professional brethren, issued the following
Circular to fourteen practising Accountants :—

15 DUNDAS STREET, 17th January 1853.

Several gentlemen connected with our profession have resolved to
bring about some definite arrangement for uniting the professional
Accountants in Edinburgh, and should you be favourable thereto I
have to request your attendance in my Chambers here on Thursday
next, the 20th Inst., at 2 o'clock.

In response to this Circular the following gentlemen invited assembled on the date named, making, with Mr. Robertson, eight present at the Meeting: Messrs. Archibald Borthwick, John Scott Moncrieff, Thomas Martin, Kenneth McKenzie, Samuel Raleigh, George Meldrum, and William Wood. Mr. Charles Pearson intimated that a prior engagement prevented him attending. Mr. Archibald Borthwick was called to the Chair, and stated that the Meeting was aware that various attempts had from time to time been made to incorporate the accountants in Edinburgh, but that such attempts had hitherto proved fruitless. That the failure was to be attributed to several causes, but that it had appeared to him and other gentlemen that means might be followed now, whereby this very desirable object might be accomplished. With this view, therefore, it had been resolved to use every effort to form a Society of those gentlemen who were recognised by the profession generally as carrying on the business exclusively of accountants in Edinburgh, and for this purpose there had been prepared and would now be read for the consideration of the Meeting a sketch of a Constitution and Rules for the formation and regulation of such an Association. The Meeting, after a careful revisal of the proposed Constitution and Rules, requested Mr. Robertson to have the same immediately put in type for further consideration, and to summon another Meeting for Saturday next, in order that the other necessary steps for constituting the Association be taken without delay.

The second Meeting was held on 22nd January 1853. Seven out of the eight gentlemen present at the previous Meeting again attended, and the following in addition: Messrs. J. J. Dickson, J. S. Ogilvy, Thomas Scott, William Moncreiff, J. M. Macandrew, and Richard Gordon. At this Meeting the proof print of the Constitution was fully considered and amended, and the Meeting, with the exception of one gentleman, who desired time to consider the matter, formed themselves into sections and arranged to wait upon those who were to be requested to join the Institute who had not yet been seen; and to report to Mr. Robertson so as to complete the roll of Members with as little delay as possible.

The next Meeting was held on 31st January, and was attended by forty-seven gentlemen, and one other apologised for absence owing to his having to leave town. On this occasion Mr. James Brown was unanimously called to the Chair. Mr. Archibald Borthwick stated that before putting to the Meeting the Motion which had been entrusted to him he would make a very few preliminary remarks. The idea of associating together the accountants of Edinburgh in one body was not a new one—it had originated many years ago; and although the attempt to do so had not succeeded at that time it had by no means been finally abandoned. After referring to the various important duties which the accountants practising in Edinburgh were called upon to discharge, he said he presumed there could be no difference of opinion as to the expediency of endeavouring by such an Association as that now proposed to have those important duties entrusted only to those who were qualified by their education and business acquirements to fulfil them with credit. That accordingly the plan now before the Meeting had been moved in lately, and that it had met with the approval of all the Members of the Profession to whom it had been communicated. That plan, they would observe, was for the Constitution, in the first instance, of a voluntary Association; but it would be an ultimate object, and probably at no distant period, to apply for a Charter of Incorporation conferring on the Institute the usual powers and privileges. The Institute would consist of Ordinary Members, being gentlemen practising at present in Edinburgh as Accountants; and of Honorary Members, being gentlemen who were formerly in practice as Accountants, and who now act as Managers of Life Assurance Companies or hold appointments from the Courts.

Mr. Borthwick moved: That the Institute of Accountants be held as constituted in terms of the Constitution and Laws then laid on the Table.

Mr. H. G. Watson seconded the Motion, which, having been put to the Meeting by the Chairman, was carried unanimously.

A Committee was thereafter appointed for the purpose of recommending to another General Meeting the names of Gentlemen to be elected as Office-Bearers of the Institute, and of making such suggestions as to the Constitution and Laws as might occur to them.

The next Meeting was held on 4th February 1853, Mr. James Brown again occupying the chair. At this Meeting a Report by the Committee which had been appointed was submitted, and in terms thereof the following Office-Bearers were unanimously appointed: *President:* Mr. James Brown; *Council:* Messrs. Donald Lindsay, Thomas Mansfield, Henry George Watson, Archibald Borthwick, Ralph Erskine Scott, Archibald Horne, Thomas Scott, and William Moncreiff; *Secretary:* Mr. Alexander W. Robertson; *Treasurer:* Mr. Kenneth MacKenzie. The Constitution and Laws of the Institute of Accountants in Edinburgh were finally approved. Rule No. 6 was in the following terms: New Members are admitted into the Institute at any General Meeting, Annual or Special. They must be proposed by one Member and seconded by another, and their election shall be carried by the votes of three-fourths of the Members present, ascertained by ballot. Ordinary Members were required to pay an Annual Subscription of £2 2s., and Honorary Members an Annual Subscription of £1 1s.

The first Annual Meeting of the Institute was held on 1st February 1854, and at this Meeting the President and Council reported that, in their opinion, the time had arrived when application should be made for incorporation by Royal Charter, and this being the unanimous view of the Meeting, the President and Council were empowered to take the preliminary steps. In May 1854 the Council approved of a draft Petition to Her Majesty Queen Victoria, which had been prepared by Mr. John Clerk Brodie, W.S., and at a General Meeting of the Institute held on 30th May this Petition was adopted, and was then and afterwards signed by all the Ordinary Members, fifty-four in number. The petition set forth:—

That the profession of Accountants, to which the Petitioners belong, is of long standing and great respectability, and has of late years grown into very considerable importance: That the business of Accountant, as practised in Edinburgh, is varied and extensive, embracing all matters of account, and requiring for its proper execution, not merely thorough knowledge of those departments of business which fall within the province of the Actuary, but an intimate acquaintance with the general principles of law, particularly of the law of Scotland; and more especially with those branches of it which have relation to the law of merchant, to insolvency and bankruptcy, and to all rights connected with property: That in the extrication of those numerous suits before the Court of Session, which involve directly and indirectly matters of accounting, an Accountant is almost invariably employed by the Court to aid in eliciting the trust: That such investigations are manifestly quite unsuited to such a tribunal as a Jury, yet cannot be prosecuted by the Court itself without professional assistance on which it may rely, and the Accountant, to whom in any case of this descripton a remit is made by the Court, performs in substance all the more material functions which the Petitioners understand to be performed in England by the Masters in Chancery: That Accountants are also largely employed in Judicial Remits, in cases which are peculiar to the practice of Scotland, as, for instance, in Rankings and Sales, in processes of Count and Reckoning, Multiplepoinding, and others of a similar description: That they are also most commonly selected to be Trustees on Sequestrated Estates, and under Voluntary Trusts, and in these capacities they have duties to perform, not only of the highest responsibility, and involving large pecuniary interests, but which require, in those who undertake them, great experience in business, very considerable knowledge of law, and other qualifications which can only be attained by a liberal education: That, in these circumstances, the Petitioners were induced to form themselves into a Society called the Institute of Accountants in Edinburgh, with a view to unite into one body those at present practising the profession, and to promote the objects which, as members of the

same profession, they entertain in common; and that the Petitioners con-
ceive that it would tend to secure in the members of their profession the
qualifications which are essential to the proper performance of its duties,
and would consequently conduce much to the benefit of the public if the
Petitioners who form the present body of practising Accountants in Edinburgh were united into a body corporate and politic, having a common
seal, with power to make rules and bye-laws for the qualification and
admission of members, and otherwise.

In June 1854 a draft Charter was adjusted, which it was
found necessary to present along with the Petition. At this
time the Council considering that the terms of the Petition
would not admit of the distinction between Honorary and
Ordinary Members which existed according to the Laws of
the Institute, instructed the Secretary to communicate with
all the Honorary Members with a view of affording them an
opportunity of signing the Petition as Ordinary Members if
desired. Seven of the Honorary Members signed the Petition and thus became Ordinary Members, six did not do so,
and accordingly ceased to be Members of the Institute.

The Royal Warrant for the incorporation of the Insti-
tute under the name of THE SOCIETY OF ACCOUNTANTS
IN EDINBURGH, was "Given at Her Majesty's Court at
St. James's the twenty-third day of October 1854," and
signed by Lord Palmerston by Her Majesty's command.
The Charter itself—which is a translation into Latin of the
Warrant, is dated 23rd October 1854, and "written to the
seal registered and sealed 11th December 1854"—was pre-
sented to the Society at the Meeting of President and
Council held on 18th December 1854, and to a General
Meeting of the newly constituted Society held on 29th
December 1854.

The Institute of Accountants and Actuaries in Glasgow
had its origin in a requisition drawn up in the autumn of 1853,
which was signed by twenty-seven accountants in Glasgow who
had commenced business there subsequent to 1st January 1841,
and addressed to fifteen accountants who had been practising

prior to that date. It requested these gentlemen to form themselves into a Committee or Society of Accountants, and to frame such a Constitution as may appear to them necessary for organising the same, containing Laws and regulations for the admission of Members, &c., which shall be applicable to all gentlemen who have commenced business as accountants subsequent to 1st January 1841. One reason for forming such a Society or Institute is thus stated:—

" The late changes and contemplated alterations in the Bankruptcy Law of Scotland point out, in a marked degree, the necessity and importance of now carrying the proposal into execution, in order that the practical experience of those parties who have hitherto been entrusted with the management of Bankrupt Estates in the West of Scotland may be properly represented and have due weight in determinating what changes require to be made upon the existing Bankruptcy Law."

The parties requisitioned—under the chairmanship of Mr. James McClelland, with Mr. Walter Mackenzie as Secretary, met on 3rd October 1853, and appointed a Committee of their number to meet a like Committee from the requisitionists to take the necessary steps.

By 9th November, with the assistance of Dr. Anderson Kirkwood as legal adviser, the draft Constitution was ready for approval, and the First Council of the Institute was nominated by the Senior Accountants out of their own number as follows :—*President :* James McClelland ; *Treasurer :* Peter White ; *Secretary :* Walter Mackenzie ; *Auditor :* Andrew McEwan ; *Committee :* Allan Cuthbertson, David Dreghorn, Robert Aitken, T. G. Buchanan, and William Anderson.

The Deed of Constitution of " The Institute of Accountants in Glasgow " was produced and signed on 14th November 1853. Intimation was sent to the Committee of the Requisitionists that the Institute was organised and that application for admission from all parties eligible might now be made. By the 16th of December 1853 forty-three gentlemen had been enrolled members of the Institute.

On 6th July 1854 it was decided to petition for the grant of a Royal Charter. The Petition, which was signed by forty - nine accountants in the City of Glasgow, set forth :—

That the profession of an Accountant has long existed in Scotland as a distinct profession of great respectability; that originally the number of those practising it was few, but that, for many years back, the number has been rapidly increasing, and the profession in Glasgow now embraces a numerous as well as highly respectable body of persons; that the business of an Accountant requires, for the proper prosecution of it, considerable and varied attainments; that it is not confined to the department of the Actuary, which forms indeed only a branch of it, but that, while it comprehends all matters connected with arithmetical calculation, or involving investigation into figures, it also ranges over a much wider field, in which a considerable acquaintance with the general principles of law, and a knowledge in particular of the Law of Scotland, is quite indispensable; that Accountants are frequently employed by Courts of Law, both the Sheriff Courts and the Court of Session, which is the supreme Civil Tribunal of Scotland, to aid those Courts in their investigation of matters of Accounting, which involve, to a greater or less extent, points of law of more or less difficulty; that they act under such remits very much as the Masters in Chancery are understood to act in England, and that they are also most commonly selected to be Trustees on Sequestrated Estates, and to act as Trustees under private Deeds of Trust on large landed Estates, and that in these capacities they have often to consider and determine, in the first instance, important questions of ranking and of competition between Creditors, and many other important questions of law relating to property; that it is obvious that to the due performance of a profession such as this a liberal education is essential, and that the object in view in the formation of the Institute of Accountants in Glasgow, of which the Petitioners are the Members, was to maintain the efficiency as well as the respectability of the professional body in Glasgow to which they belong; that it appears to the Petitioners that this object will be further greatly assisted by the formation of the Petitioners into a body corporate and politic, having a common Seal, with power to make regulations and bye-laws respecting the qualification and admission of Members, and other usual powers.

The Royal Warrant was given under date 15th March 1855 for the incorporation by Royal Charter of the Petitioners and such other persons as might thereafter be admitted as Members, into one body politic and corporate, by the name of THE INSTITUTE OF ACCOUNTANTS AND ACTUARIES IN GLASGOW. The Institute held a dinner on 7th December 1855 to celebrate this auspicious event.

The Charters thus obtained, besides the usual privileges, empowered each Society to make bye-laws, rules, and regulations not inconsistent with the terms of the Charter, to appoint office-bearers and to constitute and appoint a Committee of Examinators, "for the purpose of regulating and conducting such examinations of entrants and others as the Corporations might from time to time direct, and in such manner as they may appoint in furtherance of the objects of the Societies, and that the course of education to be pursued and the amount of general and professional acquirement to be exacted from entrants should be such as the Corporations should from time to time fix."

This purpose was immediately carried into effect, and both Societies made suitable arrangements for the examination of candidates for admission. The Societies from the first attached special importance to the practical experience of business obtained by service in an accountant's office, and all through their history they have insisted on this as an essential qualification for admission. They have also required the attendance of apprentices at University Law Classes, a rule which undoubtedly has had its effect in maintaining a high standard among those becoming members. The examinations of each Society proceed on similar lines, having been from time to time rendered more exacting with the general advance of education and the introduction of competitive examinations into business life. In 1892 the Societies, including the Society of Accountants in Aberdeen, which had been formed and incorporated by Royal Charter in 1867, realising that much labour was wasted in setting different examination papers for each of the three Societies, and that it was eminently desirable that the rules for admission and the standard of the examinations should be the same in all three Societies, entered into a joint agreement constituting a General Examining Board, and assimilated their rules relating to the admission of members. The arrangements made under this agreement have worked admirably, and the step has brought about the practical affiliation, for all public purposes, of the Chartered Accountants of Scotland, while at the same time each Society is left free to administer its own funds and manage its own local affairs.

Directly after its formation the Edinburgh Society deliberated upon a distinctive title for its members, and resolved to adopt the name of "Chartered Accountant," indicated by the letters "C.A." The same course was followed by the Glasgow Institute as well as by the Aberdeen Society when they were incorporated later. It naturally took some little time before the new name became familiar to the public or even in the mouths of the members themselves, but ere long it acquired a definite signification throughout Scotland, and when in 1880 the same designation was adopted by the English Institute, incorporated in that year, it soon became a recognised term wherever the English language is spoken. Efforts have been made in Scotland by other associations to obtain a right to use the designation or the abbreviate letters for professional purposes, but the Chartered Societies have successfully resisted such attempts, and obtained judgments which in effect reserve to the members of the Societies the exclusive use in Scotland of these professional designations.

In most matters of public interest the Societies have co-operated, and they have not neglected their duties or overlooked their responsibilities in that direction. As soon as it was formed the Edinburgh Institute proceeded to consider proposed changes in Scottish Bankruptcy Law. A Bill had been introduced into Parliament by the Lord Advocate and was down for second reading on 12th May 1853. The Council of the Institute drew up representations and submitted them

to the Lord Advocate.   The Act which was passed in 1853
being only of a limited and tentative nature, in 1855 very
careful consideration was given to a comprehensive measure
of bankruptcy reform, and a number of communications took
place with the Lord Advocate, who invited the views of both
the Edinburgh and Glasgow Societies.   The Bankruptcy
Act of 1856 was the outcome of these proceedings, and it
remains the governing Statute in Scotland to this day,
being generally recognised as having established an excellent
bankruptcy system.   Other matters connected with bankruptcy were frequently under the consideration of the
Councils of the Societies, such as the abuse of the privileges
of the Scottish Act by English Insolvents and the Fraudulent Debtors' Bills.   The Societies also early advocated the
placing of Judicial Factors, elected under the Act of 1711
and the Act of Sederunt of 1730, under the supervision
of the Accountant of Court, a reform which was effected
in 1889.

It does not appear that the Societies took any active
interest in the passing of the Companies Act, 1862, but they
considered very fully the various subsequent schemes of
Company Law Reform, drew up reports, and attended conferences on the subject.   A leading member of the Edinburgh
Society, the late Mr. George Auldjo Jamieson, was a member of
the Royal Commission which investigated the subject.   The
Forged Transfers Act was also carefully examined while passing
through Parliament, and assistance was given to the successful
movement for the reform of Private Bill Procedure in Scotland.
The Trust Investment Act, the two Local Government Bills
for Scotland, and other measures of more or less importance to
the profession, all received due consideration at the proper
time.

The various Bills promoted in Parliament from 1891
onwards for the better regulation of the profession of accountant naturally received very full consideration at the hands
of the Societies.   A Joint-Committee of the three Societies

in 1895 with much care and pains prepared a Bill applicable to Scotland, which was approved in its general terms at Special Meetings of the Members of each of the Societies, and was afterwards introduced in the House of Commons in two Sessions of Parliament. The Bill was backed by the Right Honourable J. B. Balfour, Mr. J. A. Campbell, Mr. R. B. Haldane, and other influential Scottish Members, but it did not satisfy all parties, and as the Government could not give facilities for the discussion of controversial measures of this nature it was not proceeded with. None of the other Bills to regulate the profession, which have been from time to time introduced in Parliament, has made any progress.

After the establishment of the English Institute of Chartered Accountants in 1880, and the Irish Institute in 1888, communications and conferences on matters of mutual interest took place with the Councils of these bodies, and a standing Joint Committee was established in 1902 composed of representatives of the Councils of the various Chartered Societies in the United Kingdom.

In 1896 the three Scottish Societies commenced the issue of an annual *Official Directory of Scottish Chartered Accountants,* which has proved of great value to the business community and most useful to the members themselves as a book of reference. In the beginning of 1897 *The Accountants' Magazine,* a monthly periodical, was first issued. This, although an independent publication, received the support of most of the leading members of the profession, and immediately secured an important place among technical periodicals. It has become the recognised vehicle of official intimations in Scotland, and has served to knit more closely together the members of the Scottish Societies wheresoever they carry on their professional practice.

For a considerable number of years the Edinburgh and Glasgow Societies, in conjunction with the Institute of Bankers in Scotland, have arranged courses of lectures, on some subject of mutual interest, which have been delivered under their auspices in Edinburgh, Glasgow, and Dundee. The subjects dealt with have included Partnership, Trust, Commercial, Banking and Company Law, several courses on economic subjects, Bank Book-keeping and Stock Exchange Securities; and as the lecturers chosen are invariably authorities in their respective subjects the lectures have been well attended and greatly appreciated.

In concluding this account of the Scottish Societies in their joint interests it may be mentioned that the aggregate membership of the three Societies now (November 1904) amounts to 906 and that these members are distributed as follows :—

Scotland	671
England and Ireland	138
British Colonies and Dependencies . .	60
United States of America . . .	20
Other Foreign Countries . . .	17

Admission to the Scottish Societies can only be obtained after a full term of service under Articles with a Chartered Accountant, and after attendance at certain University law classes. The examinations are three in number, preliminary, intermediate, and final. The first embraces the usual educational subjects, the second advanced mathematics and professional knowledge, the third law, actuarial science, political economy, and four papers on the general business of an accountant, under which are included book-keeping and all forms of accounts, auditing, bankruptcies, trusts, factorships, apportionments, administration and liquidation of companies, and judicial and private references, remits, and proofs. The examination fees are £1 1s. each for the preliminary and intermediate, and £2 2s. for the final.

In referring to the individual concerns of each Society the Society of Accountants in Edinburgh may first be dealt with.

The Society very early in its history contemplated the

acquisition of suitable premises in which to hold meetings and house a library. The views of the Society were, however, not always unanimous as to the places proposed, or even as to the immediate necessity of taking this step. Many different places were suggested, committees were appointed and negotiations took place, but for one reason or another nothing definite was done until 1891, when the premises No. 27 Queen Street were acquired. Queen Street was built as a residential district in the end of the eighteenth century, having fine gardens in front and a magnificent view over the Firth of Forth to the mountains of the north, but with the gradual removal of business chambers from the old to the new town of Edinburgh the houses came to occupy a central business position. The Society wisely decided not to touch the simple and chaste exterior of the house they acquired, but they reconstructed the interior and provided a suitable library and reading-room, a hall to contain about two hundred, a smoking-room, a writing-room, and a caretaker's house. This left untouched a large area at the back upon which at any future date it would be possible to erect a larger hall and additional library accommodation. Although the great bulk of the members had long desired the acquisition of premises, it is believed that few of them quite realised the extent to which they would be appreciated, and how important they would become in connection with the various agencies of the Society.

The library of the Society, which had been founded in 1865, did not reach large proportions until it was removed to Queen Street, but from that time it increased rapidly, and it now contains almost all the known works on book-keeping and accounts, most of the legal books bearing on the profession, including full sets of both English and Scottish decisions and a large number of actuarial and economic publications. Amongst the rarer books on book-keeping are copies of Paciolo (both editions), Tagliente, Gottlieb, Manzoni, Cardanus, Schweicker, Menher, Rocha, Casanova, Pietra, Petri, Passchier-Goessens, Grisogono, Moschetti, Buingha, Malynes,

Carpenter, Dafforne, Flori, Collins, Venturi, Venturoli, Colin-son, Hatton, De la Porte, Irson, Roose, and others. The aim of the Council is that the library should contain every book to which an accountant is ever likely to require to refer in connection with his business. A classified catalogue of the library was recently issued, and all new books added are notified monthly in *The Accountants' Magazine.* The reading-rooms are supplied with most of the periodicals re-lating to the profession, in whatever language, with the banking, insurance, and economic journals, and also with daily and weekly newspapers and magazines.

At one period the Society awarded bursaries and fellowships to the candidates taking the highest places in the intermediate and final examinations, but these were dis-continued as tending rather to an unhealthy competition than to that uniformly high standard in the examinations which the Council desired to see. For a number of years the Society has arranged Evening Classes for apprentices, which are con-ducted at 27 Queen Street. The subjects embraced are mathematics, book-keeping, actuarial science, law, and poli-tical economy, and they have been found most helpful in enabling apprentices to acquire that theoretical knowledge and book-learning which they can hardly be expected to obtain in their office work.

Proposals had early been made for the establishment of a Benevolent Fund for the assistance of unfortunate members of the Society, and in 1886 this idea took the more important shape of an Endowment and Annuity Fund, which was estab-lished by Act of Parliament in 1887. To this Fund all members of the Society are required to contribute £5 5s. per annum until the age of sixty-five. In return for this contribu-tion the member may elect to receive either an Endowment Assurance, payable at age sixty-five, a Life Annuity com-mencing at that age, or a Life Annuity payable to any widow he may leave. The amount of the benefit varies according to the age of the contributor at entry, and, in the case of a widow's annuity, the age of his wife. A considerable portion of the Society's accumulated funds was paid over to the Endowment and Annuity Fund at its formation, and one half of the entry money of all new members is also paid over to it, so that at its quinquennial investigations the Trustees of the Fund have so far been able to declare satisfactory bonus additions to the benefits. The Fund under the care of the Trustees now amounts to nearly £40,000.

The Society has at different times made considerable grants from its funds in aid of the Royal Infirmary, the extension of Edinburgh University, the South African War Relief Fund, the Fund for Local Meetings of the British Association, and other objects.

In 1859 the Society joined heartily in the general feeling of loyalty and patriotism which took effect in the Rifle Volunteer Movement. The Queen's Rifle Volunteer Brigade, The Royal Scots, was the first Volunteer Corps formed in Scotland under the existing Volunteer organisation, and it stands as No. 11 in order of precedence of the whole Rifle Volunteer Force.

No. 6 (Accountants') Company was formed by the Society of Accountants in Edinburgh at an early stage of the movement, its first drill having taken place on 18th July 1859. Towards the end of June of that year sixty-four members of the Society and their apprentices and clerks had intimated their desire to form a Company in the proposed Edinburgh Rifle Corps. A Volunteer Corps had been enrolled in Edinburgh on three previous occasions, viz., in 1794, 1803, and 1819. The City of Edinburgh Rifle Volunteer Corps enrolled in 1859 was the origin of the Queen's Rifle Volunteer Brigade of to-day.

The funds required to arm and equip the Accountants' Company were supplied by the Society of Accountants in Edinburgh, and by subscription among the individual members of the Society, while the cost of uniform and the annual expenditure were met by subscriptions from a few of the members of the Society and from the members of the Company.

At a meeting of those who had volunteered their services, held on 5th July 1859, Company Officers were elected by those present.   The Officers elected were :—

     Captain—John Maitland, Register House.

     Lieutenant—Thos. G. Dickson, 3 N. St. David Street.

     Ensign—Jas. Howden, 5 N. St. David Street.

Shortly afterwards many of the insurance offices in Edinburgh agreed to arm and equip those of the insurance profession desirous of enrolling in the Company.   The sanction of the Society of Accountants to this proposal was obtained, and this departure was the means of giving additional support, much needed in later years.

About one year after the formation of the Company, Captain Maitland resigning his commission, Lieutenant Dickson succeeded to the captaincy of the Company.   During Mr. Dickson's captaincy (for the period of nine years) the training of the Company was carried through with great zeal on the part of all.   Drills were held in the morning at 7 A.M., and in the afternoon at 4 P.M., such was the desire of the Volunteers of those days to attain efficiency for service.

The Muster Roll of the Company at the Royal Review of Scottish Volunteers in Holyrood Park on 7th August 1860 numbered 70.   In the year 1870, in spite of the conditions of service being relaxed, the membership of the Company had fallen to 40—less than half of its former strength.   The novelty of the movement had in a great measure worn off.   In later years the sense of a national duty has probably been its principal mainstay.   It is interesting to note in this connection that thirty years later—viz., in the year 1900—the membership had increased to over 140.

The Company has for many years past shown a particular aptitude for Rifle Shooting, and this, with proper encouragement, has now given it a first place in the Queen's Brigade.   A Challenge Trophy, with valuable prizes attached, offered five years ago for competition by shooting under service conditions among the twenty-nine companies of the Brigade, has, for the last four years in succession, been won by a team from the Accountants' Company. Individual members of the Company have also distinguished themselves on many different occasions.

A Chartered Accountants' Students' Society was formed in Edinburgh in 1886, which has each winter arranged a series of interesting addresses, lectures, and discussions on professional subjects. The Society has been successful in enlisting the interest of students and young members in the more academic aspects of their profession, and its meetings, which are held in the hall of the Society of Accountants, are, as a rule, fairly well attended. Most of the papers read are published in *The Accountants' Magazine*, and an annual volume of Transactions is issued by the Society. At 31st March 1904 the Society had 342 Ordinary and 49 Extraordinary Members.

As already mentioned, James Brown was elected the first President of the Society, and he continued in office until his death in 1864. He commenced business as early as 1812, and assumed Charles Pearson as his partner in 1835. He was a big, buirdly man, and conducted a very large business with great energy and success. He was frank and pleasant in manner, and upright and honourable in all his dealings. His portrait, presented to the Society by his partner, Mr. Pearson, hangs in the hall.[1]

Mr. Brown was succeeded by Thomas Mansfield,[2] son of James Mansfield, of Midmar, a well-known private banker of Edinburgh, and he also continued in the office of President until his death in 1868. Mr. Mansfield was a very shrewd and sound man of business, and his firm of Mansfield and Spottiswoode had an extensive practice. He was most assiduous in his attention to the affairs of the Society, which made a material advance under his Chairmanship.

The next President elected was Charles Murray Barstow,

[1] See reproduction, p. 194.   [2] See portrait, p. 194.

CHARLES MURRAY BARSTOW
1804–1885

CHARLES PEARSON
1803–1884

RALPH ERSKINE SCOTT
1804–1887

GEORGE AULDJO JAMIESON
1828–1900

who held office from 1869 to 1876. Mr. Barstow was educated in Yorkshire and was trained as an accountant under Mr. Brown, the first President. He had a good business, and questions of accounting were frequently remitted to him from the Court of Session. He was a great sportsman, and his fine figure and hearty manner were well known in the hunting field. On retiring from office the Society presented him with his portrait, painted by Robert Gibb, R.S.A., and at the same time procured a replica for the Society, which now hangs in the hall.[1] The portrait was presented to Mr. Barstow at what is believed to have been the only official dinner given by the Society, held between its formation and its Fiftieth Anniversary.

The fourth President was Charles Pearson,[2] who filled the Chair from 1876 to 1879. His father was Depute-Secretary and his grandfather Secretary of the Scottish Board of Excise. Mr. Pearson was trained in the office of James Brown, and became his partner in 1835. In 1863, after the death of Mr. Brown, he assumed as partner his own eldest son. During his career Mr. Pearson was concerned in many important professional matters, and he was a man very highly esteemed for his good qualities and cultured tastes. He died in 1884 at the age of eighty-one.

The next President was Ralph Erskine Scott,[3] who continued in office from 1879 to 1882. Mr. Scott was senior partner of the firm of R. & E. Scott, having early assumed his son Ebenezer Erskine Scott as a partner. The firm occupied a high position and had a valuable connection, especially in financial matters, for which Mr. Scott's careful and exact habits eminently fitted him. He made an admirable President.

The sixth President was George Auldjo Jamieson, who was one of the most eminent accountants of his day, and well known both in England and Scotland. In his term, which extended over the now exceptional period of six

[1] See reproduction, p. 220.   [2] See portrait, p. 220.   [3] See portrait, p. 220.

years, the Endowment and Annuity Fund of the Society
was constituted, and on retiring from the Chair he was
asked to sit for his portrait to Sir George Reid, *P.R.S.A.*
The portrait, which is a very fine work, was presented to
Mrs. Jamieson, and a replica obtained for the Society's
Hall.[1] Mr. Jamieson died suddenly in 1900 in his seventy-
third year. In the course of his active life he was connected professionally with many important concerns. He
was one of the liquidators of the City of Glasgow Bank,
and a member of Royal Commissions on the Amendment
of Company Law and on Mining Royalties. He also took an
interest in municipal affairs, and was a prominent member
of the Edinburgh Town Council for a number of years. He
did much to advance the interests of the Society during his
long connection with it. He was the guiding spirit for many
years of the Students' Society, to which he contributed a
number of valuable papers on economic and professional
subjects.

The succeeding Presidents of the Society are happily
still with us.

The fees of admission to the Edinburgh Society are £105,
and an annual contribution of £5 5s. must be paid to the
Endowment and Annuity Fund.

The Institute of Accountants and Actuaries in Glasgow
for some years after its formation had no local habitation of
its own, finding accommodation for its library and for holding its meetings in a room in the then Stock Exchange
premises in National Bank Buildings, Queen Street—recently
removed to make room for the large and imposing warehouse of Messrs. Hunter, Barr, & Co., Ltd. That the
Institute should have found accommodation in the premises
of the Stock Exchange was not unfitting, when it is called
to remembrance that the men who in 1842 founded the
Glasgow Stock Exchange Association were almost without
exception practising accountants, and that of the thirteen

[1] See reproduction, p. 220.

who formed the Institute in 1853 ten were also members of the Stock Exchange Association.

In 1873 circumstances rendered it desirable that the Institute should acquire a Hall and Library of its own, and a suitable property in West Nile Street was purchased in that year. For years these premises continued to provide all the accommodation required, but as the number of candidates coming up year by year for examination continued to increase, it was found necessary to look out for larger rooms, and accordingly the present property, situated at 218 St. Vincent Street, was purchased, and adapted to the requirements of the Institute.

From the first the attention of the Council has been given to the formation of a library worthy of the Institute, and capable of meeting all the reasonable demands of the members. In the earlier days the collection was confined almost exclusively to legal and other works bearing directly on professional subjects, but latterly the field has been somewhat widened, and many books of general literature and others bearing on local and commercial interests have been added. The collection now consists of 3400 volumes, and it is being constantly added to. The apartment in which the library is accommodated is handsome and artistic. It is comfortably furnished, and the books are so arranged as to be readily accessible.

Courses of Lectures on professional and other subjects have from time to time been given in connection with the Institute. At first these were of a somewhat intermittent character, but latterly the arrangement with the Edinburgh Society and the Bankers' Institute already referred to has resulted in a short course being delivered regularly every winter.

Tutorial Classes have also been organised for the benefit of apprentices preparing for the various examinations, and at the present time a considerable extension of these is under contemplation.

A Students' Society has been formed in connection with the Institute for aiding by Lectures, Discussions, &c., young men training for the profession. Its proceedings are conducted with much enthusiasm and ability, and it is undoubtedly proving a most valuable institution.

The Institute having been formed for purely professional objects, little has ever been done under its auspices to promote social intercourse among its members. Apart from the dinner to celebrate the incorporation of the Institute in 1855, the members have only dined twice together—once at the opening of the Hall and Library in West Nile Street on 9th March 1874, under the Presidency of Mr. William Anderson, and again on 18th March 1880, when Mr. Wyllie Guild was President. On both occasions there was a good turn-out of members and friends, and the wonder is that such pleasant and agreeable gatherings did not lead to more frequent meetings of a similar kind.

The opening of the present Hall and Library in St. Vincent Street was celebrated by an afternoon reception which was attended by representatives of the Edinburgh and Aberdeen Societies, and by a large number of the leading citizens. On the evening of the same day the President and Council received the apprentices in the Library.

The formation of a collection of portraits of eminent accountants is an object which the Council have had before them, but towards the attainment of which but little progress has yet been made. At the present time the Institute's art treasures consist of a marble bust of the late James M'Clelland presented by his son Mr. Andrew S. M'Clelland, and a portrait of the late Walter Mackenzie painted by Joseph Henderson, R.S.W., and presented by the Members—a replica at the same time being presented to Mrs. Mackenzie.

A collection has also been made of enlarged photographs of all the past Presidents, which are hung on the walls of the hall. One half of the originals have gone over to the majority, and their memories are thus kept green for the benefit of succeeding generations of accountants. The following biographical notes in reference to them may not be without interest :—

Towards the end of the second decade of the last century there entered the office of James Kerr as an apprentice a young lad from Ayr, who was destined to take, by his own energy and ability, a leading place in the profession in Glasgow, and to become the first President of the Institute —we refer of course to the late James M'Clelland.[1]

Mr. M'Clelland began business on his own account in 1824, and an extract from the circular which he then issued announcing the fact has already been given.[2] He interested himself much in the amendment of the Bankruptcy Laws, and was able to give sound and valuable advice in connection therewith. He retired from active business life in 1871 when he went to reside in London, where he died in 1879 at the age of eighty.

Mr. M'Clelland was largely instrumental in the formation of the Glasgow Institute in 1853, and in obtaining the Royal Charter of Incorporation in 1855.

He was chosen as the first President, which office he occupied until 1864.

Mr. M'Clelland was much interested in education; he was also a great phrenologist. Professor Bayne in his recently published autobiography, referring to a visit made by him to Glasgow in 1865 in pursuance of his candidature for a vacant post in the Andersonian University of the city, and to the calls he made upon the Managers, says: "Another influential Glasgow man on the management was James M'Lellan (sic) an accountant, an enthusiastic phrenologist, and a particular friend of the Combes. He was satisfied with my pretensions from his inspection of my head."

The second occupant of the President's Chair was Mr. Peter White,[3] who long filled an important and influential position in the business and social circles of Glasgow life. In his later years Mr. White devoted much of his time to the Stock Exchange, the Chair of which he occupied for

[1] See portrait, p. 200.   [2] *Ante*, p. 201.   [3] See portrait, p. 200.

several terms. He died in 1881, leaving a fortune of upwards of £200,000.

Mr. Walter Mackenzie of Edinbarnet[1] succeeded Mr. White in the Presidency in 1867, holding office till 1870. He was again elected to the Chair in 1890, and filled it till 1894. Mr. Mackenzie was privileged to do more for the Institute during his long and honourable career than any other member. He was a member of Council for forty-four years, viz., from 1853 to 1897. In addition to being twice President, he filled in succession each of the offices of Secretary, Treasurer, and Auditor. During all the time he was a member of Council, and while engaged in one of the largest accountancy businesses in the city, he devoted his energies to further the interests of the profession, and he contributed in an eminent degree to promote the prosperity of the Institute. Mr. Mackenzie died in 1898 at the age of eighty-one.

The third President was Mr. William Anderson,[2] who was elected in 1870, and being re-elected for a second term in 1873, occupied the chair till 1876. It was during Mr. Anderson's term of office that the Institute first acquired a local habitation of its own.

Mr. Anderson was a man of great professional ability combined with a most genial disposition. He became a partner of the firm of Kerrs & Anderson in 1842, and until his death in 1889 he was in the front rank of the profession in the City. In 1878 he was appointed one of the Liquidators of the City of Glasgow Bank.

Mr. George Robson[3] succeeded Mr. Anderson as President in 1876, but owing to failing health retired in 1878.

Mr. Robson was of a very quiet and unassuming disposition. He was at the same time possessed of many of the qualities that go to make a good man of business, and along with his partner, Mr. Alexander Black, he commanded in an eminent degree the confidence and esteem of a large clientèle. Mr. Robson, who was a brother of the late well-

[1] See portrait opposite.   [2] See portrait opposite.   [3] See portrait opposite.

WALTER MACKENZIE
1817–1898

WILLIAM ANDERSON
1817–1889

J. WYLLIE GUILD
1826–1894

GEORGE ROBSON
1800–1881

known Rev. Dr. Robson of Wellington Street United Presbyterian Church, Glasgow, was never married, and died in 1881, aged eighty-one years.

Mr. J. Wyllie Guild[1] filled the President's Chair from 1878 to 1881.

Mr. Wyllie Guild was a native of Edinburgh, where he received his early training. He came to Glasgow in the year 1848, and soon took a good position in the professional life of the City. He was an able and brilliant accountant. Of an enthusiastic and sanguine temperament, he was possessed of a marvellous aptitude for figures, and he positively revelled in the expiscation of complicated and involved accounts. His services were much sought after as a professional witness, in which capacity he appeared in almost all the leading cases of his time where questions of accounting were involved.

He was an enthusiastic book collector, and helped largely in the formation of the Library of the Institute. Mr. Guild died in 1894, in his sixty-eighth year.

Mr. John Graham succeeded Mr. Guild in the Presidency and filled the Chair from 1881 to 1884. It was hoped that Mr. Graham would have lived to take part in the celebration of the Jubilee of the Institute, but he was called away while these pages were passing through the press. He filled an important position in the professional life of the city, and enjoyed the respect and esteem of his fellow citizens. Mr. Graham was an enthusiastic Free-mason, and attained high rank in the Craft. His funeral, which was in accordance with the ritual of the Order, was the occasion of the greatest Masonic ceremony of the kind that had been witnessed in the city for many years.

Of the seven Presidents who have gone over to the majority, there only remains to be noticed here Mr. John E. Watson,[2] who filled the Chair from 1887 to 1890. Mr. Watson long occupied a prominent position in the business

[1] See portrait, p. 226.   [2] See portrait, p. 230.

life of Glasgow, and he had a wide circle of friends.   Amongst other appointments which he held was that of Auditor of the Glasgow Savings Bank—the largest Savings Bank in the United Kingdom.   He devoted much of his time to this work, and became quite an authority on Savings Bank Accounts and Accounting.   As a mark of the respect and esteem in which Mr. Watson was held by his fellow citizens he was presented in 1898 with his portrait, painted by Joseph Henderson, R.S.W.   The presentation was made at a large and influential meeting of the subscribers.

As an Elder in St. George's Parish Church for twenty-eight years he took a warm interest in all that concerned the welfare of the Church of Scotland, and was a well-known figure in the General Assembly.   He died in 1901, aged seventy-one years.

These brief notes of the principal events in the history of the Glasgow Institute would be incomplete without a short reference to the part which the members and apprentices have taken in the Volunteer Movement.   Before, however, dealing with the movement, which began in 1859, shortly after the formation of the Institute, it is of interest to note that in 1804, when a French invasion was thought to be imminent, and regiments of Volunteers were enrolled throughout the country, Donald Cuthbertson, then a young man of twenty-one, who, as above stated, afterwards became one of the original members of the Institute, joined the Highland Regiment of Glasgow Volunteers, and was chosen to be Lieutenant of one of the Companies.

When the present Volunteer Movement began in 1859 a Company (or Corps as it was then termed) was raised under the joint auspices of the Institute and the Glasgow Stock Exchange.

It was the 17th Company in Lanarkshire, and ultimately became E Company of what is now the 1st Lanarkshire Regiment of Rifle Volunteers.   The Company (85 strong) took part in the great Review before Her Majesty Queen

Victoria and the Prince Consort in the Queen's Park, Edinburgh, on 7th August 1860, and the officers in command on that occasion were Captain William Auld, Lieutenant J. Wyllie Guild, Ensign Alex. J. Watson (C.A. Edin.).

For many years the Company was known as the "Accountants' Company," and its connection with the Institute is still maintained—the present Captain (son of the first Captain) being a member of the Institute, and the Second Lieutenant an apprentice.

Besides, however, furnishing a Company at the beginning of the movement in 1859, the members of the Institute have all along borne their full share in the Volunteer Service, and in addition to a large number of Company officers have supplied four Colonels—viz., two to the 1st Lanarkshire Rifles and two to the 1st Volunteer Battalion Highland Light Infantry—and five Majors—viz., one to the 1st Lanarkshire Royal Engineers (Volunteers), one to the 1st Lanarkshire Rifles, two to the 4th Volunteer Battalion Scottish Rifles (The Cameronians), and one to the Glasgow Highlanders.

Of these only two, viz., the two Colonels of the Vol. Bat. Highland Light Infantry, remain on the active list. Of the remainder, one Colonel and three Majors are on the retired list, while one Colonel and two Majors are dead.

It is also worthy of note that in the dark days which followed the outbreak of the Boer War, when an opportunity was afforded for Volunteers offering for active service at the front, a contingent of nine connected with the Institute—viz., two members and seven apprentices—offered and were accepted. All of these with one exception came safely through the campaign. T. Paton Menzies, C.A., a young member of considerable promise, who had a year or two before migrated to London, died of typhoid in Ladysmith.

At the close of the war the other of the two members who went to the front received an appointment under Government in Pretoria, where he is now settled, and one of the apprentices (the son of an officer who served with distinction in India during the Mutiny) was offered and accepted a Commission in the Army.

The others all returned to civil life, and are now following the profession.

The fees of admission to the Glasgow Institute are £52 10s., with an annual subscription of £1 1s.

THE SOCIETY OF ACCOUNTANTS IN ABERDEEN was originated about the end of 1866 by Mr. James Meston and Mr. William Milne convening a meeting of accountants to be held in the office of the former. A petition for incorporation by Royal Charter was thereafter presented and granted in in due course on the 18th of March 1867.

The first President was Mr. John Smith,[1] an M.A. of Marischal College, who had served his apprenticeship as an Advocate, but practised as an Accountant from 1831. His character commanded universal respect, and his business qualifications secured for him the implicit confidence of his many clients, to whose interests he devoted the closest attention. He lived to the advanced age of eighty-six. The next President was Mr. George Marquis, who also held a very high position in the profession, and was greatly esteemed by all who knew him. The President from 1873 to 1875 was Mr. James Augustus Sinclair, who in 1890 made good his claim to the title of the Earl of Caithness. The next President was Mr. Robert Fletcher, a native of Edinburgh, who had an active and influential professional career. In 1868 he removed to London, where he established a large business. He died in 1883 at the age of sixty-five. Mr. Lunan, the next President, began life in a law office in Arbroath, and received his accountant training in Edinburgh. For a long period he was connected with railway matters in the north-east of Scotland, and afterwards was for three years a partner of the firm of Marquis and Lunan. John Crombie, the next President, commenced business as an accountant in 1857. He was a Town Councillor and Magistrate of the City, a Colonel of Volunteers,

[1] See portrait opposite.

JOHN E. WATSON
1829–1901

WILLIAM TURQUAND
1819–1894

JAMES MESTON
1821–1892

JOHN SMITH
(c) 1798–1884

and an eminent Freemason, being at one time Junior Grand Warden for Scotland.

Reference to the leading Members of the Aberdeen Society would not be complete without mention of Mr. James Meston,[1] who was Secretary of the Society from its formation until his death in 1893. He was trained under Mr. John Smith, went to London for three years, and in 1857 founded in Aberdeen the present firm of James Meston & Co. He held a number of important appointments, and rendered invaluable services to the Society.

A Students' Society was early established in connection with the Society of Accountants in Aberdeen, and is still carried on.

In 1902 the "Aberdeen Chartered Accountants' Widows' Fund" was formed, to which it is compulsory for all future members of the Society to contribute.

The dues of admission to the Aberdeen Society are £52 10s., with an annual subscription of £1 1s. A minimum annual contribution of £3 is also required to the Widows' Fund, with an Age Tax and Marriage Tax according to circumstances.

---

[1] See portrait, p. 230.

CHAPTER IV

ENGLAND AND IRELAND

EARLY ACCOUNTANTS IN ENGLAND AND WALES—GROWTH IN
NINETEENTH CENTURY—FORMATION OF FIRST SOCIETIES
—INSTITUTE OF CHARTERED ACCOUNTANTS IN ENGLAND
AND WALES—SOCIETY OF ACCOUNTANTS AND AUDITORS—
THE PROFESSION IN IRELAND—INSTITUTE OF CHARTERED
ACCOUNTANTS IN IRELAND—ISLE OF MAN AND CHANNEL
ISLANDS

THE profession of accountant did not attain a position of
importance in England or in Ireland at so early a period as in
Scotland, which was probably due in great measure to the
laws of Scotland affecting the estates of bankrupts, pupils,
and other incapacitated persons, and the practice of the Courts
of Justice, being so different in character. In England questions of accounting, which in Scotland would have been remitted to professional accountants, were dealt with by the
Masters in Chancery; and estates in bankruptcy or belonging
to persons under some legal disability were entrusted to the care
of officials of the court. The Scottish system fostered the
growth of a body of men relying on their merits for success,
the English system maintained a number of court officials and
commissioners—many of them ill-qualified to perform accounting work—and left little business for the independent
practitioner.

The accountants of England of whom we find earliest
mention were obviously teachers of book-keeping and accounts.
We have seen how the Italian method of double-entry was
introduced into this country by Hugh Oldcastle (1543) and

John Mellis (1588), both designed "Scholemaisters." Richard Dafforne of Northampton (1636) calls himself "Accountant and Teacher of the same." So also in all probability was his patron "Ralph Handson, Accomptant." John Collins, F.R.S., professed "Writing, Merchants-Accompts, and some parts of the Mathematicks," and in the introduction to the 1674 edition of his "Merchants-Accompts" mentions that he had been nominated by the Lord Chancellor "in divers References concerning Suits depending in Chancery, about intricate Accompts, to assist in the Stating thereof, which hath not been without some Emolument to myself, and to the shortning of the Charge of the parties concerned." Charles Snell, "Writing-Master and Accountant in Foster Lane, London," made a report (undated, but probably in 1721) on the books of Sawbridge & Company in connection with the collapse of the South Sea Company.[1] Richard Hayes, "Accomptant and Writing-Master of Queen Street, Cheapside," wrote on book-keeping in 1731 and 1739. It is probable that the profession in England had its origin in this class and was augmented during the early part of the nineteenth century mainly from the ranks of practical book-keepers trained in mercantile or other offices.

In a Directory of Bristol and Bath for 1787 there appears the name of "Thomas Jones, Accomptant, Thomas Street, Bristol," who was probably the immediate predecessor of Edward Thomas Jones of that city, the author of the "English System of Book-keeping," published in 1796.[2] In 1790 the *British Universal Directory* gives five names of accountants in London, two being firms. One is described as writing-master and accomptant, one as commercial accomptant, and two as accomptants and agents.[3] In the same year the *Liverpool Directory* also shows five accountants, one of them however

---

[1] See "Professional Accountants," p. 14, by B. Worthington; London 1895.

[2] John Jones, Writing-Master and Accomptant in Bristol, published six questions on Company Accounts in 1730. See "An Essay to make a Compleat Accountant," Roose, London 1760.

[3] Worthington, *op. cit.*

adding to his designation of mercantile accomptant that of dealer in tin plates![1]

In 1793–1794 the number of accountants in Bristol had increased to about 25, many of them professing other occupations as well—such as writing-master, teacher, agent, or broker. In 1794 we find two public accountants in Manchester, but by the end of the century there was only one left. In 1796 the number in Liverpool had increased to ten, including two gentlemen who in 1790 had been described as book-keepers.[2] In London in 1799 there were eleven accountants, including a firm of accountants and notaries and one writing-master and accountant.[3]

Such are the meagre records which we have been able to find of accountants in England prior to the nineteenth century. Soon after 1800 the number of persons described in the *Directories* as accountants rapidly increased, but many of them still appear to have had other occupations. Indeed, it is not unlikely that in England, as in other places, the title of accountant had been adopted by some who in Lord Brougham's phrase "could give no proper account of themselves." As regards the metropolis we find that there are 24 entries of accountants in London in *Holden's Triennial Directory* for 1809–1811,[4] 47 in *Johnston's London Commercial Guide* for 1817, 99 in *Pigot Co.'s London and Provincial Directory* for 1826–1827, and 107 in the *Post-Office Directory* for 1840. In 1850 the number had risen to 264, in 1860 to 310, and in 1870 to 467. In Liverpool the number of accountants in 1832 had increased to 37, in 1849 to 69, in 1860 to 91, and in 1870 to 139. In Manchester, while the accountants in the early part of the century did not number more than 4 or 5, they rose to 14 in 1815, 24 in 1829, 32 in 1832, 52 in 1840, 66 in 1850, 84 in 1861, and 159 in 1871. In Bristol, notwithstanding its early start, the increase was not so rapid, there being only 20 names in 1824, 24 in 1827, and 28 in 1830. In 1861 there

[1] Address by A. W. Chalmers, F.C.A. *The Accountant*, No. 431, 1883.
[2] Chalmers, *loc. cit.*   [3] Worthington, *op. cit.*   [4] Ibid.

were 74 accountants there. In Birmingham there were only 2 accountants in 1808 and in 1861 there were 45.

In Leicester we find 5 accountants in 1831, 7 in 1846, 9 in 1850, and 18 in 1862. Bradford *Directories* show 4 accountants in 1845, 8 in 1850, 9 in 1856, 13 in 1863, and 20 in 1872. The records of accountants do not go very far back in Sheffield, though 21 gentlemen formed an Association of Accountants there in March 1877. Northampton had 3 accountants in 1847, 4 in 1861, 5 in 1874, and 13 in 1879. In Nottingham there was a "Money Agent and Accomptant" in 1825, 8 accountants in 1853, and in 1872 a considerable number joined the newly formed Society of Accountants in England. In Hull the profession may be said to have originated in 1840, the business of average-stating being then combined with it.

In Wales, if Cardiff may be taken as representative of the principality, the professional accountant is of recent origin. There were 6 public accountants and appraisers there in 1863, 5 accountants in 1873, and 20 in 1880.

The first step in the organisation of the profession in England was taken by the Liverpool accountants, who, on 25th January 1870 with "considerable difficulty" formed the "Incorporated Society of Liverpool Accountants." This was soon followed by the "Institute of Accountants" in London, formed on 29th November 1870, and by the "Manchester Institute of Accountants," formed on 6th February 1871. "The Society of Accountants in England" was created on 11th January 1873, and the "Sheffield Institute of Accountants" on 14th March 1877. In May 1880 the Liverpool Society had 29 members, the London Institute 188, the Manchester Institute 103, the Society of Accountants in England 286, and the Sheffield Institute 32.

On the 29th November 1878, the Council of the Institute of Accountants advertised in the *London Gazette* that they were about to apply to Parliament for leave to introduce a Bill for incorporating the Institute. The Council invited representatives of the English Societies and other well-known accountants, not members of any Society, to confer with them, with the object of ensuring that the Bill about to be introduced into Parliament should be so framed as to promote the interests of the members of those Societies, and the profession generally. A Conference was fixed for the 14th January 1879, and several subsequent meetings were held.

A Bill was introduced into Parliament early in 1879, but eventually, on the suggestion of Lord Redesdale, a petition for a Charter of Incorporation was substituted, as being more in accordance with precedent.

The draft Charter was submitted to the late Queen, and approved by Her Majesty at the Privy Council held on the 24th March 1880; the formal grant being made on the 11th May 1880. This Charter incorporated the existing Societies into one body, THE INSTITUTE OF CHARTERED ACCOUNT-ANTS IN ENGLAND AND WALES, and made provision for the admittance of other persons as members on certain conditions.

These conditions entitled every person who had been in continuous practice as a Public Accountant for five years from 1st January 1879 to be admitted as Fellow, and every person who had, prior to the date of the Charter, been for three years in public practice or for five years employed as a public accountant's clerk, to be admitted an Associate of the Institute. The Council were also given a discretionary power of election in certain exceptions by a three-fourths majority; but for practical purposes admission to the Institute is now only obtainable by passing a preliminary examination in general education, service under articles for five years with a member of the Institute, passing an intermediate examination in book-keeping and accounts, auditing and liquidations, and passing a final examination in these subjects with the addition of bankruptcy, company, mer-cantile and arbitration law. Examination fees of £2 2s. are payable on each occasion. The entrance fees to the

Institute are £10 10s. on becoming an Associate, and a further £10 10s. on becoming a Fellow, and the annual contributions are as follows: members practising in London, Fellows £5 5s., Associates £2 2s.; members practising out-side of London, Fellows £3 3s., Associates £1 1s.; members not in practice, Fellows £2 2s., Associates £1 1s.

On the 11th May 1880, 224 Fellows, 241 Associates, 31 Associates not in practice, and 31 Associates not in England and Wales (members of the previously existing Societies residing abroad) were elected—527 in all. Before the 3rd February 1881, the number of members had increased to 1025, their applications having been received before the end of 1880. In 1891 the number was 1766, in 1901 2776, and in 1904 (September) 3177. The numbers in the larger towns in 1904 were as follows:

Birmingham	249	Liverpool	161
Bradford	44	London	1383
Bristol	73	Manchester	319
Cardiff	35	Newcastle	71
Hull	35	Northampton	13
Leeds	66	Nottingham	49
Leicester	40	Sheffield	87

The administration of the Institute is in the hands of a Council of not more than forty-five members, from whom a President and Vice-President are chosen annually, and which appoints Committees of its members for different purposes. At present there are seven Committees:—

1. APPLICATIONS.—To regulate admissions to membership; to decide whether applicants are fit and proper persons to be elected.
2. EXAMINATION.—To regulate the examinations, preside at them, and examine the papers of candidates.
3. FINANCE.—To regulate expenditure.
4. INVESTIGATION.—To examine into cases of alleged wrong-doing or unprofessional conduct of members.
5. LIBRARY AND PUBLICATION.

6. PARLIAMENTARY AND LAW.—To consider Parliamentary Bills, legal decisions, &c., which may affect the Institute or the accountancy profession.

7. GENERAL PURPOSES.—To consider any matters that do not come within the scope of the other Committees. There are also Special and Sub-Committees appointed as occasion may require. In the early years of the Institute there were: The Accountants Benevolent Association Committee, which ceased to exist when the Chartered Accountants' Benevolent Association was started in 1887; the Bankruptcy Committee and the Joint-Stock Companies Committee, which are now merged in the Parliamentary and Law Committee; the Building Committee, whose office ceased in 1894.

William Turquand[1] was the first President of the Institute and held the office for two years. He was one of the foremost Accountants of his day and was engaged in most of the important liquidations of his time. He did much to raise the status of the profession in England, and was Vice-President of the Institute of Accountants from 1870 to 1877, and President from 1877 until it was merged in the larger body in 1880. He had the best of reputations both outside of his office and in it. He died on 20th March 1894 at the age of seventy-five.

The offices of the new Institute were at first at 3 Copthall Buildings, London, E.C. But it was soon felt that the Institute should have a building of its own; and in 1888 an agreement was made to take on lease, for 999 years, a plot of land in Coleman Street Buildings (now Moorgate Place) containing about 4500 sq. ft.

Six architects were invited to send in competitive designs, and that of Mr. John Belcher, F.R.I.B.A. (now A.R.A.), was accepted. The Council also accepted the offer of Mr. Hamo Thornycroft, R.A., to design and execute a sculptured frieze, of 140 ft. in length, running round the building at the first storey, while Mr. Harry Bates, A.R.A., designed the corbel groups and other groups and figures.

[1] See portrait, p. 230.

OFFICES OF THE INSTITUTE OF CHARTERED ACCOUNTANTS IN ENGLAND
AND WALES—MOORGATE PLACE, LONDON

By permission of Mr. John Belcher, A.R.A., Architect

There was at first considerable delay through legal proceedings with regard to rights of light, but eventually the contractors, Messrs. Colls & Son, got to work, in May 1890, and the building was completed in the autumn of 1892, the December Examinations being held in the building, which, however, was not formally opened till May 1893. The building—in Italian Renaissance style—was unanimously described in the architectural papers as one of the finest erected in London for many years; and a folio volume of views, with accompanying letterpress, was published by Mr. B. T. Batsford in 1893. One of the views is here reproduced by permission.

The Library of the Institute of Accountants was purchased by the new Institute, and has been added to largely each year. At present it contains about 4200 volumes, chiefly works on book-keeping and accountancy, law books, sets of the various law reports and miscellaneous reference books; together with a large collection of Company balance-sheets, &c., in guard books.

The chief feature of the library is the collection of works on book-keeping and accounts, more than 600 in number. It includes Paciolo's *Summa de Arithmetica, Geometria, Proportioni & Proportionalita*, 1494 (the oldest printed book on book-keeping), and also the 1523 edition; Mellis' "Briefe Instruction," 1588; the 1636, 1651, 1660 and 1684 editions of Dafforne's "Merchant's Mirrour"; and many other early and interesting books.

A full catalogue of the Library was printed in 1903, including, besides the books, everything of importance in the various Accountancy magazines, and Accountant Students' Societies.

The following Provincial Societies have been formed from among the members of the Institute at various dates since its incorporation, each having a Library—viz., The Birmingham and Midland, Bristol, Leicester, Liverpool, Manchester, Nottingham, and Sheffield Societies of Chartered

Accountants, and the Northern Institute of Chartered Accountants. Grants were made by the Council to the above Societies to help in the formation of libraries, and annual grants are also made.

On the 4th November 1885 the Council passed a resolution "that it is in the interests of the profession that a meeting of members of the Institute should be held in a provincial town in the autumn of next year." Invitations were received from both the Manchester and Birmingham Societies of Chartered Accountants, and the Council decided to hold the meeting at Manchester, as that city contained the largest number of accountants of any provincial town in England. This first meeting took place in October 1886, and there have since been Autumnal Provincial Meetings in Birmingham (twice), Newcastle-upon-Tyne, Liverpool (twice), Sheffield, and again at Manchester.

At each meeting papers on matters of interest to the profession were read and discussed, and the members dined together.

Instead of Provincial Meetings there were Special Meetings in London in 1887 at the time of the Jubilee, in 1893 at the opening of the Hall, in 1897 at the Diamond Jubilee, and in 1902 at the Coronation of King Edward VII.

In 1881 the Council devoted much time to the consideration of the Bankruptcy Bill which had been introduced into Parliament by the Government, and they embodied their views in a series of observations and suggestions which were submitted to the Board of Trade, with whom a deputation from the Council subsequently had an interview.

Again in 1882 the Bankruptcy Bill had the careful consideration of the Council, who drew up and circulated a series of observations upon it.

A number of alterations suggested by the Council to the President of the Board of Trade and to the Standing Committee on Trade were introduced into the Bankruptcy Bill during its progress through the Committee. After the passing of the Act, in 1883, various alterations suggested by the Council in the Preliminary Draft of the Bankruptcy Rules were adopted.

Numerous complaints having been made as to the working of the Bankruptcy Act 1883, the Council communicated with all the members of the Institute asking them for information as to their experience. The Bankruptcy Committee held numerous meetings, and Board of Trade Officials were interviewed. The Council drew up a series of observations and suggestions as to improvements of the Act, and forwarded them to the President of the Board of Trade—they were also sent to each member of the Institute, and were approved at a Special General Meeting held on the 4th March 1885.

As the 1885 Bill for the Registration of Deeds of Arrangement was not proceeded with, the Council had a Bill prepared showing the views of the Institute as to the method in which the registration and legalisation of Deeds of Arrangement should be dealt with; and the Bill was submitted to a General Meeting on the 3rd February 1886.

The Bankruptcy Committee had under consideration Section 55 of the Bankruptcy Act 1883, and gave instructions for the preparation of amendments, repealing Section 55 and substituting other clauses. Copies were forwarded to the Inspector-General in Bankruptcy, who replied that the clauses had been referred to the legal advisers of the Board of Trade to report upon.

In 1887, in view of the forthcoming Local Government Bill, the Council addressed a letter to the President of the Local Government Board suggesting that provision should be made in the Bill that the accounts of County Boards, Municipal Corporations, and other Local Bodies should be audited only by properly qualified accountants. When the Bill was introduced into Parliament by the Government, providing that the audit of the accounts of County Councils should be conducted by District Auditors appointed by the Local Government Board, amendments were framed to secure that the audit should be conducted by "Chartered or other qualified Public Accountants appointed by the County Councils with the approval of the Local Government Board"; but these amendments were not accepted.

The Bills introduced into Parliament in 1887 and 1888 for "the consolidation and amendment of the Companies Acts 1862 to 1883" were carefully considered by the Joint-Stock Companies' Committee and the Council, who drew up a series of observations upon the Government Bill and circulated it among the members of the House of Lords. The Council took much trouble and spent much time in considering the Bill for amendment of the Bankruptcy Act 1883 and the Companies (Winding-up) Bill, and succeeded in getting important amendments made to each before the passing of the Acts in 1890.

The Savings Bank Act 1891 provided that an Inspection Committee of Trustee Savings Banks should be formed. In accordance with the scheme drawn up under the provisions of the Act, one member was to be appointed by the Council of the Institute of Chartered Accountants. The Council accordingly appointed Mr. T. A. Welton, at that time President of the Institute; and on his vacating the office in 1893, under the regulations, he was re-appointed, in accordance with the wishes of the Committee.

In 1891 the Council was successful in inducing the Board of Trade to modify the rules as to returns, &c., under the Bankruptcy Act 1883, and the Companies (Winding-up) Act 1890, so as to bring them, to a great extent, in accordance with the views of the Council. The Council prepared in 1893, and submitted to the President of the Board of Trade, a Bill providing that companies in liquidation not formally dissolved, where there had never been any assets or where the assets had been realised and distributed prior to the coming into operation of the Companies

(Winding-up) Act 1890, should be struck off the register of Joint-Stock Companies. The Bill was introduced into Parliament in 1894, but was " crowded out," and again introduced in 1895.

In 1893 a Bill was introduced into the House of Commons to arrange for the more complete organisation of the profession, and to restrain all persons from practising who were not registered as Chartered Accountants. On 25th May 1893, a General Meeting was held to consider the Accountants Bill. It was resolved: "That it is desirable to promote legislation which shall restrict public accountancy to existing or future Chartered Accountants. That if restriction cannot be obtained, then it is desirable to legislate to protect our title of ' Chartered Accountants,'" and the Council were empowered to make arrangements with the existing Societies, and to take legislative action in the direction indicated. The Bill, however, could not be proceeded with, and was withdrawn.

In 1894, four lectures were delivered before the Institute in London and also before some of the provincial Societies, and these lectures have since been printed.

A Bill for the establishment of a register and the protection of the title "Chartered Accountant" was introduced into Parliament in 1895. In 1896 a Bill was introduced to prohibit any person from stating that he is practising as a Public Accountant, and from performing certain functions as a professional accountant unless he is registered as a Chartered Accountant. On the 13th January 1897 a Bill for the amendment of the law relating to Public Accountants was submitted to a Special Meeting of the Institute; but on a poll the majority decided against it.

The Council, having considered the 1896 Companies Bill, prepared suggestions for its amendment, and forwarded them to the members of the Select Committee and to other members of the House of Lords. They nominated Mr. F. Whinney, F.C.A., the Chairman of the Parliamentary and

Law Committee, to give evidence before the Select Committee, and again in 1897 and 1898.

In 1896 the Council pointed out to the Registrar of Friendly Societies certain desirable amendments in the form of Building Societies' Accounts. The Council also submitted to the Lord Chancellor certain suggestions as to the rules to be drafted under the Judicial Trustees Act 1896.

The Council suggested an amendment to the London Government Bill 1899 providing "that at least one of the auditors shall be a qualified professional accountant, carrying on business in the Metropolis, but not necessarily a ratepayer in the particular district."

The Council endeavoured to obtain an amendment to the Audit Section of the Education Bill 1902, which would provide that the accounts of a Council of a Borough should be audited by a professional accountant, but the Clause was not debated, owing to the operation of the closure.

The articled and other clerks of members of the Institute have in most of the larger centres formed Students' Societies for mutual advancement in professional knowledge. The Birmingham Chartered Accountants Students' Society was founded in 1882 ; the Manchester Chartered Accountants Students' Society, the Chartered Accountants Students' Society of London, the Liverpool Chartered Accountants Students' Association, the Bristol Chartered Accountants Students' Society, and the Sheffield Chartered Accountants Students' Society, in 1883; and the Chartered Accountants Students' Society of Hull, the Leeds and District Chartered Accountants Students' Association, the Leicester Chartered Accountants Students' Society, and the Nottingham Chartered Accountants Students' Society, in subsequent years.

At the meetings papers are read by members and others, debates are held on matters of professional interest, examination questions are discussed, &c. Most of the papers read are printed in *The Accountant* or *The Accountants' Journal.* Several of the Societies publish "Transactions," in which the papers read, the List of Members, and the Report of the Society are included. Most of the Societies have lately joined to form a " Working Union of Students' Societies."

Following upon the formation of Societies of Accountants in England *The Accountant* newspaper was started in 1874, first as a monthly, but after a few months as a weekly publication, in which form it is still issued and circulates widely.

Five years after the amalgamation of the earlier English Societies and their incorporation by Royal Charter as one Institute, THE SOCIETY OF ACCOUNTANTS AND AUDITORS was formed.

This Society owes its inception to a meeting of accountants convened and held in London in the month of February 1885, when those present resolved to form themselves into " The Society of Accountants." The objects of this Society were stated under three heads, the chief being " To watch over and protect the mutual interests of its members." A Provisional Council was formed and regulations as to the admission of members agreed upon. The Provisional Council devoted itself mainly to obtaining the incorporation of the Society, which was accomplished on December 29, 1885, when a licence was obtained from the Board of Trade to incorporate under the title of The Society of Accountants and Auditors.

The Memorandum of Association contains the following objects *inter alia* :—

To provide a central organisation for accountants and auditors, and generally to do all such things as from time to time may be necessary to elevate the status and procure the advancement of the interests of the profession.

To provide for the better definition and protection of the profession by a system of examinations and the issue of certificates.

To promote and foster in commercial circles a higher sense of the importance of systematic and correct accounts, and to encourage a greater degree of efficiency in those engaged in book-keeping.

To provide opportunities for intercourse amongst the members, and to give facilities for the reading of papers, the delivery of lectures, and for the acquisition and dissemination, by other means, of useful information connected with the profession, and to encourage improved methods of book-keeping.

To watch over, promote, and protect the mutual interests of its members.

To assist necessitous members, and the widows and children of any other dependent kindred of deceased members.

To apply, petition for, or promote any Act of Parliament, Royal Charter, or other authority with the view of the attainment of the above objects or any of them.

The government of the Society is vested in the Council consisting of not more than 30 members in the United Kingdom. The principal office is in the City of London, and the Council has power to sanction the formation of branches under its control.

The members of the Society consisted for many years of three classes—viz.: Fellows, Associates, and students, but the election of students as members upon passing the intermediate examination ceased on September 1, 1902.

The total number of members on the roll in October 1904 was 2068, consisting of 786 Fellows, 1152 Associates, and 130 students (admitted prior to September 1902). The numbers in the principal towns, &c., were as follows:—

Birmingham	76	Leicester	18
Bradford	35	Liverpool	66
Bristol	10	London	511
Cardiff	23	Manchester	94
Edinburgh	20	Newcastle	20
Glasgow	46	Northampton	8
Hull	14	Nottingham	22
Leeds	59	Sheffield	41
Cape Colony	30	New South Wales	15
Transvaal	115	Victoria	52

The regulations as to qualification and admission of members have in their main provisions remained the same throughout. The articles and bye-laws now in force contain the following provisions as to the admission and examination of candidates :—

No person (except as provided by these presents) shall be eligible for admission as a Fellow of the Society unless he has shown to the satisfaction of the Council that he has been continuously in practice as a public accountant in the United Kingdom, the Empire of India, or any Colony or Dependency of the United Kingdom, for not less than seven years immediately prior to the date of his application, or, having passed the examination for the admission of Associates hereinafter mentioned, has been continuously in practice as aforesaid for not less than three years immediately prior to his application.

No person (except as provided by these presents) shall be eligible for admission as an Associate of the Society who is not, at the date of his application, a public accountant or a principal clerk to a public accountant, or an accountant in the service of the Government of the United Kingdom, or of the Government of India, or of any Colony or Dependency of the United Kingdom, or of a corporation or public body, and who has not passed such an examination or examinations as the Council may, from time to time, by bye-law or otherwise, determine.

All applications for admission to membership, upon being made in the forms prescribed by the Articles of Association, shall in the first place be submitted to the Examination and Membership Committee of the Council.

It shall be the duty of the Examination and Membership Committee of the Council to inquire into the professional standing and character of every applicant for admission, and the Committee's report on each case shall be laid before the Council, together with the candidate's application.

The Council shall consider each application, together with the Examination and Membership Committee's report thereon. The Council shall at their discretion determine as to the conditions upon which any applicant shall be admitted to membership, or they may adjourn the consideration of any application or postpone the election of any applicant, or they may altogether refuse to admit any applicant to membership, and their decision not to admit any applicant shall be final, and no reason shall be given for such refusal.

The examinations of the Society are the preliminary in general educational subjects, the intermediate in book-keeping and accounts, partnership and executry law, liquidations and general commercial knowledge; and the final in advanced book - keeping, auditing, liquidations, partnership and executry law and accounts, and mercantile, company, bankruptcy and arbitration law. In Scotland and in the Colonies the legal subjects included in the intermediate and final examinations may be varied to meet the requirements of Scottish or Colonial law. The examination fees are: preliminary, £1 1s.; intermediate, £1 11s. 6d.; final, £2 2s.

Articles or indentures of apprenticeship are a condition precedent to the intermediate examination, subject to the following special provisions:—

1. Clerks to public accountants (other than articled clerks) of not less than six years' continuous service, and whose age shall not be less than 22 years, may apply for permission to sit for the intermediate examination provided they have first passed or obtained exemption from the preliminary examination.

2. Candidates (other than articled clerks) who have passed the intermediate examination and attained the age of 25 years, may apply for permission to sit for the final examination. Such candidates must produce certificates from their employer or employers proving nine years' continuous service in the profession.

3. Senior clerks to public accountants who have had not less than ten years' continuous experience in the profession and have attained the age of 27 years, may apply to sit for the final examination only. Such candidates must produce certificates from their employer or employers proving their length of service, position, and character.

4. No clerk shall be admitted to membership of the Society without examination, but on a longer continuous service than is prescribed in the two preceding clauses, the Council may, at its discretion, permit an examination equivalent to the final to be substituted for the above.

It will be observed that though articles of clerkship are provided for by the Society's regulations, and are freely entered into, the Society admits to its examinations clerks to professional accountants whose experience and training are in accordance with the conditions laid down.

The entrance fees of the Society are: Fellows, £10 10s.; Associates, £5 5s.; and the annual subscriptions: Fellows, £2 2s.; Associates, £1 1s.; students, 10s. 6d.

In the year 1899 an agreement was entered into between the Society and the Scottish Institute of Accountants, a body established in Scotland in or about the year 1880, whereby the Scottish Institute became the Scottish Branch of the Society, and the members thereof were transferred to the Society's roll of membership. This agreement, which was confirmed by special resolutions passed by the members of the Society, affected 123 members.

In the year 1902 a further agreement was entered into between the Society and the Institute of Accountants in the (late) South African Republic, whereby the said Institute became the Transvaal Branch of the Society, and the members thereof were also transferred to the Society's roll of membership. This agreement was approved by special resolutions passed by the members, and was the means of adding 77 names to the roll.

The branches of the Society established before the end of 1903 were as follows: Scotland, Ireland, Victoria (Melbourne), New South Wales (Sydney), South Africa other than Transvaal (Cape Town), and Transvaal (Johannesburg). There are District Societies of Incorporated Accountants formed for the purpose of mutual intercourse and the reading of papers on matters of professional interest at Manchester, Sheffield, Birmingham, Leeds (Yorkshire Society), Cardiff (South Wales Society), Liverpool, Newcastle-on-Tyne, and Bristol (West of England Society). Students' Societies are also established in London and Birmingham.

The publications of the Society are :—

Incorporated Accountants' Year Book, containing List of Members, Articles of Association, Bye-laws of the Council, Library Catalogue, Examination Papers, &c. (yearly).
Examination Papers (half-yearly).
Incorporated Accountants' Journal (monthly).

The policy of the Society is directed towards securing the registration and control of professional accountants by Statute of the Imperial and Colonial Parliaments.

There is a London Society of Corporate Accountants, being the London organisation of the Corporation of Accountants, Limited, registered in Scotland in 1891, which is stated to have a membership of over 50 in the metropolis. "Accountants in public practice (and under certain circumstances accountants to limited companies) are eligible as members." There is also a Yorkshire District Society of Corporate Accountants.

As regards Ireland, there was a "Public Accomptant" in Dublin in 1808, as well as a "Sworn broker and accomptant," [1] but the profession was very little known there before the middle of last century. In 1850 the Dublin Directory shows 26 accountants; in 1860, 30; in 1870, 33; and in 1880, 30.

On 14th May 1888 THE INSTITUTE OF CHARTERED ACCOUNTANTS IN IRELAND was incorporated by Royal Charter, with 31 members, mostly practising in Dublin, Belfast, and Cork. The number has now increased to 62, of whom 19 are in Dublin, 34 in Belfast, and 5 in Cork.

The Charter is very similar in terms to that of the English Institute, and the conditions of admission to membership include a preliminary examination in general education, five years' service under articles with a practising Chartered Accountant, an intermediate examination

[1] Worthington, *op. cit.*

in book-keeping, auditing, executorship accounts, liquidations and bankruptcies, and advanced algebra, and a final examination in accounts, auditing, liquidations, &c., bankruptcy, company, partnership, and arbitration law, and actuarial science,

The entrance fees are £10 10s. as Associate, and an additional £10 10s. as Fellow. The annual contributions are: Fellows, £5 5s.; Associates in practice, £3 3s.; Associates not in practice, £1 1s. The examination fees are £1 1s. for preliminary, and £2 2s. for intermediate or final examination.

A branch of the Society of Accountants and Auditors was formed in Ireland in 1900, which has 31 members.

In Ireland practically all bankrupt estates are administered by a permanent Court Official, known as the Official Assignee. An accountant is, however, frequently appointed the Trustee under Deeds of Arrangement. As in other parts of the United Kingdom, the formation of Joint-Stock Companies has created a greater demand for the services of qualified accountants, and the value of good account-keeping and auditing is being more and more recognised.

Before concluding this chapter reference may be made to the Isle of Man and the Channel Islands, which, having separate governments, and making their own laws, are in a different position from other parts of the United Kingdom. The Isle of Man being convenient of access, is, it is understood, chiefly served by accountants from the mainland. There was, it is true, some years ago a local or professedly local organisation of accountants, but it fell upon evil days. The Channel Islands, which are separated from England by a troublesome strip of sea, and have different coinage, weights, and measures, give employment to a number of local accountants, and also to four or five firms of Chartered Accountants. Guernsey has recently earned some notoriety as a convenient place for the registration of Companies, which, for reasons of their own, desire to evade the more exacting conditions of registration in England, and the heavier duties payable there. There is, however, a draft ordinance at present under consideration, designed to bring the local Company Law more into conformity with that of England.

CHAPTER V

THE BRITISH COLONIES, ETC.

SOCIETIES FORMED IN MONTREAL, TORONTO, NOVA SCOTIA, MANITOBA, AND BRITISH COLUMBIA — INSTITUTES IN AUSTRALASIA—UNIFORM EXAMINATIONS—MOVEMENT FOR AMALGAMATION—OTHER SOCIETIES IN AUSTRALIA AND NEW ZEALAND — INSTITUTES IN NATAL AND SOUTH AFRICAN REPUBLIC — SITUATION IN THE TRANSVAAL— ORDINANCE OF LEGISLATIVE COUNCIL — CAPE COLONY— INDIA—CEYLON—HONG KONG—SINGAPORE—EGYPT

THE movement for the organisation of accountants begun in Scotland in 1853 and taken up in England in 1870, soon spread to other parts of the British Empire.

The first of the colonies to form an Association of Accountants was the Dominion of Canada, in the two chief provinces of which steps to that end were almost simultaneously taken. On 18th June 1879 a preliminary meeting was held in Montreal to consider the advisability of forming an Association of Accountants and of applying to the Legislature of the Province of Quebec for an Act of Incorporation. On 5th December 1879 a Provisional Council was formed, and on 24th July 1880 THE ASSOCIATION OF ACCOUNTANTS IN MONTREAL was finally incorporated under Statute of the Province. Membership of the Association is strictly limited to practising accountants in the Province of Quebec. Every applicant for admission must have attained the age of twenty-one years, and must have been in practice as a professional accountant in the city of Montreal for a period of one year at least, or have served for three years at least as clerk or apprentice with a member of the Association. An examination by a Committee of the Council has also to be undergone on the principles of arithmetic and algebra, insolvent law, book-keeping and accounts, and the practical working of insolvent and trust estates. There is an examination fee of $10, and members pay an entry money of $40 and an annual assessment which must not in any year exceed $20. In March 1904 there were 20 members of the Association.

In November 1879 some of the principal accountants and book-keepers of Toronto united for the purpose of forming an association of persons occupied in the various branches of accountancy, and in December following The Institute of Accountants and Adjusters of Ontario was organised. A constitution and bye-laws were adopted, and the Institute held regular meetings and largely increased its membership. The tests of admission to membership of the Institute were general good character and an implied knowledge of accounts, the occupation of the applicant usually being relied upon as evidence of such qualifications. In the winter of 1881 and 1882 the Institute membership had increased to about 150 persons, and it was decided to apply for incorporation. A special Act of the Legislature of Ontario giving effect to this application was assented to on 1st February 1883, by which the Institute was incorporated under the title of THE INSTITUTE OF CHARTERED ACCOUNTANTS OF ONTARIO. The intention of the incorporators was to secure incorporation on a line similar to the Royal Charter granted to the Institute of Chartered Accountants in England and Wales, but it was found impossible to get so far. The Legislature, which at that time consisted largely of representatives of the rural population of the Province, was exceedingly suspicious of anything which looked like an attempt to secure "class legislation"; and some of the most important provisions of the Act had to be modified. That the Charter was granted at all at that time was probably due largely to the fact that its

objects were stated to be distinctly educational; the Legislature took no account whatever of existing conditions, with
a view to granting any definite status to men engaged in the
practice of accounting, and for the reasons already mentioned
refrained carefully from allowing any exclusive privileges, or
attaching any official function to the profession of an accountant. The first bye-laws of the new Institute provided for
an examination for the position of Fellow; but membership
generally continued to be by the vote of the members, on the
ground of good character alone. This continued to be the
case until about 1891, when by reason of the larger measure
of recognition accorded to the profession of accounting, it
became possible to reorganise the Institute and provide for
admission to membership by examination only. When the
Council of the Institute finally determined to adopt definite
tests of membership, the roll of the Institute contained something over one hundred names, a considerable reduction from
the number at the time of incorporation. An inquiry into
the reasons for the falling-off in the membership was one of
the determining factors in their decision. It was found that
the majority of those who had joined the Institute at its
inception found no advantage to themselves by continuing
as members. To be a Chartered Accountant carried with it
no significance in the public mind. The Council carefully
reconsidered its bye-laws and provided for a series of examinations corresponding with the recognised tests in the English
societies. Under these bye-laws it was also provided that no
member, who was not a member at the time of incorporation,
should be entitled to style himself a Chartered Accountant
until he had submitted to an examination; and at the time
when the change was decided upon, there was consequently
a considerable number of members who were entitled to continue as members but were not entitled to announce themselves as Chartered Accountants, or in any such way as would
imply competency as accountants. During the ten years
that followed these non-qualified members have one by one

submitted themselves for examination or else withdrawn from membership, and it was announced that last year the sole remaining members of this class had qualified and were entitled to their certificates. The Institute now consists solely of persons who have passed the prescribed examinations, and the majority are now practising accountants.

At the time of the incorporation of the Institute there were few, if any, industrial corporations doing business within the Province, and the Insurance and Financial companies usually employed as auditors men who occupied book-keepers' positions and audited the accounts after business hours, consequently there was little for public accountants to do excepting the performance of such functions as came within the requirements of the Insolvency Act then in force. The Ontario Institute, however, by persistently placing itself before the public, and making known the nature of the tests required to enable a man to style himself a Chartered Accountant, has eventually succeeded in establishing the profession upon a sure footing. It may confidently be stated that over seventy-five per cent. of the auditing business of that Province is now performed by members of the Ontario Institute; and the public do not now ask, as formerly, what it means to be a Chartered Accountant. The educational features of the Institute's work, which were one of the chief grounds for recognition in 1883, have been preserved and pushed vigorously each winter; series of lectures have been held, the lecturers being members of the Institute who have given their services without remuneration. Up to 1891 the annual examinations were attended by an average of three or four candidates. The examinations in 1903 were attended by nearly sixty candidates. In 1900 a Students' Association was formed, and lectures were also delivered to them on the various subjects of the examinations.

Under the Act of Incorporation the Institute is empowered to grant Diplomas of Fellowship to competent members enabling them to use the distinguishing letters F.C.A. Under the bye-laws three examinations are held, the primary, the intermediate, and the final. The first is a test of general education, the second embraces book-keeping and accounts, auditing, general commercial knowledge, and statutory requirements relating to companies, partnerships, and insolvency, the third covers similar ground, but more advanced. A term of practical experience of accounts may be accepted in lieu of the primary examination, and three years' practice as a public accountant may exempt from the intermediate examination. After passing the final examination candidates are admitted Associate Members, and after five years' practice and on attaining the age of thirty they are admitted Fellows. The examination fees are $5 for the primary, and $10 each for the intermediate and final examinations. The entry money as an Associate is $20 and as a Fellow $50. The annual subscription for Fellows is $5, for Associates resident in Toronto $5, and for Associates not resident in Toronto $3. There were 83 members of the Institute in the list for 1904.

THE INSTITUTE OF CHARTERED ACCOUNTANTS OF NOVA SCOTIA was incorporated by Act of the Legislature on 30th March 1900. Candidates for admission are, at the discretion, of the Council, subjected to three examinations or tests as to their qualifications, viz., preliminary, intermediate, and final. The final examination must be passed satisfactorily before admission, and according to the Act of Incorporation the subjects are (1) the grouping and classification of accounts, (2) the opening of sets of books for a new business, (3) the methods for detecting mistakes in book-keeping, and (4) the methods pursued in the audit of a set of books. The examination fees are $2.50, or if the final examination only is passed, $5, the entry money $10, and the annual subscription $5. By the bye-laws members are entitled to sign themselves "Chartered Accountant" or any abbreviation thereof. The number of members of the Institute in

March 1904 was 14: 12 in Nova Scotia, 1 in New Brunswick, and 1 in India.

THE CHARTERED ACCOUNTANTS' ASSOCIATION OF MANITOBA was incorporated in 1886. Candidates are required to pass an examination in general accounting, company and mercantile law, &c. The Association had a membership in August 1904 of 15.

THE INSTITUTE OF ACCOUNTANTS OF BRITISH COLUMBIA was formed in Vancouver in 1904 and at the time of writing is engaged in adjusting its constitution and bye-laws.

In New Brunswick no organisation of accountants exists, which is also the position in the independent colony of Newfoundland.

In 1901–1902, as the outcome of a number of conferences, application was made to the Parliament of Canada for an Act of Incorporation of an Association of practising accountants, applicable to the whole Dominion. This application was opposed by the Chartered Accountants of Ontario, Nova Scotia, and Manitoba; but, notwithstanding, an Act received the Royal assent on 15th May 1902, incorporating six gentlemen of Toronto, three of Montreal, three of Ottawa, two of Winnipeg, one of Vancouver, one of Victoria, two of St. John, N.B., and two of Halifax, as THE DOMINION ASSOCIATION OF CHARTERED ACCOUNTANTS. Under the bye-laws the membership consists of Fellows and Associates. All members of the existing Institutes who applied for admission within one year of the passing of the Act were eligible as Associates, but only practising accountants, whose applications for membership are approved by the Councils of their respective bodies, may become Fellows. Any other applicant for membership must undergo such examination as to fitness or character as the Council may from time to time prescribe.

The bye-laws state that Fellows shall have the right to use the initials F.C.A. (Can.). Fifteen members of the Montreal Association, seven of the Ontario Institute, and one of the Nova Scotia Institute, have become Fellows of the Dominion

Association, and three members of the Ontario Institute have become Associates. At April 1904 the Dominion Association contained 33 Fellows and 15 Associates. The entrance fees are: Fellows $50, Associates $25; and an annual assessment is made not exceeding $30 for Fellows, and $15 for Associates.

In Australasia during the last twenty years there has been a great development of the profession. The colonies now comprised within the Commonwealth of Australia and the colony of New Zealand may be conveniently dealt with together, as, though they have separate laws, the differences in those affecting the practice of accountants are not so material as to result in the profession being anywhere carried on under exceptional conditions.

The following six Institutes of Accountants in Australasia have since 1899 been associated for purposes of examination of candidates for admission:—

THE INSTITUTE OF ACCOUNTANTS IN SOUTH AUSTRALIA (INCORPORATED) was originally formed as "The Adelaide Society of Accountants" on 20th November 1885, but has borne the wider title since 1889. Admission in ordinary circumstances is obtained as an Associate by passing the required examination, after three years' service with a Fellow of the Institute, or after three years' practice as a public accountant. Associates of five years' standing in practice on their own account may be admitted Fellows. The Council has, however, a power, under certain conditions, of electing as members candidates who are following the profession without requiring them to pass examinations. The entrance fee for Associates is £1 1s., and for Fellows £2 12s. 6d. The annual subscription of Fellows is £2 2s., and of Associates £1 1s. When the Institute was founded in 1885 there were 19 members. At 31st December 1903 the membership consisted of 35 Fellows and 103 Associates.

THE INCORPORATED INSTITUTE OF ACCOUNTANTS OF VICTORIA was the outcome of a meeting of thirty practising accountants held in Melbourne on 12th April 1886, and it was incorporated on 1st March 1887. Admission is obtained after passing the preliminary, intermediate, and final examinations, unless the candidate be a member of another recognised Institute, or the examinations, or any of them, shall have been dispensed with. Two years' accountancy experience is requisite before election as an Associate, and a further five years' public practice before election as a Fellow. Entrance fees: Associates £2 2s., Fellows, a further sum of £3 3s. Annual subscriptions: Fellows £2 2s., Associates £1 1s. At 1st June 1904 there were 109 Fellows and 162 Associates of the Institute.

THE QUEENSLAND INSTITUTE OF ACCOUNTANTS (INCORPORATED) was formed in Brisbane on 27th August 1891 with 18 original members. Admission as an Associate is obtained after passing the final examination, and as a Fellow after having been an Associate for five years. The Council may in special cases, however, admit Fellows and Associates who have not fulfilled the usual conditions. Entrance fees: Associates £3 3s., Fellows, a further sum of £1 1s. Annual subscriptions: Fellows £2 2s., Associates £1 1s. At 30th March 1904 the membership consisted of 25 Fellows and 24 Associates.

THE SYDNEY INSTITUTE OF PUBLIC ACCOUNTANTS was incorporated on 21st May 1894, there being then 17 members. Admission as an Associate is obtained after passing the final examination, and an Associate may become a Fellow after three years' continuous practice as a public accountant. There is a power given to the Council to modify the conditions of admission as Fellow or Associate in special cases. The desire of the Institute has always been to confine its ranks to practising public accountants. Entrance fees: Associates £2 2s., Fellows £5 5s. Annual subscriptions: Fellows £3 3s., Associates £1 1s. Membership at 31st March 1904: 25 Fellows in practice, 7 Associates in practice, and 24 Associates not in practice.

THE TASMANIAN INSTITUTE OF ACCOUNTANTS was founded on 2nd December 1897, there being 12 original members, and incorporated under the Companies Acts. Admission can only be obtained after examination. Entrance fees £1 1s. Annual subscriptions, not exceeding £2 2s. for Fellows and £1 1s. for Associates. Number of members at December 1903: 36 Fellows, 4 Associates.

THE INCORPORATED INSTITUTE OF ACCOUNTANTS OF NEW ZEALAND was incorporated in May 1894. The foundation members were nominated by the Chambers of Commerce in the four leading towns of the Colony, and a Committee of these members afterwards admitted other practising accountants who submitted satisfactory applications. Since then all new members have been admitted only after examination. Associates of five years' standing may be elected Fellows. Entrance fees: Fellows £5 5s., Associates £3 3s. Annual subscriptions: Fellows £2 2s., Associates £1 1s. Number of members at 31st July 1903: Fellows 100, Associates 43.

The uniform examinations for Australasia, to which the foregoing six Institutes submit their candidates, are as follows:—

FINAL EXAMINATION for the degree of Associate, or Fellow, or for advancement to Fellowship:—

1. Book-keeping and Accounts—two papers.
2. Auditing.
3. Rights and duties of Trustees and Receivers, and Law of Arbitration.
4. Law of Insolvency.
5. Law relating to Companies.
6. Mercantile Law.

Candidates for Fellowship must obtain a minimum of 75 per cent. of marks in five subjects, including Nos. 1 and 2, and an aggregate of 475 marks. Candidates for the degree of Associate must obtain 65 per cent. in four subjects, including Nos. 1 and 2, and an aggregate of 400 marks.

INTERMEDIATE EXAMINATION for Students :—

1. Book-keeping and Accounts.
2. Auditing.
3. Insolvency Law.
4. Company Law.

Candidates must pass in Nos. 1 and 2 with a minimum of 65 per cent. in each and obtain an aggregate of 150 marks.

The papers dealing with local law are set and examined by local examiners.

The arrangements made in 1899 among these Institutes for uniform examinations having worked satisfactorily, the idea of an amalgamation of the six Institutes concerned into one great Australasian Institute was naturally brought forward. It was at a conference in Sydney in 1901 (in the week in which the Commonwealth of Australia was founded), that the proposal was first made and the subject was further considered in Adelaide in June 1902 and at a convention in Melbourne in June 1903. At this convention all the Institutes were represented by delegates, and a draft constitution was submitted and discussed at great length. It was found impossible, however, to reconcile the various views and provide for the different circumstances, and though a draft constitution was agreed upon after the representatives of one Institute had withdrawn from the convention, it was not in all respects acceptable to the constituents of the delegates who adjusted it.

The movement accordingly came to a standstill. The main difficulty was one which is met with in most places where accountants exist, viz., the rights and position in the Institute of the accountant who is not in public practice. Another difficulty was the situation of the head office of the amalgamated body.

The Institutes already mentioned are, however, not the

only bodies of accountants in Australasia. THE FEDERAL IN-STITUTE OF ACCOUNTANTS was incorporated in Victoria in July 1894, the intention being that while the Institute should have its headquarters in Melbourne, there should be local Boards subject to the Council in the other Colonies. Examinations are held yearly, and three years' continuous practice in accounts is required of candidates presenting themselves for admission as Associates at the final examination. The Institute contained in January 1904 92 Fellows and 87 Associates located in all parts of Australia, but chiefly in Melbourne, Brisbane, and Adelaide.

THE SOCIETY OF ACCOUNTANTS AND AUDITORS OF VICTORIA was incorporated on 3rd November 1900. The Society consists of Members and of Fellows, who may either have gone through the course prescribed for students, or have satisfied the Council as to their qualifications. At September 1904 there were 13 Fellows and 87 members.

The Society of Accountants and Auditors (London) has also branches in Victoria and New South Wales with 52 and 15 members respectively.

THE CORPORATION OF ACCOUNTANTS OF AUSTRALIA, which was incorporated on 17th August 1899, has its office in Sydney. Examinations are conducted, and Associates are admitted after passing the final examination. They may become Fellows after three years' public practice. In January 1904 there were 26 Fellows and 15 Associates. The Corporation issues a quarterly journal entitled *The Public Accountant*.

THE INSTITUTE OF ACCOUNTANTS AND AUDITORS OF WESTERN AUSTRALIA was incorporated on 3rd December 1900. It instituted local examination of candidates in 1903, in which it endeavours to maintain a high standard of efficiency. In February 1904 it had 12 Fellows and 45 Associates. There are about twenty firms of accountants in Western Australia, some of them being connected with the Incorporated Institute of Accountants, Victoria.

THE NEW ZEALAND ACCOUNTANTS' AND AUDITORS'

ASSOCIATION was incorporated on 30th December 1898. The Association consists of Honorary Members, Fellows, Associates, and students, and is open to both sexes. Several ladies have been admitted. Examinations are conducted, but Fellows and Associates are admitted without examination—in the former case if they have been in practice or employed as an accountant for five years, and in the latter case if they have been employed as an accountant or assistant accountant or accountant's principal clerk for three years. The Council has also power by special resolution to admit as a Fellow or Associate any accountant who may not be eligible under these rules. At 31st December 1903 there were 155 members, of whom about 40 are marked as in public practice.

It will be seen that the profession in Australasia is fully organised and is active and vigorous. Most of the Institutes arrange periodical lectures for the instruction of their members, and Students' Societies exist in connection with some of them. Professional libraries are also established in the chief towns. Municipalities and other public bodies are beginning to appreciate the value of the services of professional accountants, who are rapidly taking up an important position in the business community.

The part of the British Empire to which we now turn as being next in interest to accountants is South Africa.

THE INSTITUTE OF ACCOUNTANTS IN NATAL was formed in 1895, the first President having been in practice as a professional accountant in Durban from about 1867. It consisted at December 1903 of 24 Fellows and 12 Associates. Associates are admitted only after examination. Fellows are also admitted after examination, but Associates of two years' standing, members of other recognised Institutes, and principals of firms in practice as accountants, may be admitted without examination. The examinations cover the usual subjects of book-keeping and accounts, auditing, mercantile, company, and insolvency law, average adjusting, and general commercial knowledge. Entrance fees :

Associates £2 2s. and £2 2s. on election as Fellows. Annual subscription : Fellows £5 5s., Associates £3 3s. The Institute has a good library at its office in Durban.

THE INSTITUTE OF ACCOUNTANTS AND AUDITORS IN THE SOUTH AFRICAN REPUBLIC was formed in 1894 with an original membership of 65, and early approached the Boer Government for a Charter of Incorporation. After considerable delay the Volksraad in 1899 approved the principle, and published a draft law, but the outbreak of the war stopped further proceedings. After the Transvaal became a British Colony an agreement dated 28th August 1902 was entered into between the Institute and the Society of Accountants and Auditors (London), by which the Institute became the Transvaal branch of that Society. There were 99 members of the Institute at that time. In February 1903 there were 95 members of the new branch, and in February 1904, 97 Fellows and 1 Associate. The branch is of course subject to the rules of the Society, and the examination of candidates for membership is under the control of the London Council. An annual subscription of £5 5s. is payable by Fellows, and £2 12s. 6d. by Associates.

In January 1903 a number of British Chartered Accountants in South Africa, several of whom had been members of the old Transvaal Institute, formed an Association under the name of THE INSTITUTE OF CHARTERED ACCOUNTANTS IN SOUTH AFRICA. At August 1904 this Association had 18 members, all but one being resident in the Transvaal. An entrance fee of £3 3s., and an annual subscription of £2 2s., are payable.

In the course of the year 1903 suggestions had been made that the profession in the Transvaal might be put on a better footing by an Ordinance of the Legislative Council of the Colony, and a Joint Committee of the above two bodies was appointed to discuss the terms of such an ordinance. This Committee after full discussion was unable to agree upon terms, and the local branch of the Society then drafted an ordinance which they promoted on their own account. Petitions were lodged with the Legislative Council by members of the Institute of Chartered Accountants intimating approval of the preamble of the draft ordinance, but desiring that certain of the general provisions thereof should be amended; and by 65 public accountants, secretaries of companies, and accountants of leading mercantile or financial houses in Johannesburg, desiring certain amendments. The Legislative Council referred the draft ordinance to a select committee, which heard evidence and found the preamble proved, but allowed considerable latitude in regard to amendments with a view to enabling the various parties interested to arrive at an understanding as to the points of difference between them. The ordinance as amended was passed by the Legislative Council in August 1904.

As this is the first law regulating the profession which has been passed in the British dominions, its provisions may be referred to in some detail. The Ordinance incorporates THE TRANSVAAL SOCIETY OF ACCOUNTANTS, which is required to keep a register of public accountants, and no one who is not registered as such "shall describe himself or hold himself out as an accountant, or as a public accountant, or as an auditor," or use any title, letters, &c., indicating that he is so, under a penalty not exceeding £100 or three months' imprisonment, but a person employed exclusively at a salary on accounts may describe himself as an accountant in relation to his employment. The persons entitled to be placed forthwith on the register are persons resident in the Transvaal who are members of the Transvaal Branch of the Society of Accountants' and Auditors, or of any of the five Chartered Societies of the United Kingdom, or of the Society of Accountants and Auditors, England, or who were practising as public accountants in the Transvaal at the date of the passing of the Ordinance, or who make written application and are considered by the Provisional Council constituted under the Ordinance fit persons to be registered "by virtue of their position and past experience." After the expiry of six months no one shall be registered unless he is resident in the Transvaal and is a member of a Society or Institute of Accountants whose membership is declared to be sufficient by the bye-laws of the newly constituted Society for the time being in force, or has passed the examinations prescribed by the bye-laws, and has had such practical experience as is required by them. The following are declared to be offences for which a registered accountant may have his name removed from the register by the Supreme Court, or be suspended from practice.

> Allowing an unregistered person who is not in partnership with himself to practise in his name as a public accountant.
>
> Sharing profits with any one not a partner or accepting commission from solicitors, auctioneers, &c.
>
> Certifying statements representing accountancy work which was not carried on under his personal supervision or direction.
>
> Allowing commission to any one for bringing him work.
>
> Improperly attempting to obtain work.
>
> Performing work in connection with disputes on condition of payment only in the event of a favourable result.
>
> Dishonourable professional conduct.
>
> Wilful breach or neglect of the bye-laws of the Society.
>
> Any acts or practices similar to the foregoing.

Any person on the register is entitled to style himself "Registered Public Accountant (Transvaal)." The Society's bye-laws are subject to the approval of the Lieutenant-Governor of the Transvaal.

The Ordinance is not all that was desired, and considerable diversity of opinion exists in the Colony as to the details of the measure, but it can hardly fail to have a beneficial effect. Although it interferes with no one in the performance of any kind of accounting work with which he may be entrusted, it ensures that only those who are registered shall be permitted to describe themselves to the public by the title which implies proper qualification for undertaking such work.

In Cape Colony a branch of the Society of Accountants and Auditors (England) was formed about ten years ago and it had 30 members in September 1904. There are also several British Chartered Accountants in practice in Cape Town and Port Elizabeth. A few members of the home Societies have also already established themselves in Buluwayo, Rhodesia.

We have now dealt with every part of the British Empire where, so far as we can ascertain, incorporated Societies of Accountants exist, but before closing this chapter we may give a short account of the position of the profession in other colonies or countries under British administration.

In INDIA a considerable number of British accountants find employment, and in the Bombay Presidency both Hindoos and Parsees are experts in figures. The Hindoo is skilful in book-keeping and in unravelling intricate accounts, and the Parsee affects also the higher duties of the auditor. The great majority of mill audits are conducted by Parsees. They are frequently interested in the capital of the concern, and they undertake the audit for a very small fee. In many cases the books are written in the vernacular and in native characters, which precludes the idea of a European desiring such audits. The Parsee is ambitious and enterprising, and many of them have sat for and obtained the London Chamber of Commerce Diploma in book-keeping and accounts. An increasing number are endeavouring to secure a business training in Great Britain. They are naturally energetic and gifted, courteous, willing, and helpful to one another.

The work of the British accountants in Bombay, Calcutta, and Madras consists almost entirely of auditing the accounts of concerns in which European capital is employed.

There are no public accountants in the native communities of CEYLON. Accounts in the native firms are mostly kept by Tamils, who are called " Kanakapulles." The rice-dealing Chetties (Tamils) keep their accounts on ola leaves. In case of winding up a business, or when disputes arise between the parties, they engage, if found necessary, some one from their own community with a knowledge of business, and in whom the parties have confidence.

It is with the European community that skilled professional accountants are employed. For the most part they are attached to firms and companies, but their number does not exceed five. There is only one professional accountant in practice solely as an accountant; but a considerable amount of the work of auditing companies' accounts and other work connected with the accountant profession is entrusted to some of the others referred to.

The accounts of railways and other works belonging to Government pass through the office of the Auditor-General.

The profession of Accountant in HONG KONG is still in its infancy, indeed, until 1902 audits and other professional work had been performed by men chosen for their lengthy experience in the business usages of the Colony, but in no sense professional accountants in the usual acceptance of the term. In 1902 a member of the English Institute commenced practice as a Chartered Accountant, and is still the only trained man.

There are in SINGAPORE seven or eight accountants of British nationality in public practice. Of these one is a Scottish Chartered Accountant, one an English Chartered Accountant, and one an Incorporated Accountant, the others being ex-bankers and merchants.

The profession is not associated or organised. In the cases of several companies the work is jointly performed by two auditors.

In this chapter reference may also be made to EGYPT, which since 1883 has been under British influence. Notwithstanding the difficulties arising from the cosmopolitan character of the country and the various languages (chiefly Arabic, English, and French), in which accounts are kept, already one or two British firms of accountants are estab-

lished in Cairo and Alexandria. Until recently the accounts
of Egyptian companies were audited by government or
bank officials of all nationalities, but of late professional
auditors have been employed in many cases. Bankruptcy
work is in the hands of so-called "experts" attached to
the "Mixed Tribunals." The Chambers of Commerce are
endeavouring to procure the appointment of better qualified
men to act in this capacity.

Previous to the reforms which have been carried out in
Egypt of recent years, all the accountant business of the
country was in the hands of Coptic clerks, who pursued a
complex system intelligible only to themselves, and of which
it would be difficult for even a skilled accountant to give
an idea. Under the pressure of more civilised institutions,
however, this archaic mode of book-keeping has now disappeared, and merchants generally employ the ordinary system
of accounts, although some slight diversities may be found in
individual cases, more especially among the Syrian and Coptic
communities.

CHAPTER VI

THE UNITED STATES OF AMERICA

THE PROFESSION ONLY RECOGNISED RECENTLY—THE FIRST
SOCIETY OF PUBLIC ACCOUNTANTS—THE MOVEMENT FOR
STATE LEGISLATION — THE FIRST C.P.A. LAW — SIMILAR
LAWS IN OTHER STATES—SUBJECTS OF EXAMINATION—
DIFFERENCE BETWEEN AMERICAN AND BRITISH SYSTEMS
—EXISTING SOCIETIES OF ACCOUNTANTS IN THE STATES
—FEDERATION OF SOCIETIES—CONGRESS AT ST. LOUIS—
CONDITIONS OF PRACTICE IN THE UNITED STATES—THE
PROFESSION IN CUBA

THE history of the profession in the United States may
be said to have commenced only about twenty years ago.
Prior to that time there were comparatively few American
public accountants.   There is one gentleman still living,
however, who commenced business in Boston in 1847, but
for a year or two he was the sole representative of the
profession in that city, and it was many years before it
was regarded with much favour.

In New York an Institute of Accounts was formed in
1882, but this was a scientific body, consisting only partly of
public accountants.

THE AMERICAN ASSOCIATION OF PUBLIC ACCOUNTANTS
was incorporated under New York State law on 20th August
1887, the object being to associate into a Society "the
best and most capable public accountants practising in the
United States."   At the first annual meeting in May 1889
this association had only 25 Fellows and 7 Associates.
During the first five years of its existence the Asso-

ciation did little. The professional accountant was then almost unknown outside of New York, and although the Association was constituted to include members over the whole Republic, it became in effect a New York body. In 1892 the Association started a school of accounts in New York under authority of the Regents of the University, but this proved a failure.

During the winter of 1894–1895 the Institute of Accounts drafted a Bill providing for the professional education of accountants, and for securing a professional title. The American Association also drafted a Bill to provide for the licensing of practising accountants, and early in 1895 both Bills were introduced in the State Legislature. A meeting attended by about sixty accountants was held in New York in March 1895, at which a Committee was appointed, which Committee resolved to support the Bill of the Institute of Accounts. Neither Bill passed, however. Next year the attempt to obtain State legislalation was renewed, and finally after much effort an Act "to regulate the profession of Public Accountant" in the State of New York was signed by the Governor on 17th August 1896.

This Act, which was the forerunner of similar laws in a number of the other States, provides that any citizen of the United States or person who has duly declared his intention of becoming such citizen, who resides or has a place of business in the State, is over twenty-one years of age and of good moral character, "and who shall have received from the Regents of the University a certificate of his qualifications to practise as a public expert accountant, shall be styled and known as a Certified Public Accountant, and no other person shall assume such title or use the abbreviation C.P.A. or any other words, letters, or figures, to indicate that the person using the same is such certified public accountant." The Regents of the University were empowered to make rules for the examinations and to appoint

THE UNITED STATES OF AMERICA   273

examiners, and they were also authorised for a period of
one year to waive the examination of any person who had
been practising as a public accountant on his own account
for more than one year before the passage of the Act. In
April 1901 the privilege of applying for exemption from
examination under this waiver clause was re-opened to 1st
September 1901.

The example of New York was followed by the State
of Pennsylvania, where after some delay an Act was passed
on 29th March 1899, by Maryland on 10th April 1900, by
California on 23rd March 1901, by Illinois in May 1903, by
Washington in March 1903, and by New Jersey in April
1904. Bills have also been introduced in the Legislatures
of Michigan, Minnesota, Wisconsin, and Kansas, but at the
time of writing have not become law.

The Acts passed in the various States, though identical
as regards the title adopted and protected, are not precisely
similar in the other provisions. In New York and Illinois
certificates are granted, examiners appointed, and rules made
for the examinations, by the University authorities; in the
other States the appointments are made by the Governor,
and the power to formulate rules appears to rest with the
examiners themselves. The clause authorising the waiving
of examination materially differs in the different States. In
Washington examination may be dispensed with if the applicant has resided for more than one year in the State,
whether he has had any experience in the profession or not.
Some diversity in the laws was probably unavoidable, and
may be necessary to meet the special circumstances of each
State, but if the title adopted is to become generally recognised in America as the stamp of high professional capacity,
it is obvious that great care must be used in the administration of the Acts and in the exercise of the powers given.
It is not quite clear whether a Certified Public Accountant of
one State is free to practise as such in another State. It is
noticed that the Illinois and New Jersey laws have a special

provision permitting this, while the others are silent on the point.

Candidates for the C.P.A. certificate are examined in theory of accounts, practical accounting, auditing, and commercial law. In New York a high-school graduation or its equivalent is required as a pre-requisite to examination, and in most of the States from three to five years' satisfactory experience in the study or practice of accounting is necessary before a certificate can be granted. So far the greater number of certificates have been issued under the waiver clause. In New York State, up to the end of 1902, 169 certificates had been so issued, while 93 had been granted to those who had passed the examinations. The failures to pass numbered 115.

The New York law makes no provision for the registration of certificates or their annual renewal. There is, however, a power to revoke any certificate for sufficient cause after notice to the holder and a hearing thereon.

The certificates are unconnected with any Society or Institute. The holder may or may not be a member of a Society. It will thus be seen that the system established in the United States is essentially different from that followed in this country. The C.P.A. certificate is analogous to our medical degree, while our method of admission to membership of an Institute is similar to the practice of the old Gilds. Each system has its advantages. The American plan prevents more effectively the misuse of the title adopted, while the British insures the benefits of association. There is greater freedom and elasticity under the British system, which is, however, accompanied by some liability to abuse.

A step of considerable importance in relation to the education of accountants was taken in New York about three years ago, when the School of Commerce, Accounts, and Finance was founded in connection with the University of New York, mainly through the exertions of individual members of the New York State Society of Certified Public

Accountants, and of that Society in its corporate capacity, assisted by the American Association. The school has the power to confer degrees, the course of study extends over three years, and for session 1904–1905 there were about 200 students. A similar school has recently been started, associated with the University of Pennsylvania.

Though membership of a Society of Accountants is not necessary in order to obtain the C.P.A. degree, there are a number of such Societies in the States. Mention has already been made of the American Association of Public Accountants, which was mainly instrumental in procuring the passage of the New York law regulating the profession. It has also assisted other States in this direction, and has established a Scholarship in Accounting in connection with the School of Commerce, Accounts, and Finance in New York. Although at first practically a New York Society, the Association has of late enlarged its scope, and at October 1904 had 107 Fellows and 39 Associates located in 15 different States. Seventy-three of the Fellows and eight of the Associates held the C.P.A. degree. Members are elected by the Board of Trustees, and Fellows must have been three years in practice on their own account or hold the C.P.A. certificate. Entrance fees: Fellows $25, Associates $10. Annual subscriptions: Fellows $10, Associates $5.

The accountants of Massachusetts have not so far fallen in with the movement for State legislation. The Society incorporated in Boston on 14th February 1901 under the name of THE INCORPORATED PUBLIC ACCOUNTANTS OF MASSACHUSETTS endeavours to establish and maintain repute for the distinctive abbreviation "I.P.A."

The Incorporated Kansas Association of Public Accountants issues C.P.A. diplomas, although no State law has been adopted there. A Charter was granted incorporating the Association.

There is given below a list of all the Societies of Accountants in the United States, with the number of members and

year of formation. With the exceptions already mentioned
all of these Societies were either formed with the view of
procuring a C.P.A. law or have been formed as the result of
such a law having been passed. Membership of those which
are designed Societies of *Certified* Public Accountants is only
open to persons who have obtained the C.P.A. certificate.

Year of Formation	NAME	Number of Members
1887.	American Association of Public Accountants . .	146
1897.	* New York State Society of Certified Public Accountants	101
1897.	* † Pennsylvania Institute of Certified Public Accountants	30
1897.	* † Illinois Association of Certified Public Accountants	40
1901.	† Incorporated Public Accountants of Massachusetts	19
1901.	* † Maryland Association of Certified Public Accountants	21
1902.	* † Washington Society of Certified Public Accountants	8
1903.	* † California Society of Certified Public Accountants	17
1903.	† Ohio Society of Public Accountants . . .	20
1903.	* The Society of Certified Public Accountants of the State of New Jersey	37
1904.	† Incorporated Michigan Association of Public Accountants	10
1904.	† Georgia State Association of Public Accountants .	8
1904.	† Colorado Society of Public Accountants . .	16
1904.	† Missouri Society of Public Accountants . .	18
1904.	Tennessee Association of Public Accountants . .	8
1904.	Louisiana Society of Public Accountants . .	8
1904.	Incorporated Kansas Association of Public Accountants	4
1904.	† Minnesota Society of Public Accountants . .	7
1904.	Wisconsin Association of Public Accountants .	11
1904.	Indiana Association of Public Accountants . .	8
1904.	Kentucky Society of Public Accountants . .	6

* These States have C.P.A. laws.
† These Societies are members of the Federation.

THE FEDERATION OF SOCIETIES OF PUBLIC ACCOUNTANTS
IN AMERICA was founded at a meeting of delegates from the
various Societies held in Washington on 28th October 1902.
The objects for which the Federation was formed as defined
in the Constitution are as follows :—

"(*a*) To bring into communication with one another the
several Associations and Societies of Public Accountants,
organised or to be organised under the laws of the several
States of the United States of America; (*b*) to encourage
the formation of State Associations of Public Accountants
in States where they do not exist; (*c*) to encourage State
Certified Public Accountant legislation on uniform lines;
(*d*) to secure Federal recognition of the profession of the
Public Accountant; (*e*) to facilitate and assist the training
of young members of the profession, and to establish a uniform
standard of efficiency in federated societies; (*f*) to disseminate
throughout the United States a general knowledge of the
objects of the Federation and of the utility of the Public
Accountants in the industrial and financial development of
the country; and (*g*) to further the interests of the profession
of the Public Accountant generally."

The bye-laws provide for the admission of one Society
from each State provided it is solely composed of public
accountants, and has at least seven members exclusive of
Associate members.   An annual contribution is required of $5
for each Fellow.   An annual convention is held at Washington
at which the State Societies are represented by delegates,
and reports are submitted from each Society.   The government of the Federation is vested in an Executive Board
consisting of the President of each Federated Society and
six delegates elected at the annual convention.   The active
management is entrusted to a small Executive Committee,
and there is also a Legislative Committee.

The Report of the annual convention held on 20th October
1903 gives evidence of much energetic work by the officers
of the Federation, and although the result in figures appears

small, it must be remembered that the difficulties are great and the circumstances exceptional. The profession of accountant has hitherto been little known and little understood in America. The States are very numerous and cover an enormous extent of country. Each State makes its own laws regulating commerce and the professions. The people as a whole are perhaps not naturally pre-disposed to the care and pains necessary for accurate accounting. The work which the Federation has undertaken is therefore no child's play; but that some such organisation was necessary if the state of the profession in the Republic was to be kept from hopeless confusion appears perfectly clear. Whether success may attend the effort to secure recognition of the public accountant by the central or Federal Government may be doubtful, but if the Federation can succeed in securing some uniformity in the State laws regulating the profession and in their administration it will have achieved a valuable work. Much also may be done in fostering the formation and growth of local Societies and in watching over the general interests of accountants.

In connection with the Louisiana Purchase Exposition or World's Fair held at Saint Louis in 1904, the Federation arranged a congress of Professional Accountants which was held on 26th, 27th, and 28th September. Representatives of the English, Scottish, and Canadian Societies of Accountants were present by invitation, and papers were read and discussions engaged in of much interest to accountants.

In addition to the Societies of Accountants and the Institute of Accounts already mentioned, there is a New York Society of Accountants and Book-keepers, answering in many respects to our Students' Societies, which publishes a useful monthly journal.

The work of an Accountant in the United States is carried on under conditions which differ considerably from those prevailing in Great Britain. The scope of business is more limited, being confined chiefly to audits and investigations. Little of the nature of liquidations or administration of trust estates comes the way of the accountant. The commercial spirit is more in evidence. American accountants freely advertise, and in sympathy with this attitude to the public they are commonly asked to estimate in competition with others for any accounting work which may require to be done. Large pieces of work have often to be carried through at high pressure, and as a consequence there is a floating population of accountants' assistants who are only taken into temporary employment by the different firms as they may require extra help. Those are not the safest kind of persons on whom to rely for efficient work. There is also a tendency among practitioners, perhaps the outcome of necessity, to employ too large a number of unqualified assistants in proportion to principals, with consequences hurtful to the profession. It can hardly be doubted too that the growing practice of forming auditing or accounting companies, in which the element of personal responsibility is completely obscured, is an unhealthy manifestation likely to prove injurious.

The present system, by which single firms undertake work in all quarters of the continent, their assistants being often engaged simultaneously at a number of different places perhaps thousands of miles apart, places a handicap on satisfactory work. The efforts of the Federation to encourage the formation of local Associations and obtain the passing of State C.P.A. laws are undoubtedly calculated to direct the development of the profession towards sounder and better lines in this respect.

Withal a good deal may be learned from our American cousins in matters of Accounting, more especially in the working of costing systems and in the devising of methods of book-keeping by which the results of the trading of huge concerns are shown with a frequency and a rapidity which would astonish accountants or book-keepers of the old-fashioned school. In most of the larger commercial undertakings systems are found in operation which have been perfected by specialists in that particular business, and which are wonderfully successful in attaining the objects aimed at.

It may not be generally known to the accountants of the United States that in the island of Cuba, which has recently been brought under American influence, their profession has for a considerable time occupied an honourable and important position. Commercial schools were established in Havanna in 1850, and from 1865 the degree of " Professor Mercantil" or " Perito Mercantil" was obtainable by a course of studies in commercial and accounting subjects. The COLEGIO DE PROFESSORES Y PERITOS MERCANTILES DE LA HABANA was founded in 1888, and is composed of those who, having obtained the degree, practise as public accountants. This Society has 51 members, and there are in all 61 accountants practising in Havanna. The School of Commerce is now associated with the University, and the diploma of "Professor Mercantil" is only granted after thorough examination in book-keeping, accounting, political economy, mercantile law, and other more general subjects. Persons who are not officially qualified as accountants are prevented from practising as such, and in the Law Courts accountants are employed whenever questions of accounting are involved. In the audit of the accounts of public companies or the administration of bankrupt estates, however, the profession has not as yet obtained any great foothold in Cuba.

CHAPTER VII

THE CONTINENT OF EUROPE

NUMEROUS SOCIETIES IN ITALY—SPHERE OF THE ACCOUNTANT
THERE—PERIODICAL CONGRESSES—PROPOSED LAW AS TO
ACCOUNTANTS—SOCIETIES IN HOLLAND, SWEDEN, AND
BELGIUM — SITUATION IN FRANCE, SPAIN, GERMANY,
RUSSIA, AND THE OTHER EUROPEAN COUNTRIES, WITH
INFORMATION AS TO THE LAW AND PRACTICE IN MATTERS
OF ACCOUNTING

ON leaving English-speaking countries, the first place to
claim attention in an examination of the position of the professional accountant is, of course, ITALY. We have already
dealt at some length with the early history of the profession
in that country, and we shall here take up the narrative at
the time from which what may be called the Italian Renaissance in accounting dates, that is to say, about thirty years
ago.

The Florence accountants, in 1876, had proposed the
holding of a National Congress of Accountants, and a Committee was appointed to promote that object. The Congress,
which was held in Rome in 1879, recommended the formation
of Colleges or Gilds of Accountants in every province of
Italy, and from this period date the numerous Colleges which
now exist. The exception is the *Reale Accademia dei Ragionieri di Bologna*, which is, however, an institution more of
a scientific than a professional character, and its members
are for the most part officials and lovers of science rather
than public accountants.

The College of Milan, formed in 1880, was the successor

of the Academy then existing; which, again, was the representative of an older college.   The College of Florence, dating from December 1879, arose out of the Committee already mentioned, and a then existing Association, the successor of two previous Societies, the first of which dated from 1869.

The following is a list of the more important Societies of Accountants in Italy, with the number of members in each:—

NAME OF SOCIETY	NUMBER OF MEMBERS
Collegio dei Ragionieri di Alessandria	37
Collegio dei Ragionieri di Bergamo	31
Reale Accademica dei Ragionieri di Bologna	95
Collegio dei Ragionieri di Biella	30
Collegio dei Ragionieri di Como	92
Collegio dei Ragionieri di Cremona	63
Collegio dei Ragionieri di Cuneo	32
Collegio dei Ragionieri di Ferrara	70
Collegio dei Ragionieri di Firenze	105
Collegio dei Periti Ragionieri Esercenti di Genova	36
Associazione Ligure dei Ragionieri di Genova	160
Collegio dei Ragionieri di Girgenti	15
Collegio dei Ragionieri di Lecce	19
Collegio dei Ragionieri di Mantova	80
Collegio dei Ragionieri di Messina	30
Collegio dei Ragionieri di Milano	400
Collegio dei Ragionieri di Modena	80
Collegio dei Ragionieri della Provincia di Napoli	130
Collegio dei Ragionieri della Provincia di Novara	65
Collegio dei Ragionieri della Provincia di Padova	71
Collegio dei Ragionieri di Piacenza	75
Collegio dei Ragionieri di Roma	150
Collegio dei Ragionieri Professionisti di Torino	34
Associazione Subalpina dei Ragionieri	70
Collegio dei Ragionieri del Friuli, Udine	68
Collegio dei Ragionieri di Venezia	50
Collegio dei Ragionieri di Verona	55
Collegio dei Ragionieri di Vicenza	41

Societies have also been formed in the following smaller towns—viz. : Ancona, Arezzo, Cagliari, Caserta, Catania, Catanzaro, Cosenza, Foggia, Forli, Massa, Palermo, Pavia, Perugia, Pisa, Portomauriz, Potenza, Ravenna, Reggio-Emilia, Rovigo, Sassari, Sodrio, Trapani, Treviso, Varese.

The annual subscriptions to these Colleges run from one to thirty *lire*. Membership is open to persons who have obtained the *Diploma di Ragioniere* of one of the Royal Technical Institutes, of which there are about sixty in the Kingdom. The course of study in accounting at these Institutes extends over four years, and includes law, political economy, book-keeping, and auditing, besides two foreign languages and other branches of general education. Most of the Colleges do not restrict their membership to practising accountants, and in many districts all the practising accountants are not embraced, there being no necessity to join any society.

The sphere of the accountant in Italy is defined in Royal Decrees dated 21st June 1885, and 2nd October 1891. It includes designing books for public and private businesses, reform of office administration and book-keeping, making up inventories and balance-sheets, unravelling accounts, auditing, liquidations, schemes of division, trusts, expert evidence, &c. There is, however, no reservation of these duties to accountants, whether with or without diploma, and in many districts lawyers and others participate in them. It should be added that the profession is better known and more generally employed in northern than in southern Italy, where as yet it has made little way.

The accounts of joint-stock companies in Italy are audited by persons elected by the shareholders, who are called Syndics (*Sindaci*), and who are frequently but not generally professional accountants. Their duties are detailed in Sections 183–185 of the Commercial Code. In bankruptcies a local roll of Trustees (*Curatori*) is drawn up by the Courts every three years, and only those persons whose names are on the roll are eligible to wind up estates. Those enrolled are in many cases professional accountants, but the list also includes many lawyers, and even engineers, architects, and others.

Since the first Congress of Italian Accountants in Rome in 1879 similar meetings, attended by delegates from the Colleges, have been held in one or other of the large towns at intervals of about three years. Exhibitions of accounting have also been arranged, the most important of which took place in Genoa in 1892.

The colleges are endeavouring to obtain an Act of Parliament for the protection of their rights, and the regulation of the profession. A Bill was recently introduced in the Chamber of Deputies, and was referred to a Parliamentary Committee to consider and report upon.

The provisions of the Bill as amended by the Committee restrict the public practice of the profession of accountant to those who are registered members of a College of Accountants, of which one is to be instituted in every province. To become a member of such a College it is necessary to hold the diploma of accountant, or to be qualified as a teacher of accounting in Technical Institutes, or to be an Associate of the High School of Commerce, or to have obtained a similar qualification prior to the present school regulations coming into force. It is also necessary to have practised accounting for two years after obtaining the diploma, to be an Italian citizen, and of age, and to have incurred no criminal penalty. Accountants in practice at the date of the Act coming into force will be exempt from the provision requiring two years' practice, and those who have been ten years in practice prior to that date will not be required to possess any degree, while those who have been only five years in practice will also be registered without having a degree, provided they pass a practical examination.

The Bill has given rise to considerable discussion and does

not appear at the time of writing to have made further progress towards adoption by the legislature.

In Italy quite a number of professional journals are published in connection with the various colleges.

Next in interest after Italy is HOLLAND, which from an early period has had a reputation for merchants' accounts. In 1711 Sir Richard Steele, in a paper which is a masterly exposition of the value of keeping proper accounts and a severe condemnation of those who affect to despise them, remarks : " When a man happens to break in Holland they say of him that ' he has not kept true accounts.' This phrase perhaps among us would appear a soft or humorous way of speaking, but with that exact nation it bears the highest reproach." [1]

The first public accountant's office in Holland was established in 1880. Before that time there were two or three industrial firms, having business in Holland and England, who had their own accountants. Since the year 1880 the number of accountants has grown steadily, and there are now about 110 accountants in public practice, of whom three do not belong to any society.

In Holland there are four societies of accountants, viz. : The Netherlands Institute of Accountants, The Netherlands Society of Accountants, The National Organisation of Accountants, and The Netherlands Academy of Accountants.

The *Nederlandsch Instituut van Accountants* is the oldest Society, having been formed in 1895. The members are divided into first and second class. First-class members are :—

1. Those who were in practice before 15th December 1894, and connected with the founders of the Institute.

2. Those who have been at least five years in practice as second-class members.

3. Those who, at the time of the formation of the Institute, were at least five years in practice.

[1] *The Spectator*, No. 174, September 19, 1711.

4. Those who passed the examination of the Institute before the 1st January 1900, and have been at least five years in practice.

Second-class members are those who have passed the Institute examination and are at least twenty-three years of age.

There are 99 members of the Institute, 75 in public practice, of whom 64 are first-class and 11 second-class members. The Institute has also 184 Associates, who must have passed one of the examinations in book-keeping before they can be admitted.

The Institute's examinations include three modern languages—besides Dutch—and general business knowledge, also book-keeping and accounts, examination of balance-sheets, calculations, statistics, finance, commercial law, bankruptcies and liquidations, and drafting of deeds and reports.

The Associates need not be in accountant practice, owing to the fact that the number of accountants' offices at the present time is too small to make it possible for all the associates to obtain places in them.

The *Nederlandsche Bond van Accountants* was formed in 1902. The members are divided in the same way as in the Institute.

First-class members are :—

1. The Founders of the Society.

2. Those who were twenty-three years of age before the 1st January 1900, have been in practice at least three years in not less than three branches of commerce or industry in businesses of sufficient importance, have passed the State examination as teacher in book-keeping, and have continued in practice since the 1st January 1900.

3. Those who have been second-class members for five years, and have been in practice during that time.

Second-class members are those who have been in practice at least three years in any branch of commerce or industry, and have passed the examination of the Society.

Nineteen of the accountants in public practice are mem-

Oprecht

FONDAMENT

Ende principalen inhout van het
Italiaens Boeck-houden.

Om van alle Partyen den Rechten Debiteur,
ende Crediteur te stellen, die selve int cort op 't groot Boeck
over te draghen: Mitsgaders een grondtlijcke onderrichtinghe,
om een yeghelijcx Reeckeninghe in *Debito*, ende *Cre-*
dito van 't groot Boeck wel te verstaen, zijnde
't voornaemste des Boeck-houdens,

NEMINEM TIMEAS. ✳ IOANNES BUINGHA. RECTE FACIENDO.

t'AMSTELREDAM.
By Willem Jansz, Stam Boeckvercooper 1627.

TITLE PAGE OF BUINGHA, 1627 (same size as original)

From Copy in the Edinburgh Chartered Accountants' Library

bers of this Society. The rules for Associates are the same as those of the Institute, but at present the Society has no Associates. The syllabus of examinations has not yet been framed.

The *Nationale Organisatie van Accountants* was formed in 1903. There are first-class members and ordinary members. Ordinary members are those who have been engaged in commerce or industry (not necessarily as accountant) for at least ten years, and have been in accountant practice for two years in different branches. They must further have reached the age of thirty years, and have passed the State examination as teacher in book-keeping, or the examination of the Organisation in book-keeping, accountancy, law, and economics.

First-class members are those who have been ordinary members for three years. Thirteen of the accountants in public practice are members of this organisation.

The *Nederlandsche Academie van Accountants* was formed in the end of 1902. It consists of two classes of members, —practical accountants, and teachers, &c., of book-keeping, the latter preponderating. It conducts examinations in book-keeping and accountancy.

The greater part of the work of accountants in Holland consists of auditing. The liquidation of companies is—as a rule—not placed under their charge. The Bankruptcy Act does not speak of accountants. In cases of temporary suspension of payment the Act prescribes an investigation by "experts," and for this investigation the Court nearly always appoints a public accountant.

There are one or two professional journals published in Holland.

We may next examine the position in SWEDEN, where only within the last ten years has the profession of accounting and auditing received any great share of public attention. Several cases having arisen which showed the need of more efficient auditing, the question was brought before the Diet in 1895, and the example of the organisation and education of professional accountants in Great Britain adduced and recommended.

On 29th December 1899 *Svenska Revisorsamfundet* (the Swedish Society of Auditors) was formed in Stockholm.

Section 4 of the rules prescribes that a person who wishes to be elected a member has to file an application with the Board, stating his age and what educational institutions he has attended, and accompanied by a certificate, issued by competent and trustworthy persons, that he possesses the requisite knowledge of book-keeping and auditing. This application is subjected to examination by a Committee consisting of three active members, after which it is brought before the Society, which has the power to grant the application or not. In 1904 the Society had 32 active members in Stockholm and 39 in other parts of Sweden. It had also 63 members not in practice. The members of the Society have no special privileges as such. The power of appointing auditors, without restriction, rests with the members or shareholders of the particular corporation or company, and the appointment of liquidators of bankrupt estates is also unrestricted. The desirability of legislation providing against irregularities in these respects having made itself felt, the Swedish Diet in 1902 requested the Government to cause a satisfactory investigation to be made into the question, whether a body of fully educated and trained accountants would be considered requisite, and, if so, what measures would be necessary to give this body a legally recognised position coupled with responsibility. It was further requested by Parliament that the Government should take into consideration whether and under what circumstances it should be deemed suitable that a minority in a company or a registered corporation with an economic purpose should have the right to resolve that a specially qualified person, outside the company or corporation, should take part in the auditing of the accounts. Both these questions are still pending.

In the meantime, throughout Sweden the work of auditing accounts and preparing balance-sheets is frequently performed by solicitors, merchants, officials, and people of various callings.

The winding-up of bankrupt estates is also performed by solicitors and other persons, chiefly merchants and manufacturers. When a person becomes insolvent the Court summons the creditors to attend a meeting at which the administrators or trustees are chosen. Of these the Court appoints one—a member of the Court or a solicitor, whose duty it is to see that the estate is legally administered—and the creditors two or more, one of whom, as a rule, is a solicitor, and the other a creditor.

There are no public accountants in NORWAY. Accounts are usually audited, in the case of the Government, by the Government Audit Department; of Municipalities, by the two elected Municipal Auditors, who are chosen by the Town Council; and of Companies, by two auditors elected at an Annual General Meeting of Shareholders.

The liquidators of bankrupt estates are usually elected by the creditors, and the name of the person elected—generally a solicitor—is then submitted to the Probate Court (*Skifteret*) for approval.

The profession of public accountant is not officially recognised in BELGIUM, nevertheless accountants are named by the Courts and tribunals in the capacity of experts to examine disputed accounts which are submitted to their jurisdiction. This has been the practice since 1831. Accountants thus appointed are men who are known by the magistrates to be the most upright and capable, and who have an irreproachable reputation. They are called *Experts Comptables*.

These accountants are entrusted by companies and managers of commercial enterprises with the making up of balance-sheets or their verification, but this is not obligatory upon each company. It has, however, been the custom for some years to name an Expert Accountant as auditor (*Commissaire*) in the constitution of joint-stock companies.

Expert Accountants are often appointed as liquidators by the Commercial Courts, and in matters of bankruptcy or suspension they are also sometimes named as assistants to the *avocats*, who alone are appointed Trustees (*Curateurs*), by the Court pronouncing the bankruptcy.

There was not until recently any Association or Corporation of Expert Accountants in Belgium. It was only in the beginning of 1903 that the older Expert Accountants thought it desirable to form an association, in the interests of justice and accuracy, for many of those employed as Expert Accountants did not know the rudiments of the accountant's profession, and were thus a cause of detriment to its good name. The *Chambre Syndicale des Experts Comptables* was formed in May 1903, in connection with the Chamber of Commerce known as the *Union Syndicale de Bruxelles*, but with absolute autonomy. The members are divided into (A) *Experts Comptables* (B) *Comptables*. The former must have acted as *Comptables* for at least ten years. The latter must be over twenty-five years of age. The election is made in General Meeting after the Committee has examined into the professional capacity and character of the candidates. The questions set cover law and practice.

In the first six months about 100 members were elected as *Experts Comptables* or *Comptables*.

In FRANCE the profession of accountant is entirely free. Any one can take the designation—even joining to it that of expert—without coming within the range of any penalty, or having to furnish the slightest proof of his capacity or integrity.

This regrettable state of matters is explained in the following manner:—Till within the last few years, the profession of accountant was considered by the public as something altogether inferior. With a few exceptions it was practised by people of little education, and of a generally mediocre standing, both intellectually and socially—people who tried, without special training, to gain a livelihood by this means after having failed in other careers. As a matter of fact, commerce and all that relates to it has no prestige in the eyes of Frenchmen, and accounting could not fail to suffer thereby.

By degrees, however, the conclusion has been arrived at that the routine of business is not a sufficient training. Schools of commerce have been established nearly everywhere, and many young men have abandoned the so-called liberal professions for this line of life.

In a certain measure this movement has been favourable to the accountant; it has given rise to the formation of a body of teachers, and to the publication of works which, though far from presenting the same interest, yet denote on the whole an appreciable amount of progress.

In spite of all this things advance very slowly, and it is not possible as yet even approximately to forecast the time when accountancy will be recruited and appreciated as it ought to be.

At the present time the people who occupy themselves with accounting may be classed as follows :—

    Teachers.
    Accountants attached to commercial concerns.
    Expert Accountants in the employment of the Law
        Courts.
    Ordinary Expert Accountants.

It is only the teachers who can exhibit official testimonials of capacity. About ten years ago two diplomas were introduced, which are given, after examination, by the Ministry of Education and the Ministry of Commerce. The examination is altogether theoretical and academic ; many candidates pass it with success, without having the slightest knowledge of business from a practical point of view, and of the difficulties it presents.

Accountants attached to commercial concerns learn to fulfil their functions by practical work. Many are old pupils of the Schools of Commerce, or have improved themselves by attending free evening classes got up by private enterprise; very rarely do any of these men rise to high appointments.

Expert Accountants in the employment of the Courts are those persons who are occasionally employed to examine contested accounts which have given rise to legal proceedings or a criminal action, and to report thereon. Their position has no characteristic of stability. Their names appear on lists made up simply on the discretion of the Magistrates of each Court, but inclusion in this list is a matter of favour, and, properly speaking, does not constitute a right on the part of those who obtain it. There is no examination or competition to undergo in order to be placed on the list. Up to the present the Expert Accountants employed by the Courts have not succeeded in forming any society or organisation.

Any one can assume the designation of Expert Accountant and offer his services in this capacity to the public without furnishing any credentials of integrity or professional attainment. There exist certain associations of accountants, but these are rather mutual benefit societies, or organisations for defending the material interests of their members, than associations for testing the capacity of those who wish to style themselves accountants.

In 1881 certain persons founded an association under the title of *Société Académique de Comptabilité*. This Society awards diplomas after examination. This is an interesting venture, which deserves to be more known and encouraged; unfortunately, through want of material resources, the *Société Académique* has not made much progress, all the more as the diploma it gives lacks effective sanction.

To sum up, French accountants are still far from

having any regular organisation, although the need for it appears more and more. The necessity of imposing certain conditions on those who wish to call themselves accountants —more particularly expert accountants—is being emphasised on all hands, in pamphlets and in the newspapers, but the question, being very complex, does not look as if it would soon be solved.

In Marseilles, where there is a branch of the *Société Académique*, there is at present a movement to form a Society of Expert Accountants.

Individuals employed as auditors (*Commissaires*) by public or private companies or firms are chosen according to their known capacity or personal standing, and are not necessarily *Experts Comptables*.

In cases of bankruptcy or liquidation the Courts employ certain individuals who are known as Syndics in Bankruptcy (*Syndics de faillites*), invested with powers from the respective tribunals. In practice some of these persons confine themselves to this work and acquire a quasi-public status in certain judiciary centres in France.

The profession of public accountant is not known in SWITZERLAND. There are no public accountants, but there are some private accountants, who are sometimes called in as experts for the examination of books for various purposes (for instance, in cases where a person wishes to purchase a business), but they are not associated or organised.

With regard to public and private corporations or companies, the Swiss law regulating the administration of such companies provides in Clause 616, Paragraph 10, that the manner in which the balance-sheet is to be drawn up and the profits calculated and paid out, and also the mode of auditing the balance-sheet, must be distinctly stated in the statutes of the company.

According to Swiss law liquidators of bankrupt estates can either be official or voluntary. As soon as one half of the original capital is no longer secured by the assets, the management of the company must immediately inform the District Court of this fact. A liquidator is then proposed, either by the creditors or by the shareholders, who is appointed by the District Court with full power to act.

The above-mentioned Swiss law deals particularly with this point in Clause 657, which runs as follows: "Should the last balance-sheet of a Company show that the original capital has become reduced by one half, the Management of the Company must forthwith call a General Meeting to announce the state of affairs.

"As soon as the claims of the creditors of the Company can no longer be covered by the assets, the Directors must inform the Court thereof, with a view to winding up the Company. It shall, however, be left to the discretion of the Court to postpone the winding up either on the proposition of the creditors or of an administrator appointed by the creditors for the protection of their common interests, and, in the meantime, to make provisional arrangements for the security of the balance of the capital."

There are no professional accountants in SPAIN corresponding to those in the United Kingdom.

Public and private corporations and companies have not, as a rule, their accounts audited, but make out their own balance-sheets and statements of affairs and lay them before the shareholders at a meeting. In certain cases when the statutes of the company provide that the accounts must be audited, the Board of Directors appoint any one in whom they have confidence to do what is required, and that gentleman need not be a professional man, or hold any title. In cases of bankruptcy a Board of Creditors appoints the liquidators. Mercantile Experts (*Peritos-Mercantiles*) or Mercantile Accountants (*Contadores-Mercantiles*) are frequently employed in these capacities. They are grouped into societies which have various names. The most important are those called *Colegeos Periciales*, the larger number of which partake of an official character, and the members undertake calculations and work of a legal kind. Such Colleges exist in Madrid, Barcelona, Gigon, Cadiz, Valencia, Almeria, Santander, Bilbao, San Sebastian, La Coruna, Malaga, Seville, Zaragoza, and Alicante. Almost all of them are of recent date.

Of longer standing are the so-called Mercantile Academies (*Academias Cientifico Mercantiles*), which have a scientific rather than a practical aim. At the present day there are only a few, the greater number disappearing when the "Commercial Schools" were founded.

Finally, in some few cities there are the Associations of Commercial Weighers and Measurers, that of Barcelona being of very ancient standing, and having acquired the character of an official institution.

The larger number of book-keepers have no official standing in Spain, seeing that they only possess practical knowledge acquired either in an office or private academy, that is to say, one that has no official character.

As regards the system of book-keeping, the most general in all houses of any importance is that of double-entry, as established by the Commercial Code. This, according to Articles 33 to 49 inclusive, lays down rules for keeping books and states which would be required and demanded in a court of law, and their legal value when found correct.

In PORTUGAL there are no public accountants, and the accounts of public and private corporations and companies are usually audited by what is termed the Fiscal Board, (*Concelho Fiscal*) consisting of commercial gentlemen elected for the purpose.

The persons who act as liquidators of bankrupt estates are persons of standing appointed for the purpose by the Judge of the Court before whom the affairs of the bankrupt estate are being investigated.

The *Associacão Portugueza de Contabilidade* (formed in 1885) never had any standing, and has long since ceased to exist.

In Berlin, and in all important towns throughout the
GERMAN EMPIRE, there are a large number of professional
accountants (*Bücherrevisoren*), but so far as has been ascertained they are not in any way associated or organised.
A considerable number of them are sworn in by the Courts
of Justice, and are admitted and act as "Sworn Experts for
Commercial Matters" in civil and criminal actions at Courts
of Law. They are appointed after due inquiry at the respective Chambers of Commerce concerning their capabilities,
and only those persons are appointed who are understood to
have a thorough commercial training, a prolonged experience,
and more particularly an accurate knowledge of book-keeping.
No examinations take place. They are not actual officials
(*Beamten*) within the legal meaning of the word, but enjoy
the special confidence of all German authorities by virtue of
their position as Sworn Experts, in which capacity, also, they
are usually called upon to audit the accounts of public and
private corporations and companies, and to make up balance-
sheets and statements of affairs of public and private concerns,
although these functions are frequently assigned to other confidential persons.

So-called *Konkursverwalter* act as liquidators of bankrupt
estates. In Berlin, and in other large cities, these *Konkursverwalter* are merchants of good position, whilst in smaller
provincial towns attornies-at-law (*Rechtsanwälte*) are mostly
selected for that purpose.

At Hamburg the persons employed to act as liquidators of
bankrupt estates are either private accountants or the official
sworn accountants. If the bankruptcy is in the hands of
the Courts of Justice, the appointment of an accountant must
be confirmed or made by the Courts.

There are no accountants in public practice in AUSTRIA
existing as a separate or associated body.

The accounts of public and private corporations, companies, banks, &c., are made up by the respective employees,
and audited in the case of companies by so-called *Revisoren*,

who are shareholders chosen by the shareholders for that purpose.

Bankrupt estates are administered by an advocate named by the Court.

All questions regarding the accounts of public and private concerns dealt with in a Court of Law are referred to so-called book-keeping experts (*Buchsachverständige*), who are appointed as occasion requires by the Commercial Courts. The persons so appointed are usually teachers in Commercial Schools, official accountants, bankers, or merchants.

Neither is the institution of public or professional accountant known in HUNGARY.

The accounts of limited companies (bound by law to render public accounts) are audited by the "Superintending Committee" of each company. The members of the Superintending Committee (at least three), are elected at the General Meeting of the shareholders for a period not exceeding three years. The duty of this Committee consists in the control of the conduct of the business of the Company: for this end it is at liberty at any time to examine the books, papers, and the cash of the Company. This Committee examines the annual accounts, the balance-sheet, and the proposals of the Board on the distribution of dividends, and reports upon these subjects to the General Meeting of the Company. Members of the Superintending Committee are not necessarily shareholders.

Balance-sheets of private concerns are made up by the owners themselves according to the requirements prescribed by the Commercial Code. In cases of bankruptcy the Court appoints a liquidator from the list of practising advocates. In cases of enquiry the Court employs, whenever needed, one or more of the sworn experts permanently appointed for such purposes.

In RUSSIA there are no public accountants. There are, of course, book-keepers, but even they are not numerous, and it is understood many wealthy Russian merchants conduct their business without the aid of any proper books, trusting a good deal to memory. It is rather a curious fact that most Russians, whether merchants, bankers, or book-keepers, in summing a column of figures use an abacus or counting frame. They are certainly very expert in its use, but as with it there is no occasion for regular tabulation of the figures, which are often scattered all over the money columns, their accounts are not very easily checked by persons who do not make use of this contrivance.

Joint-stock companies are, however, very strictly controlled, and are bound to keep proper accounts, which the Government officials have a right to examine with a view to taxation. The accounts of such companies are audited by a committee consisting of not less than five shareholders, but it is understood their examination is usually of a very superficial character. They are elected by the shareholders in General Meeting.

In the case of bankrupt estates, liquidators (not less than three in number, one of whom is elected Chairman), are appointed by the Commercial Court of the district in which the estate may be situated. As such liquidators, lawyers or their assistants, and in some cases prominent merchants, are selected. The Chairman must, however, be a lawyer. These liquidators are responsible to the Courts for the proper administration of the estates placed in their charge.

Sometimes estates which are in difficulties are carried on, without being placed in bankruptcy, by administrators appointed by the creditors at a Meeting, after having obtained the permission of the Commercial Court. Under this process accounts are made up annually, and a Meeting held at which the administration may be continued or the estate thrown into bankruptcy.

There is a journal published twice monthly in St. Petersburg entitled *Schetovodstvo*, " A Journal of Commercial and Financial Science." It deals with questions of accounting and book-keeping.

There are no professional accountants in FINLAND. The accounts of public and private corporations and companies are usually audited by ordinary legal firms (who also act as liquidators of bankrupt estates, make up balance-sheets, &c.), or by private individuals, possessing public confidence, but who have no official status.

In POLAND there are no accountants in public practice. The accounts of companies are audited by a special committee elected from amongst the shareholders. In judicial cases the Court appoints experts to balance the books, usually book-keepers from the State Bank or from the Audit Office.

In bankruptcy cases the Commercial Court appoints as Trustee (called the *syndic*) a lawyer and sometimes a member of the Court, who may invite an expert, as above mentioned, to help him to make up balance-sheets and statements.

There are practically no professional accountants in DENMARK. The Probate Court at Copenhagen always employs one gentleman, a former bank official, for winding up bankrupt and other estates. He has no appointment by any authority, and is not sworn, but he may now be said to be a professional accountant.

In the provincial towns the County Courts employ persons who, as a rule, are bank officials or merchants, to do accounting work, but there is no one who follows that occupation as a separate profession.

In ROUMANIA there are no public accountants. There is an Audit Department at Bucharest to which every Department connected with the Government throughout the kingdom sends its accounts to be audited.

Public and private companies, merchants, &c., who have their accounts audited, employ private persons, but they are not bound to have this done. Many bring their annual accounts to the Law Courts to be stamped—not audited. In any case of dispute or question occurring, accounts are not valid unless duly stamped.

In reference to bankruptcy very little action is taken. It is regarded as a private matter, and there exist no Bankruptcy Courts.

Accountants are unknown in BULGARIA. The accounts of public corporations, such as municipalities, are audited by officials appointed by the Government, while those of private companies are examined by a committee of three selected by the shareholders from their own number at the General Meetings.

In cases of bankruptcy the Court of bankruptcy appoints three liquidators, one of whom is a member of the Court, one a barrister (*avocat*), and the third a person possessed of a competent knowledge of the trade of the bankrupt.

There are no accountants in public practice in SERVIA. Banks are obliged to submit their books yearly to the Ministry for Commerce, where they are examined. In private concerns, where necessary, an accountant from the Ministry of Finance or from a bank might be called in. These accountants have as a rule studied for four years in the Commercial Academy of Belgrade, or completed similar studies abroad.

In the case of the bankruptcy of a business house a committee is appointed by the Ministry for Commerce to act as liquidators of the bankrupt estate, and in that of a private person the committee is nominated by the law courts.

In TURKEY there are no public accountants. The accounts of private and public companies are audited by private persons, usually clerks of the Imperial Ottoman Bank.

Bankrupt estates are administered by the Consulate of the bankrupt's nation, which appoints liquidators of its own choice from among the merchants of its own nation resident in Turkey.

The above applies to Europeans. The Turks have no system of any kind.

In GREECE there is no organised service of professional accountants.

The accounts of all companies and corporations, public and private, are supposed to be inspected annually by some one appointed by the Minister of the Interior, usually a member of the Civil Service. As regards large businesses such as banks, insurance companies, &c., the verification of the books is entrusted to a committee, the members of which are not considered as Expert-Accountants. Their remuneration is rather moderate.

In cases of bankruptcy the Court of First Instance appoints Trustees who have the right to employ their own accountant.

In 1903 the Government established two public Commercial Schools—one in Athens and the other in Patras—where book-keeping is taught.

CHAPTER VIII

OTHER FOREIGN COUNTRIES

SOCIETIES IN ARGENTINA, URUGUAY, AND PERU—SITUATION
IN BRAZIL, CHILE, CENTRAL AMERICA, MEXICO, AND
OTHER COUNTRIES—PRACTICE IN CHINA AND JAPAN—
JAPANESE COMMERCIAL CODE AS TO ACCOUNTS AND
BALANCE-SHEETS

AMONG countries which are not English-speaking or European it is in the Republics of South America that we find the accountant in the most advanced state.

The profession of public accountant was legally created and recognised in the ARGENTINE REPUBLIC so long ago as July 12, 1836, when it was decreed that such a person must (1) be officially declared competent; (2) be twenty-five years old, and an Argentine citizen; (3) be of good character and conduct; (4) be examined by the Appeal Court as to his knowledge of law; and (5) be examined in arithmetic and accounting by such persons as the Government should designate.

The number of recognised public accountants was then fixed at eight. Their chief work in those days was defined as all such matters of accounting as came before the Courts, as well as the division of property in cases where there were minors, or persons under curatorship.

In 1863 the limitation in number was abolished, and the profession thrown open to all who should qualify. In 1870, complaints were made that notaries and solicitors, even in cases where they were incompetent, were encroaching on the domain of the accountant. The fiscal reported at that time

(1) that the judges should comply with the regulations regarding accounts; (2) that in cases where notaries had invaded the province of the accountant, they should be entitled only to notaries' fees; (3) that where they had recovered larger fees, they should be ordered to repay the excess; and (4) that all the fiscals and defenders of minors should be advised of this, in order that they might recover such excess.

The practices complained of continued, however, and the final blow to the public accountant as a purely legal official was given some years later, when it was decided on appeal that an advocate (*abogado*, who acts as solicitor as well as barrister) was entitled, in virtue of a law of 1768, to draw up Schemes of Division, on account of his possessing a knowledge of law and arithmetic.

After years of inaction, during which the profession had fallen into insignificance, the College of Accountants was founded in Buenos Aires in 1892. It aimed at raising the standard of examinations, and at the same time recovering some of the lost privileges of the profession. In the former object it was successful, and the examinations held by the Supreme Court and the Accountancy General of the province of Buenos Aires were made considerably "stiffer." But the purely legal side of the profession was less important than formerly, and the commercial side was rapidly growing in importance. After a good deal of discussion and appeal to various branches of the legislature, it was decided by the National Ministry of Justice and Education, to remodel the regulations affecting the profession. Accordingly, in 1897, it was thrown open to foreigners as well as to Argentine citizens; and a scheme of examinations, based to some extent on that of the Scottish and English Institutes, was established. The examining body was to consist of Professors of the National School of Commerce, who were also to institute a course for the preparation of candidates. The old provincial diploma was declared insufficient in the Courts of the Federal

Capital; and the public accountant (*contador público*) once more became a recognised professional man.

Since that time the qualification has been taken by over a hundred candidates, who are almost all in practice in Buenos Aires. The preparatory course extends over two years, and embraces commercial and civil law, book-keeping in the three branches of commerce, banking and judicial work, arithmetic, algebra, and Spanish (the language of the country).

The Director of the National School of Commerce, who has recently returned from an extended tour of inspection, which embraced the Commercial Schools of the United States, England, and France, now proposes to extend the course to three years, giving in particular a longer time to the study of law.

The profession has gained in importance on the commercial side, owing to the provision in the Bankruptcy Law of 1903, that in every case of application for bankruptcy a public accountant shall be appointed by the judge from a list drawn up at the beginning of each year, to report to the creditors' meeting on the debtor's books, and give the due ranking of the creditors. His remuneration in such a case is limited to a maximum of two per cent on the assets; but he is not uncommonly appointed at the meeting as trustee (*síndico*) and in that event his charge becomes a more onerous one, and his remuneration may reach a maximum of six per cent.

It would not be surprising if a similar regulation were applied to Argentine public companies, in which the *síndico* possesses powers much more extensive than those of an auditor, though in many cases he fails to exercise them for want of sufficient knowledge of accounts. It would be a natural sequel to the Bankruptcy Laws if a regulation were passed to the effect that the *síndicos* of public companies should be selected from among the recognised public accountants.

On the whole, therefore, it may be said that the Argentine public accountant is finding his profession a more important one than formerly, in all departments save that of purely Court work. The College of Accountants now numbers about a hundred members, and it may be expected to grow in influence as the younger and more active men come to take a more prominent place in its deliberations, and turn their attention from lost privileges in the case of succession estates to the securing of recognition in commercial circles.

The profession of public accountant was created in URUGUAY on the formation of the Tribunals of Justice immediately after the Declaration of Independence in 1825, distinguishing between the book-keeper of previous times who continued to be the confidential and practical accountant of commercial houses, and the public accountant (*contador publico*) who was accepted in Courts or Tribunals of Justice as an authority on all matters of accounts, having proved his efficiency by submitting to an examination.

According to registers in the Tribunals and University 147 diplomas have been issued ; many of the holders, however, have died, others have emigrated, and at the present time probably not more than thirty actually practise as public accountants. Being a new country all nationalities are represented in the profession, the native Uruguayan predominating, followed by Argentines, Spaniards, French, Italians, &c.

In 1893 a small number of public accountants constituted the *Colegio de Contadores Publicos de la Republica Oriental del Uruguay,*" which body at present (March 1904) numbers 69 members. Up to 25th November 1889 a candidate as public accountant underwent an examination before a Court formed by the Judge of Commerce and two public accountants, and, if he satisfied them, he was given the diploma. From that date the profession was annexed to the Faculty of Scientific and Social Rights, and subjected to the rules of the University, where a four years' course is arranged.

All candidates must therefore now obtain their diplomas from the University. The programme of studies embraces a thorough knowledge, theoretical and practical, of commercial, banking, farming, navigation, and industrial book-keeping; calculations, commercial and advanced; life insurance, algebra, and geometry; civil and commercial law, especially respecting liquidation of estates and bankrupts, legal procedure; history of commerce and political economy. All persons obtaining a diploma from the University are qualified to become members of the College of Accountants.

Up to the present time most of the public corporations' and companies' accounts are audited by shareholders or persons appointed at the yearly general meetings. Most of the foreign companies are audited by persons calling themselves and accepted at home as "auditors," but without any legal authority in Uruguay. Some English companies have adopted the practice of having their accounts audited by duly authorised public accountants.

Bankrupt estates are liquidated by *Sindicos*, forty merchants being designated yearly by the *Tribunales de Justicia* to act in this capacity. The *Colegio de Contadores* is making strenuous efforts to have this changed and the duties assigned to public accountants.

In PERU a Technical Institute of Accountants (*Instituto Técnico de Contadores*) was formed in Lima in May 1900. The members consist of three classes: *First*, Expert Accountants and Auditors; *Second*, Book-keepers and Accountants; and *Third*, Students (*Aspirantes*). The Institute, with the view of strengthening its position, presented in September 1902 a petition to Congress asking for official recognition as a Corporation. This petition was favourably entertained by Congress, and it was hoped that the petition would be agreed to by the Senate of the Republic in the Session of 1904.

The Institute publishes a monthly organ entitled *El Contador*, and is endeavouring to establish a body of professional men qualified under the guarantee of the Institute for the performance of the duties of judicial accountants, liquidators, and auditors.

At present the accounts and balance-sheets of public companies, &c., are audited by shareholders named at the general meetings. Bankrupt estates are liquidated by persons named by the judge, who are chosen from a list which is composed of merchants.

There is no organised association of professional accountants enjoying official recognition in BRAZIL.

The system adopted for the auditing of the accounts of public and private corporations and companies is to entrust this work to certain of the shareholders, who form the *Conselho Fiscal* or Audit Committee.

In the liquidation of bankrupt estates the judge nominates receivers from among the creditors, who are made responsible for the administration of the estate.

And whenever the services of an expert are required for drawing up balance-sheets or statements of the affairs of public or private concerns, any private book-keeper may be appointed who has the confidence of managers, receivers, or judge, according to the circumstances of the case.

There is only one firm carrying on the profession of accountant in CHILE. Both of the partners are members of the Society of Accountants in Edinburgh.

There is no recognised body of accountants in Chile. The profession has only come to be known within the last few years, and the native merchants and business men generally are very slowly learning to understand and appreciate the work done by Chartered Accountants. The greater part of that work is done on behalf of British companies with capital invested in Chile; a little is done for Chilian firms, but the feeling among them against outside intervention is very strong.

So far as known, there is no professional audit of any of the corporation or other public accounts. In certain cases lay auditors are employed, but they have no status as auditors, and are rather in the position of inspectors. Generally, auditing is very little known, and in many cases, where known, it is considered to be work done by a species of itinerant book-keeper.

The absence of any large business centres in Chile makes it necessary for the auditor to travel all over the country, and as there are not first-class means of communication, much time is lost and trouble caused in moving up and down the coast.

The language of the country is Spanish, and though English is generally understood, the strange tongue is a factor that has to be reckoned with. The question of exchange, as between sterling and currency, is also an element which presents considerable difficulty.

As regards CENTRAL AMERICA, there are no accountants in public practice, and the profession is practically unknown. In San José there are three Chartered Accountants, members respectively of the English Institute, the Edinburgh Society, and the Glasgow Institute, but they do not practise as public accountants. The principal companies have accountants in their employment who do not accept other work. Two have their accounts audited by a gentleman in the employment of a bank, but his duties consist chiefly in examining the accounts forwarded to London, and certifying that the same are exact copies of the entries as they appear in the books of the company.

In the case of the two local banks the securities are examined and the cash counted once in each year by a committee of the stock-holders. Beyond this there is no auditing by any outside person. One feature, however, in connection with the banks, is that for ten days between the date on which the accounts are published and the holding of the meeting of stock-holders, any stock-holder is entitled to attend at the bank and examine the books and obtain any information he wishes in connection with the account of any person who has dealings with the bank, either as a depositor or as a borrower.

In addition to this there is presented at the annual meeting of stock-holders a complete detailed trial balance and also schedules showing the names of the depositors, the amount to the credit of each, the names of the borrowers and the amount lent to each, as well as very complete information of the amount for which each man is a guarantor or endorser. These schedules also show the turn-over on account current during the year. This system seems to work quite satisfactorily, and no one seems to object to the publicity given to his banking operations.

Similar conditions prevail in Guatamala, Spanish Honduras, Nicaragua, and Colombia.

In MEXICO there are many professional accountants among the Mexicans, who are generally employed to attend to the technical matters of preparing and auditing accounts and winding up bankrupt estates. They have at present no organisation, but steps are being taken with that object. In the British colony there are several professional accountants, one or two of whom belong to the English Institute of Chartered Accountants. There are also several American professional accountants, but as in the case of the Mexicans, no organisation.

Accounts of public companies are prepared by an officer of same, called *comisario*, who is responsible for their correctness. He may of course employ an auditor, but that does not relieve him from responsibility. The balance-sheet must be published yearly in the official journal. Auditors of bankrupt accounts are appointed by the Courts before which the proceedings in the matter are pending, under the supervision of the receiver.

In the French colony of ALGERIA there are no accountants following a separate profession.

The accounts of public and private corporations and companies and their balance-sheets are certified by the Chairman and the Committee, or, in some instances, the Committee appoints a *Commissaire aux Comptes,* a person of no official standing, but chosen on account of his character and knowledge of the particular business in hand. In the case of a bankruptcy, the person appointed is an official, called *Syndic de faillites*, and these Syndics form a separate body. They are named officially, and the *Tribunal de Commerce* chooses from among them the one to be appointed in each case.

As regards FRENCH INDIA there are only a few native accountants in Pondicherry and in Karikal.

When a firm becomes insolvent the affairs are looked after by the District Court, and one of the subordinate officers of the Court (*greffier*) is appointed receiver.

In SIAM there are no accountants in public practice. Public companies and corporations, which by virtue of statutory provisions or otherwise are required to have their accounts audited, appoint for that purpose a person acquainted with book-keeping. Of the persons who at present fulfil the duties of auditors one is an assistant in a local firm and three others are merchants. The same practice is adopted in the case of liquidators of bankrupt estates, and the making up of balance-sheets, &c.

In reference to CHINA it has to be borne in mind that the Empire is a very large one, and in very few things is it safe to take the practice of one place as being of general application to the whole country. It may, however, be stated, that so far as can be ascertained the science of accounting as it applies to tradesmen's accounts is well developed in China, but accountancy as a profession does not exist.

The Chinese are undoubtedly skilled in book-keeping, and their manner of keeping books corresponds more or less with the system practised in this country. In many businesses an exact entry is made of every item of cash received, and when goods are sold on credit they are entered in a book which corresponds with a day-book or invoice-book. They also keep ledger accounts, written up as ours are in the names of individual debtors and creditors, and a thorough record of stock is, in many places, kept.

All traders of any standing are in the habit of taking annual balance-sheets and making up their profit and loss accounts, and in many cases this is done three times a year at the three great feasts which are observed in China, one in the Fifth Moon, one in the Eighth Moon, and one at the close of the year. This work is usually done by some member of the business staff.

The practice with regard to bankrupts is, that if a trader is unable to meet his liabilities, he will get the assistance of some friends, call the creditors together, and try to make some arrangement with them. If this fails, the creditors then appeal to the Civil Magistrate, who takes possession of all the debtor's estate upon which he can lay hands, and realises it for the benefit of the creditors, but the proverbial corruption of a Chinese *Ya-men* (Court of Law) is such that very often the benefit obtained by the creditors falls considerably short of the actual proceeds.

At the port of Shanghai a number of British and American accountants have established themselves in practice. They audit accounts and wind up bankrupt estates.

In JAPAN professional accountants, as a separate profession duly organised and associated, do not exist. The Japanese have, however, a peculiar faculty and fondness for figures and tabulated statements, and book-keeping is systematically taught in the middle and higher schools.

There is a Board of Audit for the Government accounts, the functions of which consist, *First*, in vouching and confirming the accounts of the different branches of the Administration; *Second*, in controlling the accounts of the authorities possessing the power of issuing warrants on the Treasury; and *Third*, in verifying and confirming the general final accounts, as well as the reports on final accounts of the different departments of the State.

The accounts of public and private corporations and com-

panies generally are audited by inspectors appointed by the
companies, and holding office for one year. The following
are the provisions of the Commercial Code of Japan relating
to the keeping of the accounts of traders and the audit of
the accounts of joint-stock companies :—

TRADE BOOKS

25. A trader is bound to keep books and to record therein accu-
rately and clearly his daily business and all circumstances affecting his
property. As to household expenses only the total monthly amount need
be entered.

As to the selling transactions of a retail business, only the total
amount of each day's cash and of each day's credit sales need be separately entered.

26. A trader at the time of commencing business, and a commercial
company at the time when its formation is registered, and both also once
in each subsequent year at a fixed time, must make a general inventory of
movables and immovables, of credits and debts and of other property, and
a balance-sheet, and enter both in books specially kept for such purpose.

In the inventory a valuation must be inserted of the movables and
immovables, and of the credits and other property as at the time of
making the inventory.

27. If a commercial company distributes profits twice a year or
oftener, it must make an inventory and balance-sheet according to the
provisions of the preceding article at the time of each distribution.

28. A trader must preserve his trade books and business correspond-
ence for a period of ten years.

Such period is to be computed for each trade book from the time
when it is closed.

JOINT-STOCK COMPANIES

133. In the general meeting for organisation directors and inspectors
shall be appointed.

180. The duration of the function of an inspector is one year, but he
may be re-elected after such time has elapsed.

181. The inspectors may at any time require the directors to give
them information about the business of the company, and may examine
the management of its affairs and the condition of its property.

182. The inspectors may call a general meeting of the shareholders,

whenever they consider such a measure necessary. Such general meeting may appoint special examiners to inquire into the affairs of the company and the condition of its property.

183. It is the duty of the inspectors to examine the papers which are to be submitted to a general meeting of the shareholders by the directors, and to make a report thereon to the meeting.

186. An inspector is liable to the company and to third persons for any damage caused by his having neglected his duties.

190. The directors must submit to the inspectors the following documents one week before the day of an ordinary general meeting, namely:—

1. An inventory.
2. A balance-sheet.
3. A report on the company's business.
4. An account of profits and losses.
5. Proposals relating to the reserve fund and to the distribution of profits and interest.

191. The directors must deposit before the day of an ordinary general meeting at the principal and each branch office the documents mentioned in Art. 190 and the report of the inspectors.

The shareholders and the creditors of the company may at any time during business hours demand an inspection of the documents above mentioned.

192. The directors must submit to the ordinary general meeting the documents mentioned in Art. 190 for approval.

After such approval has been given, the balance-sheet must be published by the directors.

194. The company must appropriate at each distribution of profits at least one twentieth of such profits to a reserve fund, until the latter amounts to one fourth of the capital.

In the case of a dissolution of partnership or of the ordinary winding up of a commercial concern, liquidation is carried on by all the partners or by persons appointed by them.

Liquidators in bankruptcy are chosen from a special list, kept in each Court, of barristers practising in that Court, who are qualified to act in such a capacity.

CHAPTER IX

DEVELOPMENT OF THE PROFESSION

NATURE OF BUSINESS FIFTY YEARS AGO AND AT THE PRESENT
DAY COMPARED—DEVELOPMENT OF AUDITING—JOINT-
STOCK COMPANY LEGISLATION—LOCAL AUTHORITIES' AC-
COUNTS—BANKRUPTCIES AND LIQUIDATIONS—THE TEACH-
ING OF BOOK-KEEPING—JUDICIAL FACTORIES—GROWTH OF
THE SOCIETIES—IS THE PROFESSION OVERSTOCKED?

THE origin and progress of the profession of Accountant,
where it exists, having now been traced, and the situation
in matters of accounting of other civilised countries examined, a chapter may be devoted to the recent remarkable
development of the profession and its causes. It has been
seen that the name and the business of the accountant are at
least of respectable antiquity, but it must be admitted that the
profession, as now understood, is to a very large extent the
creation of the last fifty years. It is unnecessary to do more
than refer to the enormous advance which has taken place
during that period in every department of human thought
and energy. Every one is familiar with the great strides in
the domain of scientific invention and discovery. These have
been accompanied by a steady and rapid growth of commerce, both in regard to its volume and the complexity of
business affairs; and the course of legislation, called for by
the changing conditions of life, if it has sometimes lagged
behind the requirements of the day, has upon the whole
followed the general advance. No business or profession has
remained untouched by these changes, and we are fairly
entitled to claim that the development of this profession

has not been incommensurate with the progress in other departments.

In this advance, however, we cannot point to any striking revolution. The development has not been characterised by any startling discoveries of new principles or the introduction of entirely novel methods, but rather by the steady working out, with modifications suited to changing conditions, of those principles and methods which were already well understood and practised by the old "accomptants." New departments of work have no doubt opened themselves up to the ever increasing number of members of the profession, but they have not, on the whole, caused any undue strain on the inventive faculties. Thus it happens that the definition of an accountant fifty years ago, and the description of the kind of work he had to do, do not differ so greatly as might be thought likely, except in one or two particulars, from the terms which would be employed at the present day.

In the petition for the incorporation of the Society of Accountants in Edinburgh in 1854, which has already been quoted,[1] there is a pretty full description of the "varied and extensive" business of an accountant as practised at that time; and the Glasgow Charter, obtained in the following year, employs very similar language. In another part of this volume[2] will be found a transcript of the circular—dated 12th March 1824—in which one of the pioneers of the profession in Glasgow, Mr. James McClelland, afterwards the first President of the Glasgow Institute—intimated that he had begun business, and in it he gives a very complete account of the kind of work he professed his willingness to perform.

Some twenty years later, Mr. Robert Balfour, a highly esteemed Edinburgh accountant, full of zeal for the honour of his calling, wrote an apology for, or rather encomium of, the profession, which is well worthy of quotation. "It is

---

[1] *Ante,* p. 207.   [2] *Ante,* p. 201.

certainly," he says, writing to a friend who endeavoured to persuade him to abandon it for the Bar, "more varied than that of the lawyer, and I believe it to be certainly not less dignified.   It embraces the extensive field of insurance, which has occupied the attention of many of the profoundest thinkers that Europe has produced, and which, even yet, is in its infancy; banking, which regulates the prosperity of nations and influences the civilisation of the world; finance, whether it be the bankruptcy of a nation, or, what is often just as difficult to manage, of a private individual, and then, on the other hand, there are arbitrations where conflicting parties, placing unlimited confidence in the caution and sagacity of the accountant, voluntarily entrust him with the arrangement of their disputes.   And then, just to throw a little more variety into the profession, and lessen the constant hard thinking which would otherwise be required, there are the details of general business in which most of us to some extent engage.   It is here that the profession is little more than an infant one, and that no measures have been taken for reducing it to a proper shape.   This can be done, and ought to be done.   It is not impossible that I may to some extent be instrumental in accomplishing it, and then, I think, there will be nothing about the profession of which any one can be ashamed."

From these remarks it is apparent that the idea of placing the profession on a more regular and recognised basis was already taking shape.   At all events they were prophetic, for in a few years the Society in Edinburgh and the Institute in Glasgow had been formed, and the Chartered Accountant fairly started on his honourable, and in many cases, successful career.   It would be rash to state that every one now styling himself an accountant is a credit to the profession. Any one, with or without reason, can call himself an accountant, and although various attempts have been made to get the appellation restricted by law to those properly qualified, they have not as yet been successful.   But the public have begun to see that in the Chartered Accountant they have some guarantee of professional training and of tested knowledge, and such gibes as that of Registrar Hazlitt, that an accountant is a person "unaccountable for his actions,"[1] are now quite out-of-date.

It is interesting to compare these descriptions of the kind of work falling to the accountant of sixty or eighty years ago with the most recent definitions such as that given in the "Encylopædia of Accounting," where the duties are summarised as follows:—

Auditing and reporting on the account of companies, corporations, public bodies, societies, institutions, private firms, and individuals.

Drawing up balance-sheets, states of affairs, schemes of division, and other statements of accounts.

Investigating books and accounts with the view of certifying as to profits, accounting for losses, or tracing defalcations.

Reporting on and unravelling accounts under remits from the courts.

Designing systems of book-keeping and keeping accounts and advising thereon, acting as arbitrator or as an expert witness in judicial proceedings, and in arbitrations where matters of accounting are involved.

Acting as secretary or accountant of companies or other concerns which have not such officers of their own.

Managing as factor, appointed by the courts, the estates of persons under some legal incapacity, or as trustee or factor, estates voluntarily placed under an accountant's charge.

Winding up and distributing estates in bankruptcy, insolvency, or liquidation, including estates of persons deceased.

The point which will probably strike one most on comparing these descriptions of an accountant's duties is the entire absence from the earlier accounts of any reference to *auditing*, an omission which will be particularly noticed in the petitions for the Edinburgh and Glasgow Charters. The position this branch of work now occupies in most businesses is well brought out by the fact that in the most modern definition

[1] Worthington, *op. cit.*, p. 3.

just given it is the first mentioned; and it will be felt by most accountants that if the auditing department were left out of their business, they would be deprived of the most regular and upon the whole most remunerative portion of it. Twenty or thirty years ago this was certainly not the case, and the growth of this kind of business is probably the most striking feature in the experience of the average accountant, and is responsible for the enormous increase in the members of the profession.

Audits and auditors of a sort there no doubt were from very early times,[1] but their thoroughness may be gathered from the etymology of the word, which implies that the accounts were read over to the officials so termed. The Companies' Clauses Consolidation Act of 1845 provided for the appointment of auditors for Railway Companies who were entitled to employ accountants to assist them. Some alteration with regard to these offices was made by the Regulation of Railways Act of 1868, and it may safely be said that the audit of the accounts of all the leading railways in the kingdom is now in the hands of professional accountants.

The Companies Act of 1862 may well be termed the "accountant's friend," for it provides him with occupation (and incidentally with remuneration) at the inception, during the progress, and in the liquidation of public companies. The Act did not expressly require audit of the accounts, though the model set of regulations contained in Schedule A had such a provision; it was not till the Amendment Act of 1900 that the accounts of all limited companies required to be audited, and even yet it is not laid down by whom the audit is to be performed.

There has always been a close connection between accountants and the insurance profession arising from a certain similarity in the work involved. Many of the early members of the chartered bodies became managers or other officials

[1] See Part I. Chap. IV.

of insurance companies, and it is significant that when the Glasgow Institute obtained its Charter, it added the words "and actuaries" to its description. The oldest of the insurance companies now in existence date from about the beginning of the eighteenth century, but there have been many additions to the ranks during the past fifty years. Some of them do not fall under the Limited Companies Acts, but all of them either by private Acts or regulations are provided with auditors.

It was long before the great joint-stock banks obtained the advantage of an outside and independent audit. These institutions were illegal in England till 1826, but in Scotland four survive besides the Bank of Scotland which were established before that date. The failure of the City of Glasgow Bank in 1878 led to the Act of 1879, which provided for the limiting of shareholders' liability, and also for the audit of the accounts of all banks, with the sole exception of the Bank of England, by an independent auditor; and these bank auditors are now, almost without exception, to be found in the ranks of duly qualified accountants.

The audit of the accounts of the various councils responsible for the government of counties, municipalities, and parishes, now forms an important part of the work of an accountant. It does more than that, for, by giving him a public and official, as well as a responsible position, it has undoubtedly done a great deal to dignify and enhance the position of the profession in the public esteem. The reform of municipal corporations in 1835 was the first step in bringing about the present popular and representative system of local government. Another Municipal Corporations Act was passed in 1882; County Councils were established in England in 1888, and in Scotland in the following year, and in 1894 a similar form of government was introduced into the parishes in both countries. The affairs of the Scottish Burghs are regulated by the Town Councils Act of 1900; and in all of these Acts there will be found some provision for the audit of the public accounts.

In England, the accounts of county and parish councils are audited by Government officials, but there is another class —the nominees of the Mayor and ratepayers—who by the Act of 1882 audit the borough accounts. They are unpaid, and are seldom accountants, but in the case of the large towns there is usually a professional man appointed to "assist" the elective and the Mayor's auditors in the discharge of their duties. In Scotland the auditors of parish councils are appointed by the Local Government Board, those of county councils and burghs by the Secretary for Scotland; the larger towns which have local acts of their own usually appoint different auditors for the various departments into which their accounts are divided; but in almost every case the auditor is a duly qualified accountant.

The select Committees of both Houses of Parliament on Municipal Trading issued in August 1903 a report on the systems of audit in the English boroughs and councils. They had the benefit of listening to the evidence of several well-known accountants, and their report is emphatically un-favourable, both to the Government and the amateur auditors. They recommend that the present system be abolished, and that the three classes of local authorities—subject to the approval of the Local Government Board—should appoint auditors who are members of the Institute of Chartered Accountants or of the Incorporated Society of Accountants and Auditors. They also approved of the practice in Scotland of appointing auditors from a distance for the smaller burghs.

There is as yet no indication of these recommendations being given effect to, but there can be no doubt that they have the approval of intelligent public opinion; and in defer-ence to that supreme authority the day is probably not far distant when the accounts of all kinds of corporations, trusts, and boards, will be subjected to thorough and effective audit at the hands of duly qualified accountants.

A somewhat extreme example of the dangers affecting the present system of audit was brought to light during the proceedings in bankruptcy connected with the estate of the treasurer of a fairly populous borough in the west of England not long ago. In his examination this functionary admitted with perfect frankness that he had not always kept the borough accounts quite distinct from those of his own business, and that being in want of funds he had got an assessment laid at double the rate actually required, and had used the surplus for his own purposes. Yet the borough accounts had been duly certified as correct by the elected auditors!

What a professional auditor undertakes to do is to place his expert knowledge of figures and accounts, and his experience, at the service of his client, for the prevention both of fraud and of innocent error. To do this properly, the audit must be exhaustive, intelligent, and continuous. Much of the detail must of course be left to subordinates, but the principal should devote his best energies to the scrutiny of results and of general principles. If he fails in these obvious duties, he cannot complain if he is held liable for his neglect. Prominence was given to the responsibility of auditors in the case of the London and General Bank Limited (one of the Balfour Companies) where the auditors were found liable to repay certain dividends which had been improperly paid.

It is possible, however, to push the principle too far. No audit, however painstaking, is an absolute preventive against fraud, neither is any auditor more than human, and as we all know, it is human to err. If the auditor has shown all reasonable skill and diligence in the discharge of his duties, it is only fair that he should enjoy the same immunity as a director who has innocently erred or been wilfully deceived.

In the days when limited companies were much less numerous than they are now, and when the employment of auditors, whether of companies, firms, public authorities, or corporations was less common, the management and liquidation of estates in bankruptcy formed the larger portion of the accountant's daily work. Many members of the profession, still little beyond middle age, can look back to a time when this class of work bulked much more largely in their business than it does now ; and this is the experience of so many firms of good standing that one feels inclined to wonder what has become of this department of business. Owing to the increase of limited companies and the greater prevalence of private arrangements between debtors and creditors, it is probable that there is not comparatively so much ordinary insolvency work as there used to be. But another influence which must not be lost sight of is the *specialisation* of the various branches of the accountant profession. We have not yet lost that wide range and variety of work which has already been alluded to as one of the charms of the profession ; but there is no doubt a growing tendency on the part of firms and of individuals to devote themselves more particularly to one special branch of work. Formerly an accountant not only carried on all the varieties of what is now considered legitimate accountancy, but he frequently added to that some other more or less kindred occupation. Now we hear of men being specially marked out as railway accountants, company promoters, court accountants, bankruptcy trustees, and the like. Not only is this so, but there are accountants who look after the interests of particular trades, and to a large extent confine their practice to these. It is to be feared also that a considerable number, particularly of smaller bankrupt estates, find their way into the hands of self-styled accountants who are very ill qualified for the duties they profess to undertake, and whose main object is too often not to pay as large as possible a dividend to the creditors, but to secure on one pretext or another as large a share of the recoveries as possible for themselves.

The passing of the English Bankruptcy Act of 1869, under which official assignees were abolished and trustees appointed to realise and distribute bankrupt estates, appears to have had the effect of largely increasing the numbers of this unqualified and greedy class of practitioners, though

Mr. Justice Quain went a little too far when he remarked from the bench in 1875 that "the whole affairs in bankruptcy had been handed over to an ignorant set of men called accountants, which was one of the greatest abuses ever introduced into law."[1] This state of matters led to the passing of the Bankruptcy Act of 1883, as noted below.

The apparent necessity of protecting an indiscriminating public against this unscrupulous, but fortunately small class of men, is the excuse, if not altogether the justification, not only for plain language, such as that quoted above, but for the tendency to "officialism" which has been already remarked upon as much more prevalent in England than it is in Scotland. It appears to be the case that under the present bankruptcy administration in England, the smaller insolvent estates, which are the more apt to become the prey of the sharks of the profession, are most frequently left in the hands of the official receiver, while the larger estates, after the initial stages, are usually transferred to those of a practising accountant.

In Scotland the whole proceedings in bankruptcy are left almost entirely in the hands of the creditors, who appoint the trustee and an advising committee of three creditors termed commissioners. A certain amount of supervision is exercised by the Accountant of Court, to whom copies of the trustee's accounts must be regularly sent. The proceedings are still regulated by the Bankruptcy Act of 1856, which has been found to work very well in practice; and while in minor points it has been amended by legislation, there has been practically no alteration affecting the position of the accountant as trustee. Amending Acts were passed in 1857, 1860, 1875, and 1879. By the Debtors Act of 1880, imprisonment for debt was abolished, except in the case of alimentary debts and Crown taxes, and new *criteria* were introduced for ascertaining the position of "notour" or obvious bankruptcy, while by the same Act, the old process

[1] Worthington, *op. cit.*, p. 73.

of *cessio bonorum* was remodelled. This was followed by the Bankruptcy and Cessio Act of 1881, which made better provision for the discharge of debtors; the Civil Imprisonment Act of 1882; the Bankruptcy Frauds and Disabilities Act of 1884, which deals more sharply with undischarged debtors than formerly, and the Judicial Factors Act of 1889, which united in one person the offices of the Accountant of Court, who had charge of Judicial Factories, and the Accountant in Bankruptcy.

It is worth noticing that a year or two before the passing of the Bankruptcy Act of 1856, a Bill was introduced into the House of Lords by Lord Brougham, the purpose of which was to import into Scotland, in a great measure, the English system, with its Bankruptcy Court, Judges, Registrars, Official Assignees, and other officers; but the proposal was not received with favour and fell to the ground.

It may be enough to mention, without detailing early bankruptcy legislation in England, that the Court of Bankruptcy was first established under Lord Brougham's Act of 1831. Official Assignees took the place of the Commissioners and Trade Assignees, who formerly had charge of the ingathering and distribution of insolvent estates, and, being appointed by the Lord Chancellor, often for political reasons, had rarely any special knowledge of the duties required of them, and were thus dependent upon the solicitors employed. An attempt was now made to remedy this defect, for the official assignees were to be "merchants, brokers, accountants, or persons who were, or had been, engaged in trade." A Consolidating Act was passed in 1849 which introduced some changes and encouraged private arrangements with creditors under this Act. Debtors were required to lodge statements of their affairs, and the preparation of these statements brought many well-known accountants into prominence and repute. After being amended more than once, this Act was supplanted by the Bankruptcy Act of 1869, which was founded largely on the Scottish Act of 1856. Official

Assignees were swept away, the powers of the creditors were largely increased, and a Comptroller in Bankruptcy appointed, who occupied very much the position of the Accountant in Bankruptcy in Scotland. As already indicated, however, this Act was found to have many defects, and it was superseded by the Bankruptcy Act of 1883, which, with some slight modifications, still remains in force. This Act is too well known to need description here, but one of its most important effects was to restrict the powers granted to creditors in 1869 and restore the official element, Receivers being appointed under control of the Board of Trade to take charge of bankrupt estates, which they continue to manage unless the creditors afterwards elect a private trustee, a proceeding which is usually adopted only in the case of large estates.

It is unfortunately a matter of every day experience that limited companies as well as private firms are subject to insolvency, and in this case the proceedings are directed by the winding up clauses of the Act of 1862 and subsequent amending acts. A liquidator, or in the case of Court liquidation an official liquidator, is appointed to supersede the directors, make calls where necessary on the shareholders, and generally realise the assets for the benefit of the creditors in the first place, and after their claims are satisfied for the shareholders. In the great majority of cases this position has been filled by an accountant, and its importance to the profession may be judged from the fact that during the forty-two years which have passed since the date of the Act 87,821 companies have been registered, of which no less than 50,534 have come to an end. The Records of the Registrar do not enable us to discover what became of the many millions of capital which these companies represented, but it is to be feared that, regarded as capital, the great bulk of it came to an end also. The position of voluntary liquidator is one of very great responsibility and independence. Unfortunately the holders of office, like the trustees in bankruptcy, were not in every case worthy of the confidence reposed in them ; and the scan-

dalous delays which took place in winding up the affairs of
companies, particularly in England, led to the passing of
the Companies Winding-up Act of 1890 (not applicable to
Scotland), which considerably curtailed the employment of
accountants, as the practice, in the case of companies
wound up compulsorily, was assimilated to that pursued in
bankruptcy under the Act of 1883.

The Act of 1862 had not long been in existence before the
occurrence of the great commercial crisis of 1866, which saw
the collapse of many large and important concerns, but at the
same time established the reputation of more than one accountant and laid the foundation of some of the most respectable fortunes which have been amassed in the profession. The principal failure of that year was that of Overend,
Gurney, & Co., a well-known banking firm which had, only
ten months before, been converted into a limited company, the
value of the good-will being placed at half a million sterling.
The liquidation lasted till 1893, but the creditors were paid in
full, with interest, within four years of the liquidator's appointment, the sum paid to them being £4,913,382, 12s. 5d. The
calls on the shareholders, after tedious litigation, produced
over two millions sterling, and ·the liquidators' remuneration
was fixed at £71,946, 2s. 4d., exclusive of £14,863 for clerks'
services. This was perhaps the first important liquidation
under the Acts; those of the Balfour group of companies,
and the still more recent Whitaker Wright concerns, are
still fresh in the public mind; and while the Act of 1900
has done something to check the formation of unstable companies, their liquidation will no doubt continue to afford
steady and remunerative employment to the accountant.

The Companies Acts, beginning in 1862 and ending, for the
present, in 1900, have already been referred to as good friends
to the accountant, and two ways have been particularised,
auditing and liquidation, in which they bring grist to his mill.
But his obligation does not by any means end there. An
accountant is usually consulted, and often takes an actual part

in the formation of new and the amalgamation or reconstruction of existing companies, and his report is one of the most important parts of the prospectus. His services are required as secretary, manager, or director, and he is sometimes called in to report on particular questions of policy, or to investigate the position of affairs in distant parts of the world. In some cases an accountant has been retained, with a handsome salary, not as a member of the Board of Directors, but as a sort of financial adviser, and it is not unlikely that in years to come, the consulting accountant, freed from the cares of general practice, may have as well defined a place in our profession as the consulting physician has in that of medicine.

The employment of accountants as book-keepers is no doubt one of the humbler walks of the profession, but it need hardly be said that a thorough knowledge of book-keeping forms the most important plank in the substructure of the accountant's art. Mercantile transactions are much more complex than they were formerly, and it is a very common experience to be called upon to devise new and improved methods of keeping accounts, which will ensure not only accuracy, but, the great desideratum of the times, simplicity and saving of time. So great effect has been given to these requirements, particularly in this country and in America, that the old book-keeper would probably consider the decay of book-keeping as one of the prominent characteristics of the age. While the profession in general has obtained a much more defined and important position in this country than it has on the Continent, it would appear that the intricacies and refinements of book-keeping on the scientific Italian model have been more closely studied there than here. One can imagine the horror with which one of the old book-keepers, whose painstaking caligraphy we admire in the business books of which specimens have been given, would see the Journal to a large extent disused, and their sacred Ledger turned into a pack of cards!

No one who has had to do with the examination of

candidates for the various societies of accountants can have failed to notice the want of exact and practical acquaintance with this important subject, which affects a very large percentage of the candidates. The teaching of book-keeping in our schools used to be of a very formal and perfunctory character. It was considered a branch of the writing department, and consisted of copying out a wearisome rigmarole of details in an imaginary waste book, journal, and ledger. The teacher's own knowledge of the subject was purely theoretical, and it was little to be wondered at that he was unable to endow it with the life and interest without which no instruction can be easily conveyed. Under these circumstances the student could hardly be expected to obtain even what Dr. Johnson somewhat grudgingly admitted to the Scottish University students, "a mediocrity of knowledge, between learning and ignorance, not inadequate for the purposes of common life." But the profession is waking up to the importance of this matter, and, as the learned author just quoted observes, "where there is yet shame, there may in time be virtue." Tutorial classes, courses of lectures, and students' societies, are now the rule in most of our large towns; libraries are at the disposal of the apprentices, and in at least two places, the University of Birmingham and the New York University School of Commerce, the teaching of accountancy has been raised to the dignity of a Professor's Chair.

Reference having been made to Dr. Johnson, it may be recalled that, among remarks on most things under, and even beyond the sun, he has left on record his views on book-keeping, and it will be seen that they were not very appreciative. Replying to the pertinacious Boswell, who had praised the accuracy of a lady's account-book, he is reported to have said, "keeping accounts, sir, is of no use when a man is spending his own money and has nobody to whom he is to account. You won't eat less beef to-day because you have written down what it cost yesterday."

Boswell maintained the orthodox view of the advantages of correct account-keeping, and the record ends with the words, "this he did not attempt to answer."[1] One more classical quotation may be permitted, from another great philosopher, and it suggests the apotheosis of book-keeping: "Book-keeping by double-entry is admirable, and records several things in an exact manner. But the Mother Destinies also keep their tablets; in Heaven's Chancery also there goes on a recording; and things, as my Moslem friends say, are 'written on the iron leaf.'"[2]

In Scotland certain Court appointments are open to the practising accountant. These are known by the general appellation of Judicial Factories, and the Judicial Factor is defined as being any person judicially appointed factor upon a trust estate or upon the estate of a person *incapax* (*i.e.* pupils, minors, or lunatics). In the great majority of cases the "person" so appointed is a professional accountant.

Judicial Factors may be appointed at Common Law in the discretion of the Court, and there is a regulating Act of Sederunt, dated so far back as 13th February 1730, but still in force, which thus explains in its preamble the purpose of these appointments :—

The Lords of Council and Session, considering that they have been often applied to for appointing factors on the estates of pupils not having tutors, and of persons absent that have not sufficiently empowered persons to act for them, or who are under some incapacity for the time to manage their own estates, to the end that the estates of such pupils or persons may not suffer in the meantime, but be preserved for their behoof and of all having interest therein, &c.

They are also appointed under various Statutes. The Companies Clauses Consolidation Act (1845) authorises application by mortgagees to the Court of Session for a Judicial

[1] Boswell's "Life," March 1783.
[2] Carlyle, "Past and Present," Book III. Chap. 10.

Factor to receive the whole or part of the tolls of the under-taking indebted to them. The main Act of Parliament regulating such appointments is the Pupils Protection Act of 1849, which has been modified, but only to a slight degree, by the Judicial Factors (Scotland) Acts of 1880 and 1889, the Guardianship of Infants Act 1886, and by various Acts of Sederunt of the Court of Session carrying out details. There is consequently little to be said in regard to develop-ment in this class of work, except the increase of its volume, a feature to be observed in all the other branches of the profes-sion. A tendency may perhaps be noted in recent years to employ this method of winding up the estates of deceased or insolvent persons instead of the ordinary methods of executry and bankruptcy. The Bankruptcy Act of 1856, § 164, pro-vided for the appointment of a Judicial Factor on the estate of a deceased person in the place of trustees, and § 189 of the Judicial Factors (Scotland) Act of 1889 allows testamentary trustees to apply to the Court for a superintendence order as to the investment and distribution of the estate. In all cases, the Judicial Factor is subject to the superintendence of the Accountant of Court, who audits his accounts, fixes his remuneration, and advises the Court on applications for special powers.

The preparation of the accounts and schedules required in connection with the Government death duties is still largely undertaken by solicitors, but it is beginning to be recognised, particularly in England, that this is a kind of work more suited to the accountant.

A notable feature of the latter half of the nineteenth century is the claim made on behalf of women to take a part in professional and other work which had hitherto been reserved for the sterner sex. Their demand for admission into the ranks of the medical profession has long since passed into the realm of history. The struggle was long and severe, but it must be admitted that they were successful all along the line, and there are now few towns of any conse-

quence where the brass plate and not infrequently the neat
brougham of the lady doctor are not in evidence. They
have not been so successful in the domains of law and
divinity, though lady barristers are not unknown in Paris,
and if the public prints are to be credited not a few congregations in America, both white and coloured, are ministered
to by lady parsons. Their invasion of the accountant profession need not therefore occasion any surprise. Of course
hundreds of women find employment as typists — and to
a less extent as clerks in accountants' offices, and their
patience and manual dexterity seem to fit them admirably
for routine and mechanical work. But that was not enough,
for some years ago a memorial was presented to the English
Institute of Chartered Accountants by the Society for Promoting the Employment of Women asking for the admission
of women as members. The Council of the Institute did not
see their way to grant the petition, but a perusal of the
London Post-Office Directory records the fact that at least
four women are engaged in business as accountants, and one
of them describes herself as a public accountant. With all
respect for the undoubted genius of women, it may be
questioned if their faculties are at all specially adapted for
accountants' work at large. Still, it may be argued that any
difference between the sexes in this respect is due to long
centuries of disuse and repression. Time and experience will
show, and it is at least possible that at the end of another
fifty years lady trustees, receivers, and auditors may be as
common as lady doctors are now.

To show the remarkable development of the profession
during the last half century, it is only necessary to examine
the particulars given in earlier chapters with regard to the
societies of organised accountants throughout the world.
Fifty years ago there were only the two Scottish Societies
with a membership of little more than 100, now the membership of the various Societies in English-speaking countries
exceeds 8000. It is during the second half of the period

that much the larger portion of this increase has taken place. In 1880 there were 270 Scottish Chartered Accountants and about 1000 in England, with a very few in two newly formed societies in Canada. All the other societies, numbering some forty, have sprung up since that date. This enormous increase naturally leads to the question, has it kept pace with, or has it outrun the expansion of accountant work which has been discussed in the preceding pages? In plain language, is the profession overstocked? and further, is the competition for business induced by the numbers seeking employment a wholesome one, or is there a danger of it becoming deleterious to the best interests of the profession? Competition, it is often said, is the soul of business, because it stimulates the search for improved and cheaper methods of production. But the work of accountancy is necessarily slow, laborious, and painstaking. The details of an audit, for example, do not appear on the surface of the report, nor are they obvious to the untrained eye; but this work cannot be shortened or cheapened without damaging its efficiency and thereby endangering the reputation of the profession.

The question of over supply is one to which it is difficult to give any definite answer. The *Post-Office Directory*, which gives the names of over 1100 accountants in London, records no less than thirteen times that number of solicitors; and the political economist would argue that the eternal law of supply and demand may safely be left to solve the difficulty in its own callous way.

It is quite obvious, however, that all who are crowding into the ranks cannot possibly reach eminence or lucrative employment in the profession. Many have no natural aptitude for it, and there is always a certain proportion of men of real ability who from the lack of some not easily definable quality fail to "get on" in anything they attempt. But there is a good deal of truth in the old maxim, that there is plenty of room at the top of the profession, and men of real capacity will in general find their proper place. The aspirants who do succeed will most likely be found to be those who, starting with a certain modicum of aptitude for the work, have in addition a sound moral backbone, abundant common-sense, and that infinite capacity for taking pains which is closely allied to genius.

CHAPTER X

THE POSITION AND PROSPECT

NUMBER OF PROFESSIONAL ACCOUNTANTS—DIFFERENT COUN-
TRIES COMPARED—FORMATION OF RIVAL SOCIETIES—DE-
SIRE FOR LEGISLATIVE CONTROL—DANGERS TO BE GUARDED
AGAINST—FUTURE DEVELOPMENT

IT is believed that in the foregoing pages practically every
Society of Accountants in the world has been referred to.
Inquiry has been made at all important commercial centres,
and the only institutions that can have escaped notice are
those which either from their small size or recent formation
are very little known. The total number of members enrolled in one or other of the societies mentioned is about
11,150, and making allowance for instances of the same individual being a member of two societies, 11,000 may be
taken as the number of individual accountants. Roughly
speaking, the United Kingdom accounts for half that
number, Italy for one fourth, the British Colonies for 15
per cent., the United States for 5 per cent., and South
America, Holland, Sweden, and Belgium for the remaining
5 per cent.

Of public accountants unconnected with any society it
is impossible to make a reliable estimate. In Great Britain
they probably do not exceed a hundred or two, and in other
countries enquiry does not disclose many. The absence of
any society is itself an indication that accountants are few
in number.

In Scotland the profession may be said to be thoroughly
established and organised. The period of fifty years during

which it has been regulated there has been long enough to produce this state of matters: that substantially no active practitioner now living can have any legitimate reason for not having entered the profession through the regular channels, or for failing to possess the hall-mark of efficiency which membership of a properly conducted society bestows. Where organisation has not existed for so long a time there may be persons still alive who had passed the natural period of training for a profession, and had commenced practice before any society was formed. Such persons may fairly enough have felt no call upon them to become members of the new society. But after a lapse of fifty years very few in that position are likely to survive.

In Scotland, as in other countries, there are no doubt some individuals claiming to be ranked as professional accountants who are not members of any properly conducted society. This is likely always to be the case. It may be conjectured that many of these claims would on investigation be found to rest on somewhat slender grounds, but even in those few cases—and in Scotland they are very few—where the claim may be recognised, the reasons for having failed to pass through the regular curriculum must have been of a purely personal nature.

From the figures given in an earlier chapter,[1] it will be noticed that a considerable proportion of Scottish Chartered Accountants have found it to their advantage to betake themselves to other countries. It may therefore be held that the present needs of the country, so far as professional accountants are concerned, are fully met. There is left in Scotland one Chartered Accountant to every 6500 of the population. In England and Wales, including the Scotsmen who have crossed the border, there is only one Chartered Accountant for every 10,500 of the population. If the members of the Society of Accountants and Auditors in both countries be included the figures are: Scotland, one

[1] Page 215.

accountant for every 5500, England, one for every 7200, of the population.

These figures give a fair view of the relative strength of the profession in the two countries. It is true that many who are qualified practitioners are not in practice on their own account, and that some members of the societies may have ceased to act as public accountants, but these conditions are much the same in both countries. With the exception of the colonies of Australasia, where there has been a rapid growth in the number of accountants during the last ten years, accompanied by the formation of an apparently unnecessary number of societies, the figures are not approached by any other country in the world. In Australia and New Zealand there are thirteen different societies, and one enrolled accountant for every 4000 of the population, the proportion of accountants being greatest in the sparsely populated Colonies of South Australia, West Australia, and Tasmania, and in the Colonies of New Zealand and Victoria. It is possible that the existence of so many societies, in several cases operating in the same districts, has brought about the inclusion of more names than would otherwise have been the case. In Italy the proportion of accountants who are members of societies to population is one in 13,000.

A drawback which frequently accompanies the earlier years of the organisation of a new profession is the formation of rival societies, as an examination of the foregoing pages will show. It is something more than a mere question of the " ins " and the " outs," or at least it assumes a more complex form. When a society is first proposed, the promoters cannot be expected to undergo a professional examination, as, if they were, the society would probably never be formed. The course usually followed is, that all recognised practitioners within the area of the proposed association are invited to become original members without examination, and the society having been formed, rules are adopted regulating the admission of future members. If the society is to attain any standing, these rules must provide for an efficient test of the candidates' fitness.

Unless these proceedings are gone about with very great care and discretion, there will be three classes of "outs" who are likely to give trouble to the new society before it has attained much strength and public standing. These are, *First*, men who were invited to join the movement, and did not then think it worth their while, but who afterwards saw cause to change their minds; *Second*, men worthy of being invited who were unwittingly overlooked; *Third*, men deemed by the promoters unworthy of being included, but who themselves held a different opinion. The probability is that such men, if they are at all numerous, will form a new society within a few years. Again, if the community is a large one, this new body will meet with exactly the same difficulty, though most likely at a point a little lower down the professional scale, and a third society may be formed. The operation may even be several times repeated.

It is unfortunate for the profession when this state of matters arises, and some considerable time may elapse before it can emerge from the consequent confusion. Eventually, however, with the assistance of a discerning public, the mingled elements may be expected to resolve themselves into the qualified and the unqualified. For its members to be ranked as qualified a society must consistently require of all entrants a sufficient general education, ample practical training, and full professional knowledge, tested by periodical examinations open to the searchlight of public criticism.

Where the condition referred to has arisen it is sometimes proposed to restore immediate order by Act of Parliament. State laws have been passed in many of the United States of America and also in our new Transvaal Colony, but in these cases the opportunity was taken of imposing State regulation practically from the commencement, a much easier matter than to interfere with an established condition. In the latter case there are two considerations which do not in any important degree enter into the question in the former : *First*, whether, having regard to what may be called vested interests, the enactment of a satisfactory law is practicable ; and, *Second*, whether any law which could be passed would effectually remove the grievances and abuses alleged to have grown up.

This is not the place to enter upon a discussion of the various proposals of the kind which have been before the legislative assemblies of this and other countries, but we may express the opinion that so far as Great Britain is concerned accountants will do well in the meantime not to place much reliance on the State coming to their help. It is contrary to the traditions of British legislation to interfere with the natural development of any calling or industry. Most of the other professions have grown up without the aid of a foster-mother, and although in the particular cases of law and medicine Acts of Parliament have been passed in comparatively recent times for their regulation, it may be questioned whether the results have been as beneficial as was anticipated. An examination of the Amending Acts upon the Law Agents (Scotland) Act 1873 will show how difficult it is to reach finality in such a matter. In establishing the systems of registration which are the chief features of legislation of this kind precisely the same difficulties are met with as in the formation of societies, and in a more aggravated form. Unless every one is allowed on the register at the outset the Bill is not permitted to pass. If every one is registered the profession is given a set back which it cannot possibly recover for many years.

What the Societies and the individuals comprising them may with more profit address themselves to is to maintain the strictest code of professional morality, to aspire to the highest standard of professional skill, and to cultivate the broadest spirit of professional brotherliness. These things are not achieved by Act of Parliament, or even greatly assisted thereby.

The profession needs the guidance and watchful care which association in societies only can provide. There are dangers in the modern trend of business which should be well looked to. Perhaps the most important is the tendency to allow the personal element to be obscured. The accountant must not forget that he is a professional man, and that like other professional men he must attend to his work himself. His is not a business which can be devolved on managers or carried on at branches like a bank or mercantile concern. If he is to be successful, he must give everything his "personal attention." He may employ *assistants*, but not *substitutes*, and he must not seek to escape from the fullest measure of personal responsibility. "A long and laborious tract of attention" was Sir Walter Scott's phrase.[1] But in these days the profession has become infected with the commercial spirit, and we not only see many branch establishments carried on, but even Accounting and Auditing Companies formed,[2] where the personal element is completely obliterated.

Another danger is the tendency to specialisation, to which reference has already been made.[3] This is likely to exercise a narrowing influence on the individual, and to destroy his character as a good all round "man of affairs" of the type of him to whose counsel men like Sir William Forbes were "accustomed to resort on every emergency."[4]

Let us hope that it is on broad lines the profession of accountant will continue to be developed. There is still room for greater method and accuracy in business, greater clearness and promptitude in exhibiting results. Joint-stock enterprise is by no means exhausted, and bankrupts we have always with us. But there are other directions where the services of the accountant might, it seems to us, with advantage be utilised. Why, for instance, should not his assistance more frequently be invoked in settling disputes such as those between Labour and Capital, or why should not the adjustment

[1] See *ante*, p. 197.   [2] See *ante*, p. 279.
See *ante*, p. 322.   [4] See *ante*, p. 186.

of an Income Tax Return of profits, where a difficulty has arisen, be left to an accountant?

It would be unbecoming in us to say more, but we hope we have said enough to show that the prospects of the profession are bright and that its sphere is likely to expand. Sixty years ago Robert Balfour said of it, "It is certainly more varied than that of the lawyer, and I believe it to be certainly not less dignified;"[1] and later, Dr. John Brown described it as "an important and severe profession."[2] These epithets were applied to the profession in Scotland when it occupied a much less important position than at present, and they can now be given a considerably wider geographical application. Yet in many parts of the civilised world the accountant is still unknown. In other parts where he has only just presented himself before the public, these words of wise and far-seeing men may perhaps strengthen his courage and endue him with a proper pride; and for further encouragement, let us only add in conclusion that, if we read the signs of the times aright, a far greater measure of development all over the world awaits the profession during the next fifty years than that which we have witnessed during the half century which has just elapsed.

[1] See *ante*, p. 315.   [2] See *Accountants' Magazine*, vol. i. p. 155.

APPENDICES

APPENDICES

APPENDIX No. I

BIBLIOGRAPHY OF BOOK-KEEPING

A CHRONOLOGICAL LIST OF PRINTED BOOKS ON BOOK-KEEPING UP TO THE YEAR 1800

NOTE.—*Many of the books in this list have been examined and the particulars of the entries verified. Where otherwise, the entries for the most part have been taken from the " Elenco cronologico delle opere di computisteria e ragioneria venute alla luce in Italia," 4th Edition, 1889, and from " The Origin and Progress of Book-keeping," by B. F. Foster, London, 1852.*

FRÀ LUCA PACIOLO, DA BORGO SAN SEPOLCRO.

Summa de Arithmetica, Geometria, Proportioni et Proportionalità.—Venice, 1494, folio.
Another edition, Toscolano, 1523, folio.

HEINRICH SCHREIBER (*Henricus Grammateus*).

Rechenbüchlin, Künstlich, behend vnd gewiss, auff alle Kauffmann-schafft gericht.—Erfurt, 1523.
Other editions, 1545, and *Frankfort*, 1572.

GIOVANNI ANTONIO TAGLIENTE.

Considerando io Ioanni Antonio Taiente quanto e necessaria cosa a li nostri magnifici getilhomeni & adaltri mercatanti el laudabile modo de tenere conto de libro dopio cioe, el Zornale el Libro conlalphabetto secondo el consueto de questa inclita Citta di Venetia, &c.—Venice, 1525, 4to.

ANONYMOUS.

La tenuta del libro mastro pel negoziante e il possidente.—1525, 4to.

ANONYMOUS.

Opera che insegna a tener libro doppio et a far partite, e ragion de Banchi, e de Mercantie a riportare le partite novamente stampata.—Venice, 1529, 16mo.

JOHAN GOTTLIEB.

Ein Teutsch vertendig Buchhalten für Herren oder Gesellschafter inhalt Wellischem process, &c.—Nuremberg, 1531.

Zwey Künstliche und Bestendige Buchhalten, das erste, wie einer für sich selbst oder Gesellschaffter handeln soll, das ander, fur Factorey wie man auch Wahre mit.—1546 (?).

Another edition, Nuremberg, 1592, sm. 4to.

DOMENICO MANZONI, da Oderzo.

Quaderno doppio col suo giornale secondo il costume di Venetia.—Venice, 1534, 4to.

Quaderno doppio col suo giornale, novamente composto, et diligentissimamente ordinato, secondo il costume di Venetia.—Venice, 1554, 4to.

Libro mercantile ordinato col suo Giornale et Alfabeto per tener conti doppi al modo di Venetia.—Venice, 1540, 4to.

Other editions, Venice, 1564, 1565, 1573, 1574.

HIERONIMUS CARDANUS.

Practica Arithmeticae et mensurandi Singularis.—Milan, 1539, 8vo.

Another edition, Leyden, 1663.

HUGH OLDCASTLE.

A profitable Treatyce called the Instrument or Boke to learne to knowe the good order of the kepyng of the famouse reconynge, called in Latyn, Dare and Habere, and in Englyshe, Debitcr and Creditor.—London, 1543, 4to.

JAN YMPYN CHRISTOFFELS.

Nieuwe Instructie Ende bewijs der lo-offelijcker Consten des Rekenboecks ende Rekeninghe te houdene nae die Italiaensche maniere, &c.—Antwerp, 1543.

Nouuelle Instruction et Remonstration de la tres excellente fciĕce du liure de Compte, pour compter & mener comptez, a la maniere d'Itallie, &c.—Antwerp, 1543.

A notable and very excellente woorke, expressyng and declaryng the manner and forme how to kepe a boke of accomptes or reconynges, verie expedient and necessary to all Marchantes, Receiuers, Auditors, Notaries, and all others. Translated with greate diligence out of the Italian toung into Dutche, and out of Dutche into Frenche, and now out of Frenche into Englishe.—London, 1547.

GASPAR DE' TEXADA.

Suma De arithmetica pratica y de' todas Mercaderias Con la 5 orden de contadores.—Madrid (?) 1545, 4to.

WOLFFGANG SCHWEICKER, Senior.

Zwifach Buchhalten, sampt seine Giornal desselben Beschlus auch Rechnung zuthun &c. Durch Wolffgang Schweicker Senior von Nürnberg jetzt in Venedig wonend mit allem fleis gemacht und zusamen bracht.—Nuremberg, 1549, folio.

VALENTIN MENHER de KEMPTEN.

Practicque brifue pour cyfrer et tenir Liures de Compte touchant le Principal train de marchandise.—Antwerp, 1550.

Another edition, Lyons, 1591.

Practicque povr brievement apprendre à Ciffrer, & tenir Liure de Comptes, auec la Regle de Coss, & Geometrie.—Antwerp, 1565, 8vo.

BARTOLOMEO FONTANA.

Ammaestramento novo che insegna a tener libro.—1551.

JAMES PEELE.

The maner and fourme how to kepe a perfecte reconyng after the order of the most worthie and notable accompte of Debitour and Creditour set forthe in certain tables with a declaracion thereunto belongyng.—London, 1553, folio.

The patheway to perfectness in the accomptes of Debitour and Creditour : in manner of a dialogue very pleasant and proffitable for Marchaunts and all other that minde to frequent the same, once againe set forthe and very much enlarged, &c.—London, 1569, folio.

ALVISE CASANOVA, da Venezia.

Specchio lucidissimo, &c.—Venice, 1558, 4to.

ANTICH ROCHA.

Compendio y breue instruction por tener Libros de Cuenta, Deudas, y de Mercaduria : muy prouechoso para Mercaderes, y toda gente de negocio, traduzido de Frances en Castellano.—Barcelona, 1565, 8vo.

PIERRE SAVONNE.

Antwerp, 1567.

An enlarged edition, Geneva, 1614.

BENEDETTO COTRUGLI, da Ragusi.

Della Mercatura et del Mercante perfetto.—Venice, 1573, 8vo.

The MS. written in 1463.

MICHIEL COIGNET.

Antwerp (?), 1573.

Don ANGELO PIETRA, da Genova.

Indirizzo de gli economi, osia ordinatissima instruttione da regolatamente formare qualunque scrittura in un libro doppio, &c.—Mantua, 1586, folio.

JOHN MELLIS.

A briefe instruction and maner how to keepe bookes of Accomptes after the order of Debitor and Creditor, & as well for proper Accompts partible, &c. Newely augmented and set forth by John Mellis, Scholemaister.—London, 1588, 8vo.

NICOLAUS PETRI DAVENTRIENSES.

Practicque omte Leeren Rekenen Cypheren ende Boeckhouden met die Reghel Coss, ende Geometrie.—Amsterdam, 1588, 8vo.
Other editions, 1595, 1596, and 1605.

ELEIUS EDUARD LEON MELLEMA.

Boeckhouder na de conste van Italien met twee partijen.—Rotterdam (?) 1590.

BARTOLOME SALVADOR de SOLORZANA.

Libro de Caxa y manual de Cuentas de Mercaderes. Compendio para tener y regir los libros de Cuentas de Mercaderes.—Madrid, 1590.

BARTHELEMY de RENTERGHEM.

Instruction nouvelle pour tenir le livre de compte ou de raison, selon la façon et manière d'Italie.—Antwerp, 1592.

PASSCHIER-GOESSENS.

Buchhalten fein kurtz zusamen gefasst und begriffen, &c.—Hamburg, 1594, folio.

MARTINUS WENCESLAUS.

Boeckhoudens Instruction. —— (?) 1595.

W. P.

The Pathway to Knowledge. Conteyning certaine briefe Tables of English waights, and Measures. . . . And lastly the order of keeping of a Marchant's booke, after the Italian manner, by Debitor and Creditor . . . . Written in Dutch, and translated into English by W. P.— London, 1596, 4to.

MARTIN VAN DEN DYCKE.

Demonstration claire et brève de la tenue des livres.—Antwerp (?) 1598.

ZACHARIE de HOORBECKE.

Middelburg, 1599.

SIMON STEVIN of Bruges.

Livre de compte de prince à la manière d'Italie en domain et finance ordinaire, &c.—Leyden, 1602, folio.

Verrechnung van Domeinen, ende vorstelyke Boeckhouden.—Amsterdam, 1604.

Mathematica hypomnemata.—Leyden, 1605–1608, folio.

JAN COUTEREELS.

Den vasten styl van Boeckhouden.—Middelburg, 1603.

MICHEL van DAMME.

Rouen, 1606.

SIMON GRISOGONO, da Zara.

Il Mercante arricchito del perfetto quaderniere, overo specchio lucidissimo nel quale si scopre ogni questione che desiderar si possa per imparare perfettamente a tenere Libro Doppio, &c.—Venice, 1609, 8vo.

GIO. ANTONIO MOSCHETTI, da Venezia.

Dell' Universal trattato di libri doppii, ne' quali con regole universali et essempi particolari ampiamente s' insegna il modo di girar in scrittura doppia qual si voglia negotio mercantile.—Venice, 1610, 4to.

NICOLAUS WOLFF.

Kurtze Dochgrundliche und Aigentliche beschreibung eines Ordentlichen rechten Buchhaltens wie solches ein jeder inn seinem Handel und Gewerb oder Hauszhalten gebrauchen vnnd führen kan, &c.—Nuremberg, 1610, folio.

JOHN TAP.

The Pathway to Knowledge, &c.—London, 1613, 8vo.

(A reprint of W.P. above.)

HENDRICK WANINGHEN van CAMPEN.

Tresoor vant Italiaens Boeck-houden, waer in begrepen staet, Een Memoriael, Iournael, ende Schult-Boeck, &c.—Amsterdam, 1615.

Another edition by Ioannes Buingha.—Amsterdam, 1639, folio.

JAN WILLEMSZ VON LÖWEN.

De Gulden School ofte Instructie vant Italiaens Boeck-houden.—Amsterdam, 1616.

ANDREA MONARI, DA CENTO.

Nuova tariffa nella quale con prestezza e facilitá si comprende il dare et havere di ogni mercantia, &c.—Bologna, 1620.
Other editions, 1714, 1743, 1761, 1782, 1783, 1800, 12mo.

JEAN BELOT.

Instruction sur la tenue des livres italienne en vingt leçons.—1621.

GERARD MALYNES.

Consuetudo, vel Lex Mercatoria, or, The Antient Law-Merchant.—London, 1622, folio.
Other editions, 1636, 1656, 1686.

ANONYMOUS.

La scrittura doppia. Memorie ricavate da alcuni discorsi del conte Locatelli.—1624.

IOANNES BUINGHA.

Oprecht fondament ende principalen inhout van het Italiaens Boeckhouden, &c.—Amsterdam, 1627, 8vo.

ANTOINE VAN NEULIGHEM.

Exposé de la Tenue des Livres Italienne.—1630.

MATHIEU THOMAS.

1632.

I. CARPENTER, GENT.

A most excellent instruction for the . . . keeping merchants bookes of accounts by way of Debitor and Creditor . . . and . . . here is adioyned the practice by an example of the Inventory, Journall, and Lidger, &c.—London, 1632, folio.

MATTEO MAINARDI, DA BOLOGNA.

La scrittura mercantile fatta e riordinata, &c.—Bologna, 1632, folio.
L'Economo overo la Scrittura tutelare, Scrittura mercantile formalmente regolata, &c.—Bologna, 1700, folio.

JACOB VAN DER SCHUERE.

Kort onder-richt over het Italiaens Boeckhouden.—1634.

JEAN ANDRÉ.

Paris, 1636.

RICHARD DAFFORNE of NORTHAMPTON, ACCOUNTANT.

The Merchants' Mirrour, or Directions for the perfect ordering and keeping of his accounts. Framed by way of Debitor and Creditor after the (so tearmed) Italian manner.—London, 1636, folio.
Other editions, 1651, 1660–1684.
The Apprentices Time-Entertainer accomptantly; or, A Methodical means to attain the Exquisite Art of Accomptantship. . . . Also, the form of a Book for Charges of Merchandize. . . . By John Dafforne.—London, 1670, 4to.
The English Merchant's Companion: . . . Wherein the perfect Method of Merchants Book-keeping, and other matters relating to Traffick, is compleatly demonstrated.
4th edition, London, 1700. 4to.

LODOVICO FLORI, DA PERUGIA.

Trattato del modo di tenere il libro doppio domestico col suo esemplare.—Palermo, 1636, folio.
Other editions, Rome, 1667; 1677, folio.

GIOVANNI DOMINIC PERI.

Il Negotiante, &c.—Genoa, 1638, 4to.
Other editions, 1649, 1662, 1672, 1697, 1707.

CLAUDE BOYER.

Lyons, 1645.

GIOV. LUCA CAMPACCIO.

Breve discorso sopra l'aritmetica pratica e della scrittura mercantile.—Rome, 1650, 12mo.

JOHN COLLINS, FELLOW OF THE ROYAL SOCIETY.

An Introduction to Merchants-Accompts.—London, 1652.
Other editions, 1664–1665, 1674–1675, 1697, folio.

BASTIANO VENTURI.

Della scrittura conteggiante di possessioni.—Florence, 1655, folio.

CHRISTOPHOR ACHATIUS HAGER.

Buchhalten über Proper Commission und Compagnia Handlungen.—Hamburg, 1654, folio.
Another edition, Hamburg, 1695.

FRANÇOIS LEGENDRE.

Paris, 1658.

350 APPENDIX

DAVID KOCK.

De luchtende Fackel van het Italiaens Boeck-houden. Republished by B. H. Geestevelt.—Amsterdam, 1658, sm. 4to.

ABRAHAM LISET, Gent.

Amphithalami: or, The Accomptants Closet, Being an Abbridgment of Merchants-accounts kept by Debitors and Creditors.—London, 1660, folio. Another edition, London, 1684.

Don GIACOMO VENTUROLI, da Bologna.

Scorta di Economia, o sia dialogo di scrittura famigliare.—Bologna, 1666, 4to.

SBERNIA ONOFRIO PUGLIESE, da Palermo.

Prattica economica numerale ed anche "Giornale del libro Maestro" nella quale s'insegna il modo di tenere regolarmente i libri di conti, &c.— Palermo, 1671, 4to.
Other editions, 1678, 1745.

ANDREA ZAMBELLI, da Brescia.

Il ragionato, o sia trattato della scrittura universale.—Milan, 1671, 4to. Mercantesche dichiarationi della scrittura doppia.—Brescia, 1681, 4to.

M. DE LA PORTE.

La Science des Negocians et teneurs de livres ou instruction generale, &c.— Paris, 1673, oblong 4to.
Le Guide des Negociants et Teneurs de livres.—Paris, 1685.
Other editions, Paris, 1704, 1712, 1714, 1716, 1748, 1754, 1770, 1792, do.

JACQUES SAVARY.

Le Parfait Negociant.—In 2 vols., Paris, 1675.

STEPHEN MONTEAGE.

Debtor and Creditor made easie: or, a short Instruction for attaining the Right Use of Accounts, &c.—London, 1675, 4to.
Other editions, 1682, 1690, 1708.
Instructions for Rent-Gatherers Accompts, &c., Made Easie; by the Author of the Book, entituled, Debtor and Creditor.—London, 1683, 4to. Another edition, 1708.

JOHN VERNON.

The Compleat Counting-house; or the young Lad taken from the Writing-School, and fully instructed . . . in all the Mysteries of a Merchant, &c. —London, 1678, 8vo.
Other editions (3rd) 1698, (5th) 1722, 12mo.

BIBLIOGRAPHY OF BOOK-KEEPING 351

ROBERT CHAMBERLAIN.
The Accountant's Guide or Merchant's Bookkeeper.—London, 1679, 4to.

ROBERT COLINSON.
Idea Rationaria, or the Perfect Accomptant, Necessary for all Merchants and Trafficquers; Containing the True Forme of Book-keeping, According to the Italian methode, &c.—Edinburgh, 1683, folio.

CLAUDE IRSON.
Methode pour bien dresser toutes sortes de comptes a parties doubles, par debit et credit, et par recette, depense, et reprise.—Paris, 1687, folio.

FRANCESCO GARATTI, DA VENEZIA.
Saggio di Scrittura doppia di mercantie e cambi.—Venice, 1688, 8vo.
Another edition, 1711.

ABRAHAM DE GRAAF.
Instructie van het Italiaans Boeckhouden, &c.—Amsterdam, 1693.

ANDREAS CHRISTOPHORUS RÖSENER.
Tractatus Juridicus de Libris Mercatorum.—Leipsic, 1694, 4to.

EDWARD HATTON.
The Merchant's Magazine, or Trades Man's Treasury, &c.—London, 1695, 4to.
Other editions, 1707, (6th) 1712, 1719, 1726.

GEORG NICOLAUS SCHURTZ.
Nutzbare Richtschnur der Loblichen Kauffmannschafft, das ist neuvermehrt vollkommenes Buchhalten oder grundliche Univeisung dieser preisz-würdigen Wissenschafft, &c.—Nuremberg, 1695, folio.

JOACHIM RADEMANN.
Buchhaltens-Ubung denen in solcher Wissenschafft practicirenden abermahl vorgestellet in einer—1. General-handlung; 2. Auff Lissabon furnirten Compagnia-handlung; 3. Schiff-Rehderen; und dann 4. Verwaltenden Vormundschafft.—Hamburg, 1698, sm. 4to.

P. GIRAUDEAU.
L'Art de tenir les livres en parties doubles.—1700.
Another edition, 1769.
Art de dresser les Comptes des Banquiers, Negociants et Marchands.—Geneva, 1746.
Another edition, 1754.

P. J. M. [PAUL JACOB MARPERGER.]

Probir-Stein der Buch-Halter oder selbstlehrende Buch-Halter-Schul allen angehenden Buch-Haltern Kauffleuten und Handels-Bedienten.—Salseburg, 1701, 12mo.

GIACOMO AGOSTINETTI.

Cento, e Dieci Ricordi, che formano il buon fattor di villa.—Venice, 1704, 8vo.

H. DESAGULIERS.

Grondig onderwijs in het Italiaansch boekhouden.—1705.

Other editions, Amsterdam, 1732, 1741, 1760 (4to).

T. R.

The Gentlemans Auditor: or, a new and easie method for keeping accompts of Gentlemens Estates, &c.—London, 1707, 4to.

CHARLES SNELL, WRITING-MASTER.

A guide to Book-keeping according to the Italian method.—London, 1709.

Accompts for Landed-Men: or, a plain and easie form which they may observe in keeping accompts of their estates.—London [1710?], folio.

ABRAHAM NICHOLAS.

The Young Accomptant's Debitor and Creditor; or An Introduction to Merchants' Accounts, after the Italian Manner, &c.—London, 1711, 18mo. Another edition, London, 1713.

JOH. AYRES.

Arithmetick Made Easie For the Use and Benefit of Trades-Men. 12th Edition; with an Appendix on Book-keeping by Charles Snell.—London, 1714, 12mo.

ANONYMOUS.

The Gentleman Accomptant: or an Essay to unfold the Mystery of Accompts by Debitor and Creditor, &c. Done by a Person of Honour [R. North].—London, 1714.

WILLIAM KELLY.

The Merchant's Companion, being a complete System of Book-keeping both in Theory and Practice.—Cork, 1714.

ALEXANDER MACGHIE.

The Principles of Book-keeping explain'd.—Edinburgh, 1715, 8vo, and 1718, 4to.

THOMAS KING.
An Exact guide to book-keeping by way of debtor and creditor.—London, 1717, 4to.

ALEXANDER MALCOLM.
A New treatise of arithmetick and book-keeping, &c.—Edinburgh, 1718, 4to.
A Treatise of book-keeping; or merchants accounts.—London, 1731, 4to. 2nd edition, 1743.

WILLIAM WEBSTER, WRITING-MASTER.
An Essay on book-keeping according to the true Italian method of debtor and creditor, by double entry, &c.—London, 1719, 8vo.
Other editions, 1721, 1726, 1731, 1740 (7th), 1744, 1747, 1749, 1772 (15th), 1779, 8vo.

N. H.
The Compleat Tradesman; or, the Exact Dealer's Daily Companion, &c.—London, 1720, 12mo.

BERTRAND FRANÇOIS BARRÈME.
Traité des parties doubles ou méthode aisée pour apprendre en parties doubles les livres du commerce et des finances.—1721.

ALEXANDER BRODIE, GENT.
A New and Easy Method of Book-keeping; or instructions for a methodical keeping of Merchants' Accompts, &c.—London, 1722.

SAMUEL RICARD.
L'art de bien tenir les livres de comptes en parties doubles a l'Italienne.—Amsterdam, 1724, folio.

ANONYMOUS.
The Complete English Tradesman, 2nd edit.—London, 1727, 8vo.

RICHARD HAYES.
Modern Book-keeping, or, the Italian Method Improved.—London, 1731. 2nd edition, 1739.
The Gentleman's Complete Book-keeper.—London, 1741, 8vo.

JOHN CLARK, WRITING-MASTER, &c.
Lectures on Accompts; or, Book-keeping after the Italian manner, &c.—London, 1732.

JOHN MAIR.

Book-keeping Methodiz'd; or, a methodical treatise of merchant-ac-compts, according to the Italian form, &c.—Edinburgh, 1736, 8vo.
Other editions, 1741, 1752 (4th), 1757, 1760, 1765 (8th).
Book-keeping Moderniz'd: or merchant-accounts by double entry, &c.
—Edinburgh, 1768, 8vo.
Other editions, 1773, 1784, 1789 (5th), 1793, 1797, 1800, 1807.

HUSTCRAFT STEPHENS.

Italían Book-keeping reduced into an Art.—Dublin, 1737, 8vo.
Another edition, 1754, 8vo.

GIUSEPPE VERGANI.

Istruzione della scrittura doppia economica, &c.　Milan, 1738, 8vo.
Another edition, Milan, 1773, 8vo.
Esemplare per la pratica della scrittura doppia economica.—Milan, 1741, folio.
Other editions, Milan, 1744, 1774, 1780 (Venice), 1781, folio, 1782, 8vo.

Don CARLO BUSCEMI, da Palermo.

Lo scritturale mercantile.—Palermo, 1739, 8vo.

D. GIUSEPPE CARLO AMATO ed URSO, da Palermo.

Il Microscopio dei computisti ossia istruzioni di economia pratica.—Bassano, 1740, folio.
Another edition, 1788.

ANONYMOUS. [BALUGANI PELLEGRINO.]

Instruzione brevissima per formare con metodo qualunque scrittura in un libro doppio, coll'esemplare dello stesso libro e suo giornale.—Modena, 1745, folio.

CLAUDE PERRACHE.

Nouvelle Méthode de tenir les Livres marchands d'une manière très sûre et très facile.—Brussels, 1748.

JOHN LONDON, Merchant.

A Complete System of Book-keeping after the Italian Method.—London, 1748.
The Art of Book-keeping made easy to the young and inexperienced.—London, 1751.

THOMAS CROSBY, Schoolmaster.

Book-keeping after the Modern way of Debtor and Creditor.—London, 1749.

JAMES DODSON, TEACHER OF THE MATHEMATICS.

The Accountant: or the method of Book-keeping Deduced from Clear Principles.—London, 1750, 4to.

ANONYMOUS.

A Treatise of Book-keeping after the Italian Method; By a Book-keeper. London, 1750.

TOMMASO DOMENICO BREGLIA, DA NAPOLI.

L'idea dello scritturale, ovvero Trattato della scrittura doppia baronale, &c.—Naples, 1751.

WILLIAM WESTON.

The Complete Merchant's Clerk; or British and American Compting House, &c.—London, 1754, 8vo.

PIETRO PAOLO SCALI, DA LIVORNO.

Trattato del modo di tenere la scrittura dei mercanti a partite doppie, cioè all'italiana e descrizione del bilancio della prima e della seconda ragione.—Leghorn, 1755, folio.

WILLIAM STEVENSON.

A serious advice to Tradesmen showing them the inconveniences they lye under . . . by not learning Book-keeping, &c.—Edinburgh, 1756, 12mo.

J. P. AUBERT.

Kort dog duidelijk onderwijs van 't Italiaans Boeckhouden, 1758.
Another edition, Amsterdam, 1782.

BENJAMIN DONN.

The Accountant: containing an Essay on Book-keeping by Single and Double Entry.—London, 1758.
The Accountant and geometrician: containing the doctrine of circulating decimals, logarithms, book-keeping, &c.—London, 1765, 8vo.

S. DUNN.

The New Method of Book-keeping, showing how merchants may keep their books after a more easy and correct manner than hath hitherto been practised, and also know by inspection what has been gained or lost.—London, 1760.

RICHARD ROOSE.

An Essay to make a compleat accomptant: in two parts. I. A Treatise of book-keeping according to the true Italian method, &c.; II. The solution of 18 questions in company accompts, &c.—London [1760 ?], 8vo.

GIOVANNI SAPPETTI, DA COSENZA.

Elementi di commerzio ossia Regole generali per coltivarlo, appoggiate alla Ragione, alla Pratica delle nazioni ed alle autorità de'scrittori di questa materia.—Genoa, 1762, 8vo.

W. EVERARD.

Mercantile Book-keeping; or a Treatise on Merchants' Accounts.— London, 1764.

JOHN COOKE.

The Compting-house assistant; or book-keeping made easie, &c. 2nd edition, London, 1764, 12mo.

WILLIAM GORDON, OF THE GLASGOW ACADEMY.

The Universal accountant, and complete merchant. In two volumes. 2nd edition, Edinburgh, 1765, 8vo. Other editions, 1770 (3rd), 1777, 1788. The General counting-house, and man of business.—Edinburgh, 1766, 8vo. 2nd edition, 1770.

NICOLAS STRUYCK.

Inleyding tot het Koopmans Boeckhouden.—Amsterdam, 1768.

ANONYMOUS.

A Lecture upon Partnership Accounts, Foreign and Domestic, by a Merchant. 2nd edition, London, 1769.

WILLIAM SQUIRE.

The Modern Book-keeper; or Book-keeping made easy.—London, 1769.

M. F. FÖRTSCH.

Instructie of grondige onderrichting over het Italiaansch boekhouden, 2nd edition.—Amsterdam, 1769, 4to.

DANIEL DOWLING.

A Complete system of Italian book-keeping according to the modern method. 2nd edition, Dublin, 1770; 3rd edition, 1775, 8vo.

D. FENNING.

The Youth's Guide to Trade, as it is now practised.—London, 1772.

GEORGE FISHER.

The Instructor: or, young man's best companion; containing . . .
merchants accompts, &c.
New edition, Edinburgh, 1772, 18mo.
Other editions, 1779 (23rd), 1810 (30th).

JOHN SEALLY.

The Accountant's companion: . . . with a course of book-keeping by
single entry.—London, 1773, 12mo.

SAMUEL FRIEDRICH HELWIG.

Anweisung zur leichten und grundlichen erlernung der Italienischen
doppelten Buchhaltung.—Berlin, 1774, 8vo.

THOMAS CHAPMAN.

Chapman's introduction to business.—London [1774], 12mo.

WARDHAUGH THOMPSON.

The Accomptant's Oracle; or key to science, being a treatise of common
arithmetic; in two volumes; vol. 1 (arithmetic); vol. 2, a compleat
practical system of book-keeping, &c.—York, 1777, 8vo.

WILLIAM PERRY.

The Man of business and gentleman's assistant; containing arithmetic
and book-keeping by single and double entry.—Edinburgh, 1774, 8vo.
3rd edition, 1777.

S. THOMAS.

The Economist; or, housekeeper's accompts made easy, after the Italian
method: the like not extant.—Newcastle-upon-Tyne, 1779, 8vo.

RAFFAELLO SECCHIONI, DA FIRENZE.

Scrittura di Possessioni per bilancio.—Florence, 1774.
Another edition, Florence, 1782, 4to.

ANONYMOUS.

La scrittura doppia economica rischiarata.—Milan, 1774, folio.

ANONYMOUS.

An Easy introduction to book-keeping . . . for the improvement of
young accountants.—1776, 8vo.

MATTHEW QUIN.

Quin's Rudiments of Book-keeping; comprised in Six plain Cases, &c.—London, 1776, 8vo.
Third edition, 1779.

ROBERT HAMILTON, LL.D.

An Introduction to Merchandize, &c.—Edinburgh, 1777, 8vo.
Other editions, 1788, 1799 (4th), 1802.

JOHN SEDGER.

The Rudiments of Book-keeping.—London, 1777.

WILLIAM WOOD.

Book-keeping familiarised.—Birmingham [1777 ?], 8vo.

JAMES SCRUTON.

The Practical Counting House.—Glasgow, 1777.

THOMAS DILWORTH.

The Young Book-keeper's Assistant, shewing in the most plain and easy manner, the Italian way of stating Debtor and Creditor, &c.
7th edition, London, 1777.
Other editions, 1781, 1784, 1793, 1796, 1801, 1828, 1839, 1856, 1870.

CHARLES HUTTON.

A Complete treatise on practical arithmetic and book-keeping.
5th edition, 1778.
Other editions, London, 1796, 18mo, 1801 (11th), 12mo, 1806, 1834 (18th).

SANTI GIUSTI, DA PISTOIA.

Elementi di aritmetica pratica, &c.—Pescia, 1778, 8vo.
Another edition, Pistoja, 1792, 4to.

DON CARL' ANTONIO MONTI, DA MODENA.

Instruzione brevissima per formare regolarmente qualunque scrittura in libro doppio, &c.—Vicenza, 1779, 4to.

SAMUEL EDWARDS.

A Complete System of Book-keeping, according to the modern method practised by Merchants and others.—Dublin, 1781.

WM. TAYLOR.

A Complete System of Practical Arithmetic (includes book-keeping).—Birmingham, 1783, 8vo.

JEAN JACQUES IMHOOF.
L'Art de tenir les livres en parties doubles.—Vevey, 1786, 4to.

FERERIO ANTONINO FARGHISCOC.
Trattato di scrittura mercantile e di scrittura economica.—Venice, 1786, folio.

BENJAMIN BOOTH, MERCHANT.
A Complete System of book-keeping by an improved mode of double entry, &c.—London, 1789, 4to.

GIUSEPPE FORNI, DI PAVIA.
Trattato teorico pratico di scrittura doppia.—Pavia, 1790.

JOHN SHAW.
Book-keeping epitomized: a compendium of Mair's Merchants-accompts.—Leeds, 1794, 12mo.

EDWARD THOMAS JONES.
Jones's English System of Book-keeping by Single or Double entry.—Bristol, 1796, 4to.

JAMES MILL.
An Examination of Jones' English System of Book-keeping, in which the insufficiency of that mode of Keeping Accounts is clearly demonstrated, and the superiority of the Italian method fully established.—London, 1796.

JOSEPH COLLIER.
A Defence of Double Entry, with a new arrangement of the Journal and objections to "Jones' English System."—London, 1796.

THOMAS KNOLLES GOSNELL.
An Elucidation of the Italian Method of Book-keeping, with free observations on Jones' English System.—London, 1796.

JOHN MATTHEWS.
A New and Perfect Model of a Set of Books for the Shopkeeper or Retail Trader, comprised in two Books only.—Bristol, 1796.

EDMOND DÉGRANGE.
La Tenue des Livres rendue facile ou Nouvelle Méthode d'enseignement, &c.—1797.
Other editions, Paris, 1800, 1801, 1802, 1804, 1806.

J. H. WICKS.

Book-keeping Reformed ; or the Method of Double Entry so simplified, elucidated, and improved, as to render the practice easy, expeditious, and accurate.—Egham, 1797, 4to.

C. BUCHANAN.

The Writing-master and Accountant's Assistant, &c.—Glasgow, 1798, 4to.

JOHN SHIRES.

An Improved Method of Book-keeping.—London, 1799.

P. J. MIGNERETS.

La science des jeunes négocians et teneurs de livres.—Paris, 1799, 2 vols., oblong 8vo.

JOHN WILLIAMSON FULTON.

British Indian Book-keeping : a new system of double entry, exemplified in a variety of compendious methods.—Bengal, 1799.
Another edition, London, 1800, 8vo.

APPENDIX No. II

LISTS OF DECEASED SCOTTISH ACCOUNTANTS, WITH NOTES[1]

EDINBURGH

A

ADAM, ROBERT; born (c.) 1824; died April 7, 1899; City Chamberlain of Edinburgh from 1847-1895.

AINSLIE, WALTER; died (c.) 1787.

ALEXANDER, JOHN, 1812-1826.

ALISON, ALEXANDER; died December 31, 1805.

ALLAN, ROBERT; died December 1803.

ALLAN, WILLIAM, 1830-1844.

ALLISTER, DAVID, 1835-1852.

ANDERSON, CHARLES, 1822-1838.

ANDERSON, JAMES, 1822-1829.

B

BAILLIE, JOHN MENZIES, C.A.; born April 24, 1826; son of R. G. Baillie of Culterallers; educated at High School, Edinburgh; apprentice of William Moncreiff; in business from 1849 to 1880, when he succeeded to estate of Culterallers; partner—Wm. Moncreiff; Original Member of Society; died October 6, 1886.

BAIN, DONALD, 1815-1865.

BAIRD, HUGH JAMES, 1844-1848.

BALFOUR, JAMES, Advocates' Close, 1786; Charles Street, 1790; Old Posthouse Close, 1794; born (c.) 1735; died October 20, 1795.

---

[1] The information given in these lists as regards the earlier names has been compiled from Almanacs, Directories, and a variety of other sources. In the absence of other statement the dates given are those during which the names appeared in published lists of accountants. The later information has been principally obtained from the records of the Societies.

BALFOUR, ROBERT, C.A.; born June 24, 1818; son of James Balfour of Pilrig, W.S.; educated Edinburgh Academy and University; apprentice to William Paul; commenced business 1842; partner—Patrick Brodie; from 1846 Edinburgh Secretary, City of Glasgow Life Assurance Co.; Original Member of Society; died August 14, 1869.

BALGARNIE, JAMES HOGARTH, C.A.; born 1829; apprentice of C. M. Barstow; commenced business 1850; elected Member March 29, 1855; died January 10, 1879.

BALGARNIE, NORMAN, C.A.; born October 12, 1865; son of J. H. Balgarnie above; apprentice to Murray & Romanes; admitted February 1887; died on board S.S. Dominion for South Africa, October 6, 1902.

BALLANTYNE or BANNATYNE, ANDREW, Calton Hill; died September 9, 1804; in Ramsay's Bank for thirty-eight years.

BALLINGALL, WILLIAM, 1835–1849.

BARRON, JOHN, C.A., 1837; Depute Clerk of Teinds; Original Member of Society; died November 1, 1873.

BARSTOW, CHARLES MURRAY, C.A.; born January 11, 1804; son of Captain Barstow, Kelso; educated in Yorkshire; trained with James Brown; commenced business in 1828; Original Member and Third President of Edinburgh Society; partners — James Latta, Robert Cockburn Millar; died November 10, 1885.

BELL, ROBERT, 1797–1805.

BERWICK, DAVID, 1848–1858; Manager, Insurance Co. of Scotland, 1845–1847.

BLACK, MAURICE, C.A.; born Kirkcaldy, October 8, 1865; apprentice of J. Campbell Penney; admitted February 1, 1888; practised in London; lost in the Stella near the Channel Islands in April 1899.

BOGGIE, WALTER, Fountainbridge, 1786.

BORTHWICK, ARCHIBALD, C.A.; born 1811; son of Patrick Borthwick; first Manager of National Bank of Scotland; educated Edinburgh High School and University; trained with J. A. Cheyne; Secretary Life Insurance Co. of Scotland from formation till 1834; practised as Accountant in Edinburgh, 1834–1838; first Manager City of Glasgow Insurance Co., 1838–1839; resumed practice, 1839; partners—Samuel Raleigh, James Howden, J. A. Molleson; Original Member of Society; died July 3, 1863.

BORTHWICK, JAMES; in 1811 designed "Merchant, Leith"; Manager, North British Insurance Co., 1824–1858; designed Accountant from 1830; died 1863.

BOSWALL, THOMAS, Custom House Stairs; Captain Honourable Company of Golfers, 1758; died (c.) 1778.

BOWIE, PETER, Castlehill, 1774–1775.

BREMNER, HUGH, corner of South Bridge, 1790; died February 20, 1804.

BREWIS, JOHN, C.A.; born in 1854 at Eshott Hall, Northumberland; educated High School, Edinburgh, and University; apprentice to Howden & Molleson; admitted February 1879; partners—G. Todd Chiene, J. Scott Tait, R. D. Rainie; died February 11, 1900.

BRIGGS, D. C., 1831–1845.

BRINGLOE, FRANCIS ADAM, C.A.; born in Edinburgh, September 14, 1847; educated Edinburgh Academy and University; apprentice to Lindsay, Jamieson, & Haldane; admitted February 1, 1871; partners— J. Campbell Penney, J. Maxtone Graham; on Council of Society, 1884–1888, auditor, 1898–1901, collector of Annuity Fund, 1901–1903; died April 10, 1903.

BRODIE, PATRICK; born February 17, 1817; educated at Haddington and Edinburgh University; trained in office of William Paul; practised 1842–1844; partner — Robert Balfour; Secretary, Scottish National Insurance Co., 1844–1846; Manager, British Linen Co. Bank, Glasgow, 1846–1860; and Manager at head office from 1860 till death on March 3, 1867.

BROUGHTON, CHARLES, W.S., son of Edward Broughton of the Excise; in business from 1806; died November 10, 1823.

BROWN, JAMES, C.A.; born 1786; son of Rev. James Brown of Newbattle; educated Edinburgh High School and University; Original Member, and First President, Edinburgh Society; partner—Charles Pearson; died February 2, 1864.

BROWN, JAMES ADAM, C.A.; born March 1817; eldest son of James Brown, C.A.; educated Edinburgh Academy and University; trained with Brown & Pearson; Original Member of Society; assumed name of " McKerrell-Brown"; died June 1, 1896.

BRUCE, ARCHIBALD, 1816–1849; Joint City Accountant, 1820–1825.

BRUCE, JAMES, 7 York Place, 1796–1825; Accountant to City of Edinburgh, 1796–1820.

BRUCE, WILLIAM, 1803.

BUCHAN, JOHN; born 1756; died May 18, 1808; was Accomptant to General Post Office.

BUDGE, HENRY, C.A.; born at Grantown in 1835; son of Henry Budge, Excise Officer; trained with James Brown and Kenneth Mackenzie; elected Member, February 4, 1863; died May 27, 1873.

BURKE, FRANCIS; born January 20, 1795; son of John Burke, Edinburgh; educated Edinburgh High School and University; in business from 1825; died June 4, 1847.

C

CALLENDER, HENRY, C.A., 1843–1873; Original Member; ceased Membership in 1873; sometime Treasurer of City; Manager, Scottish Life and Mercantile Insurance Co.

CALLENDER, WILLIAM; born 1804; died November 13, 1837.

CAMERON, ROBERT, 1821–1831.

CAMPBELL, ALEXANDER, 12 S. Frederick Street, 1805.

CAMPBELL, D., 1822–1829.

CARPHIN, JAMES RHIND, C.A.; born Edinburgh, January 22, 1835; educated Edinburgh Academy and University; apprentice to R. E. Scott; admitted February 4, 1857; in practice till 1881, when appointed Chamberlain of Merchant Company; died April 6, 1897.

CARTER, FREDERICK HAYNE, C.A.; born August 24, 1817; trained with Keith & Horne and William Low; commenced business 1840; partners— A. B. Tawse, Fred. W. Carter; Original Member; died February 3, 1886.

CASTLE, J., 1844–1850.

CHALMERS, ALEXANDER; Accountant-General to Board of Excise in Scotland; Accountant to City of Edinburgh from 1717 to 1759; died at Birmingham on a tour for his health, September 13, 1760.

CHALMERS, ROBERT; Accountant to City of Edinburgh for some time prior to 1796.

CHAPLIN, THOMAS ROBERTSON, C.A., 1848; died 1857; Original Member; partner—David Robertson Souter.

CHEYNE, JAMES AUCHINLECK, W.S.; born 1795; son of N. R. Cheyne, bookseller, Edinburgh; designed Accountant from 1820; from 1831 Manager of Life Insurance Co. of Scotland; died June 21, 1853.

CHIENE, GEORGE TODD, Senr., C.A.; born at Crail, August 21, 1809; son of Captain John Chiene, R.N.; educated Crail and Edinburgh High School; trained with Paul & Mackersy; in business in Edinburgh from (c.) 1850; admitted March 29, 1855; died June 17, 1882.

CHIENE, GEORGE TODD, C.A.; second son of G. T. Chiene, Senr., C.A.; born October 30, 1844; educated Edinburgh Academy and St. Andrews and Edinburgh Universities; apprentice to Lindsay, Jamieson, & Haldane; admitted February 1869; partners—John Scott Tait, John Brewis; died September 5, 1900.

CHRISTIE, ROBERT, C.A.; born in Dunfermline, 1791; trained in the country and with a W.S. in Edinburgh; for a time a partner in firm of Keith, Christie, & Horne, and afterwards practised on his own account; in 1831 first Manager of Scottish Equitable Insurance Co.; retired in 1861; Original Member of Society; died 1863.

CHRISTIE, ROBERT, JUNR., C.A; born (c.) 1819; son of Robert Christie, C.A.; Assistant Secretary, Edinburgh & Northern Railway Co.; afterwards Edinburgh Secretary, Northern Assurance Co.; Original Member; died March 24, 1874.

CLEGHORN, JAMES; born 1776; son of William Cleghorn, Merchant, Dunse; educated at Dunse, and Edinburgh University; tenant farmer in Wigtownshire, 1806–1815; Editor of *Farmers' Magazine* and *Edinburgh Monthly Magazine*; Accountant in Edinburgh from 1824; founder and first Manager of Scottish Provident Institution; published a treatise on Widows' Funds, 1833; died May 1838.

CLERK, SAMUEL, 1820–1846; partner—James Morison, for a short time.

COCKBURN, PATRICK, 1804; died 1837; first Auditor Scottish Widows' Fund; partner—Charles Selkrig.

CORMACK, DAVID, C.A., 1829; Original Member; died August 27, 1867.

COWAN, ROBERT CAMERON, M.A., C.A.; born April 13, 1836; son of Hugh Cowan, Banker, Ayr; educated Ayr Academy and Glasgow University; apprentice to D. Lindsay and G. A. Jamieson; admitted February 1864; partner—A. T. Niven; Member of Council, 1895–1898; died August 19, 1898.

COX, CLEMENT HENRY, C.A.; born St. Pauls, Knightbridge, March 14, 1875; apprentice to F. W. Carter; admitted February 1898; died June 5, 1901.

CRAIG, ALEXANDER, C.A.; trained with Mansfield & Spottiswoode; admitted March 29, 1855; died November 1897.

D

DALL, THOMAS, C.A.; born at North Berwick, October 10, 1826; admitted March 29, 1855; partner—Hugh Miller; died March 20, 1880.

DAWSON, ALEXANDER, Cowgatehead, 1774.

DICK, ALEXANDER, 1804; died December 10, 1823.

DICK, ANDREW, 1825–1852.

DICKIE, HENRY DAVID, son of William Dickie, who was the first Secretary Caledonian Insurance Company; in 1812 succeeded to his father's office; in 1828 became Joint-Manager; in 1830, Manager; retired in 1861, and died in August 1863.

DICKIE, JOHN, of Corstorphine; Accountant-General Excise Office; died (c.) 1775.

DICKSON, FRANCIS, C.A.; apprentice to James Wilkie, afterwards to T. G. Dickson; admitted February 1873; died August 13, 1900.

DICKSON, JAMES, 1823–1836.

DICKSON, JAMES JOBSON, C.A.; born at Edinburgh, November 24, 1811; son of Rev. David Dickson, D.D., St. Cuthberts; educated High School and University; trained with Paul & Mackersy; commenced practice in 1835; for a time in partnership with Archibald Horne, afterwards on own account; Original Member; died December 4, 1891.

DICKSON, WILLIAM, 1830–1832 and 1842–1849.

DICKSON, WILLIAM PURDIE, C.A.; born in Edinburgh, April 17, 1870; apprentice to J. M. Macandrew & Hugh Blair; admitted February 1894; died June 15, 1902.

DONALDSON, JAMES, 1836–1848.

DOUGLAS, CHRISTOPHER, C.A.; born at Kelso on October 20, 1827; son of Captain Pringle Home Douglas, R.N.; educated at Kelso; trained with Archibald Borthwick; Original Member of Society; died February 3, 1882.

DOUGLAS, ROBERT HARDIE, C.A.; admitted February 4, 1855; ceased to be a Member on February 2, 1887.

DRUMMOND, ARTHUR, C.A.; born in Edinburgh, May 30, 1870; apprentice to Charles Prentice; admitted February 3, 1892; died February 13, 1904.

DUFF, DONALD, 1855–1858.

DUFF, JOHN, 1830–1840.

DUNDAS, GEORGE, C.A.; apprentice to Keith & Horne; Original Member; left Edinburgh for New Zealand; died October 1870.

DUNDAS, JAMES, of Ochtertyre, W.S.; born 1752; in practice from 1794; partner—Robert Wight; died April 2, 1831.

DUNLOP, ALEXANDER, JUNR., C.A.; born December 18, 1835; son of Alexander Dunlop of Clober; apprentice to A. Borthwick & Samuel Raleigh; admitted February 1,¹ 1860; Assistant-Accountant in Bankruptcy; died January 19, 1888.

E

ELDER, WILLIAM; died March 12, 1824.

ELLIS, JAMES, C.A.; apprentice to James Howden & J. A. Molleson; admitted February 5, 1873; went to Dublin, practised as a C.A. there, and died on September 28, 1878.

EMSLIE, FRANCIS, 61 Nicolson Street, 1807.

ESSON, GEORGE AULDJO, C.A.; born August 13, 1813; trained in Aberdeen; went to Donald Lindsay's office in 1837 and became his partner on January 1, 1838; appointed Accountant in Bankruptcy, October 31, 1856; Original Member of Society; died March 13, 1888.

EWART, PETER, 1834–1840.

F

FAIRLEY, T. S., 1831–1848.

FALKNER, FREDERICK, C.A.; born Edinburgh, November 21, 1853; apprentice to David Marshall; admitted February 7, 1883; died August 19, 1889.

FARQUHARSON, ALEXANDER OGILVIE, of Haughton (nephew of Francis); in practice in 1764; died October 15, 1788.

FARQUHARSON, FRANCIS, of Haughton; died 1770.

FARQUHARSON, FRANCIS, of Haughton (son of Alexander); born (c.) 1772; died January 21, 1808.

FERRIER, CHARLES, of Baddinsgill; born (c.) 1774; in business from 1804; died May 1, 1850.

FINLAY, HENRY ALEXANDER, C.A.; son of G. L. Finlay; apprentice to F. W. Carter; admitted February 4, 1863; left Edinburgh for India; died 1872.

FITZSTRATHERN, W., LL.D., 1826–1830.

FLEMING, D. W., 1834–1835.

FLEMING, THOMAS, 1826–1829.

FORBES, JAMES ALLAN, C.A.; born Edinburgh, July 3, 1864; apprentice to Charles Prentice; admitted February 3, 1886; died July 25, 1892.

FORMAN, ALEXANDER; son of John Forman, Stirling; born (c.) 1778; died March 7, 1853.

FORMAN, ROBERT, C.A.; son of J. N. Forman, W.S.; born Edinburgh, February 3, 1839; apprentice to William Moncreiff & J. M. Baillie; admitted February 5, 1862; partner—Andrew Paterson; died February 25, 1899.

FORREST, JOHN, 1793–1803.

FORREST, WILLIAM H., 1843–1851.

FRASER, ALEXANDER, 1800–1805.

FRASER, ALEXANDER, 1814–1839.

FRASER, EVAN, 1800–1803.

FRASER, JOHN, 1848–1851.

FRASER, JOHN CHARLES, C.A.; assistant to Accountant of Court; Original Member; died September 1864.

FRASER, JOHN WALKER, C.A.; born April 3, 1876; son of Rev. James Fraser, United Free Church, Dalkeith; apprentice to Carter, Greig & Co.; and for some years with Richard Brown & Co.; admitted July 1900; commenced practice January 1904; died September 18, 1904.

FYFE, ARCHIBALD, 1836–1844.

G

GALLAWAY, WILLIAM ; born (c.) 1771 ; designed Accountant from 1823 ; died April 1851 ; for portrait see Crombie's "Modern Athenians."

GARDINER, WILLIAM, C.A. ; son of James Gardiner, S.S.C. ; apprentice to Thomas Martin ; admitted February 7, 1867 ; left Edinburgh for India in 1877 ; died (c.) 1882.

GIBSON, ARCHIBALD, C.A. ; born 1793 ; son of Archibald Gibson, W.S. ; partner—William Scott Moncrieff, Senr. ; Original Member ; died 1869.

GIBSON, THOMAS, C.A. ; born Duddingston, June 3, 1871 ; apprentice to R. C. Millar ; admitted February 2, 1898 ; died Rhodesia, July 6, 1902.

GIRVAN, ANDREW, 1818–1841.

GLENDINNING, EDGAR, C.A. ; apprentice to W. A. Wood ; admitted February 3, 1892 ; died 1893.

GOLDIE, GEORGE, 1826–1861.

GORDON, JAMES, 1773–1780.

GORDON, RICHARD, C.A. ; in business from 1830 ; Original Member of Society ; died May 1865.

GORDON, WILLIAM, of the Academy, Glasgow, author of "The Universal Accountant," first published about 1760 ; died in Edinburgh December 12, 1793.

GRAHAM, PETER, 1834–1836.

GRANT, LUDOVIC, 1780 ; died at Smithfield, September 3, 1793.

GRANT, THOMAS, C.A. ; son of Rev. Dr. Grant of St. Andrews ; Manager of Savings Bank ; Original Member ; died 1855.

GREENFIELD, JAMES ROBERT, C.A. ; born November 14, 1874 ; son of James Greenfield, Banker, Reston ; apprentice to Hugh Blair ; admitted February 1, 1899 ; died at Johannesburg, South Africa, August 3, 1904.

GREEN, HUGH JOHN MACKAY, C.A. ; born Edinburgh, November 25, 1870 ; apprentice to C. W. W. Thomson ; admitted February 1, 1893 ; died May 4, 1899.

GREIG, ALEXANDER, 1800–1835 ; partner—Francis Farquharson (?).

GREIG, DAVID, 1824–1831.

GREIG, JAMES THOMAS McDOWELL, C.A. ; born February 13, 1864 ; apprentice to J. Campbell Penney ; admitted February 3, 1886 ; died July 19, 1902.

GREIG, JOHN, 1812–1835.

GREIG, WILLIAM, 1817–1839.

GREY, EDWARD SIMPSON, C.A. ; born Edinburgh, March 3, 1863 ; apprentice to Lindsay, Jamieson, & Haldane ; admitted February 3, 1886 ; latterly resident in London ; died January 11, 1902.

GRIEVE, JOHN, 1817–1851.

GRIFFITH, JAMES, 1845–1850.

H

HAGART, FRANCIS DAVID VALENTINE, C.A.; born (c.) 1852; son of J. V. Hagart, S.S.C.; apprentice to Thomas Scott & Thomas Scott, Junr.; admitted February 6, 1878; died October 3, 1897.

HAMILTON, JOHN; born February 20, 1827; son of Col. James Hamilton; educated Edinburgh Academy and University; apprentice to A. Borthwick; died May 8, 1852.

HAMILTON, ROLAND, 1834–1848.

HAY, JOHN, Blackfriars' Wynd, 1773; died March 31, 1790.

HENDERSON, ALEXANDER, 1800–1803.

HEPBURN, JOHN, 1773; died March 18, 1800; Accountant-General of Excise.

HERD, DAVID; born at Marykirk, October 1732; son of John Herd, farmer; Chief Clerk to David Russell, Accountant, from (c.) 1760; died Edinburgh, June 10, 1810.

HILL, JOHN, 1805; died December 9, 1818.

HOGARTH, GEORGE, 1836–1840.

HOME, A. F., 1853 to (c.) 1870.

HOPE, ARCHIBALD; sometime Accountant in Edinburgh, afterwards Secretary to Royal Bank; died June 13, 1790.

HORNE, ARCHIBALD, C.A., of Balvarran; born 1795; in business from 1824; Original Member; Member of Council, 1856–1860; partners— J. J. Dickson, William Keith, Robert Christie; died July 30, 1862.

HORSBRUGH, HENRY MONCREIFF, C.A.; born September 3, 1858; apprentice to A. Gillies Smith; admitted February 4, 1880; partner— F J. Moncreiff; Member of Council, 1887–1890; died October 17, 1892.

HORSBURGH, ROBERT, 1825–1836; partner—G. Marjoribanks.

HUIE, A., 1839–1845.

HUNTER, JOHN, C.A. and W.S.; born 1801; son of Professor Hunter, St. Andrews; Original Member; Auditor of Court of Session, 1849–1866; died December 3, 1869.

HUTTON, JOHN, 1807–1830.

I

INGLIS, STEWART, 1801–1803.

IRELAND, THOMAS, 1853–1866.

IVORY, HOLMES; son of Thomas Ivory, Dundee; commenced business, 1827; partner—Kenneth Mackenzie; Manager, Scottish National Insurance Co., 1841–1853; died May 13, 1855.

J

JAMIESON, ALEXANDER, C.A.; born March 1, 1809; son of Robert Jamieson, W.S.; commenced business, 1839; Original Member; Member of Council, 1870–1874; died July 13, 1878.

JAMIESON, GEORGE AULDJO, C.A.; born May 1, 1828 ; son of Dr. Jamieson of Aberdeen; educated Aberdeen University; trained in Aberdeen, and also with Lindsay & Esson, Edinburgh; partner of Lindsay, Jamieson, & Haldane; Original Member of Society; Member of Council from 1861 to 1865, 1866–1870, 1871–1875, and from 1888 to 1891; Examinator from 1873 to 1882; Sixth President from 1882 to 1888; died July 18, 1900.

JAMIESON, GEORGE ROBERT CLAUDE AULDJO, C.A., son of above ; born Inveresk, August 25, 1872; apprentice to Lindsay, Jamieson, and Haldane; admitted July 20, 1899; died September 15, 1902, from injuries received in Boer War, where he served as Lieutenant, Scottish Horse.

JEFFREY, WILLIAM, 1831–1843.

JOHNSTON, JOHN, 1838–1848.

JUNNER, J. M., 1846–1863.

K

KAY, ROBERT, Sandiland's Close, 1786.

KEAY, ALEXANDER, 1793; died July 21, 1804.

KEITH, ALEXANDER, W.S., of Ravelston and Dunnottar; born July 15, 1763; in practice as accountant from 1812; died February 20, 1819.

KEITH, WILLIAM, born 1748; third son of Alexander Keith of Ravelston and Dunnottar; commenced business, 1780; died at his house at Corstorphine Hill, October 22, 1803.

KEITH, WILLIAM, third son of William Keith above; born (c.) 1785; commenced business, 1820; partners—Robert Christie, Archibald Horne; died (c.) 1852.

KERR, DUGALD CAMPBELL, C.A.; apprentice to David Cormack; admitted March 29, 1855; died 1859.

KERR, WILLIAM H., 1821–1840; published in 1836 "Considerations regarding the State of Affairs of the City of Edinburgh."

KING, JOHN, 1793.

KINNEAR, DAVID, 1851; left Edinburgh for Montreal (c.) 1855.

KIRKLAND, JAMES, Lauriston; 1774–1780.

KIRKWOOD, CHARLES, 1840–1864.

KNOX, ROBERT, 1793.

L

LAMOND, ALEXANDER, 1817–1856.

LATTA, JAMES, C.A.; born in Renfrewshire, 1821; educated High School, Edinburgh; apprentice to C. M. Barstow; admitted March 29, 1855; partner—C. M. Barstow; died April 13, 1874.

LAURIE, WILLIAM, 1836–1854.

LIDDELL, JOSEPH MACK, C.A.; son of Joseph Liddle, S.S.C.; born (c.) 1825; trained with D. S. Peddie; practised for a time in Perth, afterwards in Edinburgh; Original Member; resigned in 1857 on leaving Edinburgh.

LINDSAY, DAVID, Castlehill; died 1786.

LINDSAY, DONALD, C.A.; born in Forfarshire, 1796; son of James Lindsay-Carnegie of Boysach; trained with Alexander Pearson, W.S.; commenced business, 1823; Original Member; Member of Council, 1855–1859; senior partner, Lindsay, Jamieson, & Haldane; retired 1867; died December 17, 1876.

LOGAN, JAMES WILKIE, C.A.; apprentice of Archibald Borthwick and James Howden; admitted February 12, 1864; died August 1901.

LOUNDS or LOWNES, JAMES, Morocco's Close, 1774; Accountant of Excise; died May 12, 1797.

LOW, ALEXANDER; born September 15, 1799, at Langton, Berwickshire; commenced business, 1832; partner—Thomas Martin; Manager, Life Association of Scotland, 1840, till his death on June 25, 1847.

LOW, WILLIAM, C.A.; commenced business, 1827; Original Member; died August 1855.

LYLE, JAMES R, 1823–1840.

LYON, GEORGE, 1844–1854.

Mc

M'BEAN, WILLIAM, C.A.; apprentice of J. M. Macandrew; admitted June 27, 1860; practised in Dundee and afterwards in Edinburgh; died December 7, 1878.

M'CUAIG, COLIN, C.A.; born August 25, 1839; apprentice to Mansfield and Spottiswoode; admitted February 12, 1864; entered service of Scottish Union Insurance Co., and became Actuary in 1890; Examiner, 1891; Member of General Examining Board, 1893; Trustee of Endowment Fund; died August 5, 1904.

MACDONALD, JOHN, 1841–1850.

MACDOWALL, JAMES, 1832–1836.

MACDOWALL, P., 1817; died December 31, 1826.

M'EWAN, MATTHEW CLARK, C.A.; born Edinburgh, October 5, 1865; son of Rev. Thomas M'Ewan; apprentice of F. & W. Carter; admitted February 1, 1888; partner of Carter, Greig, & M'Ewan; went into business in America and died at Chicago, April 14, 1899.

MACGREGOR, JAMES, C.A.; born Edinburgh, November 15, 1854; apprentice of James Brown; admitted February 3, 1886; died June 30, 1892.

M'GREGOR, JOSEPH, 1821–1846.

M'GREGOR, PATRICK, 1820–1840.

MACGREGOR, T. M., 1827–1848.

M'KEAN, JOHN, W.S.; son of Andrew M'Kean of Locharwoods; born May, 4, 1794; designed Accountant 1818–1839; Second Manager, Scottish Widows' Fund; died January 3, 1839.

MACKENZIE, JOHN; born April 1, 1812; trained with William Paul; partners—William Paul, William Moncreiff; Manager, Scottish Widows' Fund, 1839–1859; thereafter Treasurer of Bank of Scotland; died June 26, 1900.

MACKENZIE, KENNETH, C.A.; son of Richard Mackenzie of Dolphinton, D.K.S.; born July 17, 1812; commenced business, 1837; Original Member; Treasurer, 1853–1863; Member of Council, 1863–1867, and 1869–1873; partners—Holmes Ivory, William Spens, George Todd, J. Turnbull Smith; died September 16, 1880.

MACKERSY, LINDSAY; son of Rev. Mr. Mackersy, Whitburn, 1818–1835; partner—William Paul.

MACLAGAN, DAVID, C.A.; born October 9, 1824; son of Dr. David Maclagan; educated Edinburgh High School; in 1840 went to Scottish Union Insurance Co.; in 1847 Manager, Insurance Co. of Scotland; in 1862 Secretary to Alliance Assurance Co. in London; in 1866 Manager, Edinburgh Life Assurance Co.; Original Member; died March 30, 1883.

MACLEISH, ALEXANDER A., 1838–1841.

M

MABEN or MABON, JOHN, 1839–1851.

MAITLAND, JOHN, C.A.; born 1803; son of Sir Alexander Gibson Maitland, Bart., of Cliftonhall; commenced business, 1834; partner—William Wood; Original Member; Member of Council, 1860–1864; first Accountant of Court, 1850; died January 23, 1865.

MANSFIELD, THOMAS, C.A.; son of James Mansfield of Midmar, Banker; born March 3, 1800; commenced business in 1825; Original Member; Member of Council, 1853–1859, and 1863; Second President, 1864–1868; partner—Robert Spottiswoode; died July 20, 1868.

MANSFIELD, THOMAS JOHN, C.A.; born February 18, 1843; son of Thomas (above); apprentice of Mansfield & Spottiswoode; admitted February 1, 1871; partner—Robert Spottiswoode; died November 14, 1876.

MANSON, WILLIAM, 1817–1822.

MARJORIBANKS, G., 1825–1838; partner—Robert Horsburgh.

MARSHALL, ARCHIBALD, 1832–1854.

MARSHALL, DAVID, C.A.; born Edinburgh, April 3, 1829; son of William Marshall, Goldsmith; educated High School; apprentice to Borthwick and Raleigh; Original Member; partner—F. A. Marshall; died May 30, 1897.

MARSHALL, JAMES, 1824–1831.

MARTIN, JAMES, C.A.; born October 3, 1846; son of Thomas Martin; apprentice of Thomas Martin; admitted February 3, 1869; Member of Council, 1885–1888; partner—Thomas Martin; died January 18, 1893.

MARTIN, THOMAS, C.A.; trained with Alexander Low; Original Member; Member of Council, 1873–1877 and 1883–1884; partners—Alexander Low, Samuel Raleigh, James Martin; died April 7, 1884.

MATHIESON, JAMES, 1780–1803.

MAUGHAN, F. T., 1846–1851.

MAUGHAN, JOHN, 1828–1832.

MAXTONE, JAMES; born June 1819; son of Anthony Maxtone of Cultoquhey, Perthshire; on succeeding his Uncle to estate of Redgordon, Perthshire, took additional name of Graham; trained with Lindsay & Esson; in lists, 1848–1852; died August 1900.

MELDRUM, GEORGE, C.A.; born 1812; commenced business, 1842; held appointments from Free Church of Scotland; Original Member; died October 12, 1876.

MICHIE, ALEXANDER, 1800; died June 24, 1808.

MIDDLEMISS, JOHN ALEXANDER, C.A.; born September 19, 1861; apprentice to John Edward Dovey; admitted February 4, 1885; practised in London; died January 12, 1905.

MILLAR, ARTHUR WELLESLEY, C.A.; apprentice of Henry Callender; admitted February 1, 1871; died February 1899.

MILLAR, THOMAS, 1830–1831.

MILLAR, THOMAS H., 1845–1850.

MILLER, HUGH, C.A.; born Edinburgh, April 28, 1843; apprentice of Thomas Dall; admitted February 5, 1868; partner—Thomas Dall; died July 14, 1896.

MILLER, THOMAS, 1842–1852.

MITCHELL, FRANCIS, 1800; died February 19, 1810.

MITCHELL, GEORGE THOMSON, C.A.; born September 3, 1812; son of Robert Mitchell, Airth; Original Member; resigned January 31, 1865; died July 19, 1894.

MITCHELL, HUGH, 1834–1853.

MOFFAT, LEWIS ROSE, C.A.; apprentice of John Taylor; admitted February 7, 1883; died January 8, 1885.

MOINET, JOHN; born 1805 of French descent; described as an accountant from 1842; in 1835 Secretary, in 1861 Manager, Caledonian Insurance Co.; retired 1875; died July 11, 1879.

MOIR, WALTER, 1800–1825.

MOLLESON, JAMES ALEXANDER, C.A.; born 1839; son of Dr. Molleson, Forfarshire; apprentice to Borthwick & Raleigh; admitted February 1 1860; partners—A. Borthwick, James Howden; Examinator, 1882–1889, Member of Council, 1890–1894; died January 5, 1901.

MONCREIFF, FRANCIS JEFFREY, C.A.; born August 27, 1849; son of Lord Moncreiff of Tulliebole; educated Edinburgh Academy and University; apprentice to Lindsay, Jamieson, & Haldane; admitted February 3, 1875; partners—A. Gillies Smith, H. M. Horsbrugh, T. P. Laird; Member of Council, 1881–1885 and 1898–1900; died May 30, 1900.

MONCREIFF, WILLIAM, C.A.; third son of Sir James Wellwood Moncreiff' Bart., of Tulliebole; born September 28, 1813; commenced business, 1842; partners—William Paul, John Mackenzie, J. M. Baillie, A. G. Smith; Accountant of Court, 1865–1889; Original Member; Member of Council, 1853–1855, 1856–1860, 1861–1865, and 1866–1868; died August 31, 1895.

MONCRIEFF, DAVID SCOTT; second son of William Scott Moncrieff; born (c.) 1800; short time in business; died November 5, 1875.

MONCRIEFF, JOHN SCOTT, C.A.; fourth son of William Scott Moncrieff; born March 4, 1811; partners—William Scott Moncrieff, C. W. W. Thomson; Original Member; Member of Council, 1868–1872; died February 25, 1889.

MONCRIEFF, WILLIAM SCOTT, of Newhalls, afterwards of Fossoway; born April 7, 1766; son of Robert Scott Moncrieff of Newhalls; commenced business, 1800; partners—Archibald Gibson, John Scott Moncrieff; died December 6, 1846.

MORISON, PATRICK, C.A.; son of James Morison, Perth; born August 7, 1825; trained with James Morison and Lindsay & Esson; commenced business, 1850; Original Member; partner—A. T. Niven; retired from bad health; died October, 20, 1880.

MORTON, WALTER, opposite the Guard, 1774–1780; Accountant of Excise and Writing Master.

MUIR, JOHN, 1835–1852.

MUNRO, ANDREW, 1844–1849.

MURRAY, DAVID, C.A. ; born November 1787 ; commenced business, 1826 ; last Deputy Controller of Excise for Scotland ; Original Member ; died February 24, 1877.

MURRAY, GEORGE, C.A. ; son of Rev. Mr. Murray, North Berwick ; commenced business 1835 ; Original Member ; Member of Council, 1876–1880 ; died April 19, 1884.

MURRAY, JOHN, 1829–1832.

MURRAY, JOHN, 1835–1854.

MURRAY, ROBERT, C.A. ; trained with William Wood ; admitted December 29, 1854 ; Assistant to Accountant of Court ; practised in Dundee from 1861 till his death in 1870.

MURRAY, WILLIAM, 1843–1855 ; son of David (above) ; left Edinburgh.

MYLNE, GEORGE ; son of Thomas Mylne of Mylnefield ; born 1762 ; a merchant in London and member of Lloyds' ; Accountant in Edinburgh, 1822 ; Manager, Edinburgh Life Assurance Co., 1824 ; retired, 1833 ; died January 11, 1835.

MYRTLE, WILLIAM, C.A. ; born in Edinburgh, May 31, 1818 ; son of John Myrtle ; commenced business, 1851 ; Original Member ; died April 22, 1902.

N

NAIRNE, ALEXANDER, 1786 ; died at Paisley, September 22, 1804.

NOBLE, ERIE MACKAY, C.A. ; apprentice to Richard Wilson ; admitted February 1, 1871 ; resigned membership, 1875.

O

OGILVY, JAMES, 1813–1852.

OGILVY, JAMES, Junr., C.A., 1849 ; Original Member ; died April 1876.

OGILVY, JOHN, C.A. ; born July 8, 1830 ; apprentice to David Robertson Souter ; admitted March 29, 1855 ; died July 20, 1894.

OGILVY, JOHN SPENCE, C.A., 1838 ; Original Member ; left Edinburgh for Australia ; died December 12, 1871.

OLIPHANT, ROBERT LINDSAY, C.A. ; born March 5, 1841 ; son of Robert Oliphant of Rossie ; apprentice to G. A. Jamieson ; admitted February 12, 1864 ; died January 13, 1866.

P

PATERSON, ANDREW, C.A. ; born February, 1821 ; admitted March 29, 1855 ; retired from business, 1890 ; died February 25, 1900.

PATERSON, ANDREW MURRAY, C.A. ; commenced business, 1852 ; Original Member ; died 1861.

PATERSON, DAVID, 1817; left Edinburgh 1829 (?) for a position in the Treasury.

PATERSON, JAMES, 1826–1860.

PATON, THOMAS, 1827–1838.

PAUL, WILLIAM; son of Rev. William Paul, St. Cuthberts; born June 10, 1786; partners—Lindsay Mackersy, John Mackenzie, William Moncreiff; died January 15, 1848.

PEARSON, CHARLES, C.A.; born Edinburgh, 1803; son of David Pearson, Depute Secretary to Board of Excise; educated High School and University; trained with James Brown; partners—James Brown, David Pearson; Original Member; Examinator, 1855–1873; Member of Council, 1864–1867, 1868–1872, 1873–1876; Fourth President, 1876–1879; died October 17, 1884.

PEAT, JOHN C., Leith, 1823.

PEDDIE, DONALD SMITH, C.A.; second son of Rev. James Peddie, D.D.; trained with David Paterson; commenced business, 1831; Original Member; ceased to be a Member, January 3, 1883.

PETRIE, W. H. F. S., 1821–1829.

PETTY, JAMES, 1845–1854.

POLLARD, JAMES, C.A.; born Dublin, May 24, 1845; apprentice to John Scott Moncrieff; admitted February 5, 1873; Member of Council, 1894–1898; Magistrate of City of Edinburgh; partners—William Pollard, George Bird; died September 26, 1901.

PRENTICE, CHARLES, C.A.; apprentice to George Murray; admitted February 5, 1868; died February 23, 1892.

R

RAINIE, ROBERT, C.A.; son of William; born Edinburgh, December 7, 1818; trained in his father's office; Secretary of Life Association; admitted February 1, 1860; died March 29, 1882.

RAINIE, WILLIAM; born at Ormiston, October 15, 1788; son of David Rainie, Dean of Guild, Aberdeen; in practice from 1832; died April 24, 1850.

RALEIGH, SAMUEL, C.A.; born January 8, 1815; Original Member; Examinator, 1855–1882; partners—Archibald Borthwick, Thomas Martin; a liquidator of Western Bank, 1857; Manager of Scottish Widows' Fund, 1859; retired in 1881; died July 26, 1882.

RAMSAY, GEORGE, C.A.; born 1809; son of Thomas Ramsay and grandson of Sir James Ramsay of Banff; in practice from 1838; Original Member; Manager of Scottish Union Insurance Co.; died September 11, 1887.

RAMSAY, JAMES, 1774–1784.

REID, JAMES, 1835–1853.

REID, SYLVESTER, W.S.; born 1780; son of James Reid, Huntly; Depute-Clerk of Teinds; designed Accountant from 1817; died May 8, 1842.

RENTON, JAMES, 1815–1852.

RHIND, CHARLES, 1780–1788.

RHIND, J., 1838–1850.

RICHARDSON, JAMES, 1835–1853.

ROBERTSON, ALEXANDER WEIR, C.A.; born January 21, 1819; son of James Saunders Robertson, W.S.; educated Edinburgh Academy; trained with Archibald Bruce, Patrick Cockburn, and Donald Lindsay; in practice from 1842; Original Member; Secretary, 1853–1863; Treasurer, 1863–1879; partner—James Alexander Robertson; died January 17, 1879.

ROBERTSON, CHARLES, C.A.; admitted March 29, 1855; short time in business; retired to his estate of Kindace in Ross-shire, where he died in October 1903.

ROBERTSON, JOHN, 1786; died April 13, 1801.

ROBERTSON, JOHN HUSSEY, C.A.; born in Edinburgh, May 17, 1870; apprentice to Moncrieff & Horsbrugh; admitted February 1, 1893; for a short time in business in Edinburgh; went to Brazil and afterwards to New York, and became partner of Menzies, Robertson & Co.; died at New York, September 13, 1900.

ROBERTSON, THOMAS, 1822–1847.

ROSS, DAVID, 1773; in 1780 Secretary to the Post Office; died July 14, 1789.

RUSSELL, CLAUD; son of John Russell of Roseburne, W.S., and nephew of David; born July 12, 1769; died July 8, 1846.

RUSSELL, DAVID; son of John Russell of Braidshaw, W.S.; born August 8, 1722; died April 2, 1782.

RUSSELL, ROBERT, 1851–1854.

RUSSELL, WILLIAM, C.A.; in practice from 1825; Original Member; died in November 1871.

S

SAWERS, EDWARD, 1832–1841.

SCHENIMAN, FERDINAND, 1836–1843.

SCOTT, DAVID, C.A.; born December 22, 1830; son of Andrew Scott, W.S.; trained with D. S. Peddie; admitted March 29, 1855; Member of Council, 1879–1883; died May 5, 1898.

SCOTT, DAVID DUNDAS, 1841–1843.

SCOTT, EBENEZER, 1839–1843.

SCOTT, EBENEZER ERSKINE, C.A.; born May 3, 1839; son of R. E. Scott; apprentice to R. E. Scott; admitted February 6, 1861; partners— R. E. Scott, T. Bennet Clark; Member of Council, 1887–1891; died June 10, 1897.

SCOTT, JAMES, 1816–1831.

SCOTT, JOHN, 1843–1853.

SCOTT, RALPH ERSKINE, C.A.; born August 27, 1804; trained with David Paterson; in practice from 1836; Original Member; Member of Council, 1859–1863, 1864–1868, 1870–1874, 1877–1879, 1882–1886, and 1887; Fifth President, 1879–1882; partner, E. Erskine Scott; died May 7, 1887.

SCOTT, THOMAS, C.A.; born June 26, 1799; son of Rev. Mr. Scott of Newton; trained with James Brown; in practice from 1823; Original Member; Member of Council, 1853, 1858–1862, 1864–1866, 1867–1871, and 1874–1878, died June 1, 1883.

SCOTT, WILLIAM, 1817–1831.

SCOTT, WILLIAM BELL, C.A.; born March 26, 1862; son of Archibald Scott; apprentice to J. Turnbull Smith; admitted February 3, 1886; died January 22, 1899.

SELKRIG, CHARLES, in practice from 1786; partner—Patrick Cockburn; died November 14, 1837.

SIMPSON, ALEXANDER JAMES, C.A.; son of Dr. Archibald Simpson, London; apprentice to James Haldane; admitted February 4, 1885; died in London, June 1903.

SIMSON, JAMES, 1835–1842; founded bursaries in connection with Edinburgh Presbyteries.

SINCLAIR, A. H., 1835–1852.

SINCLAIR, JAMES, 1848.

SKIRVING, JAMES, 1825–1827.

SLATE, WILLIAM, 1832–1839.

SMITH, ADAM GILLIES, C.A.; born Dreghorn, November 30, 1827; son of Rev. Robert Smith, D.D. of Aberdeen; educated Aberdeen University; apprentice to Donald Lindsay; admitted March 29, 1855; Assistant to Accountant in Bankruptcy; partners—Messrs. McClelland, Glasgow, William Moncreiff, F. J. Moncreiff; Manager, North British and Mercantile Insurance Co., 1880–1894; Member of Council, 1874–1878, 1879–1881; Examinator, 1887–1891; died January 8, 1900.

SMITH, ARCHIBALD, 1813–1840.

SMITH, JOHN, 13 South Richmond Street, 1800–1803.

SMYTH, DAVID, 1850–1851.

SOUTER, DAVID ROBERTSON, C.A.; afterwards Souter-Robertson; succeeded his uncle, J. Robertson Chaplin; in practice from 1832; Original Member; Member of Council, 1854–1855; died November 10, 1888.

SPALDING, WILLIAM, 1835–1844.

SPENCE, JAMES THOMAS, C.A.; born April 18, 1837; apprentice to Samuel Raleigh; admitted February 1, 1865; died March 16, 1888.

SPENCE, JOHN, 1820–1828.

SPENS, WILLIAM; born September 6, 1807; son of Dr. Thomas Spens, grandson of Dr. Nathaniel Spens; trained with Paul & Mackersy; commenced business in 1832; partner with Kenneth Mackenzie for five years; in 1839 Manager, Scottish Amicable Life Assurance Society; died August 22, 1868.

SPOTTISWOODE, ROBERT, C.A.; native of Perthshire; in practice from 1837; partners—Thomas Mansfield, T. J. Mansfield; Original Member; Member of Council, 1869–1873; died November 4, 1876.

STENHOUSE, WILLIAM, 1800–1828.

STEUART, CHARLES EDWARD, C.A.; apprentice to Wood & Hanna; admitted February 2, 1876; died April 12, 1884.

STEVEN, GEORGE, Baxter's Close, 1774–1775.

STEWART, ALEXANDER, 1816; died April 19, 1822.

STEWART, JAMES, 8 Shakespeare Square; 1800–1805.

STEWART, JOHN, C.A.; born (c.) 1868; apprentice to Francis Dickson; admitted July 29, 1895; died June 21, 1901.

STEWART, JOHN, JUNR., 1814–1835.

STEWART, MALCOLM, 1842–1850.

STEWART, WILLIAM, 1835–1851.

STUART, JAMES JARDINE, C.A.; born Edinburgh, October 4, 1857; apprentice to Charles Prentice; admitted February 2, 1881; died February 11, 1895.

STUART, JOHN; native of Banffshire; in practice from (c.) 1784; connected with the Board of Trustees; died (c.) 1837.

STUART, P., 1842–1848.

STUART, WILLIAM; son of John Stuart (above); educated in London; trained with Henry Mackenzie, W.S., and with his father; in practice from 1839; Attorney to H.M. Exchequer, Edinburgh; died November 5, 1855.

SYM, JAMES, 1844–1850.

T

TAWSE, ALEXANDER BONAR, C.A.; son of Andrew Tawse, W.S.; admitted March 29, 1855; partner—F. H. Carter; died 1858.

THOMSON, ADAM; born at Dailly, Ayrshire, October 28, 1776; son of Rev. Thomas Thomson, Parish Minister; educated at Dailly; trained in Banking House of Sir William Forbes; in practice from 1819–1843.

THOMSON, ALEXANDER, Potterrow, 1780; Deputy Cashier of Excise; died November 30, 1806.

THOMSON, ALEXANDER, 1835–1852.

THOMSON, CHARLES WILLIAM WOODROW, C.A.; born (c.) 1828; son of Rev. Mr. Thomson of Newbattle; trained with Archibald Borthwick; Original Member; Member of Council, 1878–1882, and 1889–1890; partners—John Scott Moncrieff, H. K. Shiells; died February 13, 1898.

THOMSON, JOHN; born (c.) 1733; author of "The Universal Calculator or the Merchants, &c., Assistant," published in 1784; died September 19, 1807.

THOMSON, WILLIAM THOMAS; born February 25, 1813; son of William John Thomson, R.S.A.; trained with William Paul; Secretary, Standard Insurance Co., 1835; Manager, 1837–1874; Consulting Actuary till death on September 16, 1883.

TODD, GEORGE, C.A.; born December 15, 1813; son of George Todd; in practice from 1843; partner—Kenneth Mackenzie; afterwards Secretary of Standard Insurance Co.; Manager of Scottish Equitable Insurance Co.; Original Member; died June 6, 1873.

TROTTER, ARCHIBALD, of the Bush; in practice from (c.) 1753–1760; died October 22, 1784.

TURNBULL, PATRICK, C.A.; born near Coldstream, February 26, 1835; apprentice to D. Robertson Souter; admitted February 3, 1858; in practice in Edinburgh from 1866; died January 17, 1887.

TURNER, W. A., 1822–1836.

V

VEITCH, JOHN, 1845–1849.

W

WALKER, DAVID, 1812–1817.

WATERSTON, WILLIAM, 1834–1846; author of "A Cyclopedia of Commerce," published in 1843.

WATSON, GEORGE; born November 23, 1645; eldest son of John Watson, Merchant, Edinburgh; bred a merchant; sent to Holland to learn bookkeeping, &c.; accomptant to Sir James Dick of Prestonfield, and on his own account; First Accountant of Bank of Scotland; Founder of George Watson's Hospital; died April 3, 1723.

WATSON, HENRY GEORGE, C.A.; born 1791; son of Captain Watson, R.N.; in practice from 1825; partner—T. G. Dickson; Original Member; Member of Council, 1853–1857, 1859–1863, and 1864–1868; died July 2, 1879.

WATSON, JAMES; born in Edinburgh, 1811; educated High School and University; apprentice to David Paterson; partner—James Cleghorn; succeeded him as Manager, Scottish Provident Institution, in 1838; retired 1890; died 1893.

WATT, PETER, 1827–1839; author of several books on Life Assurance.

WHITE, WILLIAM ADAM, C.A.; born October 2, 1864; apprentice to John Walker, and subsequently partner; admitted February 2, 1887; died November 26, 1897.

WHITSON, THOMAS, C.A.; born Blairgowrie, January 15, 1835; apprentice to George Auldjo Jamieson & James Haldane; admitted February 7, 1872; partner in Lindsay, Jamieson, & Haldane; died October 15, 1895.

WIGHT, ROBERT, 1807–1835; partner—James Dundas.

WIGHT, ROBERT, Junr., 1818–1839.

WILKIE, JAMES, C.A.; born at Haddington (c.) 1815; in practice from 1841; Original Member; Member of Council, 1865–1869; Manager, National Guarantee & Suretyship Association; died November 18, 1871.

WILLIAMSON, JAMES, 1845–1850.

WILSON, EDWARD LIDDELL, Junr., C.A.; born October 3, 1872; son of E. L. Wilson of Hillpark, Bannockburn; apprentice to Brewis & Rainie; admitted July 1904; died at Dumfries, November 22, 1904.

WILSON, ROBERT, 4 So. Charlotte Street, 1800–1819.

WILSON, WILLIAM, C.A.; born Kirkpatrick-Durham, March 27, 1870; apprentice to J. Turnbull Smith; admitted February 1, 1893; died June 30, 1896.

WOOD, WILLIAM, C.A.; born 1812; son of John Philip Wood, Auditor of Excise; in practice from 1841; partners—John Maitland, T. C. Hanna; Original Member; Examinator in 1855–1857; Member of Council, 1858–1862, 1867–1871, and 1876–1880; Treasurer, 1879–1892; died December 15, 1892.

WOTHERSPOON, WILLIAM, 1809; First Manager Scottish Widows' Fund; died November 16, 1818.

WRIGHT, H. G., 1837–1846.

WRIGHT, T. G., 1818–1850.

WRIGHT, WILLIAM BURT, C.A.; born May 3, 1848; apprentice to William Wood and T. C. Hanna; admitted February 7, 1877; died January 19, 1894.

Y

YOUNG, GEORGE, 1829–1848.

GLASGOW

A

AITKEN, JAMES; in *Directory*, 1821.

AITKEN, ROBERT, C.A.; Original Member of the Institute; in partnership with Walter Mackenzie under the firm of Aitken & Mackenzie; Chairman of the Stock Exchange 1865–1868; died July 19, 1890.

ALLAN, ROBERT; in *Directory* from 1832.

ANDERSON, JAMES; in *Directory*, 1820–1839.

ANDERSON, JAMES, C.A.; a brother of William (see below); admitted a member of the Institute in 1856; died January 6, 1890.

ANDERSON, WILLIAM, C.A.; an Original Member of the Institute; in partnership from 1842 with James and Henry Kerr, under the firm of Kerrs & Anderson, and afterwards—on the death of James Kerr, and assumption of John A. Brodie—of Kerr, Anderson, & Brodie, now Kerr, Andersons, & Macleod; President of the Institute from 1870–1876, a double term; appointed a liquidator of the City of Glasgow Bank in 1878; died November 13, 1889.

AULD, WILLIAM, C.A.; an Original Member; trained in the office of James M'Clelland; in partnership (1) with Andrew MacEwan (see below) under the firm of MacEwan & Auld, and (2) with J. Wyllie Guild, under the firm of Auld & Guild. The firm of Auld & Guild was afterwards dissolved, when Mr. Auld entered into partnership with the son of his former partner, Andrew MacEwan, under the firm of Auld & MacEwan; Chairman of the Glasgow Stock Exchange, 1870, 1874, and 1878; died January 30, 1885.

B

BAILLIE, JOHN; in *Directory*, 1783.

BANNATYNE, ANDREW, C.A.; trained in the office of J. Wyllie Guild; admitted a member of the Institute in 1862; died January 29, 1885.

BARCLAY, HUGH BROWN, C.A.; trained in office of J. Wyllie Guild; admitted a member of the Institute in 1870; became a member of the firm of Mackenzie, Aitken, & Barclay in 1870; laid aside by illness shortly thereafter, and died March 3, 1892.

BELL, WILLIAM; in *Directory*, 1818.

BLACK, ADAM ELLIOT, C.A.; trained in office of Moore & Brown; admitted a member of the Institute in 1877; in partnership with Alexander Fleming under the firm of Fleming & Black; a very capable volunteer officer—held the rank of Major in the Lanarkshire Engineer Volunteers; died suddenly May 31, 1893.

BLACK, ALEXANDER, C.A.; an Original Member of the Institute; in partnership with George Robson under the firm of Black & Robson; a prominent member of the Stock Exchange; killed in a railway accident at Pennilee, near Paisley, September 8, 1880.

BOAZ, JAMES; in *Directory* from 1821–1829.

BRODIE, JOHN ALISON; trained in office of William Moncreiff (Edinburgh); a partner of firm of Kerr, Anderson, & Brodie from 1853–1870; a leading member of the Glasgow Stock Exchange; died 1879.

BROWN, THOMAS; in *Directory* from 1832.

BROWN, WILLIAM, C.A.; trained in office of Robert McCowan; admitted a member of the Institute in 1857; partner first of the firm of McCowan and Brown, and latterly of the firm of Moore & Brown; died June 13, 1889.

BROWN, WILLIAM STEWART, C.A.; trained in office of Auld & Guild; admitted a member of the Institute in 1877; in partnership with J. Gibson Fleming under firm of Brown & Fleming—now Brown, Fleming, and Murray; died January 14, 1888.

BUCHANAN, THOMAS; in *Directory* from 1832.

BUCHANAN, THOMAS GRAY, C.A.; an Original Member; also a member of the Glasgow Stock Exchange, of which he was Vice-Chairman from 1844 till 1864; died July 31, 1871.

BURNSIDE, JAMES; in *Directory*, 1820.

C

CAIRNS, CHARLES, C.A.; admitted a member of the Institute in 1853; devoted himself to the Stock Exchange, of which he was a member; died in 1883.

CAMERON, GRAEME; in *Directory* from 1824–1827.

CAMPBELL, B.; in *Directory* from 1828–1829.

CARRICK, WILLIAM; in *Directory* from 1820–1840.

CARSWELL, W. J., C.A.; admitted a member of the Institute in 1857; died in 1885.

CHARLES, JOHN; in *Directory* from 1825–1835 (Measurer, Factor, and Accountant).

CHRISTIE, JAMES; in *Directory* from 1823–1840.

CHURCH, WILLIAM, JUNR., C.A.; admitted a member of the Institute in 1857; died January 1, 1887.

COLQUHOUN, A.; in *Directory* from 1829.

COWAN, WILLIAM, C.A.; trained in the office of James S. Duncan; admitted a member of the Institute in 1853; died August 5, 1881.

CRAIG, ROBERT, C.A.; trained in the office of James Gourlay; admitted a member of the Institute in 1857; a member of the firm of Thomson, Ritchie, & Craig—now Thomson, Jackson, Gourlay, & Taylor; died June 11, 1864.

CRICHTON, HUGH; in *Directory* from 1832–1840.

CUNNINGHAM, CHARLES, C.A.; in business as an Accountant from 1843; admitted a member of the Institute in 1853; was also a member of the Glasgow Stock Exchange; died April 30, 1861.

CURRIE, MALCOLM; in *Directory* from 1829.

CUTHBERTSON, ALLAN, C.A.; an Original Member of the Institute; a brother of Donald (see below), with whom he was in partnership under the firm of D. & A. Cuthbertson, now D. & A. Cuthbertson, Provan, and Strong; died January 19, 1864.

CUTHBERTSON, DONALD, LL.B., C.A.; admitted a member of the Institute in 1853; having then, according to his application, been in business as an Accountant for forty years; his name appears in the *Directory* for 1813; he was trained in the office of his father, William Cuthbertson, whose name appears in the *Directory* from 1787 as a "Merchant," but who appears to have devoted himself much to Accountant business (as was not uncommon at that period), and who, according to an article which appeared in the papers on Donald's death, in 1864, "was believed to be the man who originated the Accountant profession in this City." Donald was a distinguished student both at the High School and the University; a lieutenant of volunteers in 1804; a Magistrate of the City; one of the first Directors and for many years Auditor of the Scottish Amicable Life Assurance Society; Secretary of the Royal Asylum for Lunatics, Gartnavel, from its opening till his death, which took place on December 8, 1864.

D

DENOVAN, WILLIAM; in *Directory*, 1832–1840.

DREGHORN, DAVID, C.A.; an Original Member of the Institute; a Magistrate of the City; took a deep interest in the Volunteer movement, holding the rank of captain in the early days; died November 21, 1875.

DUNCAN, WILLIAM THOMSON; trained in the office of J. Wyllie Guild; entered into partnership with Maclean Brodie; afterwards assumed as a partner by Robert McCowan, with whom he carried on business under the firm of McCowan & Duncan; died April 12, 1885.

DUNLOP, JAMES; in *Directory*, 1820.

E

EADIE, JOHN; in *Directory*, 1828–1829.

EASTON, ROBERT; in *Directory*, 1828.

EASTON, ROBERT, C.A.; trained in office of White & Gairdner; admitted a member of the Institute in 1867; assumed as a partner by Peter White; latterly carried on business under firm of Robert Easton & Co.; was also a member of the Glasgow Stock Exchange; died June 10, 1884.

F

FERGUSON, WILLIAM; in *Directory*, 1813.

FINDLAY, JAMES; in *Directory*, 1818–1828.

FLEMING, ALEXANDER, C.A.; trained in the office of Black & Robson; admitted a member of the Institute in 1878; carried on business in partnership with Arthur Elliot Black (*supra*) under the firm of Fleming and Black; died April 21, 1903.

FLEMING, J. GIBSON, C.A.; trained in the office of M'Clelland, M'Kinnon, and Blyth; admitted a member of the Institute in 1880; carried on business in partnership with William Stewart Brown (*supra*) under the firm of Brown & Fleming—now Brown, Fleming, & Murray; died January 13, 1895.

FLEMING, JOHN, C.A.; admitted a member of the Institute in 1853, having been in business as an Accountant from 1843; died in 1866. A shocking murder of a servant girl took place in his house in Sandyford Place during the absence of the family from town in the summer of 1862; the trial of the accused, Jessie McLachlan—a former servant of the family—caused an immense sensation.

FORRESTER, ROBERT, C.A.; admitted a member of the Institute in 1854; was also a member of the Glasgow Stock Exchange; died December 16, 1866.

FOULDS, JOHN CHRISTIE, C.A.; an Original Member of the Institute; was also a member of the Glasgow Stock Exchange; left Glasgow many years ago for the West Indies, where his wife had property; is believed to be dead.

FRASER, JAMES EDWARD, C.A.; trained in the office of Findlay, Kidston, and Goff; admitted a member of the Institute in 1897; entered the service of the African Lakes Co. Ltd., and died in Central Africa, March 28, 1899.

G

GAIRDNER, CHARLES, C.A.; trained in the office of James M'Clelland, and afterwards served with Peter White, by whom he was assumed as a partner in 1845—the firm being White & Gairdner; appointed a Liquidator of the Western Bank in 1857, and Manager of the Union Bank of Scotland in 1862; died February 18, 1899.

GALBRAITH, JAMES; in *Directory*, 1827.

GALT, JAMES, C.A.; admitted a member of the Institute in 1869; carried on business with John C. Reid, under the firm of Reid & Galt; died November 23, 1889.

GIBSON, JOHN; in *Directory*, 1783.

GILROY, JOHN; in *Directory*, 1820.

GLASSFORD, WILLIAM; in *Directory*, 1827–1840.

GOURLAY, JAMES, C.A.; an Original Member of the Institute; having been in business as an Accountant from 1841; a Magistrate of the City, and as such took an active part in promoting the Loch Katrine Water Scheme, by which an abundant supply of water has been introduced to the City of Glasgow; became Agent for the Bank of Scotland at its Lauriston Branch, Glasgow, in 1855; died May 17, 1872.

GOURLAY, JOHN, C.A.; admitted as a member of the Institute in 1870; carried on business on his own account for a number of years, and latterly became a partner in the firm of Thomson, Jackson, Gourlay, & Taylor; died May 12, 1897.

GRAHAM, JOHN, C.A.; an Original Member of the Institute; trained in the office of his uncle, William Lang, who took him into partnership under the firm of Lang & Graham; after various changes the firm ultimately became Grahams & Co., as it now remains; Mr. Graham served for various periods on the Council and was President 1881–1884; died November 14, 1904, aged seventy-six.

GRAHAM, PATRICK, C.A.; trained in the office of his father's firm, then J. & W. Graham; admitted a member of the Institute in 1882; served on the Council from 1900; became a partner with his father under the firm of Grahams & Co.; was an enthusiastic volunteer, and attained the rank of Hon. Lieutenant-Colonel in the Glasgow Highlanders; died January 21, 1903.

GRANT, HECTOR; in *Directory*, 1813.

GRAY, ALEXANDER; in *Directory*, 1832–1837.

GREIG, DAVID; in *Directory*, 1832–1837.

GUILD, DAVID RAMSAY, C.A.; trained in the office of Joseph Grant, W.S., Edinburgh, and also of his brother, J. Wyllie Guild, with whom he entered into partnership; admitted a member of the Institute in 1855; was also a member of the Glasgow Stock Exchange; died March 9, 1874.

GUILD, J. WYLLIE, C.A.; trained in the office of Ivory & Mackenzie, W.S., Edinburgh; came to Glasgow in 1848; admitted, in 1853, a member of the Institute, in the formation of which he took a leading part; filled the office of Secretary of the Institute from 1867–1870; and of Treasurer from 1831; was President 1878–1881; the firms as a partner in which he carried on business, were successively J. W. & D. R. Guild, Guilds and Touch, Auld & Guild, J. Wyllie Guild & Fisher, and latterly, J. Wyllie Guild & Scott; he was also a member of the Glasgow Stock Exchange; died January 4, 1894.

H

HARVIE, ANDREW; in *Directory*, 1829–1840.

HAY, ADAM; in *Directory*, 1832.

HAY, FREDERICK A., C.A.; trained in the office of S. Easton Simmers; admitted a member of the Institute in 1898; died July 17, 1902.

HERROT, JOHN; in *Directory* from 1821.

HILL, THOMAS; in *Directory* from 1783.

J

JAFFRAY, WILLIAM; in *Directory*, 1821–1840.

JAMIESON, WILLIAM, C.A.; trained in the office of MacEwan & Auld; admitted a member of the Institute in 1854; died 1855.

K

KAY, DAVID; in *Directory* from 1803–1829.

KEITH, HENRY, C.A.; trained in the office of Mitchell & Watson; admitted a member of the Institute in 1873; was also a member of the Glasgow Stock Exchange; died October 2, 1897.

KENNEDY, DUNCAN; in *Directory* from 1813–1829 (*Edinburgh Gazette,* 1802).

KERR, JAMES; in *Directory* from 1805–1842; trained in office of David Kay (*supra*); founder of the business now carried on under the firm of Kerr, Andersons, & Macleod.

KERR, HENRY, C.A.; son of James Kerr (*supra*), in whose office he was trained; admitted a member of the Institute in 1853; in partnership with William Anderson, from 1842, and also with John A. Brodie, from 1853, under the firms first of Kerrs & Anderson, and latterly Kerr, Anderson, and Brodie; was also a member of the Glasgow Stock Exchange; died December 9, 1874.

L

LAMB, DAVID F., C.A.; trained in the office of Carson & Watson; admitted a member of the Institute in 1894; in partnership with his brother, under the firm of J. S. & D. F. Lamb; died June 8, 1903.

LECK, HENRY, C.A.; trained in the office of Kerrs & Anderson; admitted a member of the Institute in 1853; became an extensive dealer in heritable property; purchased the estate of Hollybush near Ayr, where he died February 20, 1890.

LECKIE, WILLIAM; in *Directory* from 1826.

LEITCH, JAMES; in *Directory* from 1828.

LOUDON, DAVID; in *Directory* from 1823–1827.

LUMSDEN, ROBERT, C.A.; trained in the Bank of Scotland; one of the Liquidators of the Western Bank; admitted a member of the Institute in 1862; died December 25, 1898.

Mc

McARTHUR, JOHN; in *Directory*, 1827–1837.

MACCALL, JOHN C., Junr., C.A.; trained in the office of J. & W. Graham; admitted a member of the Institute in 1875; assumed as a partner by Messrs. Graham under the firm of J. & W. Graham & Maccall; died at Gibraltar, April 6, 1888.

M'CLELLAND, JAMES, C.A.; trained in the office of James Kerr (see above); began business on his own account in 1824; his firms were successively M'Clelland & Bogle, M'Clelland & Mackenzie, M'Clelland Son & Smith, M'Clelland Son & Co., which afterwards became M'Clelland, Mackinnon, and Blyth, then M'Clelland, Mackinnon, & Co., and is now M'Clelland, Kerr, & Co.; Mr. M'Clelland was for many years the leading Accountant in Glasgow; he was the first President of the Institute, and occupied that honourable position for ten years; he ultimately retired to London, where he died on October 24, 1879.

M'CLELLAND, JAMES, Junr., C.A.; son of above; was trained in the office of M'Clelland & Mackenzie; admitted a member of the Institute in 1855; became a partner with his father under the firm of M'Clelland Son and Smith—afterwards M'Clelland Son & Co.; died March 29, 1866.

McCOWAN, ROBERT, C.A.; admitted a member of the Institute in 1853, having been in business as an Accountant since 1844; was long Treasurer of the Institute; his firms were successively, McCowan & Brown, McCowan and Houston, McCowan & Duncan; died March 1880.

McCUBBIN, DAVID, C.A.; admitted a member of the Institute in 1853, having been in business as an Accountant since 1847; died May 4, 1870.

McDONALD, ROBERT; in *Directory*, 1832–1837.

McDOUGALL, JOHN; in *Directory*, 1813.

MACEWAN, ANDREW, C.A.; an Original Member of the Institute; trained in the office of James M'Clelland; began business in 1834; entered into partnership with William Auld (see above) in 1836, under the firm of MacEwan & Auld; was the first Auditor of the Institute, and would have succeeded Peter White as President, but died June 11, 1866.

McFARLANE, DUNCAN; in *Directory* from 1828–1835.

MACFARLANE, GEORGE, C.A.; admitted a member of the Institute in 1853, having been in practice as an Accountant in Glasgow since 1847; entered into co-partnery in 1865 with James Hutton under the firm of MacFarlane & Hutton—now MacFarlane, Hutton, & Patrick; died December 21, 1881.

McGAVIN, JOHN; in *Directory* from 1821.

McINTOSH, JOHN; in *Directory*, 1820–1840.

McKAY, RODERICK; in *Directory* from 1820.

MACKENZIE, WALTER, of Edinbarnet, C.A.; an Original Member of the Institute; trained in office of James M'Clelland, who afterwards assumed him as a partner under the firm of M'Clelland & Mackenzie; in 1835 he left Mr. M'Clelland and joined Robert Aitken (see above) under the firm of Aitken & Mackenzie—afterwards Mackenzie, Aitken, and Barclay, and now Mackenzie, Aitken, & Clapperton; was a member of Council for forty-four years, viz., from 1853–1897, and occupied successively the offices of Secretary, Treasurer, and Auditor; was twice President, viz., from 1867–1870, and from 1890–1894; was also a member of the Glasgow Stock Exchange; died January 24, 1898, aged eighty-three.

McKIM, THOMAS, C.A.; received his training in the office of Black & Robson, and became a member of the Institute in 1879; entered into partnership with his brother under the firm of T. & G. B. McKim; died July 4, 1904, aged fifty-three.

MACKINNON, WILLIAM, C.A.; trained in the office of James M'Clelland (see above), by whom he was ultimately assumed as a partner under the firms of M'Clelland, Mackinnon, & Blyth, afterwards M'Clelland, Mackinnon, & Co.; admitted a member of the Institute in 1867; died May 7, 1891.

McKIRDY, J. L., C.A.; admitted a member of the Institute in 1853, having previously carried on business as an Accountant in Glasgow since 1844; died 1856.

McLAREN, HAMILTON; in *Directory* from 1829-1840.

McLEAN, WILLIAM, C.A.; admitted a member of the Institute in 1853, having previously practised as an Accountant in Glasgow since 1842; was also a member of the Glasgow Stock Exchange, of which he for many years held the office of Secretary; died February 19, 1893.

McLEAN, WILLIAM, JUNR., C.A. (son of above); admitted a member of the Institute in 1869; was also a member of the Glasgow Stock Exchange, of which he was Chairman, 1882-1883 and 1885-1886; he carried on business in partnership with his brother David under the firm of W. & D. Maclean; died September 15, 1893.

M'LENNAN, THOMAS B., JUNR., C.A.; trained in the offices of John Wilson and Stirling, and Brown, Fleming, & Murray; admitted a member of the Institute in 1898; died January 26, 1901.

McNAUGHTAN, WILLIAM, C.A.; admitted a member of the Institute in 1853, having previously practised as an Accountant in Glasgow from 1846; died February 5, 1864.

MACNICOLL, ARCHIBALD, C.A.; admitted a member of the Institute in 1853, having, after serving six years as apprentice and clerk to an Accountant, been in business as such for five years; went to London in 1854, where he died March 19, 1894.

McOMISH, JAMES; trained in office of McCowan & Houston: afterwards with Thomson, Johnston, & Jackson; entered into co-partnery with his brother John (see below), under the firm of J. & J. McOmish—now McOmish & Arthur; died February 18, 1892.

McOMISH, JOHN, C.A.; trained in office of his brother James (above); admitted a member of the Institute, 1886; entered into partnership with his brother (as above); died June 3, 1891.

McPHAIL, JOHN; in *Directory* from 1820.

McPHUN, HUGH; in *Directory* from 1823.

McQUEEN, A.; in *Directory* from 1832.

M

MAIN, JOHN T., M.A., C.A.; trained in the office of the North British and Mercantile Insurance Co., Edinburgh, and afterwards with Kerr, Andersons, & Muir, by which firm he was assumed as a partner, it then becoming Kerr, Andersons, Muir, & Main; admitted a member of the Institute in 1876; was also a member of the Glasgow Stock Exchange; died June 7, 1896.

MAIR, ROBERT ALEXANDER, C.A.; trained in the office of Reid & Galt, and afterwards served with Moore & Brown; admitted a member of the Institute in 1871; entered into partnership with Robert Reid, under the firm of Reid & Mair; died March 14, 1898.

MALCOLM, JOHN; in *Directory*, 1827–1837.

MARTIN, JAMES; in *Directory*, 1829–1835.

MEIN, ALEXANDER; in *Directory*, 1820–1840.

MENZIES, T. PATON, C.A.; trained in the office of Maclean Brodie and Forgie; afterwards served with W. & W. B. Galbraith, and eventually went to London; volunteered at the outbreak of the Boer War for service at the front, and died of fever in Ladysmith, May 28, 1900.

METHVEN, JAMES; in *Directory* from 1820–1840.

MILLER, GEORGE; in *Directory*, 1828.

MILLER, GEORGE, C.A.; trained in the office of Aitken & Mackenzie; admitted a member of the Institute in 1869; was also a member of the Glasgow Stock Exchange; entered into partnership, (1) with Theodore Keyden under the firm of Miller & Keyden, and, (2) with George Slimmon under the firm of George Miller & Slimmon; died March 10, 1887.

MILLER, JAMES, C.A.; trained in the office of Alexander Sloan; admitted a member of the Institute, 1898; entered the employment of L. Talbot Crosbie, Factor and Commissioner for Scotstoun Estate; died May 21, 1902.

MILLER, JOHN, C.A.; admitted a member of the Institute in 1853, having previously been practising as an Accountant in Glasgow since 1845; was also a member of the Glasgow Stock Exchange; carried on business with James H. Ferguson under the firm of John Miller & Ferguson; afterwards with his grandson, William Quaile, C.A., under the firm of John Miller & Quaile; died September 23, 1894; aged seventy-nine.

MITCHELL, MONCRIEFF, C.A.; admitted a member of the Institute in 1853, having practised as an Accountant in Glasgow since 1849; entered into partnership, (1) with Alexander Wylie under the firm of Wylie and Mitchell, (2) with Alexander James Watson, C.A. (Edin.), under the firm of Mitchell & Watson, which afterwards became Mitchell, Watson, and Wink; died March 17, 1886.

MOFFAT, ALEXANDER; in *Directory*, 1827.

MOFFAT, GEORGE, C.A.; born 1839; trained with Aitken & Mackenzie; admitted a member of the Institute in 1867; partner of J. & G. Moffat; died December 16, 1904.

MONCRIEFF, WILLIAM; in *Directory*, 1823.

MONKHOUSE, RICHARD; in *Directory*, 1818.

MORISON, C.; in *Directory*, 1818–1840.

MORRISON, JOHN; 1818–1828.

MUDIE, WILLIAM, Junr., C.A.; admitted a member of the Institute in 1857, having been practising as an Accountant since 1845; ceased to be a member in 1892; died September 1904.

MUIR, JAMES, C.A.; trained in the office of Kerr, Anderson, & Brodie; was admitted a member in 1870, in which year he was assumed as a partner by his employers, the firm then becoming Kerr, Anderson, & Muir, and afterwards Kerr, Andersons, Muir, & Main; died December 18, 1898; was engaged for the Crown in the trial of the Directors of the City of Glasgow Bank.

MUNRO, JOHN; in *Directory*, 1829–1838.

N

NEWBIGGING, J.; in *Directory*, 1829.

O

ORD, GEORGE; in *Directory* from 1824–1840.

OUTRAM, DAVID EDMUND, C.A.; admitted a member of the Institute in 1853, having previously been in practice as an Accountant and Share-broker in Glasgow since 1845; was also a member of the Glasgow Stock Exchange, of which he was Chairman in 1881–1882; died October 31, 1893.

P

PAISLEY, JAMES; in *Directory* from 1813–1826; (*Edinburgh Gazette*, 1805).

PATON, JAMES; in *Directory*, 1820.

PAUL, HENRY; in *Directory*, 1820.

PORTER, M.; in *Directory* from 1818–1826 (" Accountant, Teacher of Book-keeping, &c.").

PROVAN, MOSES, C.A.; trained in the office of D. & A. Cuthbertson; admitted a member of the Institute in 1856; assumed as a partner by his employers under the firm of D. & A. Cuthbertson & Provan, now D. & A. Cuthbertson, Provan, & Strong; died February 21, 1871.

R

REID, JOHN C., C.A.; trained in the office of James Gourlay; admitted a member of the Institute in 1853; carried on business in partnership (1) with William Tolmie, under the firm of Tolmie & Reid, and (2) with James Galt, under the firm of Reid & Galt; died August 5, 1894.

REID, WILLIAM, C.A.; trained in the office of White & Gairdner; admitted a member of the Institute in 1856; died 1863.

RENNIE, THOMAS; in *Directory*, 1828 ("Writing Master and Accountant").

RHIND, THOMAS; in *Directory*, 1832–1834.

RITCHIE, ALEXANDER, C.A.; trained in the office of James Gourlay; admitted a member of the Institute in 1853; carried on business in partnership with James Thomson, under the firm of Thomson and Ritchie—now Thomson, Jackson, Gourlay, & Taylor; died December 15, 1860.

ROBERTSON, JAMES ALEXANDER, C.A.; served his apprenticeship with Honeyman & Drummond; was afterwards for a time with Reid & Mair; was admitted a member of the Institute in 1880; went afterwards to London and was for many years in the office of Good Son & Co., Chartered Accountants there; falling into bad health he died at Greenwich, March 29, 1904, aged fifty-seven years.

ROBERTSON, JOHN D.; in *Directory*, 1825–1835.

ROBERTSON, LAURENCE, C.A. trained in the office of M'Clelland and Mackenzie; admitted a member of the Institute in 1854; carried on business as an Accountant and Stockbroker, first on his own account, and then in partnership with his brother, under the firm of L. & R. H. Robertson; was also a member of the Glasgow Stock Exchange, of which he was Chairman in 1878–1879–1883; died December 31, 1893.

ROBERTSON, ROBERT HOPE, C.A. (brother of Laurence); served an apprenticeship of five years with Bannatyne & Kirkwood, Writers, Glasgow; thereafter for two years was a clerk in the office of Dundas and Wilson, C.S., Edinburgh; then entered into partnership with his brother in Glasgow, under the firm of L. & R. H. Robertson; admitted a member of the Institute in 1861; was also a member of the Glasgow Stock Exchange, of which he was Chairman in 1892–1893; died January 7, 1903.

ROBERTSON, T. C., C.A.; trained in the office of McFarlane & Hutton; admitted a member of the Institute in 1877; died April 1, 1887.

ROBSON, GEORGE, C.A.; admitted a member of the Institute in 1853, having previously practised as an Accountant in Glasgow; carried on business as an Accountant and Stockbroker in partnership with Alexander Black, under the firm of Black & Robson; was also a member of the Glasgow Stock Exchange; was elected President of the Institute in 1876, but retired owing to the state of his health in 1878; died February 2, 1881, aged eighty-one.

ROSE, WILLIAM; in *Directory*, 1820.

S

SANDERS, GILBERT; in *Directory*, 1820–1840.

SANDERSON, J.; in *Directory*, 1818–1828 ("Writing Master and Accountant").

SCOBIE, ROBERT, C.A.; admitted a member of the Institute in 1853, having previously practised as an Accountant in Glasgow; died 1857.

SCOTT, JOHN; in *Directory*, 1825.

SCOTT, ROBERT; in *Directory*, 1824.

SHAND, EDWARD M., C.A.; trained in the office of Moore & Brown; went to Calcutta and became a partner in a firm of Chartered Accountants in that city; died there, October 3, 1901.

SHAW, JAMES; in *Directory*, 1826.

SLOANE, FRANCIS NAPIER, C.A.; trained in office of McFarlane & Hutton; admitted a member of the Institute in 1887; died June 16, 1901.

SMITH, ALEXR. HUTCHESON, C.A.; trained in the office of Patrick Rattray, by whom and his brother he was afterwards assumed as a partner under the firm of Rattray Bros. & Smiths; retired in 1888; died November 12, 1904.

SMITH, JAMES; in *Directory*, 1828.

SMITH, JAMES, C.A.; admitted a member of the Institute in 1854, having previous to commencing practice as an Accountant in Glasgow served in the office of John Whiteford M'Kenzie, W.S., Edinburgh; retired in 18—, and died July 18, 1880.

SMITH, JOHN; in *Directory*, 1818–1832 ("Writing Master and Accountant").

SMYTH, JAMES; in *Directory*, 1828.

STALKER, SAMUEL; in *Directory*, 1783.

STEEL, THOMAS; in *Directory*, 1832 ("Corn Factor and Accountant").

STEWART, JOHN, C.A.; trained in office of Carson & Watson; afterwards served for four years with Thomson, Jackson, Gourlay, & Taylor; died March 11, 1894.

STEWART, WILLIAM; in *Directory*, 1832.

STRONG, DAVID; in *Directory*, 1818.

STRONG, J. ROXBURGH, C.A.; trained in office of MacEwan & Auld; afterwards served with Auld & Guild; admitted a member of the Institute in 1870 : assumed as a partner by Moses Provan, whom he succeeded as sole partner of the firm of D. & A. Cuthbertson, Provan, & Strong; served several times as a Member of Council, and was elected auditor in 1898, which office he held at the date of his death; died November 1, 1899.

SUTHERLAND, D.; in *Directory*, 1824.

SWAN, JOHN R., C.A.; trained in office of John L. McKirdy; admitted a member of the Institute in 1855 : died 1873.

SYM, JAMES; in *Directory*, 1832.

T

THOMSON, JAMES, Junr., C.A.; admitted a member of the Institute in 1853, having previously practised as an Accountant in Glasgow, first as a partner in the firm of James Thomson & Son, and afterwards in partnership with Alexander Ritchie under the firm of Thomson & Ritchie, now (after various changes in the interim) Thomson, Jackson, Gourlay, and Taylor; died December 12, 1885.

TOD, ROBERT; in *Directory*, 1818.

TOD, ROBERT, Junr.; in *Directory*, 1818.

TODD, RUTHVEN C., C.A.; served apprenticeship with William Alexander, W.S., Edinburgh; author of Alexander's "Digest of the Bankruptcy Laws"; afterwards served in the offices of William Russell, Accountant, Edinburgh, and John C. Foulds, C.A., Glasgow; admitted a member of the Institute in 1855; was also a member of the Glasgow Stock Exchange; died August 10, 1887.

TURNBULL, JAMES; in *Directory*, 1824–1838.

TURNER, WILLIAM E., C.A.; trained in office of Moores, Carson, & Watson, and served afterwards in office of Mitchell & Smith; admitted a member of the Institute, January 30, 1900, and died on the 14th of the following month.

W

WADDELL, ARCHIBALD; in *Directory*, 1826–1840.

WALKER, DAVID; in *Directory*, 1823.

WALKER, PETER, C.A.; admitted a member of the Institute in 1854; trained in the City of Glasgow Bank, and afterwards practised as an Accountant; died March 8, 1886.

WALLACE, ROBERT; in *Directory*, 1813–1827.

WATSON, ALEXANDER JAMES, C.A. (Edinr.); born Edinburgh, February 6, 1831; apprentice to William Low, afterwards with F. H. Carter; admitted March 29, 1855; entered into partnership in Glasgow with Moncrieff Mitchell, C.A. (*supra*) under the firm of Mitchell & Watson; died May 16, 1892.

WATSON, JAMES, 1824; began life as an Accountant, but ultimately became a Stockbroker; was the "father" of the Glasgow Stock Exchange, of which he was Chairman for many years; became Lord Provost of Glasgow and received the honour of knighthood from Queen Victoria; died August 14, 1889.

WATSON, JOHN E., C.A.; admitted as a member in 1855, having previously practised as an Accountant in Glasgow; served on the Council and was President from 1887–1890; died April 18, 1901.

WATSON, LAURENCE HILL, C.A.; trained in office of M'Clelland, Mackinnon, & Co., afterwards M'Clelland, Mackinnon, & Blyth; entered into partnership with David S. Carson, under firm of Carson & Watson, afterwards Moores, Carson, & Watson; died as the result of an accident in the hunting-field, January 27, 1893.

WHITE, GEORGE; in *Directory*, 1827.

WHITE, PETER, C.A.; born 1810; an Original Member and first Treasurer of the Institute; carried on business as an Accountant and Stockbroker in partnership with Charles Gairdner under the firm of White and Gairdner; served on the Council and was the second President of the Institute, filling the chair from 1864 to 1867; was also a member of the Glasgow Stock Exchange, of which he was Chairman, 1868–1870 and 1871–1874; died June 5, 1881.

WHITE, THOMAS; in *Directory*, 1824.

WIGHT, ROBERT; in *Directory*, 1818 (" Law Accountant ").

WILKIE, JAMES, C.A.; admitted a member of the Institute in 1853, having previously been in business in Glasgow as an Accountant and Sharebroker; was also a member of the Glasgow Stock Exchange; died February 16, 1883.

WILSON, J.; in *Directory*, 1813–1818.

WILSON, WILLIAM; in *Directory*, 1783.

WINK, GEORGE, C.A.; admitted a member of the Institute in 1853, having previously been in business as an Accountant in Glasgow since 1846; carried on business in partnership with John Wight under the firm of Wink & Wight, and afterwards with his son under the firm of George Wink & Son; died June 17, 1869.

WOODSIDE, ARCHIBALD, C.A.; admitted a member of the Institute in 1853, having previously been practising as an Accountant in Glasgow since 1843; died 1867.

Y

YOUNG, JOHN; in *Directory*, 1829.

REST OF SCOTLAND

A

ANDERSON, JAMES, Aberdeen; in *Directory* from 1858–1861.

B

BRAND, ALEXANDER, C.A., Aberdeen; in *Directory* from 1855; Original Member of the Society; died in 1876.

BUDGE, DAVID, Aberdeen; in *Directory*, 1850–1852; Accountant to North British Australasian Investment Company, and removéd with it to London.

C

COPLAND, WILLIAM, Aberdeen; Town Clerk Depute in 1796.

CROMBIE, JOHN, C.A., Aberdeen; born in 1832; trained with Mr. Robert Dyce, Advocate; in *Directory* as a Writer, 1851; Accountant, 1858; Original Member and President of the Society; a Magistrate of the City; died on 11th November 1898.

E

ELGEN, WILLIAM, Aberdeen; in *Directory*, 1824–1847; also mentioned as a Teacher of Mathematics, &c.

F

FLEMING, JAMES, Kirkcaldy; from (*c.*) 1790; educated at Blairgowrie and Perth; father of " Pet Marjorie."

FLEMING, JOHN, Dundee; Writing-Master and Accountant, from 1834.

FLETCHER, ROBERT, C.A., Aberdeen; born and educated in Edinburgh; trained with Provincial Assurance Co.; in *Directory*, 1848, Sharebroker; 1852, Accountant; Original Member and President of the Society; partner—James A. Murray; removed to London in 1868; partner there —Robert Mackay; died June 12, 1883, aged 65.

G

GALEN, BAILLIE, Aberdeen; described as a Professional Accountant in connection with Report of Select Committee of House of Commons, 1819.

GRAY, JOHN, C.A., Aberdeen; in *Directory* from 1879; trained with James A. Murray; partners—James A. Murray, James Strachan; died 1890.

GREIG, JOHN K., C.A., Aberdeen; in *Directory* from 1876; trained with Marquis, Hall, & Milne; partner—James Meston; died 1902.

H

HAMMOND, THOMAS L., Dundee; Writer and Accountant from 1840.

HARDIE, JAMES, Aberdeen; City Chamberlain; died October 19, 1840, aged 67.

I

IRONS, J. M., C.A. (Gl.); trained in office of Mackay & Mess, Dundee; admitted a member of the Institute in 1895; died July 7, 1903.

K

KENNEDY, WILLIAM, Aberdeen; born 1758; a Writer in 1783; author of the "Annals of Aberdeen"; made an elaborate report on the Town's affairs in 1820; died in 1836.

L

LESLIE, JOHN GRANT, C.A., Aberdeen; in *Directory* in 1835; Original Member of the Society; Commissary - Clerk Depute; died in 1874.

LESLIE, ROBERT, Aberdeen; in *Directory*, 1853–1856.

LUNAN, WILLIAM, C.A., Aberdeen; son of the parish minister of Kinnettles; trained with Mr. Macdonald, Arbroath, and Donald Lindsay, Edinburgh; in *Directory* from 1851; Original Member and President of Society; partner—George Marquis; died May 5, 1903, aged 84.

M

MACALDOWIE, JOHN, Aberdeen; born 1818; in *Directory* from 1858; Manager of Aberdeen Property & Investment Building Society; died January 1888.

MACLEISH, JOHN, Perth; from (c.) 1850.

McNICOL, JAMES, Dundee; in *Directory*, 1829–1833.

MAITLAND, WILLIAM, Aberdeen; in *Directory*, 1853–1862.

MARQUIS, GEORGE, C.A., Aberdeen; born at Fochabers (c.) 1802; in *Directory* from 1837; Auditor of the Aberdeen Corporation Accounts; Original Member and President of Society; partners—William Lunan, Harvey Hall, William Milne; died January 21, 1875.

MASSON, ANDREW, Aberdeen; in *Directory*, 1831–1867; Accountant to Aberdeen Fire and Life (now Northern) Assurance Company; afterwards in general practice.

MESS, JOHN, C.A. (Gl.); trained in the office of John Edward Dovey (Edinburgh); admitted a member of the Institute in 1882; entered into partnership with Alexander Mackay, Dundee, under the firm of Mackay & Mess; died January 17, 1902.

MESTON, JAMES, C.A., Aberdeen; born at Kintore, February 25, 1821; trained with Blaikie & Smith, Aberdeen; in *Directory* in 1850 as a Writer, in 1854 as an Accountant; Original Member and Secretary and Treasurer of the Society from its commencement until his death; partners—Andrew Davidson, J. K. Greig, Walter A. Reid; died August 6, 1892.

MILNE, ALEXANDER, Aberdeen; in *Directory*, 1851–1866.

MILNE, JAMES, C.A., Aberdeen; in *Directory* as Writer 1856–1867; as Accountant 1867–1888; a President of the Society; died December 17, 1888, aged 51.

MURRAY, JAMES ADAMSON, C.A., Aberdeen; in *Directory* from 1857; Original Member of the Society; died in 1879.

MORICE, GEORGE, Aberdeen; in *Directory*, 1857 and 1858, as an Accountant and Average-Stater.

MORISON, JAMES; born 1798; son of James Morison, Publisher, Perth; trained with Selkrig & Cockburn; partner—Samuel Clerk; removed to Perth (c.) 1827; founded firm of J. & R. Morison there; died 1878.

MOWAT, WILLIAM, Aberdeen; in *Directory*, 1858–1866.

MURRAY, ROBERT, C.A. (Ed.); in Dundee, 1861–1870; see page 375.

MYLES, DAVID C.A. (Gl.); admitted a member of the Institute under Rule 9 in 1891, having previously been in practice as an Accountant in Dundee for twenty-five years; died June 7, 1898.

MYLES, WILLIAM, Dundee; from 1842; partner—David Myles, C.A.; died in 1879, aged 72.

N

NOTMAN, R. R., Aberdeen; in *Directory*, 1840–1854; Manager of Aberdeen Fire and Life (now Northern) Assurance Company.

R

RITCHIE, ROBERT B., C.A. (Gl.); admitted a member of the Institute under Rule 9 in 1891, having been previously in practice as an Accountant in Dundee for twenty-three years; died February 17, 1900.

ROBERTSON, ROBERT, Perth; from (c.) 1825.

S

SINCLAIR, JAMES AUGUSTUS, C.A., Aberdeen; born May 31, 1827; son of Colonel J. S. Sinclair, R.A., practised in Aberdeen from about 1850 until 1890, when he became Earl of Caithness; Original Member and President of Society; died in London in 1891.

SMITH, JOHN, C.A., Aberdeen; born at Woodside (c.) 1798; graduated M.A. of Marischal College; trained with John Ewing, Advocate; in *Directory* as Advocate from 1824; Accountant from 1831; Original Member and first President of Society; partner—John Blaikie; died at Paris, May 5, 1884.

STEELE, WILLIAM, C.A., Aberdeen; practised from 1852; Original Member of Society; died 1870.

STIVEN, WILLIAM, C.A. (Gl.); admitted a member of the Institute under Rule 9 in 1895, having previously carried on business as an Accountant in Dundee since 1856: died December 27, 1899.

STRACHAN, A., Aberdeen; in *Directory*, 1851-1855.

STRONACH, ALEXANDER, JUNR., Aberdeen; in *Directory*, 1860-1898.

STUART, ROBERT MOODY, C.A. (Edinr.); born Edinburgh, March 17, 1846; son of Rev. Alexander Moody Stuart, D.D., of Free St. Luke's, Edinburgh; educated Edinburgh Academy and University; apprentice to Thomas Martin; admitted February 5, 1868; commenced business in Dundee in 1869; partner—J. C. Robertson; died June 22, 1896.

STURROCK, JOHN, JUNR., Dundee; Writer and Accountant from (c.) 1834: died in 1865.

SUTHERLAND, HECTOR, Aberdeen; in *Directory*, 1859-1863.

APPENDIX No. III

FIFTIETH ANNIVERSARY OF INCORPORATION

1. THE SOCIETY OF ACCOUNTANTS IN EDINBURGH

THE fiftieth anniversary of the Incorporation by Royal Charter of the Society of Accountants in Edinburgh was celebrated by a Dinner given in the North British Station Hotel, Edinburgh, on the evening of Monday, 24th October 1904. The President of the Society, Mr. Frederick Walter Carter, received the guests and presided at the Dinner. There were present as the guests of the Society the following gentlemen :—

The Right Hon. Sir Robert Cranston, Lord Provost of Edinburgh; the Right Hon. the Earl of Rosebery, K.G., K.T., Lord Lieutenant of the County of Midlothian; the Right Rev. John McMurtrie, D.D., Moderator of the General Assembly of the Church of Scotland; the Rev. Robert Gordon Balfour, D.D., Moderator of the General Assembly of the United Free Church of Scotland; the Right Rev. John Dowden, D.D., LL.D., Bishop of Edinburgh; the Most Rev. James Augustine Smith, D.D., Archbishop of St. Andrews and Edinburgh.

The Right Hon. Lord Kinross, Lord Justice General; the Right Hon. Sir J. H. A. Macdonald, K.C.B., Lord Justice Clerk; the Right Hon. Lord Kinnear; the Right Hon. George, Lord Young; the Hon. Lord Adam; the Hon. Lord McLaren; the Hon. Lord Trayner; the Hon. Lord Kincairney.

Sir William Turner, K.C.B., Principal of the University of Edinburgh; Sir Ludovic J. Grant, Bart., Professor of Public Law; Mr. James Mackintosh, B.A., Professor of Civil Law; Mr. John Rankine, K.C., Professor of Scots Law; Mr. John L. Mounsey, W.S., Professor of Conveyancing.

Sir James Guthrie, President of the Royal Scottish Academy; Mr. T. S. Clouston, M.D., President of the Royal College of Physicians; Brevet-Colonel L. A. Hope, C.B., A.D.C., Director of Supplies and Transport of the Forces in Scotland; Col. C. W. Carey, Commanding the Highland Light Infantry; Lieut.-Colonel A. B. McHardy, C.B., Chairman of Prison Commissioners for Scotland; Sir James Balfour Paul, Lyon-King-of-Arms.

The Right Hon. Charles Scott Dickson, K.C., M.P., Lord Advocate; Mr. David Dundas, K.C., Solicitor-General for Scotland; Mr. G. Falconar

Stewart, Secretary of the Local Government Board for Scotland; the Hon. Alex. O. Murray, Master of Elibank, M.P. for Midlothian; Sir John Batty Tuke, M.D., M.P. for the University of Edinburgh; Mr. George McCrae, M.P. for East Edinburgh; Mr. George M. Brown, M.P. for Central Edinburgh.

Messrs. Charles C. Maconochie, Advocate, Sheriff of the Lothians and Peebles; Donald Crawford, K.C., Sheriff of the County of Aberdeen, &c.; John Wilson, K.C., Sheriff of the County of Caithness, &c.; James A. Fleming, K.C., Sheriff of the County of Dumfries, &c.; C. Kincaid Mackenzie, K.C., Sheriff of Fife and Kinross; Henry Johnston, K.C., Sheriff of the County of Forfar; Christopher N. Johnston, K.C., Sheriff of the County of Inverness, &c.; Andrew Jameson, K.C., Sheriff of the County of Perth; John C. Guy, Advocate, Sheriff-Substitute of Midlothian; A. Edward Henderson, Advocate, Sheriff-Substitute of Midlothian.

Mr. J. S. Harmood-Banner, F.C.A., President of the Institute of Chartered Accountants in England and Wales; The Hon. George Colville, Secretary of the Institute; Messrs. Alfred A. James, F.C.A., George W. Knox, F.C.A., and Francis W. Pixley, F.C.A., Past Presidents of the Institute; Messrs. T. A. Wykes, F.C.A., President of the Leicester Society of Chartered Accountants; A. A. Gillies, F.C.A., President of the Manchester Society of Chartered Accountants; T. E. Shuttleworth, B.A., F.C.A., President of the Sheffield Society of Chartered Accountants; Robert Stokes, F.C.A., President of the Institute of Chartered Accountants in Ireland; Wm. G. Rayner, President of the Society of Accountants and Auditors; Wm. Densham, Melbourne, Member of Council of the Incorporated Institute of Accountants, Victoria; Andrew Williamson, C.A., President of the Association of Scottish Chartered Accountants in London.

Mr. Thomas Jackson, C.A., President of the Institute of Accountants and Actuaries in Glasgow; Messrs. A. S. M'Clelland, C.A., John Wilson, C.A., and James Hutton, C.A., Past Presidents; Robert Reid, C.A., R. C. Mackenzie, C.A., A. J. Fergusson, C.A., Thomson McLintock, C.A., John Mann, Junr., C.A., George A. Cadell, C.A., and D. Johnston Smith, C.A., Members of Council; Alexander Sloan, C.A., Secretary, and T. A. Craig, C.A., Treasurer; Ninian Glen, C.A., David Strathie, C.A., Joseph Patrick, C.A., and Alexander Moore, Junr., C.A., Examiners; William Turner Green, C.A., Bombay.

Mr. James Milne, Junr., C.A., President of the Society of Accountants in Aberdeen; Messrs. G. G. Whyte, C.A., Alex. Ledingham, C.A., Harvey Hall, C.A., and Alexander Machray, C.A., Past Presidents; George Dickie, C.A., and A. S. Mitchell, C.A., Members of Council; Walter A. Reid, C.A., F.F.A., Secretary, and Charles Williamson, C.A., Examiner.

Messrs. William J. Dundas, C.S., Crown Agent for Scotland; E. P. W. Redford, Secretary to the General Post-Office in Scotland; Alfred C. Trevor, Comptroller of Stamps and Taxes for Scotland; A. G. G. Asher, W.S., County

Clerk of Midlothian; N. Ballingall Gunn, F.I.A., President of the Faculty of Actuaries in Scotland; Captain Ross, Chief Constable of the City of Edinburgh; Richard Clark, J.P., D.L., Chairman of Edinburgh Parish Council; Professor George Chrystal, General Secretary of the Royal Society of Edinburgh; Messrs. Richard Mackie, Provost of Leith, and W. S. Brown, City Treasurer of Edinburgh.

Sir John Cheyne, K.C., Vice-Dean of the Faculty of Advocates; Messrs. A. A. Grainger Stewart, LL.B., Treasurer of the Faculty of Advocates; J. T. Clark, Librarian of the Faculty of Advocates; George Powell McNeill, LL.B., Collector of the Widows' Fund of the Faculty of Advocates; C. R. A. Howden, Advocate; Charles T. Cooper, Advocate, Clerk of Court; P. W. Campbell, W.S., Clerk of Court; James McIntosh, S.S.C., Auditor of the Court of Session.

Messrs. John Cowan, W.S., Treasurer of the Society of Writers to His Majesty's Signet; William Stuart Fraser, W.S., Fiscal of the Society of Writers to His Majesty's Signet; Charles Cook, W.S., Collector of Widows' Fund of the Society of Writers to His Majesty's Signet; James R. Notman, W.S., Substitute-Keeper of His Majesty's Signet; John P. Edmond, Librarian of the Society of Writers to His Majesty's Signet; A. Scott Ireland, S.S.C., President of the Society of Solicitors in the Supreme Courts; Charles Ritchie, S.S.C., Hon. Treasurer and Collector of the Society of Solicitors in the Supreme Courts.

Messrs. George Anderson, Treasurer of the Bank of Scotland; Hamilton A. Hotson, Manager of the British Linen Company Bank; Andrew Aikman, General Manager of the Commercial Bank of Scotland, Ltd.; Thomas Hector Smith, General Manager of the National Bank of Scotland, Ltd.; John Henderson, Manager of the North of Scotland Bank, Ltd.; William Baird, Secretary of the Institute of Bankers in Scotland; Archibald Hewat, Manager of the Edinburgh Life Assurance Co.; Walter A. Smith, Manager (in Scotland) of the English and Scottish Law Life Assurance Association; James Murray, Manager of the National Guarantee and Suretyship Association, Ltd.; Thomas Kyd, Manager of the Northern Assurance Co.; George M. Low, Manager of the Scottish Equitable Life Assurance Society; H. E. Marriott, Manager of the Scottish Metropolitan Life Assurance Co., Ltd.; Henry Brown, Manager of the Century Insurance Co.; A. Gibbon Thomson, Manager of the Life and Health Assurance Association, Ltd.; Harry Armour, Manager of the Scottish Accident Life and Fidelity Insurance Co., Ltd.; Robert Cumming, General Manager of the Scottish County and Mercantile Insurance Co., Ltd.; David Paulin, Manager, Scottish Life Assurance Co., Ltd.

Messrs. F. Faithfull Begg, Stock Exchange, London; T. S. Thomson, President of the Edinburgh Stock Exchange; John Sullivan, Secretary of the Edinburgh Stock Exchange; John Harrison, Master of the Merchant Company; William Grant, Treasurer of the Merchant Company;

Alexander Heron, S.S.C., Secretary of the Merchant Company; Walter B. Blaikie, Chairman of the Edinburgh Chamber of Commerce; James H. Warrack, Chairman of the Leith Chamber of Commerce.

Messrs. James Chatham, F.F.A., F.I.A., Actuary of the Assurance Fund of the Society of Accountants; R. S. Aitchison, M.D., F.R.C.P.E., Medical Officer; J. S. Mackay, LL.D., and H. H. Browning, Examiners for the Chartered Accountants of Scotland; W. Kinniburgh Morton, S.S.C., Lecturer in Law for the Society; A. B. Clark, M.A., Lecturer in Political Economy; M. Mackenzie Lees, F.F.A., Lecturer in Actuarial Science; T. C. Jack, Publisher, and C. E. Green, Publisher.

The following Original Members of the Society, viz:—

Thomas G. Dickson, C.A.; James Howden, C.A.; Alexander T. Niven, C.A.

There were also present the following other Members of the Society:—

Messrs. R. S. Aitchison; J. Shiels Alexander; W. A. Alexander; Cecil L. Anderson; W. A. A. Balfour; L. B. Bell; George Bird; Hugh Blair; Patrick A. Blair; Edward Boyd, *Auditor;* J. Wilson Brodie; H. H. McKerrell Brown; James McKerrell Brown; John Brown; Richard Brown, *Secretary;* J. Hamilton Buchanan; Norman Cairns; George H. Carphin; Frederick Walter Carter, *President;* J. K. Chalmers; D. A. Clapperton; T. Bennet Clark; Reginald Collie; William Home Cook; Alexander Cowan; Francis Cowan; J. D. Cowan; James Craig; Fred J. Crawford; W. J. Croall; Alastair Currie, London; G. W. Currie; H. T. Cuthbert; John Dalgleish, London; Charles L. Dalziel; A. Bashall Dawson; George Deas; J. Campbell Dewar; Leonard W. Dickson; Mowbray Douglas; J. E. Dovey; Thomas Dymock; Garnet W. Edmunds; A. Dodds Fairbairn, London; A. D. Ferguson; Albert A. Finlay, Paris; George A. Fraser; Hugh S. Hope Gill; J. Ker Goalen; James Gordon; Kenneth M. Gourlay; John Stuart Gowans; B. M. Graham; J. R. Leslie Gray; William Greenhill; James Greig; P. A. Guthrie; Herbert W. Haldane; James Haldane; W. G. C. Hanna; William Hardie, Greenock; Charles Hay; J. Milne Henderson; Thomas G. Herriot; Alexander T. Hunter; John Johnston; T. P. Laird; Archibald Langwill; Robertson Lawson, London; George Lisle; Alastair W. J. Livingstone, London; Edward A. Mackay, London; Alexander MacKelvie; C. P. Maclagan; J. A. McLaren; D. A. McLennan; J. M. MacLeod, Glasgow; J. A. H. Macnair, London; C. E. W. Macpherson; Hugh Macrae; F. W. Martin; Thomas S. Martin; W. C. Maughan, Musselburgh; Robert C. Millar; Thomas J. Millar; John F. Moffatt; Francis More, Junr.; Alexander Morrison; Charles Morton; A. W. Mosman; R. M. Muirhead; James Mylne; P. Nisbet; David R. Noble; Robert T. Norfor; George Oliver; David F. Park, London; Norman G. Park; Alexander J. Paterson; C. J. G. Paterson; David Pearson; J. Campbell Penney, *Accountant of*

Court; James Pringle; R. D. Rainie; H. B. Rettie; J. A. Robertson-Durham; J. H. W. Rolland, London; James Romanes; Hugh Rose; F. A. Ross; Henry L. Sanderson; William Saunders; W. P. Scott; J. Stewart Seggie; Robert Shiell; H. K. Shiells; William Sime; C. M. Smart; P. W. Smeaton, London; A. Davidson Smith; C. Maitland Smith; J. Aikman Smith; John Smith, C.B., London; J. Turnbull Smith, LL.D.; W. C. Steven; R. Sidney Stewart; D. F. Sutherland; A. W. Tait, London; Fred. Tod; George A. Touch, London; A. D. L. Turnbull; H. L. Usher; James Walker; John Walker; George E. Watson; H. M. D. Watson; J. T. Watson; George Watters; C. F. Whigham; John Wilson; and Allan R. Yule.

The following apologies for inability to be present were reported by the Secretary:—The Prime Minister, who expressed much interest in the Society, but was obliged to keep himself as free as possible from public engagements during the autumn recess; the President of the Board of Trade, who, though at one time he hoped to be present, ultimately found that his engagements prevented him; the Colonial Secretary, who was obliged to be in London, but expressed his best wishes for the success of the meeting; the Attorney-General, who was compelled to be in London for the opening of the Law Courts; the Secretary for Scotland, who was abroad; the Earl of Leven and Melville, Lord Keeper of the Privy Seal, who would not be in Scotland at the time; the Earl of Errol, Hereditary High Constable; Lord Balfour of Burleigh, late Secretary for Scotland, who expressed himself as very desirous of attending, but afterwards found that family arrangements prevented him; Lord Robertson, of the Supreme Court of Appeal, whose engagements stood in the way, but who tendered his congratulations on the fiftieth anniversary of the Society; the Duke of Montrose, Keeper of His Majesty's Signet; Sir Charles B. Logan, Deputy-Keeper of His Majesty's Signet, who was to be absent from Edinburgh; Sir Henry Campbell-Bannerman, whose engagements did not admit of his accepting the invitation; Mr. R. B. Haldane, K.C., who had also another binding engagement; the Lord Provost of Glasgow, who had an important engagement in that city; the Lord Provost of Aberdeen; Lieut.-General Sir Charles Tucker, K.C.B., and his aide-de-camp, who were absent from Edinburgh; Colonel Lord Playfair, who, though originally accepting, had been obliged to leave home; Colonel Trevor, Lieut.-Colonel Blackett, Colonel Duff, Colonel Broadwood, Colonel Kippesley, Sir James Gibson Craig, Baronet, Convener of the County of Midlothian, who, though at first accepting, found that family arrangements interfered with his presence; Sir Lewis M'Iver, Bart., M.P., who had been looking forward to the privilege of meeting the Society in its corporate capacity, but had received an urgent call to London; Sir Andrew Agnew, M.P.; Lord Kelvin, President of the Royal Society of Edinburgh, who was in England at the time; Sir Patrick Heron Watson, President of the Royal College of Surgeons; Sir Henry Littlejohn, Medical Officer for Public Health, on account of a family bereavement; Sir Kenneth Mackenzie, Bart., King's and Lord Treasurer's Remembrancer; Sir Stair Agnew, Registrar-General and Keeper of the Records, who had to be in London; Mr. Reginald M'Leod, C.B., Under-Secretary for Scotland, who at the last moment was obliged to go to London; Sir Henry Craik, K.C.B., who also, though intending to be present, was detained in London; Lord Moncrieff, Lord Kyllachy, Lord Stormonth Darling, Lord Low, Lord Pearson, the Moderator, Free Church of Scotland, the Vice-President of the Local Government Board for Scotland, the Dean of the Faculty of Advocates, the Sheriff of Lanarkshire, the Sheriff of the County of Ross, &c.; the Sheriff of the County of Berwick, &c.; the Sheriff of the County of Ayr; Mr. James M. Macandrew, C.A., an original member of the Society, who was deeply interested in the proceedings, and up to the last day or two had hoped to be present, but was advised by his doctor not to venture; Mr. Richard Wilson, C.A., whose state of health also prevented his attending; Mr. H. Sydney Merritt, C.A., of Valparaiso, who sent a cablegram conveying his best wishes; and many others.

Letters or telegrams of congratulation were also reported from the following societies of accountants unable to send representatives:—

The Montreal Association of Accountants, who adopted the following resolution at their Annual General Meeting: "Recognising the high position and prestige of the Society of Accountants in Edinburgh as the oldest incorporated society of accountants in existence, the Montreal Association, being the oldest association on this continent in point of organisation and incorporation, desire to tender their hearty congratulations to the Edinburgh Society on the occasion of the fiftieth anniversary of their incorporation by Royal Charter, expressing at the same time the sincere hope that they will enjoy in the future an even greater degree of prosperity than they have experienced in the past."

The Institute of Chartered Accountants in Ontario.

The Dominion Association of Chartered Accountants, who sent "congratulations upon this unique event, and best wishes for the Society's continued prosperity and usefulness."

The Institute of Chartered Accountants of Manitoba expressed "their good wishes for the future welfare of the Society of Accountants in Edinburgh."

The Incorporated Institute of Accountants, Victoria, "offered to the Edinburgh President, Council, and Members the most sincere and hearty congratulations of the Institute on the attainment of the fiftieth anniversary of their Society, and wished to the members of the Society long life and prosperity and the utmost success in the jubilee celebrations, and to the Society itself ' Perpetual Succession ' and increase in numbers."

The Sydney Institute of Public Accountants sent "'all good wishes for the Society's continued prosperity and usefulness."

The Tasmanian Institute of Accountants telegraphed: "The President, Council, and Members of the Tasmanian Institute of Accountants offer their hearty congratulations to the President, Council, and Members of the Society of Accountants in Edinburgh on this the occasion of the fiftieth anniversary of the incorporation of their Society."

The Queensland Institute of Accountants "wished to express the most cordial good wishes and congratulations."

The Institute of Accountants of South Australia wrote: "'Trusting your celebration will be a conspicuous success."

The Incorporated Institute of Accountants of New Zealand telegraphed: "Much regret Institute of Accountants of New Zealand cannot be represented at fiftieth anniversary of your Society. Please convey heartiest congratulations and good wishes for a successful gathering."

The Corporation of Accountants of Australia telegraphed: "Heartiest congratulations."

The Federal Institute of Accountants, Melbourne, wished the Society every success.

The Society of Accountants and Auditors of Victoria: By unanimous resolution the Council "tendered to the Society of Accountants in Edinburgh their hearty congratulations upon the attainment of its jubilee, together with sincere wishes for its continued prosperity and success in all its endeavours to further the interests of the profession of accountancy."

The New Zealand Accountants' and Auditors' Association telegraphed: "We, the New Zealand Accountants' and Auditors' Association (Regd.), tender our warmest congratulations on the occasion of your Institution attaining its jubilee. We wish you a prosperous future. We hope that the present accountancy gathering in Edinburgh, under your auspices, will be the means of cementing the good fellowship existent amongst members of the profession. We congratulate Scotland upon having first established professional accountancy upon its present basis, and upon such excellent world-wide results, being parallel to the development of Operative Masonry. We in Maoriland hope to vie in friendly emulation with our antipodean contemporaries, and tender our greetings in the national phrase of our land, 'Kia ora! kia ora!' (Good luck!)"

The Institute of Accountants in Natal: President wrote conveying "to the President, Council, and Members of the Society of Accountants in Edinburgh the congratulations of his Council, Members, and himself on the auspicious occasion."

The American Association of Public Accountants.

The Federation of Societies of Public Accountants in the United States of America.

The New York State Society of Certified Public Accountants.

The Illinois Association of Public Accountants sent cordial greetings, "and wish you a continuation in the future of the success that has marked the past."

The Pennsylvania Institute of Certified Public Accountants sent " hearty congratulations upon this occasion, and our best wishes for the continued and enlarged usefulness of the Society of Accountants."

The California Society of Certified Public Accountants.

The Incorporated Michigan Association of Public Accountants tendered "congratulations and assurances of our right good-will."

The Missouri Society of Public Accountants.

The Maryland Association of Certified Public Accountants extended their most sincere congratulations and best wishes for the future.

The Accademia dei Ragionieri, Bologna, sent their best wishes and congratulations, and at same time forwarded two medals of the Academy, as testifying their homage to the Society.

The Collegio dei Ragionieri, Florence, attested their homage.

The Collegio dei Ragionieri di Mantova presented the assurance of their high esteem.

The Associazione Ligure dei Ragionieri, Genoa, sent their congratulations and good wishes.

The Collegio dei Ragionieri della Provincia di Padova pronounced a vote of applause in favour of the Society, and sent their sincerest wishes for the continuance of its success and prosperity.

The Collegio dei Ragionieri della Provincia di Napoli wrote "applauding your noble initiative, we wish a great prosperity to your Society, and present you our respects."

The Collegio dei Ragionieri di Milano. The President of the College wrote: " I hope you will accept my best wishes and those of my colleagues for the prosperity of your esteemed Society, which has all our sympathy and sincere admiration."

The Société Académique de Comptabilité, Section de Marseilles, "addressed all their sympathies to the Society."

The Chambre Syndicale des Experts Comptables, Brussels, presented their sincere salutations.

The Nederlandsche Academie van Accountants wished to express sincere good wishes.

The Svenska Revisorsamfundet, Stockholm, telegraphed: "President, Council, Members, Society of Accountants and Auditors in Sweden, greet and cordially congratulate you on the attainment of your fiftieth anniversary in the grand development of the organisation of accountants and auditors. Your position is a proud one—we hail you with sincere affection."

El Instituto Tecnico de Contadores, Peru.

The Colegio de Contadores de la Republica Oriental del Uruguay sent cordial greetings.

The Colegio de Professores y Peritos Mercantiles de la Habana assured the Society of their highest consideration.

The following dinner was served:—

	HUÎTRES NATIVES
	TORTUE CLAIRE
Amontillado	CRÊME REINE, DAME BLANCHE
	TURBOT, SAUCE RICHE
Liebfraumilch 1893	JULIENNE DE FILETS DE SOLES À LA DIABLE
	TERRINES DE CAILLES À LA PATTI
	SELLE D'AGNEAU AUX PRIMEURS POMMES GOURMETS
Deutz & Geldermann's 1893	NÉIGE AU CLICQUOT
	FAISAN TRUFFÉES SALADE DE CŒURS DE LAITUES
	PÊCHES FRAMBOISÉES ANANAS GLACÉ DANS SON FRUIT
Liqueurs	CORBEILLE DE FRIANDISES
Château Margaux 1890	CANAPES WALTER SCOTT
	DESSERT
Sandeman's Port 1890	CAFÉ DOUBLE

Music was contributed by a band under the direction of Mr. H. Dambmann.

The President, in proposing "The King," said: My Lords and Gentlemen,—In no part of his Majesty's dominions will he find more loyal and devoted subjects than in his good and ancient City of Edinburgh. Its citizens have not forgotten when, as Prince of Wales, his Royal Highness sojourned among them as a student. Since then, through a busy life of keen observation, his Majesty has acquired a deep and intimate knowledge of human nature—a knowledge which he uses with unerring instinct. It is perhaps by this, more than by his royal birth and exalted station, that his Majesty attracts that strong and healthy allegiance which his subjects are privileged to render him. My Lords and Gentlemen, I have the distinguished honour to ask you to join with me in wishing long life, good health, and, above all, continued peace to our Sovereign, his Gracious Majesty—"The King."

The toast was loyally pledged.

The President, in proposing "The Queen, the Prince and Princess of Wales, and the other Members of the Royal Family," said: My Lords and Gentlemen,—Many of you will remember a day—nearly forty-two years ago—when a fair young Princess left her Fatherland and crossed that sea which centuries ago had been dominated by her ancestors—those hardy Norsemen—to wed our own Prince of Wales. You will also recollect how she received from the British people a warm and enthusiastic welcome, with every good wish for long life to the Prince and his winsome bride. These good wishes of 1863 have, by the grace of God, been verified, and we now find the daughter of the venerable Danish Sovereign sharing the throne with our King as his Queen and Consort. Undoubtedly she now forms one of the brightest jewels in the crown of his Majesty. The Prince of Wales, with his charming Consort, as well as the other Members of the Royal Family, vie with each other in showing their interest in the home-life of the people, especially where there is sickness and suffering. In this they set a noble example. Our thoughts and sympathies to-night, however, lie with our soldier-Duke, still an invalid in this very building. We cannot sufficiently thank God for sparing the life of the illustrious patient—for to have escaped with his life in such an appalling accident appears nothing short of a miracle. You will all be glad to unite with me in expressing our most respectful sympathy with the Duke and Duchess, coupled with the sincere wish that his Royal Highness will soon be himself again and able to resume his important duties. My Lords and Gentlemen, I have the honour to give you the toast of "Her Majesty Queen Alexandra, The Prince and Princess of Wales, The Duke and Duchess of Connaught, and the other Members of the Royal Family."

Sir Ludovic J. Grant, Bart., gave the toast of "The Imperial Forces."
He said: Mr. Chairman, My Lords, and Gentlemen,—The fifty years
which have elapsed since the incorporation of the Society of Accountants
have been productive of few developments more remarkable than that
which is indicated by the present title of the toast which it is my
privilege to propose. In 1854, the year of the Society's foundation,
Great Britain was at war—with Russia as it happened—and the fighting
forces at the country's disposal consisted of the navy and the army of
the British Isles; in 1904, the year of the Society's jubilee, the country,
I am thankful to say, finds itself at peace, at the present moment at
any rate. But the forces which are ready to answer our country's call,
if fighting has to be done, include now the Volunteers as well as the
navy and army, and they are drawn not only from the British Isles,
but from the entire circuit of the British Empire. I need not tell you
that the toast, under its new and comprehensive title, is to the full as
worthy to be pledged with enthusiasm as it was in the days of old.
The Imperial forces have given abundant proofs—some of them too
recent to need recapitulation—that in dash and determination, in
stamina and patient endurance, and in all soldierly qualities, they are
the equals of the old warriors of ages which are gone. Moreover, I
would remind you, in filling your glasses to the Imperial Forces, that
you are pledging not only the brave and gallant men, but you are
pledging the very unity of the Empire itself.

I wish that I might stop here, but that may not be. It is impossible
for me to sit down without reminding you that the recent nocturnal
vagaries of imperial forces other than our own have imparted a very
special and a very solemn significance to the toast of the Imperial
Forces of the British Crown. Far be it from me to attach undue importance to the circumstances under which this toast is being pledged
to-night, or to assign a gravity to events which they possibly may not
possess. We are still groping in the dark. It is conceivable that the
crisis may be averted by methods not involving war and completely
compatible with the national dignity and honour; and that, I need
hardly say, is a consummation devoutly to be wished. But we must
not disguise from ourselves that the recourse to the arbitrament of
arms may conceivably be the only way; and what I would say is this,
that if the worst must come to the worst, I am sure that we can count
with implicit confidence upon the Imperial Forces to meet every
emergency as it arises, and to grapple with every circumstance, whether
by land or sea, in a manner worthy of the finest traditions of British
warfare. It is in the spirit of confidence that I invite you to drink

this toast, which I have the honour to couple with the name of a gallant officer who has won distinction on many fields, Colonel Hope.

Colonel Hope, C.B., in reply, said: Allow me, in the first place, to congratulate the previous speaker on the earnest manner in which he has addressed us upon a subject which at the present time we feel very deeply. The duty of responding to the toast of his Majesty's Forces is at the present moment fraught with difficulties. Sir Ludovic Grant has alluded to the painful incident of our fellow-countrymen who, whilst employed peacefully fishing, were fired upon, some of them being killed, and some of them left to drown. This would appear to be the culminating point of the indignities with which our merchant fleet has been treated lately. I am sure you will all regret that we have not here a representative of the navy—of which we are so proud—to tell us, what we hardly need to be told, that the navy is prepared and ready to do whatever it may be called upon to do. These are anxious moments, and hasty actions or hasty words may bring on a general conflagration. Still, we must remember that our country, the empire to which we belong, has practically been insulted; and we must, if we are to remain the leading nation, insist upon a full and ample apology,—though it is hard to imagine what apology can be sufficient to meet the case of the poor wives and children who have been made widows and orphans by this action.

Well, our army is now passing through a state of transition, and it is difficult to touch on any theme concerning it which is not a subject of anxious consideration by the powers that be. We only know that we are soldiers, and we do our best to carry out the orders that we receive, leaving it to the authorities to decide whatever system they think will get us into the state of efficiency that is required by modern conditions. Whatever may be said of the system, I think you need only turn and look at the recent campaign in Thibet, where the Imperial Forces, British and native, under the command of a fellow-countryman of ours—Macdonald—have shown a high state of organisation and splendid powers of endurance in a terrible climate. We have only to look at that campaign to realise that, after all, the British army, to which we have the honour to belong, is not quite in such a hopeless state as many people seem to think. Many here have had something to do with the Volunteers, or have relatives in the auxiliary forces. We know that the Volunteers have a difficulty in finding time for any considerable amount of training; but the powers have hit upon a method whereby the services of those who are so situated, as well as the services of men who have more time for training, can be utilised.

Mr. Robert Burnett sang with fine effect "The March of the Cameron Men."

In proposing the toast of the evening, "The Society of Accountants in Edinburgh," the Lord Advocate (Mr. Charles Scott Dickson, M.P.) said: I have the honour to propose for your acceptance the toast of "The Society of Accountants in Edinburgh." Fifty years ago the Society obtained its incorporating charter, and to-night this large and impressive gathering has assembled to celebrate its jubilee. It is impossible, on an occasion like the present, not to look back, and, to some extent, to compare the times that have passed with those in which we are now living. There are probably few professions which can show a greater contrast between the present and the past during the time we have to deal with than the profession of the accountants. So far as I can see, in Scotland at any rate, the profession of accountants began to be recognised in the seventeenth century. I find, in a volume published in Edinburgh by a citizen of this famous city, Robert Colinson, near the close of the seventeenth century, under the sonorous title of "Idea Rationaria, or the Perfect Accomptant"—addressed to "The Merchants in Edinburgh, and all other lovers of this profitable science"—that apparently at that time the business of the accountant was only beginning to be known in Scotland. And the reason I so put it is that, prefaced to the volume, were two laudatory poems—poetry I do not think nowadays we associate much with accounting, but it was different in that time—two laudatory poems by a gentleman, I presume, of influence and position, commending the art and science of accounting to those who were engaged in mercantile pursuits; and, if you will pardon me, I would like to quote a few lines from the first of these poems :—

> "This was the famed and quick invention,
> Which made Venice, Genoa, and Florence rich,
> The then Low Countries (in all senses such),
> By this art now speak High and mighty Dutch.
> Which noble art, when it augments our store,
> This shall admire, and the next age adore."

All of you who are interested in the subject, and choose to study the volume, will find that the rest of the poem is as quaint as the passage I have quoted. So began towards the close of the seventeenth century a subject which had attractions for the Scottish mind of such a kind that within forty years another citizen of Edinburgh, writing on the science of accounting, and professing to have his book recommended by the most famous accountants in North Britain, dedicated his volume to the Right Honourable the Lord Provost and his brethren in council, and recorded apologetically that he wrote upon such a subject, as to which he had been preceded by what he called a great crowd of authors. Practically, I am afraid, progress was not rapid. It may be that we lawyers were more attentive to our interests then than we are now, because I find that in the beginning of the eighteenth century remits in actions of accounting by the Court of Session were made not to accountants, but to advocates or other persons of integrity and position in the city. I am sorry to say—well, I am not sorry; it is the fact—that before the century was past, what has now become the recognised practice in such matters was adopted by the court, and remits were made, as they ought to be, to the accountants. In the last century, as the complexity of business and trade accounts increased, as the intricacy of modern finance grew more intricate, and especially owing to the great development of joint-stock companies, the demands made upon the skill and experience of the professional accountants increased to such an extent that their numbers were augmented and their position was advanced much beyond what it had been; and before the middle of the century Parliament had enacted that auditors of joint-stock companies should employ such accountants as they required to enable them to deal with the accounts of the companies with which they were concerned. Down to that time no standard of proficiency was required for the accountant. There was no settled course of training, and no curriculum. Any one who pleased was entitled to term himself an accountant and to begin business. It was in these circumstances, in this city of Edinburgh, that the accountants—ever foremost, as those who have been privileged to meet them regard them as entitled to consider themselves—resolved to apply for a Charter of Incorporation. Accordingly they did so apply in 1853, and they obtained their Charter, just fifty years ago to a day, on the 23rd of October 1854. Since then the designation of Chartered Accountant has become well recognised and honoured all over the country.

The example of the Edinburgh accountants was quickly followed in Glasgow,—and Glasgow, I am sorry to find, was a year behind Edinburgh,—in Aberdeen, in England, and all over the country, and, if the list of apologies read by the Secretary is to be trusted, as I am sure it may, in the Colonies, and wherever civilisation is known. The science of professional accounting is now practised by many, but among them all, this, the pioneer Society of Accountants in Edinburgh, is, I venture to say, still holding its own. Much has been done by the accountants during the last fifty years. No longer is there any doubt as to the position of the Chartered Accountant. He who aspires to enter that profession must undergo a long course of office training. He must be a university man. He must be familiar not only with business accounts and with the methods of trade and commerce, but he must know not a little law; and, if he desires to rise to the higher places in his profession, he must be skilled in actuarial science and in economics. The result is that all of us who are favoured to meet them frequently,—and happily or unhappily we lawyers have that fortune often,—recognise them always to be men of capacity and skill, men of resource and suggestiveness, men of sterling integrity, men fitted to be what they are—honoured members of a learned profession.

Gentlemen, the Chartered Accountants of Scotland have done much. They have made an honoured designation for themselves. They have created indeed a learned profession and a literature of their own. There is still something to be done. For example, there is the definition of terms as to what is the precise line to be drawn between capital and income, what assets are included and excluded, and above all what is fixed and floating capital. Oh, the terrors of these conundrums, not only for the Chartered Accountants, but for my learned friend on my right (the Lord Justice-Clerk), and those who sit in council with him. If our Chartered Accountants could only solve these problems then indeed they would be the most learned profession, I venture to think, we know. But they have, as I have said, done much. They have earned for their profession a status and a position which it never enjoyed before.

If I have said but little directly on the subject of the toast which I am now to ask you to drink—"The Society of Accountants in Edinburgh,"—why need I say much? I have been present at many gatherings; I think few of us have been present at a more representative gathering than that at which we now are. Mr. President, on your right you are supported by him who represents the municipalities of the country (Lord Provost Sir Robert Cranston); on your left by one who has worthily filled the highest office in the State (Lord Rosebery); you have with you as your honoured and honouring guests the dignitaries of our Churches. Learning and Art are represented by the Principal of our University and by the President of our Academy. You have also represented our captains of industry, our merchant princes, those who, like myself, as a member of the Bar, are brought more closely perhaps into contact with the members of your society than any other class in the community, and who reciprocate always the kindness, courtesy, dexterity, and ability with which in the most trying cases their efforts are supported by the Chartered Accountants. You have raised not only your special branch of your profession, but all branches of your profession, to a position which makes it worthy to take its place amongst the best and most learned and better equipped of our professions in the land.

Gentlemen, in giving you the toast of "The Society of Accountants in Edinburgh," I desire to couple with it the name of your President. I am sure of this, speaking as I do in so distinguished a company as this, representative of the arts and sciences, industries and commerce, and all the varying relations of life which make up our complex modern society—speaking in the presence of very many representatives of other associations of your profession, I use no words of idle compliment or of fulsome flattery when I say that in this his native city, as a man of skill and of capacity, a man worthy to occupy the President's Chair of your Association in this your Jubilee year, no more fitting representative could have been found than our friend Fred Carter. I give you "The Society of Accountants in Edinburgh," coupled with the name of our Chairman, the President.

The President, in reply, said : My Lord Advocate, my Lords, and Gentlemen,—It is with considerable diffidence that I rise to respond on behalf of the Society over which I have the honour to preside, to the toast which my right honourable and learned friend has so ably and with so much humour proposed. As to the inception of the Edinburgh Society, the first step was taken on 17th January 1853 by Mr. Alexander Weir Robertson, the well-known and worthy father of our eminent colleague, Mr. Robertson-Durham. Within a fortnight sixty-five accountants formed a society, which they named the "Institute of Accountants in Edinburgh," under the presidency of Mr. James Brown, the distinguished grandfather of two of our colleagues here to-night. One year later, at the first annual meeting of the Institute, the President and Council reported that "in their opinion the time had now arrived when application should be made for incorporation by Royal Charter, and this being the unanimous view of the meeting, the President and Council were empowered to take preliminary steps." Following thereon, a petition, signed by sixty-one members of the Institute, was presented to her late Majesty, and on 23rd October 1854—exactly fifty years ago —a Royal Charter incorporating the Institute under the name of "The Society of Accountants in Edinburgh," was given by her Majesty's Court at St. James's, signed by Lord Palmerston by her Majesty's Command, written to the Seal, registered 11th December 1854, and sealed at Edinburgh on the same date.

Among the powers granted in the Charter was one for regulating and conducting the examination of entrants, as well as the course of education to be pursued. These powers were immediately put in force, and for fifty years the training of our young accountants has been made a special study, with the satisfactory result that entrants have now attained a high standard of efficiency. In illustration of that, I may relate a rather amusing incident. When examining some years ago a very youthful aspirant to professional fame, I asked him the usual preliminary question, "Define the terms, debtor and creditor?" Being of a methodical and mathematical turn of mind, he considered the question carefully before answering, and then wrote down, "A debtor is some one who owes something to somebody"—an eminently satisfactory answer. He then tackled the other term, and knowing that one side of a ledger account was termed the "debtor," whilst the other side was called the "creditor," he naturally came to the conclusion that the one was exactly the converse of the other, so he proceeded to reverse his former answer, with the following amusing result: "A creditor is no one who owes nothing to nobody." But to resume: later, in 1892, the Glasgow, Aberdeen, and Edinburgh Societies entered into a joint agreement, constituting a General Examining Board to deal with candidates from all three Societies. This enabled a higher and more equal standard to be maintained, and the arrangement has worked out admirably. During the past fifty years the Society has often been enabled to do useful public service in considering, discussing, and frequently advising the law officers of the Crown and others upon commercial questions requiring new legislation, and several necessary measures embodying many of the Society's suggestions subsequently found their way through Parliament, and have been placed upon the Statute-Book.

Among some of the beneficial products for which the Charter is responsible are a well-managed endowment and annuity fund for members and their widows, an energetic students' society, a professional Magazine published monthly, a hall and well-stocked library, a strong and efficient company in the Queen's Rifle Volunteer Brigade (Royal Scots), of which my right honourable and gallant friend on my right (Sir Robert Cranston) is the clever commandant; and lastly, and what perhaps is considered the most important, a popular golf club. During the half century, under the able guidance of a dozen of our leading members who have successively filled the Chair, the Society has grown and prospered, and now numbers some 415 members. Of the sixty-one original members who petitioned for the Charter, alas! only four survive. Three of these, Mr. Thomas Goldie Dickson, Mr. James Howden, and Mr. Alexander Thomas

Niven, are with us here to-night as honoured guests. The remaining one, Mr. James Maclean Macandrew, the *doyen* of the Society (and also my own old and kind master), is, I regret to say, prevented by temporary indisposition from being with us. Perhaps I may here be permitted to offer all four of them, in your name, our most hearty congratulations, and our earnest and sincere wish that they may yet be spared for many years to look back with pleasure and satisfaction on well-spent and useful lives, as well as upon the thriving Corporation of which they were the pioneers.

Our fifty years' experience has, I think, definitively proved that the profession of accounting forms a link, a somewhat important link, in the chain of our judicial and commercial systems; and so long as we accountants retain the confidence of the general public and that of his Majesty's Judges, we shall feel that our Charter of 1854 has not only attained the object of the petitioners, but has far exceeded their most sanguine expectations. I cannot conclude without mentioning that our able and efficient Secretary will shortly publish an interesting work entitled "History of Accounting and Accountants," which will deal with the subject from its earliest stages to the present day, a work which will fittingly mark the celebration of our jubilee.

My Lord Advocate, I scarcely know how to thank your Lordship for the complimentary manner in which you introduced the toast, and for the many kind things you said of our Society and of myself. My Lords and Gentlemen, pray accept our sincere thanks for the hearty way in which you have responded, and for the honour you have done us here to-night.

Lord Rosebery, in proposing the toast of "The City of Edinburgh," said: Mr. Chairman, my Lords, and Gentlemen,—I besought of the Secretary that, as one who lives in the country, and who must therefore leave soon, and one who is therefore not yet a citizen of Edinburgh, though the soaring ambition of that city may some day include me in its limits, I might be allowed to leave without saying anything to-night. And, indeed, gentlemen, I felt some alarm at attending this dinner at all. To dine with the Chartered Accountants represented to me rather an austere duty than a genial festivity. I looked up—being very ignorant of the subject —in Mr. Lisle's admirable "Encyclopædia of Accounting" which adorns my library, for a definition of what an accountant was, and I saw what I cannot help considering a somewhat bare and jejune description of an accountant as "one who is skilled in accounts." I think that a barren description—too comprehensive, although I confess it would exclude myself—but infinitely too comprehensive in itself, for it would certainly comprehend a great number of the persons who are now doing penal servitude in various parts of his Majesty's dominions. My own personal definition of an accountant, or rather a Chartered Accountant—there is no affinity whatever between a Chartered Accountant and a chartered libertine —would be that he is a sort of financial conscience. And to dine with 300 financial consciences did strike me as very appalling, until I was informed that it was only half and half—that there was a liberal dilution, and that of the 300 who dined, only 150 would be Chartered Accountants. Mr. Chairman, I listened with the greatest admiration to the speech of the Lord Advocate, but I think I can supply him with an earlier accountant, although, naturally, not a chartered one, than any he suggested. I believe the earliest accountant in Edinburgh was one Andrew Halyburton, who lived in the fifteenth century, and whose accounts are or should be on view at the General Register House in this city. I supply that piece of archæology for the subsequent rumination of the Society at some future meeting.

Now, sir, I come to the subject of my toast, which I am only too anxious to advance, and I confess that I am somewhat distressed to find any connection between the subject of accountants and the subject of the city of Edinburgh. There was a time—before the concession of the Charter to the Society of Accountants—when it would have been a matter of some delicacy to speak of accountants to the city of Edinburgh, because, as you read in "Don Quixote," you must not speak of the halter in the house of the hanged, and our good and great city did undergo some stress of financial embarrassment. That, however, is now altogether removed. I do not know who is the accountant employed by the city of Edinburgh, and I should be loath to-night to inquire, but I am sure that all the money the city spends is for the best. I think that sometimes its conceptions are on a very great scale. I am not sure that it does not sometimes build for posterity, oblivious of the fact that posterity will never build for it. At any rate I am certain of this, that there is nothing in the accounts of the capital of Scotland which any Chartered Accountant would not readily pass. I wish that that sentiment were received with more enthusiasm. As I have said, I am not a ratepayer of the city of Edinburgh, though I don't know how soon I may be one. But at any rate, sure I am of this, that even if the accountants will not cheer the sentiment to which I invite their enthusiasm, yet at any rate they will say this, that there are no items in the more magnificent projects of the city which might make a Chartered Accountant for a moment turn blue—a colour to which I suspect a Chartered Accountant's visage very readily turns—and that that expenditure is concerned with the highest and the best interests of the city of Edinburgh itself. Again the enthusiasm is not what I should wish. But now, at any rate, I will evoke your enthusiasm by giving the toast of "The City of Edinburgh," coupled, and I have never coupled it with more pleasure, with the health of our genial and excellent Lord Provost.

Lord Provost Sir Robert Cranston, in reply, said: Mr. Chairman, —It is my first duty on behalf of my colleagues and myself to tender to you our warmest thanks for your kind invitation here and also for your hospitality. I ventured to hope that my Lord Rosebery, when speaking of the city of Edinburgh, would have been more kind than he has been. His lordship gave forth certain statements which he had expected would have been received with more enthusiasm, and it would appear that his lordship judged from that that the present Lord Provost, Magistrates, and Town Council of the city of Edinburgh were not quite in accordance with his lordship's ideas in regard to the spending of money. I regret to learn that from his lordship, because I was under the impression that Lord Rosebery was a citizen of Edinburgh. (Lord Rosebery: "Not a ratepayer.") Well, my lord, I am sorry you are not a ratepayer, and if I may take the liberty of saying so, your lordship may be a ratepayer in another city where you pay a great deal more and get less benefit than you would derive from the city of Edinburgh. But whether his lordship is a ratepayer of the city of Edinburgh or not, is not a matter of consequence on the present occasion, for his lordship is a citizen of the world. He is one whose name is perhaps dearer to Edinburgh than to any other part of Scotland, but he is well known and admired over the whole world. I wish that his lordship would become a citizen and ratepayer of the city of Edinburgh. Lord Rosebery has said that he found it difficult to trace a connection between accounting and the subject of his toast, but if his lordship would attend a ward meeting in the city he would learn a good deal that he had not previously known. For the ordinary ratepayer is an excellent accountant, and knows far more about the city's affairs than any accountant in the city of Edinburgh. If you were to attend, say, a meeting of the St. Andrew's Ward electors, you would find some one talking in a fashion that might suggest that he knew more about the finances of the city than my friend M'Crae, not to speak of myself or Treasurer Brown. These men think they have a thorough knowledge of what they talk about; but I am afraid that the critics are, in many instances, men who seldom take any interest in the city's affairs except at Ward meetings. It is to be hoped that some of these critics will enter the Town Council.

Lord Rosebery has made allusion to a book in his library which he had consulted for a definition of the word "accountant." I can tell Lord Rosebery that the man who wrote that book is the accountant to the city of Edinburgh. I am sure that no one in this room will deny the fact that the fifty years of the existence of your Society has also been a period of great improvement in the city of Edinburgh. Mr. Howden, Mr. Dickson, and Mr. Niven—and Mr. Macandrew, who is not present—have seen how wonderful the change has been. I do not think that in carrying out these improvements the Town Council have gone very far wrong. We are trying to make the city more beautiful, and I know that no one is prouder of the city of Edinburgh than Lord Rosebery is. We have been doing all we possibly can, and if our efforts have not come up to his lordship's standard, it has been for want of ability and not for want of desire upon our part. Our desire has only one end—the watching of the welfare of the city. I can speak for myself, and I know I speak also for every man in the Town Council, when I say that while we may differ on some things, we are all at one in seeking to maintain the honour of the city of which we are all so proud. If there are evils still to be removed—and I admit that there are many—I think, looking back on the past fifty years, we have no reason to be ashamed of what we have done for the city. To-day, in the matter of taxation, we are lower than in other cities, and our citizens obtain greater benefit than ever they did before. Sir Robert concluded by saying that two years of his term of office as Lord Provost had still to run, and that he hoped to be able to continue to uphold and keep unsullied in every respect the city's great historic name.

Another song was here given by Mr. Burnett.

Mr. George A. Touch, London, in proposing the toast of "Other Accountant Societies," said : Mr. Chairman, my Lords, and Gentlemen,— We are a characteristically modest people, we Scots, but I think we may well be proud of the way in which the profession of Chartered Accountancy, which was inaugurated in this city fifty years ago, has grown and increased in importance, as was evidenced by the wonderful list of messages from kindred societies read to us to-night by Mr. Richard Brown. From the serene height of a great achievement we can review the great armies of organised accountants, chartered and incorporated, which have sprung into existence since that time fifty years ago, all animated by a single desire to maintain a high standard of professional efficiency and integrity, all filled, I believe, with a filial regard for the old Edinburgh Society, all inspired by a feeling of awe and reverence for every individual member of that Society as representing the most venerable caste in the hierarchy of accountancy. To all of us, especially to the youngest members, it gives the comfortable feeling of having been the pioneers of a great modern profession. The founders of this Society were far-seeing men, but I doubt whether any of them, even my old friend and master, Mr. A. T. Niven, whom I rejoice to see here to-night, I doubt whether even he foresaw that, within little more than a generation from the time when those sixty-one gentlemen founded the first Society of Chartered Accountants, the Chartered Accountants in the United Kingdom would be numbered in their thousands, and that numberless societies of accountants would have sprung into existence in every quarter of the globe. The great English Institute alone has now upwards of three thousand members, of whom only sixteen, I believe,—and these the hardiest of them,—have invaded Scotland. I hesitate to say how many Scottish Chartered Accountants have invaded England. The great majority of the English Chartered Accountants still remain in England, browsing on the fat pastures of England, which I have always regarded as the natural hunting-ground of the industrious Scot. We do not, however, grudge their presence; it is a tribute to the civilising influences of the North. That Institution is well represented to-night by Mr. Harmood-Banner, its distinguished President, by Mr. Pixley, its ex-President, and the author of the most popular book in the accountant's library, "Pixley on Chartered Accountants' Charges," and by my friend, Mr. James, another ex-President, and many other well-known members.

When I first went to London the English Institute was only three years old, though it followed other societies which had been in existence in London, Liverpool, and Manchester, since the seventies. Since that time its members have increased out of all proportion to the increase in the population, so that it is a simple calculation to discover how long it will take at the present rate of progress until every man in England and Wales is a member of the Institute of Chartered Accountants in England and Wales. These thousands of Chartered Accountants, each one equally ready to reorganise the affairs of an empire, or to perform an operation for financial appendicitis on a greengrocer, came into their professional being in response to the requirements of modern business. A nation develops the professions which it needs, just as it is sometimes threatened with the rulers it deserves. Upon this principle we may assume that Chartered Accountants appeared in Edinburgh first of all in obedience to a natural law, because it was in Edinburgh that the greatest need for independent audits existed. This scientific explanation of Edinburgh's priority ought to be soothing to Glasgow; but Glasgow was a good second, and her membership now is greater than ours. I am glad to say that the Glasgow Society is represented here to-night by their President, Mr. Thomas Jackson. Glasgow men are prominent in London. Last year's President of our little Association of Scottish Chartered Accountants in London was a Glasgow man, Mr. John Annan. Mr. Annan is a species of professional bigamist, inasmuch as he allied himself to the English Institute while still united to the Glasgow Society. Our present President is another Glasgow man, Mr. Andrew Williamson, who up to now has led a blameless life. We must not forget to mention our brethren in Aberdeen, who are represented here to-night by Mr. James Milne, their President, or the Institute in Ireland. Nor should I omit to refer, in speaking to this toast, to the Society of Accountants and Auditors, represented here by Mr. W. G. Rayner, which is surely earning for itself a worthy place in the profession.

In the British Colonies this profession of Chartered Accountants has been making rapid headway. There are institutes in nearly every state in the Dominion of Canada; there are institutes or societies in every state of the Commonwealth of Australia; there is one in New Zealand; and there are several in South Africa. There are many on the Continent of Europe; but I think it is in the United States of America that the greatest development of the profession is going to take place in the immediate future. Already the University of New York has established a degree in accountancy. I wonder when the venerable University of Edinburgh will grant a degree in accountancy or in finance or commerce. Here, surely, is an opportunity for Glasgow to get ahead of Edinburgh. If the authorities of Glasgow University desire to know who are most worthy of that new degree, I may tell them that they will find no more deserving recipients than the survivors of the original founders of this Society in Edinburgh and of the Glasgow Society. Gentlemen, it would take up too much time to mention in detail the numberless societies of accountants to which our good wishes go out to-night. I believe there are something like one hundred of them; and if I mentioned all of them some enthusiast might possibly think it his duty to drink their health individually, as well as collectively. I want not only to drink to their prosperity, but I should like to see a federation of the accountants' societies of the world, or at least of all those societies which exist in lands where the Scottish language or its English or American variants are spoken. We already have an affiliation of the Scottish societies. I would like England, Scotland, and Ireland to affiliate; and when that takes place I hope that one of the first things they will turn their attention to will be the regularising of the use of this word " accountant," which Lord

Rosebery referred to as being used by many gentlemen now undergoing penal servitude in his Majesty's prisons.

I will not take up your time further, though I have barely touched the fringe of the subject. I give you, my lords and gentlemen, the toast of "Other Accountant Societies," coupled with the name of the President of the greatest of them all, Mr. Harmood-Banner of the Institute of Chartered Accountants in England and Wales.

Mr. Harmood-Banner, in replying, said: Mr. Touch, Mr. President, my Lords, and Gentlemen,— It is my privilege, first, to thank you on behalf of our own society and the other societies for the invitation which you have accorded to us to be present to-night at your magnificent banquet. I feel a personal pride in being present, in that I have just left a large Congress of Chartered Accountants who met in Liverpool at the autumnal gathering, at which, to quote Lord Rosebery's expression, there were 400 financial consciences, to discuss matters affecting our profession, and I come fresh from the enthusiasm of these meetings, at which the desire to improve the profession was so conspicuous. Our Institute has a membership of 3200 out of a total, I think, of 4300 Chartered Accountants, and therefore, though ours is much younger than yours, on the ripe and fat plains of England we have increased in twenty-four years to a number largely in excess of what barren Scotland has apparently given to the Chartered Accountants' profession; and if we consider the position in connection with the other societies for which I respond, we number pretty nearly half of the whole. I was very glad that the Secretary named the other societies who responded with their kind wishes in connection with this interesting occasion, but he omitted one which ought at the present time to be very conspicuous amongst us, and that was the Japanese. I was interested to see the other day in an account of the Yokohama Specie Bank a certificate, full and complete, signed by two names which I cannot venture to give you. The Japanese understand and appreciate the profession, and it is perhaps to the organisation which they have adopted not only in accounts but in every system of their Government that may be owing the magnificent victories which they are now attaining. Now our societies and the other societies are very grateful to the Edinburgh Society for the fact that they have kept in high honour during fifty years the profession to which they belonged. In the olden times in England the accountant was deemed to be a man who failed in every other profession,—the tradesman who had failed, the solicitor who had lost his practice, or any one else who had been unsuccessful,—and though there were always men who stood high, it was not the great profession that we would have expected it to be. But in Scotland we know that, from the very first, among the members of the bar, the writers to the signet, the bankers, and the commercial element of the country, the Chartered Accountant was respected, and attained a very high position, and therefore we feel it a great privilege that we were entitled to come into that heritage and add that name to our society in England. In America they call themselves Certified Accountants, and they wished that they had the name of Chartered Accountants, because when you add "Chartered," and numbers increase, you go with sledge-hammer force to bring about any results you may wish to attain, and to raise your profession.

Now there was a reference made to our harmonious working together, and to the Scottish societies joining with the English Society in the work in which they wished to excel. Well, there is rather a difficulty about this. We have watched Scotsmen, and we have been bound to see that a united profession does not always mean a great success. It sometimes leaves one body with all the cash and no responsibility, and another body with all the responsibility and none of the cash; and therefore, while we have been considering this junction together, the Irish Society, the Scottish Society, or the English Society have not been able to discover a way in which they could bring about a fusion that would be acceptable to all. The question of pounds, shillings, and pence is not predominant in Scotland, but it has an influence that affects us in England. There is one way in which something might be done, and that is in connection with our examinations and educational facilities. Our institutes and societies are very much like universities. We coach and educate our students, examine them, and give them the degree of Chartered Accountants, and it does seem rather absurd that if an Englishman wants to go up to Scotland he must go through an English university, and a Scotsman who comes to London must go back to Scotland to get his degree, or, as we have sometimes suggested, must found a university of his own in London. I think that somehow we ought to arrange that an Englishman in Scotland should get his degree there, and a Scotsman in London ought to be able, through the Institute, to get his there. That, however, is a dry subject and rather deep; but as it was mentioned I felt bound to say that there are one or two ways in which we might manage that union, which would be effective in giving us better organisation and better recognition. But the great way, and the way in which we shall gain most recognition, is by upholding in our profession a very high degree of professional integrity and honour. Celt and Saxon, we shall all strive to serve the spirit and purpose of our profession, and fight not for ourselves only, but for the growth, honour, and dignity of all interested amongst us. I thank you exceedingly for the way you have received this toast.

Mr. James Haldane, in giving "The College of Justice," said: At the top of the College of Justice are the Senators, and I may explain for the benefit of our friends from England that that is another name for the Judges of the Court of Session, the Supreme Court in Scotland. Then after the Judges come the Faculty of Advocates, presided over by the Dean of the Faculty, who is elected by the suffrages of his fellows, and who at present is Mr. Asher, a man of the highest talent and integrity in the profession. We have then Writers to the Signet, and also the Solicitors before the Supreme Court. Together with this toast I propose the health of Lord Kinross, the Lord Justice-General and President of the Court of Session. I need not in his presence say anything about him, except that he is a man of the highest talent and ability, a man of great legal knowledge, and both in public and private he is well known as a man of the greatest urbanity, and possessed of the kindest of hearts.

Lord Kinross, in replying, said: Mr. Chairman, my Lords, and Gentlemen,—I thank you very warmly for the extremely kind manner in which this toast has been proposed and received. As Mr. Haldane has reminded us, the College of Justice is a comprehensive body, and therefore the toast I have to reply to is also a comprehensive one. At one time, while Scotland was a poor country, with very little trade and very little commerce, the Courts were largely occupied by the consideration of feudal questions relating to land and matters of that kind, but with very little that concerned trade and commerce. All that has long ago been changed, and now that Scotland has become a great mercantile country, having trade relations extending all over the world, the College of Justice in its different degrees has to deal with matters very largely concerning the trade and the mercantile interests of the country. It, of course, could not fail to be gratifying to the members of the College to know, under these circumstances, from such an important body as that which is assembled here, that the manner in which in their several degrees they perform their duties is appreciated so highly. I can say this, from long experience in different departments of the College, that I am sure every member of it who has had much experience, or indeed any, will always have a very appreciative and a very grateful recollection of the assistance which he has received in the performance of his duties from the accountants. We very often have questions of great complexity before us in the Court of Session, as to which differences of opinion may quite legitimately exist; but we always find that the opposing views are placed before us with an ability and a clearness by the accountants, who are now quite a cosmopolitan profession—are indeed placed before us in such a way that if there is any error made it is at all events not due to the enlightenment which we get from them, and I am sure that every one who has been concerned in the administration of justice, in whatever degree he may have been concerned, must very heartily share in the felicitations and the congratulations appropriate to this most interesting occasion—the Jubilee of this Society.

"The University of Edinburgh" was given by Sheriff Jameson, who, in the course of his remarks, said: I think that the Society of Chartered Accountants will be the first to acknowledge the debt of gratitude which they owe to the University of Edinburgh for the position which we have heard to-night that they have attained, and that the skill and knowledge by which they are distinguished is due very much, I am sure, to the teaching that they have received within the walls of the College. They are not unmindful of that, for it appears from the regulations of the Society that they encourage entrants to take university degrees by remitting such as do so a year of their apprenticeship. They compel them also to attend the classes of Scots Law and Conveyancing, and they also enjoin their apprentices to attend such other lectures on special subjects as the Society may approve and recommend; as, for instance, the classes of Political Economy and Commercial Law in the University of Edinburgh. Now I am quite sure that the distinction that Scottish accountants have all along held, and this Society has held, has been due in no small measure indeed to those wise regulations which have forced the apprentices of this Society to educate themselves in law and political science before becoming practising members of their profession. You do not expect me at this late hour of the evening, I am sure, to enter upon a history of the University of Edinburgh. For that history I refer you to the excellent volumes by the late Sir Alexander Grant; but I may say that, since the College of Edinburgh was founded in 1583—it became a university in 1708—it has, with very few backsets, had a splendid record of progress. Things have gone up and down, as is the case with every other institution in the world, and for thirty years there raged what might be called the thirty years' war between town and gown in Edinburgh. It was settled finally by the Universities Bill of 1857–58, drawn up by a great predecessor of the Lord Justice-General, the late Lord Justice-General Inglis. The numbers of this University certainly have been most remarkable. I think this may interest the Society of Accountants, as it deals with figures. The

College started with some 80 or 90 students. By the end of the seventeenth century there were about 600. In 1789 they rose to 1000; in 1825 to 2260, and then they fell away in 1868 to 1565. Then the turn came, and in the year of the tercentenary of the founding of the College, the 300th year of its existence, they had no fewer than 3340 students, of whom 1732 were students in medicine. I think this is a record that any university might be proud of, and when we look back we may think of those who directed the fortunes of the University and brought it to its present state of excellence. Among those who have done so in recent years, no one has excelled the gentleman whose name I have to couple with this toast, Sir William Turner, the present Principal.

Mr. Touch has reminded us that we in Scotland are very proud of the many excellent men we send to England to fill positions of importance there. The English, however, sometimes have a little bit of a return match, and that they certainly have in Sir William Turner, who came from England to Scotland, and who now fills with such acceptance the Chair of the leading Scottish University. Sir William Turner first came here in 1854 as senior demonstrator to the late Professor Goodsir. With what loyalty Goodsir was served by Sir William Turner in these days only those who are acquainted with the University can fully appreciate. It was with universal approbation that in 1867 he himself was appointed to the Chair. Since then he has shown himself not only a great teacher and a great scientific observer, but an admirable business man and an admirable organiser of the forces of the University; and accordingly it came to pass that when the Chair of the Principalship fell vacant on the retirement of Sir William Muir, every one turned to Sir William Turner as the proper man to take the exalted position. Since he was connected with the University he has filled almost every office of importance in it connected with his own faculty. He has been Dean of the Faculty of Medicine, President of the Royal College of Surgeons, a member of the General Medical Council, and last, but not least, a most enthusiastic and efficient officer of the University Company. He has filled every post to which he was called with an energy and ability which is the admiration of all who have watched his splendid career. I ask you to drink his health along with the toast of "The University of Edinburgh."

Sir William Turner, in his reply, said: The toast which has just been proposed by Sheriff Jameson is one that I would venture to say is worthy of a somewhat lengthened reply, but a few minutes ago I observed that the Lord Provost left the room, and I am apprehensive that he will shortly appear accompanied by several officials in dark-blue uniform, wearing heavy boots with square toes, and asking of you, What do you here at this hour? With this feeling of apprehension before me, then, you must allow me in a very few words to express to Sheriff Jameson and the company my cordial thanks for the good words that he has said of the University, and for the cordial way in which you have received those words. It is a great pleasure to me to find that the Society of Accountants does not limit itself to the multiplication table or to the framing of accurate balance-sheets, but that it has a great feeling of hospitality, and, moreover, that it has the most kindly feeling towards the University in which its members receive at least a part of their training. We are delighted to receive them as pupils, and I hope that the number of the pupils will not diminish. We have been told what an admirable field the rich pastures of England give to the Scottish accountant. May the Scottish accountants then increase in numbers, and may they, therefore, grow fat on those grand fields of which we have just been told. If they do increase in numbers the University will benefit; but we have been told that the University might do something more for the budding accountant than it has done up to this time. Well, this question of the increase in area of the university education is one which is paramount at the present time. It is the subject of grave consideration on our part, and if we get the means of increasing the area of education we shall, I have no doubt, do our best to meet the wants of the nation at the time.

Mr. John Harrison, the Master of the Merchant Company, proposed the health of the Chairman, and in doing so said: I wish to congratulate this great company on its Chairman, on the gentleman who is presiding over the meeting to-night. We all know how much for weal or for woe any meeting is in the hands of its Chairman, and I congratulate the Society of Accountants in Edinburgh on the tact and judgment and supreme common sense with which our Chairman has presided to-night; and I cannot help congratulating Mr. Carter also on having had the honour to preside over such a gathering. It will be to him, I do not doubt, a life-long pleasure that he was in the Chair at the jubilee meeting of the Society with which his own and his father's name has so long been associated.

The Chairman in responding said: You really do me far too much honour, for I feel that I have done so little to merit the kind expressions of the Master of the Merchant Company. It has been a great pleasure to my colleagues and myself to welcome our guests here to-night, and I thank you all for your distinguished presence. My Lords and Gentlemen, I beg to assure you of my grateful appreciation of the honour you have done me.

2. THE INSTITUTE OF ACCOUNTANTS AND ACTUARIES IN GLASGOW

The Fiftieth Anniversary of the Incorporation by Royal Charter of the Institute of Accountants and Actuaries in Glasgow, was celebrated by a Banquet held in the Grosvenor Restaurant, Gordon Street, Glasgow, on the evening of Wednesday, 15th March, 1905. The President of the Institute, Mr. Thomas Jackson, received the guests, and presided at the Banquet. There were present as the guests of the Institute the following gentlemen :—

The Hon. Sir John Ure Primrose, Bart., Lord Provost of Glasgow ; the Hon. Lord Ardwall; the Hon. J. C. Burns ; Sir Henry Craik, K.C.B., LL.D.; Sir John Cheyne, K.C. ; Sir David Richmond ; Sir Hector Clair Cameron, M.D. ; Sir William M'Ewen, M.D., LL.D., F.R.S. ; Sir John Shearer ; Mr John M'Kie Lees, LL.B., K.C., Sheriff of Dumbarton, Stirling, and Clackmannan ; Mr. C. J. Guthrie, K.C., Sheriff of Ross and Cromarty ; Mr. John Boyd, Advocate ; Mr. Thomas A. Fyfe ; Mr. W. G. Scott Moncrieff, Advocate ; Mr. Mark G. Davidson, LL.B., Advocate ; Mr. A. O. M. Mackenzie, Advocate, Sheriff-Substitute of Lanarkshire ; Lieut.-Col. George T. Beatson, C.B., M.D., V.D.; Very Rev. Donald Macleod, D.D., one of His Majesty's Chaplains for Scotland ; Rev. Pearson M'Adam Muir, D.D. ; Mr. A. G. Burns Graham, Convener of the County of Lanark.

Mr. Alan F. Baird ; Mr. D. C. M'Vail, M.B. ; Mr. David Murray, LL.D. ; Mr. Robt. Muir, M.D., Professor of Pathology ; Mr. Henry Jones, M.A., LL.D., Professor of Moral Philosophy ; Mr. Andrew Gray, LL.D., F.R.S., Professor of Natural Philosophy—Members of the University Court. Mr. Alan E. Clapperton, B.L., Secretary of the University Court.

Mr. George G. Ramsay, LL.D., Professor of Humanity ; Mr. William Jack, LL.D., Professor of Mathematics ; Mr. Archd. Barr, D.Sc., C.E., Professor of Civil Engineering and Mechanics ; Mr William Smart, LL.D., Professor of Political Economy ; Mr. John Glaister, M.D., Professor of Forensic Medicine ; and Mr. William Shaw, Lecturer on Mercantile Law ; Mr. Archd. Craig, LL.D., Clerk of the General Council—all of the University of Glasgow.

Lieut.-Col. Smith Park, 1st Lanarkshire Royal Engineers (Volunteers); Colonel J. D. Young, V.D., 2nd Vol. Batt. H.L.I.

Mr. J. Campbell Penney, C.A., Accountant of Court ; Mr. James M'Intosh, S.S.C., Auditor of the Court of Session.

Mr. Henry E. Clark, C.M.G., President of the Faculty of Physicians and Surgeons ; Mr. James Fleming, President of the School of Art ; Mr. Wm.

Robertson Copland, President of the Technical College ; Mr. Wm. Jacks, LL.D., President, and Mr. W. F. G. Anderson, Vice-President of the Chamber of Commerce ; Mr. James Goldie, Deacon Convener of the Trades House ; Mr. Thomas Dunlop, Chairman of the Corn Trade Association ; Mr. Wm. Cuthbert, Chairman of the Glasgow Shipowners' Association ; Mr. W. D. Gillies, Chairman of the Iron Exchange ; Mr. Samuel M. Taylor, American Consul, and President of the Consular Corps ; Mr. John Keppie, President of the Institute of Architects.

Mr. W. Weir Grieve, Sheriff-Clerk of Glasgow ; Mr. James Nicol, City Chamberlain ; Mr. James N. Hart, Procurator-Fiscal ; Mr. George Neilson, LL.D., Burgh and Police Court Procurator-Fiscal ; Mr. James V. Stevenson, Chief Constable of Glasgow.

Mr. Frederick Walter Carter, C.A., President of the Society of Accountants in Edinburgh ; Messrs. Leonard W. Dickson, C.A., Wm. Home Cook, C.A., D. N. Cotton, C.A., Hugh Blair, C.A., Archd. Langwill, C.A., A. T. Niven, C.A., And. Scott, C.A., C. E. W. Macpherson, C.A., and T. P. Laird, C.A., Members of Council ; Richard Brown, C.A., Secretary and Treasurer ; Edward Boyd, C.A., Auditor ; R. Cockburn Millar, C.A., and J. A. Robertson Durham, C.A., Examiners ; W. C. Maughan, C.A.

Mr. James Milne, Jun., C.A., President of the Society of Accountants in Aberdeen ; Messrs. George Dickie, C.A., George G. Whyte, C.A., Members of Council ; Harvey Hall, C.A., and Alex. Machray, C.A., Past Presidents.

Messrs. George W. Knox, B.Sc., F.C.A., Past President, and the Hon. George Colville, Secretary of the Institute of Chartered Accountants in England and Wales ; Mr. Robert Stokes, F.C.A., President of the Institute of Chartered Accountants in Ireland.

Mr. Jas. Alex. Reid, Dean of the Faculty of Procurators in Glasgow ; Messrs. Geo. B. Hoggan, Chas. Macdonald Williamson, Wm. Gillies, W. Boyd Anderson, Members of Council ; J. Guthrie Smith, Clerk ; John F. Orr, Auditor ; A. Millar Bannatyne, Mark Bannatyne, Robert Brodie, John J. Coats, John Fleming, H. B. Fyfe, Jas. Mackenzie, Allan M'Lean, J. Colin Mitchell, Jas. Muirhead, Thos. Stout, John Turnbull, Timothy Warren, and Alex. Watt, Members of the Faculty.

Messrs. Robert Gourlay, LL.D, Manager, Bank of Scotland ; David Wilson, General Manager, Clydesdale Banking Co., Ltd. ; A. S. Michie, Cashier, Royal Bank of Scotland ; David Rennie, Agent, Commercial Bank of Scotland, Ltd. ; Walter Ritchie, Agent, British Linen Company Bank.

Messrs. N. Ballingall Gunn, President of the Faculty of Actuaries in Scotland, Manager, Scottish Amicable Life Assurance Society ; Archibald Hewat, F.F.A., Manager, the Edinburgh Life Assurance Company ; Adam K. Rodger, Manager, Scottish Temperance Life Assurance Co., Ltd.

Mr. Charles K. Aitken, Chairman, and Mr. Horace A. Gifford, Secretary, of the Glasgow Stock Exchange.

Messrs. Jas. Crawford, M.A., Lecturer in Actuarial Science; John A. Todd, B.L., Lecturer in Law and Political Economy; J. S. Mackay, LL.D., and H. H. Browning, M.A., Examiners for the Chartered Accountants of Scotland.

Messrs. J. Carfrae Alston; John Anderson, Jun.; J. W. Arthur; Hugh Brown; John J. Burnet, A.R.A.; M. Pearce Campbell; David Cooper; John G. Couper; Wm. J. Chrystal; John T. Cargill; Robt. Crawford, LL.D.; Nathaniel Dunlop; D. M. Crerar Gilbert; James Gray; J. D. Hedderwick; E. C. Hedderwick; Joseph Henderson, R.S.W.; Arthur Kay; Robert Kedie; James Kirkwood; William Lorimer; James Maclehose, M.A.; I. P. Maclay; Walter Macfarlane; D. Hope Mac-Brayne; Thomas Mason; Robert Millar; John E. Nelson; Paul Rottenburg.

Mr. John Mann, Sen., the only surviving Original Member of the Institute.

There were also present the following other Members of the Institute:—

P. H. Aikman; Arthur Chas. Aitken; S. F. Alexander; Alex. Allan; W. J. Anderson; John Annan; Henry M. Arthur; William Auld; R. H. Ballantine; Dugald Bannatyne; Maurice James Bell; R. Marr Benzie; William R. Berry; D. Kirkpatrick Blair; Thomson Brodie; Alexander Herbert Brown; Charles L. Brown; A. R. H. Buchanan; George A. Cadell; James Campbell; D. S. Carson; D. S. Carson, Jun.; Alexander M. Carstairs; James Carswell; Robert Carswell; W. Y. Chrystal; Lewis Clapperton, M.A.; Robert H. Clark; Crawford Cook; Albert E. R. Copeland; Spiers C. E. Costigane; David Cowan; Edward H. Stanley Craig; T. A. Craig; James Dalrymple; James M. Davies, Jun.; Alex. D. Deas; Robert Dempster; William Mulley Dempster; J. L. Doran; James Drummond; William Dunlop; John Dunn, Jun.; P. J. Erentz; A. J. Fergusson; Robert Fleming; W. Hamilton Fleming; John Forrest; W. G. France; Robert D. Fraser; James A. French; Charles D. Gairdner; Walter Galbraith; W. B. Galbraith; George F. Gilchrist; Ninian Glen, M.A., F.F.A.; William H. Goff; Thomas Gordon; John W. Gourlay; William Graham; John B. Grieve; David Guthrie; Thomas Guthrie; Robert J. Hardie; Arthur Hart; James M. Hart; David A. Hay; Alexander B. Home; T. M. Hunter; Edward Hutchison; James Hutton; James C. Ireland; Patrick G. Irvine; Harry Jackson; Thomas Jackson, Jun.; James Johnston; Thomas Kelly; Charles Ker, M.A.; J. M. Kerr; David W. Kidston; John U. C. King; James S. Lamb; William Lamont; John Lauder; Alexander J. Law; John M.

Lochhead; Robert A. P. Love; Jas. Cowan MacBain; George A. Macdonald; Robert Macfarlan; A. S. Macharg; E. Simpson Macharg; Alexander Macindoe; Alexander Mackay; James R. Mackay; Robert C. Mackenzie; Hugh M. Mackie; Robert M. Maclay; Harold Macleish; John M. Macleod; Norman Macleod; Hugh Macmillan; William M'Callum; T. Frederick M'Ewan; Robert M'Farlane; George B. M'Kim; James M'Lay; Wm. M'Lay; Thomson M'Lintock; William M'Lintock; Thomson L. M'Lintock; William M'Millan; Andrew C. M'Morland; John Mann, Jun., M.A.; J. Sinclair Marr; Alexander Mitchell; Matthew Mitchell; R. D. M. Mitchell; Alex. Moore, Jun.; James A. Murdoch; Robert Murdoch; R. A. Murray; Wm. W. Naismith; Walter Nelson; James D. Norrie; J. H. Parker, B.L.; James B. Paterson; James C. Paterson; Robert Paterson; Joseph Patrick, M.A.; Stephen M. Rae; Thomas Barbour Ramsay; David Rattray; Robert Reid; Robert A. M. Reid; David A. Richmond; T. Eaton Robinson; John Munn Ross; A. B. Birkmyre Scott; Hugh L. Service; William Sharp; S. Easton Simmers; Thomas Ord Sinclair; Alexander Sloan; D. Norman Sloan, B.L.; Archibald Smith; D. Johnstone Smith; Robert E. Smith; Robert J. Smith: John D. Steel; Henry M. Steele; George H. Steven; J. Angus Steven; Henry C. Stewart; James S. Stewart; J. W. Stewart; Percy Stewart; Ralph R. Stewart; Alexander W. Stiven; David Strathie; Thomas W. Tannock; Chas. Taylor; David Taylor; Douglas D. Taylor; James Taylor; Wm. John Taylor; Alfred A. Todd; George F. Todd; John T. Tulloch; John Vallance, Jun.; William Waddell; C. D. R. Walker; Andrew Wallace; T. W. M. Watson; P. Stewart White; John B. Whyte; George W. Wight; James Herbert Wilson; James Wilson; John Wilson; W. B. Wilson.

Apologies for inability to attend were reported by the Secretary from, among many others, Lord Inverclyde, who expected to be present, but was unavoidably prevented; the Very Rev. Principal Story, who was unfortunately unable to attend; the Members of Parliament for the City and County, who were engaged in the House of Commons; Mr. J. S. Harmood-Banner, M.P., who was also detained by his Parliamentary duties; Sir James Bell, Bart., who had unexpectedly to go abroad; Mr. Wm. Guthrie, Sheriff of Lanarkshire, Mr. A. S. M'Clelland, C.A., and Mr. Robert Blyth, C.A., who were, at the last moment, prevented from attending.

Communications of a congratulatory nature were reported from the following Societies of Accountants, who were unable to send representatives :—

The Dominion Association of Chartered Accountants, Canada; the Institute of Accountants in South Australia; the Incorporated Institute of Accountants of Victoria; the Society of Accountants and Auditors of Victoria; the Incorporated Institute of Accountants of New Zealand; the New Zealand Accountants' and Auditors' Association; the Institute of Accountants in Natal; the Federation of Societies of Public Accountants in the United States of America; the American Association of Public Accountants; the New York State Society of Certified Public Accountants; the Pennsylvania Institute of Certified Public Accountants, Philadelphia; the Maryland Association of Certified Public Accountants, Baltimore; the Illinois Society of Certified Public Accountants, Chicago; the California Society of Certified Public Accountants, San Francisco; the Incorporated Public Accountants of Massachusetts, Boston; Collegio dei Ragionieri della Provincia di Como; Collegio dei Ragionieri, Florence; Compagnie des Experts-Comptables Agréés des Bouches-du-Rhone, Marseilles; Chambre Syndicale des Experts-Comptables, Brussels; Svenska Revisorsamfundet, Stockholm. A congratulatory telegram was also received from the Members of the Institute practising in Johannesburg.

After dinner the President proposed the toasts of "The King" and "The Queen, Prince and Princess of Wales, and other Members of the Royal Family," which were cordially pledged.

Sir Henry Craik, in proposing "The City of Glasgow," said: Two centuries ago your city had a population of some 13,000 people. Its chief attributes in the words of many travellers were, that it was one of the trimmest and most picturesque little towns in Great Britain. These are perhaps not among the good qualities which we would now first think of ascribing to it. It needed all the political insight which Sir Walter Scott ascribes to Andrew Fairservice to predict the future of that little township. It needed all the sagacity and the prophetic instinct of Bailie Nicol Jarvie—that most respected citizen—to predict the greatness of Glasgow when he rode out to meet Rob Roy in the company of Francis Osbaldistone over that withered heath, as Scott says, clothed in the barest vegetation in God's earth, which now is the source of one of your greatest streams of wealth, and is inhabited by a teeming population which draws livelihood and work from it. But long after Bailie Nicol Jarvie had slept with his father, the Deacon, Glasgow was still but a petty city. It was years after that that its ruin or its safety depended upon whether Parliament would make a grant of £10,000 to recoup it for the losses it had suffered in the Rebellion. Your annual valuation now is over five and a half millions. Was there ever in the history of nations such an advance—such a miraculous story of prosperity? But even within the life of many of those now present, what an advance there has been! We have seen Glasgow advancing two or three miles into the country on every side. We have seen her old landmarks pass away; we have seen the city take on a new aspect within our lifetime. And now what do we see? You are the second city in the Empire—second to none in that spirit of corporate unity which places you even above the metropolis. Your argosies are in every harbour over the civilised world. The fleets built in your dockyards hold a proud position on every sea. The products of your markets pass into every land. And I wonder in what bourse or in what financial confederation the proceedings of the great Society who are our hosts to-night are not considered with care and with a just estimate of their importance in the world? But I am well aware that you here would have little patience with me, were I merely to paint my picture of the greatness of your city and mine in roseate colours, and to pretend that there was not a reverse to the shield. We cannot, I fear, in these days of busy factories, emulate the neatness, the trimness, or the purity that met the eyes of Bailie Nicol Jarvie and Andrew Fairservice. But science has done much for us in this—science combined with wise municipal government may perhaps do more; and although we may not reach back to the time when—according to the veracious historian— St. Mungo drew herrings from the Clyde, we may still see perhaps somewhat of a less thick incense arising from the smoke of the manufacturing altar.

But there is also a more serious side from which you, the citizens of Glasgow, have no need to turn. We know that the great armies of commercial advance do not move forward without carrying upon their flanks a vast number of undesirable camp-followers. We know that inseparably connected with that advance there are the grim figures of poverty, of ignorance, of disease and of crime. And I make bold to say, as a native of Glasgow, that you have faced the difficulty, that you have not forgotten in your prosperity those who have not reaped their full share in that prosperity; that beside your commercial advance you have not lagged behind in the race of charity. You have organised— as few municipalities have organised—great societies for the relief of the poor, a vast machinery of benevolence; you have given full force to the impulse of your charitable feelings; and in no great city are there more merchant princes who are ready to spend and to be spent in the work of relieving their fellow-men. You have advanced in commercial greatness; you have done more—you have risen to the responsibilities of greatness.

But this does not end your activities. In art you stand in a position of which you may well be proud. Founded by a Glasgow citizen, your art collections stand high amongst the collections of Europe. You have a School of Art that I may well say, from personal knowledge, is second to none in the kingdom. And you have ´a school of artists which has originality and nerve enough to have drawn upon itself keen and, I may say, perhaps somewhat acrimonious criticism, which is its highest compliment. And speaking as an alumnus of our University, it would ill become me to leave out of account in reckoning the greatness of your city the ancient University with which your fame is linked. We are proud of the name that she has borne, of the children she has nourished, and the teachers of whom she can boast. Is it not worth mentioning in a commercial gathering like this, that amongst those teachers she can reckon the pioneer of the great masters of economic science, and that in our own day she can count as her Chancellor that man whose name makes the pulses of all Glasgow citizens beat quicker, the chief living master of applied science in the world. With such aids and allies, with such a commercial future, with such a stream of charity, with such artistic instincts, with such a solid foundation of sound learning to keep her company, long let Glasgow flourish.

The Lord Provost, in responding, agreed that the historic past told a story of wondrous progress. It told a story of resolute sagacious men who perceived their opportunity, and who with vision somewhat wide believed in their hearts that they had come to a wealthy heritage, and that they administered the affairs of a coming city, that had broad and wide foundations. It remained for us their sons to justify the trust given to us, and to take such measures that that trust shall be preserved along the lines of sound administration, and ensure a city not only with a past, but which we earnestly and devoutly hope shall have still a future. Proceeding, the Lord Provost said—I am all the more encouraged to take this view from the fact that to-night I am the guest of the Institute of Accountants and Actuaries. Accountant and actuary suggest a domain, a function, and a duty which are of very great value to a corporate body; because the members of a corporate body acting as trustees for the citizens are subject in their economic progress to the survey of accountants and actuaries, and if they receive the full approbation of the accountants who survey their economic line of travel, if they receive the approval of a body on whom increasingly stringent duties of observation and survey have been imposed, then they can take heart and go on their way.

But I cannot forget the beautiful allusion to that altar from which never-ending incense arises, in which I perceive a very courteous and genial allusion to the fact that we have still much to do in the material sphere to render our city not only lovable but tolerable. I thought Sir Henry Craik might even have ventured further and spoken of the intolerable din that is one of the appanages of city life, a din so distracting that one would bestow a laurel wreath on the man that could so transform the conditions of paving in the city that life might have some little quiet and reflectiveness even there. Further, and I have often spoken on this theme before, I would that the lofty ideal he has struck of citizenship were more impressed upon the community. And particularly to-night, addressing a representative gathering such as we seldom have in Glasgow, I would again uplift the standard of citizenship, and say to you, with the vast concerns many of you have to guide, that in view of the deep-rooted problems affecting the economic life of the great city with which you are in Glasgow in intimate contact, some of you might spare some little time from these engrossing pursuits to qualify and regenerate and augment the forces that guide the destinies of the city. If you neglect that, as I fear too many of you do, then hear your Cassandras predict the coming decay of civil economy; listen to them, and while you listen say " I too was an accomplice in the act." If you will relegate the destinies of the city to the caprice of an uneducated constituency in many cases, then the blame is yours, the responsibility is yours, and the final disaster if it comes will be your heritage justly earned. But I have a very firm conviction that in all that pertains to a city with traditions like Glasgow, and in all that affects the well-being of the city, we shall not lack recruits to continue the line of sound progress, and that in order that we may hold our position as a city and as a community, not only in our local circumference but in the wider circumference of the empire of which we are a part, every loyal and true citizen will seek to equip us with that methodised knowledge which is power, with that wide outlook on obligation and responsibility which is an inherent part of citizenship, and with that pride of city which can only be attained by devoted and unselfish effort on the part of every individual in the community.

Lord Ardwall, in submitting the toast of "The Institute of Accountants and Actuaries in Glasgow," said: We do not know when the profession of accountant first began or much about its early history, although I rather think that Pharaoh must have got somebody to audit Joseph's very large corn accounts. Coming down to mediæval times, I find that the first Society of Accountants—they called it a college in those days—was founded in Venice in the Middle

Ages, and one is not surprised to find that it was in that city that accountants were first found to be necessary. It was then the great emporium of commerce between East and West, and we have heard something about merchants of Venice and the sprinkling of Shylocks which inhabited that city. It is remarkable how closely this Society resembled in its objects those of the present day. It insisted on accurate training in accounting and on studies under various learned Doctors, and its rules of admission were very strict. Similar societies were afterwards started in Milan and in Bologna, and from that day to this there has always been a profession of accountant in Italy, with some interruptions; and it is a remarkable thing that, putting aside Italy and putting aside Holland, where indeed there were not Societies of Accountants, but where great attention was given to accurate book-keeping, that this little country of ours, Scotland, is the country in which the profession of Accountant has been most thoroughly and most rapidly developed in modern times. In Edinburgh and Glasgow, in the end of the eighteenth century, the accountants were known as a separate profession. In Glasgow especially they were brought into prominence by the number of failures which occurred owing to the revolt of the American Colonies.

Again, in 1793, there was a very great commercial crisis in Glasgow. There were no fewer than twenty-six banking Companies came to grief, and you will admit that was a situation which called for the services of Accountants. Accordingly we find that there was a gentleman then whose name is still well known in Glasgow through his descendants, Mr. Walter Ewing Maclae of Cathkin, designed a Merchant and Accountant. He appears under this designation in the early numbers of the *Glasgow Directory*, and he is referred to as being one of the most reliable and best accountants of the day. That closed the eighteenth century, but it is interesting to note, that there are two firms still practising in Glasgow whose origin can be traced back to that time—I refer to the firms of Messrs. D. & A. Cuthbertson, Provan, & Strong, and Messrs. Kerr, Andersons, & M'Leod.

Time went on, and the profession flourished with the advance of business of various kinds both in Glasgow and Edinburgh, until on this day fifty years ago the Royal Warrant was given for the Incorporation by Royal Charter of certain petitioners and such other persons as might thereafter be admitted as Members into one body politic and corporate by the name of the Institute of Accountants and Actuaries in Glasgow. That is the occurrence that we are here to celebrate to-day. I shall leave it to the Chairman to give you authentic and reliable details of the history of this excellent Institute. Soon after the incorporation of the Institute, its Members, on the invitation of the Lord Advocate of the day, along with the Edinburgh Society, took part in the adjustment of the clauses of the 1856 Bankruptcy Statute, and the best thing that can be said of the results of their labours is this—that that Statute has continued to the present day as the Bankruptcy Code of Scotland with very few alterations, and has been found to work most admirably in every respect. But it must not be supposed that that Statute created the Bankruptcy Law in Scotland, or that the Incorporation of this Society or of the Edinburgh one the year before was the creation of the body of gentlemen who were fit to cope with the difficulties, legal and accounting, which were raised by bankruptcy. For eighty years at least previous, the Bankruptcy Law of Scotland had been developed by a series of eminent lawyers, of whom by far the greatest was Professor George Joseph Bell, whose great work, which deals almost exclusively with law from the point of view of bankruptcy, is an authority not only in Scotland but in England, and is recognised as one of the leading authorities in the excellent Law Courts of our brethren across the Atlantic in the United States. During the same time there had grown up as practical administrators of the law throughout Scotland a body of accountants second to none in the ability with which they discharged the delicate and difficult duties which devolve upon a trustee in bankruptcy. I think my friend on my left, Mr. Knox, will admit that in England they were not so favourably situated, and that when very properly they reformed their bankruptcy law on the lines of the Scottish law, though they found some very excellent and great accountants in London and elsewhere, one of their difficulties was to find throughout England generally such a body of men as Scotland had had for eighty years past in its accountants.

Of course the important matter to which the Institute devoted its attention was the education of members, and I do not think that the public can be too thankful to the various accountant Societies for what they have done in the direction of training men for the very difficult and delicate duties which devolve upon accountants in this country. These Societies have all along, and this one in particular, attached special importance to the practical experience obtained in accountants' offices. They have always regarded this as an essential qualification. Then from time to time they have added requirements. They have made their apprentices study law, they have made them study political economy, they have made them study actuarial science, so that I think we may pride ourselves justly in Scotland upon this, that we have a body of accountants in Glasgow and elsewhere who are thoroughly competent men well furnished for their work, possessing besides, owing to the excellent training they are compelled to receive, the character of men of integrity and reliability, which is perhaps the most important qualification that an accountant can have.

I should like for one moment to say that in proposing this toast there are recalled to my memory many who have now passed away, and who took a great part in the institution of this Society. With your two first Presidents—Mr. James M'Clelland and Mr. Peter White—I, as a lad, had slight and pleasant acquaintance, having met them here and there in the houses of friends. Your third President—Mr. Walter Mackenzie, my esteemed and beloved uncle—of course I knew very well indeed, and I can only say this of him, and I may be permitted to say it, although a relative, that I never knew a man of stricter integrity, of greater business shrewdness, combined at the same time with a most lovable and genial disposition to all who ever came in contact with him. That he loved to work for this Society I need tell none of you present, because you recognised what he had done for you by the presentation so highly valued by him a few years before his death of his portrait painted by one of your eminent Glasgow artists. I also had the pleasure of the acquaintance of Mr. William Anderson, another of your Presidents. He, too, was a man of great professional ability, of most genial disposition, and most gentlemanly character. I met him in connection with the liquidation of the City Bank, and I know that it was very largely by his efforts, especially in Glasgow and the West, that the liquidation was so successfully carried through. Another President of yours I knew also very well, and that was Mr. Wyllie Guild. My experience of him was chiefly as a professional witness, and I can only say that I never, in my somewhat long experience of thirty-five years, knew a better professional witness than he was. He expounded his own views with a wealth of imagery and illustration which often affected the obdurate hearts of a British jury; and woe to the Counsel who rashly attempted to cross-examine him. He was not severe upon any Counsel who cross-examined him. He just overwhelmed him with a bland cloud-like mass against which no ill-nature on the part of Counsel could prevail, which no incisive questions could penetrate. Mr. Wyllie Guild was left standing in the box, leading everybody who heard him to think that he was absolutely right, that he alone, of anybody in the Court, knew anything about the case, and that those who differed from him were exceedingly to be pitied. Another gentleman I may be allowed to mention—a gentleman who was a great personal friend of my own in later years. He was not a President of the Society. I have no doubt he would have been, but for his too early death.

He was the late Mr. William M'Kinnon. He, I think, very nearly equalled Mr. Wyllie Guild as a professional witness, but his style was totally different. He was quiet, cool, and incisive in his examination, and then when he came to cross-examination, I can only say this, that the Counsel who cross-examined him had generally very little to congratulate himself upon, because Mr. M'Kinnon always began by stating his case very meagrely, if I may say so, and he had always up his sleeve a number of additional facts and figures with which he overwhelmed the unfortunate Counsel. Those who knew him well, unless they had some uncommonly good thing up their sleeves on which they could rely to controvert some of the propositions he had brought forward, came to know that they had very much better leave Mr. M'Kinnon alone. I refer to both these gentlemen as being in my day two of the greatest professional witnesses I have met, and I may say this for them at the same time that if you ever put a straight question to either of them which admitted of a plain answer they never hesitated to give it, even though it was against their own case. They gave it honestly and straightforwardly.

In these fifty years of your history you have done a great deal for the education of the members of the profession, and I have no doubt that I am safe in confidently predicting that in the future as in the past you will be able to send forth men able to aid the Society in the various ways that an accountant can. I think you should cultivate—and I would ask the younger members of the Society to do so—a very high view, a very high opinion of your own profession and of the part it plays in modern society. In the first place, as we all know, Chartered Accountants are employed very largely as factors on the estates of deceased persons, and upon the estates of those who are unable to attend to their own estates. It is in these capacities that an enormous amount of human happiness or human misery is placed in their hands, and I am bound to say that my experience of them as a lawyer has been that their influence is invariably for good. They take an interest, a personal interest I should say, in the affairs of those who are put under their charge, and they discharge their duties towards them as gentlemen, and I may add, as Christians. But that is not the only thing that accountants have to do ; I regard them in one sense as seekers after truth, not indeed in the high and somewhat vague paths of philosophy, but in the ordinary paths of business life. It is theirs to unravel the skeins of disordered accounts, to find out the truth regarding the affairs of men and Companies and Institutions, and they have to exercise in that pursuit the greatest accuracy and care and pains. I am glad to think that this part of their duties too they perform in a faithful and diligent manner, aided as they are by the excellent training which this Institute and other Societies insist upon them getting. But further, there are really great public and national interests in their hands, because as auditors of public companies, as advisers of great captains of industries, they have an immense power to use for good if they so choose. In doing so they may be taken into the higher regions of economics and actuarial science, and this Institute tries to provide that they shall be equipped for that. But when one thinks of the complexity of the questions they have to address themselves to, one is impressed with the idea that really they cannot be too highly educated for the purpose. The balance-sheet and accounts of profit and loss seem common enough phrases, but they both involve very highly specialised forms of abstract thought. In the balance-sheet the accountant lays his iron hand upon an industry at some particular moment and says, " Now at this particular date there is what the industry has, here is what it has to do." Profit and loss account again is another matter. That seeks to treat of matters as in the ordinary flow of business, and to settle those tremendously puzzling questions as to what shall be deducted from profit and what shall be charged to revenue and what to capital, and all those kinds of questions which really enter almost more into economic science than into mere accounting and book-keeping. But a good accountant will be furnished for all that. I have only to say that in the interest of the public, I think vigilance is more and more required on the part of gentlemen belonging to this profession, because I think there is a tendency among some sets of companies and some sets of businesses not to carry everything to revenue that they ought to do, but to carry to capital. I think this not only may apply to industrial businesses, but even, if I may venture to say so, my Lord Provost, to municipal accounts, and therefore, I would invite accountants here to be exceedingly strict with accounts of every person carrying on business, from the least even to the greatest, not excluding the accounts of this great city.

Such, as I have tried to set before you, are some of the interests which you have to guard, and some of the important duties which you have to perform. In view of these, and knowing how much this Institute has aided in the past towards helping you to the performance of these duties, I ask you to drink to the continued and increasing usefulness and prosperity of the Institute of Accountants in Glasgow.

The President, in responding, after narrating the circumstances connected with the formation of the Institute (fully described on pp. 208–211 hereof) said : I am pleased to see with us to-night the sons of several of the first Members of the Institute; and while it must be a source of gratification to them to find that the Institute, of which their fathers were the pioneers, has grown and prospered, we who are now the Members thereof cannot but feel grateful to those who rendered such good service at the beginning. Since the Institute was formed the trade and commerce of the country have largely increased, and consequently the profession of accounting has become a much more general and important one, especially since the introduction of the Limited Liability Act. The duties of accountants have become more varied and responsible, requiring a higher and more liberal education. When the Institute was formed the duties of the accountant in Glasgow were largely confined to dealing with bankrupt and insolvent estates; now, however, they are largely investigation, auditing, and company work, and present legislation all tends to make the auditor more and more responsible. Under the Companies' Acts an auditor could not pass a balance-sheet such as the one prepared by a Paisley merchant of former times. He was very careful to ascertain all his liabilities—which was a good feature—but when he came to his assets he simply looked round his warehouse and said, the first row of shelves will pay one creditor, naming him—another row will pay another creditor, and so on; then addressing his assistants he said, "The rest is all my own and we need go no further."

Of the forty-nine members who petitioned for the Charter, only one survives—Mr. John Mann, Senior—who I am pleased to see is with us to-night, and while offering our congratulations to Mr. Mann, I am sure I express the sentiments of every member of the Institute when I say that we hope he may be long spared to go in and out amongst us, and to look with satisfaction from the small beginnings of the Institute to its present flourishing position.

During the past half-century and under the able guidance of our leading Members the Institute has steadily increased and now numbers 454 Members, many of whom are filling important positions in all parts of the world as accountants and otherwise. There are 56 of our Members in England—46 in London alone; 16 in South Africa; 7 in India; 6 in the United States; 3 in Australia; 3 in China; 2 in Central Africa; 2 in Central America; and others in Canada, Ceylon, Japan, Polynesia, Straits Settlements, and South America.

In former times the leading merchants of Glasgow—particularly the West Indian merchants—conducted the liquidation of estates. All that is now changed—fifty years' experience has proved that the profession of accounting forms an important part of our legal and mercantile systems, and so long as we accountants act our part with ability and integrity, we shall feel that our Charter has fulfilled the object of its petitioners.

Mr. Arthur Hart, in proposing "Other Accountant Societies," said: You will have gathered from the list of apologies which was read by our Secretary, Mr. Sloan, that the profession of accounting is pretty well scattered over the whole earth; and that if accounting be not co-extensive with civilisation, it is at all events co-extensive with commerce, which is pretty much the same thing. And leaving for a moment the United Kingdom, I would call your attention to the fact that our kindred beyond the seas have established many flourishing Institutes. To take Canada as the first instance. In that great Dominion there are Institutes of Accountants in nearly every Province. You will also find in Melbourne, in Tasmania, in New Zealand, in South Australia, in Natal, and in the Transvaal, well-organised Associations of Accountants. And if you go to the United States of America you will find there the designation C.P.A., which being interpreted means "Certified Public Accountant," almost as familiar as the well-known C.A. of brass plates nearer home. I need not tell you how gladly we would have welcomed this evening representatives from those distant shores, as well as from many parts of the Continent, where associations with kindred objects to our own have grown up and are now flourishing. Along with ourselves two features distinguish nearly the whole of these bodies—namely, a constantly increasing membership, and an honest endeavour to raise the status of the Societies, either by raising the qualifications or by introducing a severe entrance examination. We feel honoured to-night in having present with us a large number of very distinguished representatives of other kindred Societies. And I am sure no exception will be taken if I allude in the first place to the gratification which it affords the Glasgow Society to have with them to-night the President, certain Members of Council, and other Members of the Edinburgh Society. The Edinburgh Society is the premier Association. It is only about five or six months ago that it received from all parts of the world, and from every section of professional and commercial life, tributes and congratulations upon having achieved the Jubilee of its Incorporation, and I would ask Mr. Carter and the other gentlemen from Edinburgh who are present, although it may appear a little belated, to accept in this great assembly of gentlemen gathered in the west a renewal of these congratulations, and the expression of our sincere felicities that their Society has arrived at this important stage of its career. We are accustomed to hear it said that the British Parliament is the mother of Parliaments.

I think with equal truth it may be said that the Edinburgh Institute is the mother of Accounting Institutes in far distant lands; for her sons and her example and her methods have served to build up these Associations, and to bring them to the point of success at which they now find themselves. We are also honoured by the presence of a representative of the English Institute of Accountants—Mr. Knox. The English Institute is a very large one—consisting I think of about 3200 members. Mr. Knox takes the place to-night of Mr. Harmood-Banner, who holds a very distinguished place in the annals of accounting. It is, I daresay, known to you that Mr. Harmood-Banner had the distinguished honour of being returned as a Member of Parliament for one of the Divisions of Liverpool a few weeks ago, and I cannot help thinking that it must be gratifying to all those who tremble for the ark of British solvency and of British credit that Mr. Harmood-Banner has been returned to Parliament, where, of course, he is in a position to check the accounts, and apply his mind to the other delinquencies of the Chancellor of the Exchequer. We have also with us to-night the President of the Irish Institute—Mr. Stokes; and Mr. Milne of the Aberdeen Society of Accountants. I need not tell this company that Aberdeen, Edinburgh, and Glasgow are knit together by a very close bond of union, because in the year 1893 they combined in order to secure a uniform examination for all those who desire admittance to the ranks of accounting. There are others present whom I would gladly name, but I do not wish to detain you. I hope that all those representatives will convey to their several Associations the assurance of our high regard and goodwill. We desire to remember them all here to-night, and along with them I may also say the whole brotherhood of the accounting profession under whatever sky they may be serving, satisfied that they along with us are endeavouring to uphold and to advance the interests of our common profession.

Mr. Carter, the President of the Edinburgh Society, in reply, mentioned that he had lately received a copy of a Vancouver newspaper in which there appeared the following short notice :—

PROVINCIAL LEGISLATURE

" Mr. Macgowan presented a Petition from Mr. William Thomas Stein, a Member of the Society of Accountants in Edinburgh, and others, for leave to introduce a Bill to incorporate the Chartered Accountants' Institute of British Columbia."

This, he said, is only one of many similar cases, where the young accountant, confident of his ability and resource, leaves his native land to seek his fortune in some far distant clime, and, fully alive to the advantages of co-operation, sooner or later adopts the same procedure as that used by the Founders of his Institute. Although it is probably useless to hope that the law of England and that of Scotland will ever be assimilated, I do not think it at all improbable that, in the near future, we may see Chairs founded and endowed in our leading Universities, where degrees in "Accountancy" may be obtained, which will add lustre to our profession. Accountants have become so useful to the community, that they now form a distinct requirement in the daily routine of the State, and anything which tends to increase their efficiency and utility should form the subject of careful consideration by the various Executives. Of late years, proposals have been made as to a possible federation of the Chartered Societies of the United Kingdom. In this, I know we would secure the good-will and hearty co-operation of the great English Institute, the able members of which, like ourselves, are desirous of doing everything they can to strengthen the profession, but there are many and serious initial difficulties involved in such a scheme. Suggestions have also been made relative to the registration of the individual members of the five Chartered Societies, and their inclusion in one Roll or Register, to secure uniformity in educational standards, and in the general practice of accountancy. This appears to me a more feasible project than the larger scheme of federation, and, if unburdened with unacceptable or unworkable conditions, and having due regard to the rights and privileges of particular Institutes, it is certainly worthy of consideration. We must all deplore the unexpected death which occurred last Wednesday of Mr. Alfred Augustus James of the English Institute, a past President, and a gentleman whose counsel and opinion were greatly valued. He, as Chairman of a joint Committee, had been giving this subject his careful attention. In any case, experience has shown that union is strength and that knowledge is power, and one happy result will certainly follow this important function of to-night, and that held in Edinburgh in October last. These Jubilee gatherings, the first of their kind, whilst marking an important cycle in the history of accounting, have largely assisted to draw together the various units of the profession, to promote good-fellowship and mutual respect, and to foster joint interest and wellbeing, and I hope I reflect the feelings of many here present, when I candidly state that never have I been more proud of my colleagues in all parts of the world, nor felt more desirous of securing their good opinion and respect, than in this, the Jubilee year of our two oldest Corporations.

Mr. G. Walter Knox, F.C.A., also responded, and said that as the son of a Scot he felt himself amongst brethren. In referring to the late Mr. James he stated that his whole life and soul were thrown into the interests of the Institute in London, and generally of accountants throughout Great Britain and Ireland. In tendering the heartiest congratulations of the English Institute to that of Glasgow, Mr. Knox said: Our aims are the same, our profession is the same, and we are one in our desires. There can be no jealousy between us, excepting possibly when some of us in England come up to Glasgow, or some of you in Glasgow come down to London. For you, Mr. President, have said that no fewer than forty-six Members of your Institute have gone to London. Now, so far as we have come across them we find them to be exceedingly good men; but though they are with us they are not of us, and I only wish that some plan could be brought about whereby there might be greater union in localities of Members of our various Institutes who happen to reside there.

Lord Ardwall, in his very excellent speech, for which I am sure we are all very grateful, referred to the question of England being behindhand in the matter of the establishment of our Institute, and he is quite right; I venture to say that if we had had in the 'sixties and 'seventies an Institute, such as we have now, guiding the 1869 Bankruptcy Act, the 1883 Act would never have been enacted—an Act which in my opinion has not been for the benefit of the public at large. The 1869 Act simply wanted amending in the direction of better supervision of trustees and more stringent action with regard to debtors; but we had not such a Society then as you had. We are scarcely half your age, but we have at any rate the benefit of young manhood, and we are endeavouring by every effort on our part to uphold the status of the profession, and hoping in co-operation with yourselves and with our friends in Ireland, to form ultimately some broad, large, and comprehensive body.

Mr. Robert Gourlay, LL.D., in giving the University of Glasgow—one of the three founded in Scotland before the Reformation, and only forty years younger than that of St. Andrews, the oldest — said: In the history of human things, there is to be found no grander conception than that of the Church of the fifteenth century, when it resolved in the shape of the Universities to cast the light of knowledge abroad over all the Christian world. Some of us to-night recall with reverence and pleasant memories the old College in the High

Street of Glasgow, with its quaint courts, its low ceilings, and dingy class-rooms. But whether we of an older generation think of the old College, or the new on the heights of Gilmorehill, we must feel that it has been a bountiful Mother to all who have ever been privileged to spend happy days within its walls. We have in these later years given to Cambridge Sir Richard Jebb, the foremost Grecian of our times. To Oxford, a Master in Philosophy—Dr. Edward Caird. To London, a great Chemist—Sir William Ramsay; and to the world our own Lord Kelvin, the greatest scientist of his age. This is a great and wealthy city, and we are all proud of our University. I could wish that pride to take a practical shape, and the good example of many of our American cousins followed by helping our University with funds to enable it to keep abreast of the requirements of the age, in Science, in Medicine, in Law, and in the Arts.

Professor Ramsay in reply said: Lord Ardwall told us that the Society which I have the pleasure of addressing to-night is a Society given up to the pursuit of truth. That is the great object for which the University exists, and I cannot help feeling to-night, when addressing what I think I may say is the most intellectual audience of the most intellectual profession that could be gathered together in the city of Glasgow, how it is that this Society is not represented, as Mr. Carter suggested it should be, by a Chair in the University. We gladly recognise in the University the excellence of the Actuarial and Accounting Examination. I may venture to say that we who have spent our lives in trying to raise the standard of education in Scotland have felt that this Society in Glasgow has been one of the most valuable of handmaids and assistants in that work. Long may it continue to be so. The University has embarked very largely in great schemes of building rendered necessary by science. You have only to go to Gilmorehill and you will see that new temples of learning and of research are springing up on every side. We shall have to meet the difficulties created by these new temples by-and-by, and I feel confident that the citizens of Glasgow will not be backward in maintaining those buildings after they have been so munificent in contributing to their creation.

Mr. James A. Reid, Dean of the Faculty of Procurators, in proposing "The Chairman," said: I have known Mr. Jackson long; I have known him well; and I am convinced of this, that no more delightful, no more capable man of business exists in this country. I am sure that the members of the Glasgow Institute of Accountants may well congratulate themselves in having him as their President to-day. We who are guests congratulate ourselves equally that we have had him as our Chairman and our host.

The Chairman suitably replied, after which the company separated.

During the evening a programme of music was rendered by the Grosvenor orchestra, and songs by Mr. Walter Lewis.

On the evening of 17th March the Associates and past and present apprentices of the Institute were entertained at a Smoking Concert. The attendance was large, and the proceedings were most successful.

INDEX

INDEX